AN EXPLORATION OF CHRISTIAN THEOLOGY

AN EXPLORATION OF CHRISTIAN THEOLOGY

DON THORSEN

Baker Academic
Grand Rapids, Michigan

Published by Baker Academic
a division of Baker Publishing Group
P.O. Box 6287, Grand Rapids, MI 49516-6287
www.bakeracademic.com

Baker Academic edition published 2010
ISBN 978-0-8010-4786-2

Previously published in 2008 by Hendrickson Publishers

Printed in the United States of America

The Library of Congress has cataloged the original edition as follows:
 Thorsen, Donald A.D.
        An exploration of Christian theology / Don Thorsen.
            p. cm.
        Includes bibliographical references and indexes.
        ISBN 978-1-56563-236-3 (alk. paper)
        1. Theology. I. Title.
    BT75.3.T46 2008
    230—dc22   2007037389

Cover Art: The cover image incorporates three of the many line art drawings done for this book by the author, Don Thorsen. The three images encompass central concerns dealt with in Christian theology: church tradition, the living community of Christ, and the worldwide scope of the Christian message.

10   11   12   13   14   15   16   7   6   5   4   3   2   1

To my daughters
Liesl, Heidi, and Dana,
whose love encourages me, and
whose questions both challenge and inspire me.

CONTENTS

Foundations

Creation

Humanity

Sin

Jesus Christ

The Holy Spirit

Salvation

The Church

The Future

ABBREVIATIONS

Biblical and Apocryphal Books

Gen	Genesis
Exod	Exodus
Lev	Leviticus
Num	Numbers
Deut	Deuteronomy
Josh	Joshua
Judg	Judges
1–2 Sam	1–2 Samuel
1–2 Kgs	1–2 Kings
1–2 Chr	1–2 Chronicles
Neh	Nehemiah
Esth	Esther
Ps(s)	Psalm(s)
Prov	Proverbs
Eccl	Ecclesiastes
Isa	Isaiah
Jer	Jeremiah
Lam	Lamentations
Ezek	Ezekiel
Dan	Daniel
Hos	Hosea
Mic	Micah
Nah	Nahum
Hab	Habakkuk
Zeph	Zephaniah
Zech	Zechariah
Mal	Malachi
2 Macc	2 Maccabees
Matt	Matthew

Rom	Romans
1–2 Cor	1–2 Corinthians
Gal	Galatians
Eph	Ephesians
Phil	Philippians
Col	Colossians
1–2 Thess	1–2 Thessalonians
1–2 Tim	1–2 Timothy
Heb	Hebrews
Jas	James
1–2 Pet	1–2 Peter
Jude	Jude
Rev	Revelation

General Abbreviations

B.C.E.	before the Common Era
ca.	circa
cf.	*confer,* compare
ch(s).	chapter(s)
d.	died
e.g.	*exempli gratia,* for example
ed(s).	editor(s), edited by, edition(s)
esp.	especially
etc.	*et cetera,* and the rest
ibid.	*ibidem,* in the same place
KJV	King James Version
n.	footnote
no.	number
NRSV	New Revised Standard Version
repr.	reprinted
rev.	revised
RSV	Revised Standard Version
trans.	translator, translated by; transitive
vol(s).	volume(s)

PREFACE

Let me invite you to explore Christian theology—what Christians believe, value, and practice. This is no easy task! Over the centuries, Christians have held a variety of viewpoints, yet there is a family resemblance among Christians that is recognizable and describable.

In exploring the full Christian tradition, we are likely to run into a variety of family members. We will meet aunts and uncles who live far away. We will meet some we never knew we had! Some relatives will be friendly; others will be odd; and others will be outright embarrassing. Fortunately, some relatives will be quite familiar—some a comfort and some inspiring. All these represent important members of the family we call Christian.

The study of Christianity in general, and of Christian theology in particular, is not a study like other studies. From a Christian perspective, these studies are critically important. If people are created in God's image, it is imperative that they learn about God as well as themselves. Such understanding is critical for their individual and social well-being in life here and now. Studies in Christian theology are also imperative for the eternal well-being of people, which only God can provide. In a sense, these studies are a matter of life and death for the present and future welfare of people.

Ever been to a family reunion?

A Parable

Jesus tells the story about a wealthy man who hosted a great banquet (Luke 14:15–24). Guests are invited, and the food is prepared. However, one by one all of the guests make excuses and do not come to the celebration. This disappoints the man, so he invites anyone outside his house—friend or stranger, religious or non-religious, male or female, rich or poor—to come in and enjoy the feast that had been prepared.

Jesus probably told this parable in order to challenge people about their willingness to share in the kingdom of God. People are invited to participate in the kingdom, but they have to respond to God's invitation if they want to enjoy its benefits. People have a choice.

When it comes to studying the beliefs, values, and practices of Christianity, so much has been prepared and provided. Sometimes the feast seems too bountiful! Yet, we cannot enjoy it if we do not partake of the feast. It does not matter how we get to the feast—only that we respond to the invitation.

About the Book

This book is an invitation to explore Christian theology as people conceive it in various church traditions, both past and present. It serves as an introduction designed for readers unfamiliar with Christian beliefs, values, and practices as they developed in church history. Although the intent is to provide a simple presentation of theology, the ideas discussed represent a profound summary of Christianity.

Come explore!

This book is a simple, ecumenical introduction to Christian theology. It is *ecumenical* because different views of theology are presented in ways that do justice to prominent historic attempts by Christians to describe their beliefs, values, and practices. It is *simple* because the book is intended to be suggestive rather than exhaustive in its treatment of theology.

No doubt some readers will consider the book too ecumenical or not ecumenical enough. Likewise, some readers will consider the book too simple or not simple enough. Regardless of the shortcomings of the book, I hope that readers will find themselves sufficiently drawn to the topic of theology that they will want to continue reflecting upon their understanding of God and of matters related to God.

Like those in the parable of the great banquet who were invited to share in the kingdom of God, one has to come and explore the content of this book in order to enjoy its benefits. Those who come will come away satisfied.

An Analogy

My daughters enjoy playing competitive soccer with the American Youth Soccer Organization (AYSO). Like many other "soccer dads," I have become increasingly involved with volunteering, coaching, and refereeing soccer games.

One of the things I appreciate most about AYSO is its philosophy: they want everyone—kids and parents—to have a soccer experience that is "safe, fair and fun." In many ways, that philosophy serves as an analogy for what I want to accomplish in this book about Christianity. Let me explain.

First, I want to present Christian beliefs and practices in a way that is *safe*. You do not need to fear a hidden theological agenda in this book because I will be upfront about what I want to accomplish and how I want to accomplish it. Like everyone, I have a particular religious and personal background, which I will share later on. Our backgrounds influence us, whether we like it or not! They affect how we *speak* about Christianity as well as what we *hear* about it. Recognizing and acknowledging our backgrounds represents one of the benefits of the supposedly postmodern era in which we live; we have to admit that any

Unsafe at any speed?

general statements we make are influenced by the *particular* aspects of our lives. That particularity, however, does not have to prevent us from making general statements, even general statements about God! We must be modest in what we claim, but we all must make some kinds of claims. Otherwise, we could not say anything! Thus, I will try to provide a safe context in which to learn about basic Christian beliefs, values, and practices.

Second, I want to present Christianity in a way that is *fair*. Many different church traditions will be presented in this book. I have tried to talk about those that have been most influential in church history and in modern times, in shaping Christian beliefs, values, and practices. For example, I talk about Roman Catholicism, Orthodox churches, and a variety of Protestant traditions, movements, and churches that largely make up what we call Christianity. I have included references to many of the smaller traditions, especially among Protestants, that are often overlooked, even in supposedly ecumenical introductions to Christianity. Due to the limitations of time and space, however, I cannot talk about all of them. I apologize in advance to anyone I have overlooked. It is my desire to become ever more inclusive in recognizing the variety of contributors to the richness and diversity of the Christian tradition.

Third, I want to present Christianity in a way that is *fun*. As a long-time university professor, I know that students often consider academics and fun to be mutually exclusive. As a compassionate response to their lament, I wrote this introduction to Christianity with the intent of studying it

Trying to maintain a balance

with more wit and visual aids than one usually finds in introductory textbooks. I hope that my attempts at humor will not distract anyone from the seriousness with which I undertake this study. I often tell my students that it is not enough for me to want to read a paper they wrote that is technically correct; I want to enjoy reading what they write!

At the end of each chapter, there are study questions for further reflection that are intended to help readers ponder more deeply their own views on the topics covered. Some people consider the study of theology to be so theoretical that they have difficulty recognizing its practical applications. I think that theology is very practical because ideas—including religious ideas—have a powerful impact upon how people live. The questions are intended to help readers make connections between what they read, think, and value and how they practically live their lives on a day-to-day basis.

Theology and Scripture

Since this book is an *introduction* to theology, emphasis is placed on how Christians have viewed various religious beliefs, values, and practices throughout church history. Theology deals with Christian understandings of God and of matters related to God. Of course, Christians believe that God relates to everyone and everything, so theology is potentially quite broad. In this book I discuss God, creation, humanity, sin, salvation, spirituality, and eschatology, or what people may expect (or not expect) in the end times.

Christian views mentioned in the book are based, one way or another, upon Scripture, though specific biblical passages may not always be mentioned or interpretive differences evaluated. This is not a biblical studies book per se, so it does not intend to study Scripture verse by verse, chapter by chapter. Instead, when Bible passages are mentioned, they refer to representative or illustrative portions of Scripture. Such passages serve more to illustrate than prove what is said. References to the Bible should certainly not be thought of as proof-texts for particular theological points of view. Readers may not always understand why particular Christians or church traditions believe the way they do. Nevertheless, remember that they claim scriptural evidence for their beliefs, values, and practices, even if others are not persuaded by their interpretation of Scripture.

A historical and critical understanding of Scripture is assumed for this introduction to theology. However, issues of biblical interpretation will only occasionally arise in the course of discussion. As essential as these studies are to theological understanding, it is impossible to go into such deliberations at length in an introductory text. Be aware that such concerns exist and will be mentioned to the extent that they help readers understand the various traditions of Christian-

What is the relationship between the Bible and theology?

ity. To be sure, different views of the Bible and interpretive approaches to it greatly impact theological conclusions.

Church and Denomination References

Numerous references will be made to church history and to particular churches and denominations. This book is not a church history, however, so background for such institutions will not generally be elaborated. Historical references are made throughout the book to the degree that they help present the variety of Christian beliefs, values, and practices.

Some references are made to the worldwide Christian church, and other references are made to specific churches and denominations. Such specificity is usually avoided, but sometimes it is necessary to mention particularities in order to clarify theological distinctions. For example, references are often made to Catholic and Orthodox churches, though references to specific branches within these churches—such as the Roman Catholic Church or specific Orthodox churches—are seldom used because these are not the only bodies that make up the larger church traditions. Even so, most references to Catholicism will refer to Roman Catholicism, since it overwhelmingly serves as the primary example of Catholic beliefs, values, and practices. There are many similarities between the Roman Catholic Church and other branches of Catholicism, as well as between the Catholic tradition and Orthodox churches. In order to acknowledge the varieties of similar church traditions, general references to the Catholic and Orthodox churches are preferred to specific ones.

Dueling churches?

Protestantism is very diverse, and it is often difficult to speak on behalf of all Protestant traditions. Protestantism will sometimes be contrasted with Catholicism, since the interaction between Protestant and Catholic Christians is crucial for understanding Christianity worldwide as well as in the West. When it is theologically important to distinguish between various Protestant traditions, this will be done. Certainly balance is needed in making references to so many churches, denominations, and theological traditions. I will do my best to maintain a balance that fairly treats Christianity as a whole, as well as its constituent individuals, churches, and denominations.

About the Author

Finally, I promised to tell you a little about myself. I am a professor of Christian theology at Azusa Pacific University, a non-denominational Christian institution of higher education located in southern California. My academic background is eclectic: I undertook a comparative approach to religious studies at Stanford University, an evangelical approach to religious studies at Asbury Theological Seminary, a Reformed approach to religious studies at Princeton Theological Seminary, and a Methodist approach to religious studies at Drew University, where I earned a Ph.D. in Theological and Religious Studies.

A beach bum wannabe

I am unaccountably proud of the fact that I am a third-generation Californian—an oddity (an oddity, that is, if one cannot say that all Californians are odd). As a kid, people often got the impression that I was a "PK"; however, I never figured out how they knew I was a "plumber's kid!" I grew up attending churches in the holiness tradition, though throughout my life I have attended a variety of churches in a variety of locales throughout the United States. Now I attend an independent church in southern California.

Acknowledgments

There are many people I want to thank for their help and encouragement with this book. First, I want to thank my family—my daughters Liesl, Heidi, and Dana. I dedicated this book to them. Second, I want to thank my colleagues who gave constructive and deconstructive input to the writing of this book. In particular, I want to thank Steve Wilkens, Keith Reeves, and Lane Scott. Third, I want to thank my niece Freya Thorsen, who helped me with initial research. I also want to thank several students, who helped me with research, writing, editing, and visual aids for the book. They include Halee Scott, Kari Morris-Guzman, Nicole Renaud, Jim Fisk, Dale Nelson, and Gary Myers.

I want to thank the publishers, editors, and other staff at Hendrickson Publishers for their backing and editorial assistance. In particular, I want to thank Shirley Decker-Lucke, Mark House, and Sara Scott for helping me through the last stages of publication, and Patrick Alexander for helping me through the initial stages.

Finally, I want to thank those of you who read this book. It is my hope that it will inform and humor you, interest and broaden you, challenge and inspire you. I have invited you to explore Christian theology, and I trust you will join the expedition!

Don Thorsen

FOUNDATIONS

Always be ready to make your defense to anyone who demands from you an accounting for the hope that is in you; yet do it with gentleness and reverence.
(1 Peter 3:15–16)

THEOLOGY

1.1 Introduction

The Bible tells of the time Jesus walked with his disciples in the vicinity of Caesarea Philippi, a site of pagan worship. While walking, Jesus asks his disciples, "Who do people say that I am?" In response, the disciples give several answers. They mention how some people consider him to be John the Baptist returned from the dead. Others consider Jesus to be one of the ancient prophets like Elijah, who re-appeared to the Jewish people. Finally, Jesus asks his disciples who they think he is. Peter blurts out that Jesus is the Messiah, "the anointed one," appointed by God to bring about redemption and liberation (Mark 8:27–29; cf. Hebrew, *mashiah,* "the anointed one"; Greek, *Christos,* "the Christ").

The disciples contemplating who Jesus is

Peter's declaration serves as a pivotal point in the development of the gospel (Greek *euangelion,* "evangel," "good news") accounts of Jesus' life and ministry. It represents a theological statement about Jesus. That is, Peter describes Jesus—the Messiah—in relationship to God and suggests how that relationship potentially affects the Jewish people and others.

Over the centuries, the Christian understanding of Jesus as the Messiah has gone through a variety of interpretations. Some have questioned what the people in the Bible understood and expected the Messiah to be. Others have questioned whether Jesus was self-conscious of being the Messiah or whether his messianic role was only determined at a later time by the early church. Still others have questioned the relevance of Jesus' messianic role for today. Regardless of the types of questions we ask, they remain theological questions because they concern our understanding of Jesus in relationship to God. In fact, any questions we ask that are somehow related to God are theological questions.

> **What is theology** but faith seeking understanding? When we believe in God, God wants belief that is mature and confident.
>
> God also wants us to share our faith in ways that reflect Scripture, church history, critical thinking, and experience that is relevant.

All of us are "practicing theologians" when we think to ask about God or any matters related to God. We may not be professional theologians, just as we may be neither professional doctors nor plumbers. But just as we become practicing doctors when we bandage a cut finger or practicing plumbers when we unclog a drain, we become practicing theologians when we reflect upon or talk about God. All of us are doing theology when God becomes a part of our considerations.

1.2 What Is Theology?

The first time I took a course in theology, a student sitting next to me asked a question on the first day of class that perturbed the professor. The professor responded caustically by saying that the student obviously did not understand the nature of theology and so should not be in the class. (Wasn't the reason I was taking a course in theology because I didn't know what it was?) The professor's response was very intimidating because I was unable to think of a precise definition for theology. So, immediately after class, I rushed to my desktop dictionary and looked up the word. In its simplest meaning, theology represents the study of God and all things related to God (which basically includes everything!).

The etymology of the word "theology" comes from the Latin word *theologia,* which is derived from the Greek words *theos* ("God") and *logos* ("word, language, discourse, study"). Theology can be used to describe any study of God. But in this book we are looking particularly at the Christian study of God.

1.3 Theology and Scripture

In a sense, Scripture represents theology, since it describes God and things related to God. Of course, Christians usually consider biblical teaching to be different from other theological discussion or sources of religious authority. The Bible is considered special revelation, inspired by God. It gives examples of early theo-

---

DESKTOP DICTIONARY

theology *pl.* theologies n. the science which studies God and all that relates to him, including religion and morals. Christian theology has many branches, e.g., ascetical (dealing with training in virtue), dogmatic (the formulation of doctrine), moral (the behavior of man in the light of his final destiny), mystical (contemplation of union with God), natural (in which God is known by the light of human reason alone), pastoral (dealing with the care of souls) and positive (dealing with revealed truth)

THE NEW LEXICON
WEBSTER'S DICTIONARY OF
THE ENGLISH LANGUAGE

logical reflection and different approaches taken by Jewish and Christian authors. For example, it is helpful to contrast some of the approaches taken to describe Jesus in Scripture. Let us look at the Gospels of Luke and John, two of the four gospels in the New Testament. Luke introduces his story of Jesus the following way:

> Since many have undertaken to set down an or-
> derly account of the events that have been fulfilled
> among us, just as they were handed on to us by
> those who from the beginning were eyewitnesses
> and servants of the word, I too decided, after
> investigating everything carefully from the very
> first, to write an orderly account for you, most ex-
> cellent Theophilus, so that you may know the
> truth concerning the things about which you have
> been instructed. (Luke 1:1–4)

Luke doing careful historical investigation

Luke's gospel is written to Theophilus, a person of prominence that Luke calls "most excellent." In his account, Luke intends to do his best to present a historical account of the life story of Jesus. Accordingly, Luke refers to eyewitness accounts as well as to careful investigation for the orderly account he intends to write. Luke wants to give careful attention to all the details in order to present the best history of Jesus to date.

John's gospel takes a different approach to describing the life and ministry of Jesus. John begins his story of Jesus in the following way:

> In the beginning was the Word, and the Word was with God, and the Word
> was God. He was in the beginning with God. All things came into being
> through him, and without him not one thing came into being. What has
> come into being in him was life, and the life was the light of all people. (John
> 1:1–4)

John immediately takes his introduction far beyond the historical facts about Jesus. Indeed, John contends that Jesus is divine, participated in creation, and redeems life through the light he brings. John's introduction represents a more theological approach to discussing Jesus. He presents a cosmic, eternal perspective of Jesus, which implies far-reaching implications about the nature and works of Jesus.

Both presentations of the gospel represent valid and important contributions to Christian understanding. They emphasize the historical and theological dimensions of Christianity and the ongoing need to uplift both dimensions. Together, they affirm necessary parts of Scripture as well as ongoing needs to study Christianity with great breadth and consequence.

In this book, I will examine all aspects of Scripture, including the historical facts of the life and ministry of Jesus. Yet, I will do much more. I will summarize Christian teachings that look at the "big picture." I will look at the implications

John looking at the "big picture"

of biblical and Christian teachings for addressing a myriad of issues related to God and, as I already said, all things related to God.

Any attempt at describing the gospel message of Christianity runs the risk of being "a stumbling block to Jews and foolishness to Gentiles" (1 Cor 1:23). It represents a stumbling block to Jews because Jesus claimed to fulfill so much of the Hebrew Bible—what Christians call the Old Testament. It represents foolishness to Gentiles because the story of Jesus, his crucifixion and resurrection, includes so much that seems rationally and empirically—as well as culturally—objectionable. Ironically, the New Testament claims that the story of Jesus reflects both the *wisdom* and *power* of God for those who believe in him (1 Cor 1:17).

1.4 The Meaning of Theology

In trying to comprehend the meaning of theology, it is helpful to analyze several definitions put forth by contemporary theologians. Each definition contributes to a holistic understanding of theology that defies the particularity of each. I chose three definitions based on their diverse approaches to the subject matter, which will lead us to a more integrative view of theology. In defining theology, they also discuss the task and methods of theology.

1.4.1 First Definition

Trying to determine the meaning of theology

Thomas Oden (1931–) is a contemporary Protestant theologian who provides a traditional definition of theology:

> Theology . . . is reasoned discourse about God gained either by rational reflection or by response to God's self-disclosure in history. Christian theology is the orderly exposition of Christian teaching. It sets forth that understanding of God that is made known in Jesus Christ. It seeks to provide a coherent reflection on the living God as understood in the community whose life is "in Christ."[1]

Oden emphasizes the logical way in which people attempt to talk about God. Knowledge of God is derived in two primary ways: The first way pertains to knowledge that can be determined by use of reason alone; the second way pertains to knowledge that can be determined by investigation into the revelation of God.

Theology that is Christian presents, in an orderly fashion, the teachings of the Christian church (the community of believers) about God and all things related to God. In the early church, theology fulfilled a very practical need to summarize basic Christian teachings. Today, theology continues to function like a map that encapsulates Christian teachings.

Theology is *christocentric*, that is, it focuses on Jesus Christ as the preeminent revelation of God. This focus underscores the authority of Scripture as the source of information and investigation about Jesus Christ. Thus Christian theology is dependent upon revelation, centered primarily in words of the Bible.

The goal of theology is to construct a coherent worldview that places God and Jesus Christ in proper relationship to people and to the world as a whole. In particular, Christian theology is done by those who are themselves Christian—those who are "in Christ." Although anyone can do theology, theology that is distinctively Christian is done within the context of faith.

Constructing theology?

1.4.2 Second Definition

Francis Schüssler Fiorenza (1941–) is a contemporary Catholic theologian who provides a similar albeit distinct definition of theology:

> Theology is a fragile discipline in that it is both academic and related to faith. As an academic discipline, theology shares all the scholarly goals of other academic disciplines: it strives for historical exactitude, conceptual rigor, systematic consistency, and interpretive clarity. In its relation to faith, theology shares the fragility of faith itself. It is much more a hope than a science. It is much more like a raft bobbing upon the waves of the sea than a pyramid based on solid ground.[2]

Schüssler Fiorenza focuses on the fragility of theology, that is, on the human character of people reflecting on issues related to a transcendent God. By definition, that which is transcendent surpasses our finite human understanding. Still people speak of God because of God's revelatory self-disclosure to us.

Theology is also fragile because of its dual character. Theology is an academic discipline, like other branches of learning, which uses scientific methods that include induction and deduction. Theology is also a matter of faith, which involves belief, trust, and loyalty to God. Such faith appears fragile from a human perspective because it reflects a personal association with God that defies rational and empirical analysis. But paradoxically, Christians do believe that their faith, as well as their study of theology, benefits from historical exactitude, conceptual rigor, systematic consistency, and interpretive clarity.

The academic study of theology does not always appear or feel as if it contributes to faith in God. There seems to be an inherent antagonism between a faith that can be intensely personal and private and the academic study of theology that can be intensely impersonal and public. However, because most Christians believe that "all truth is God's truth," the academic study of theology is not inherently harmful to faith but conducive to it.

Schüssler Fiorenza describes theology more as an expression of hope than of science. In church history, Christians have often described theology as a science. This is because, as I have already said, theology strives for historical exactitude, conceptual rigor, systematic consistency, and interpretive clarity. In the middle ages, theology was considered the apex (or "queen") of the sciences. But today, people more often think that the faith dimension of theology gives it more the appearance of "bobbing upon the waves of the sea than a pyramid based on solid ground."[3] This does not necessarily mean that the solidity of the divine foundation of theology is totally absent. It means that the task of theology is an ongoing human endeavor hopeful of appropriately establishing Christian faith today.

Bobbing on the theological waves of the sea

1.4.3 Third Definition

Paul Tillich (1886–1965) is another Protestant theologian who provides a definition of theology that emphasizes the need to correlate our beliefs in reference to the contemporary human situation:

> Theology, as a function of the Christian church, must serve the needs of the church. A theological system is supposed to satisfy two basic needs: the statement of the truth of the Christian message and the interpretation of this truth for every new generation. Theology moves back and forth between two poles, the eternal truth of its foundation and the temporal situation in which the eternal truth must be received.[4]

Tillich underscores the church-centered function of theology. If the church is not responding to the immediate needs of its own people, it is not functioning appropriately. Likewise, if the church is not responding to the needs of the world as a whole, it is not functioning appropriately.

Tillich, like many other Christians throughout church history, developed an extensive theological system. His system allows for expansion and development in areas that are relevant to the human situation.

Theology is not self-sealing. That is, it remains open to new insights about the truth of the Christian message and to its applications for every new generation. In this sense, theology is always reforming, just as the Protestant Reformers intended. It is a living expression of people's understanding of God and of God's relationship to them and to the world.

Theology is a dynamic enterprise that tries to integrate what is believed to be divine truth and the particular, human, finite context in which that truth must be received, understood, and applied. Discerning what is true and knowing how to integrate or contextualize it appropriately represents a tremendous challenge in a world in which there are so many personal and social challenges. What are the contemporary needs of people today? What are the needs of society? How does our theology speak to those needs, and how does our theology lead us to act appropriately? The dynamic interplay between eternal truth and temporal situation provides a fertile context in which theology becomes exciting and relevant for today.

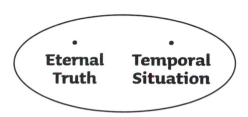

1.5 The Divisions of Theology

Theology functions in a variety of ways. Thus far we have only spoken of it in general terms. But there are various divisions of theology that help us learn the nature and extent of its relevance.

There is more than one way to divide the functions of theology. Sometimes theology is used to encompass biblical, historical, philosophical, and theological studies. But more precisely theological studies refer to biblical, historical, systematic, philosophical, and practical theologies. *Biblical* theology organizes the theological teachings in the Bible according to prominent biblical themes. *Historical* theology studies the development of theology from biblical times to the present. *Systematic* theology arranges Christian beliefs, values, and practices in an orderly and comprehensive manner. *Philosophical* theology interacts with philosophy in establishing theology. *Practical* theology applies Christian beliefs to the church and the world.

All of these theological studies overlap with one another and are interdependent. The approach of this book will be predominantly systematic, which involves arranging Christian beliefs, values, and practices in an organized or methodical way. Topics include the study of revelation, authority, Scripture, God, creation, Jesus Christ, Holy Spirit, salvation, spirituality, church, sacraments, and eschatology. Several of these topics will be subdivided into separate chapters because some topics are more extensive than others. Altogether, they provide an orderly and comprehensive introduction to Christianity.

Branches of Theology

1.6 Augustine: A Classic Model of Theology

Augustine of Hippo (354–430) is the most widely known and respected theologian in church history. His influence extends far beyond that of

Christianity because Augustine had tremendous impact upon the development of Western philosophy, historiography, and literature. The prominence of his theological understanding remains influential today. So, an investigation into who he was and what he believed remains a model for how we approach theology today.

Augustine argued that we have knowledge (Latin, *scientia*) of sense experience, which is adequate (albeit uncertain) for living in a world that is temporal and changing. But we do not have the ability to understand the eternal and unchanging aspects of ourselves, the world, and God. Only God provides wisdom (Latin, *sapientia*) adequate for understanding certain things.

God reveals wisdom primarily through the Bible, which represents God's special revelation to humanity. Revelation provides that which reason alone cannot know. Although God establishes the validity of rational knowledge, people must submit themselves to the authority of God's revelation in order to have sufficient understanding.

All people depend upon authority of one sort or another. We submit to the authority of parents, teachers, governments, and so on. This submission represents an act of faith. Augustine considered faith to be thinking with assent, particularly assent to God and to God's revelation. Augustine notably said, "Understanding is the reward of faith. Therefore do not seek to understand in order to know, but believe in order that you may understand."[5] Our understanding leads us to the point of faith because faith is not unreasonable. But it is the experience of faith that brings true intellectual and spiritual enlightenment.

This enlightenment may occur as a sudden flash of insight or understanding. Augustine participated in this type of enlightenment at the time of his conversion. Some have interpreted his experience as being almost mystical in orientation because of the sense of union Augustine felt with God. Although Augustine emphasized the need for divine illumination, he considered faith and reason to be complementary.

Over the centuries, many Christians have looked to Augustine as a model for how to approach theology. One may study theology for a variety of reasons, but one should not first seek understanding in order to believe. As noted above, Augustine urges us, "Believe in order that you may understand."[6] A classic reformulation of this approach was later articulated by Anselm (ca. 1033–1109), an influential Medieval churchman and theologian, who stated, "For I do not seek to understand so that I may believe; but I believe so that I may understand. For I believe this also, that 'unless I believe, I shall not understand' (Is. vii.9)."[7]

1.7 Theology and Apologetics

One of the most important objectives of Augustine's theology was *apologetics*. Apologetics represents the defense or explanation of Christian beliefs, values, and practices in a way that is well-reasoned and relevant to life. In the ancient church, apologetics was sometimes a matter of life and death, since Christians were martyred for their religious affirmations. Apologetics represented an important need of the growing church to defend Christianity from its critics and persecutors. By the time Augustine wrote, Christians were not formally persecuted. However, they continued to be blamed for problems in the Roman Empire, including the sack of Rome in 410. In response to such criticisms Augustine wrote such famous books as *The City of God*, which answered criticisms about whether the Roman Empire had been weakened by Christianity.

Every age and period of history raises new questions or revives ancient ones. Therefore, apologetics continues to be an important part of Christian theology. Christians have an ongoing need to answer questions and criticisms raised against it. While the purpose of this book is to provide an introduction to theology, I will address a few of the questions and criticisms that have been leveled against the church. For example, I will discuss the following apologetic issues:

Augustine defending Christianity

- Does God exist?

- How much can we know about God?

- By what authority or authorities do Christians make decisions about what they believe, value, and practice?

- How reliable is Scripture?

- To what degree does God determine what happens, and to what degree are people free to choose for themselves?

- Did God create everything, and how does creation relate to evolution?

- If God is almighty and loving, why does evil occur?

- How are people saved, and what happens to those who have never heard of Jesus Christ?

It is important for Christians to respond to challenges against essential beliefs, values, and practices. Some apologetic issues have caused strife and division. However, the focus of this book is not apologetics, and certainly not polemics against detractors of Christianity. Instead, the focus has more to do with introducing the breadth and depth of theology. Hence, the subject matter will be more irenic than polemic.

1.8 Theology and Ecumenism

What keeps the trajectory of Christian theology on track? What prevents it from spiraling out of control into corrupt or irrelevant directions? In theory, there is nothing that guarantees that theology will not become woefully distorted in one way or another. Certainly we can imagine a variety of theological trajectories that we—you or I—consider to be pretty much out of touch with reality, much less with Scripture and church history. But by what "reality" do we

evaluate theology? There are, of course, a variety of realities or criteria by which to judge theology. There are religious, personal, social, cultural, and intellectual criteria, among others.

Historically, the church has believed that the Holy Spirit safeguards God's revelation to humanity. Christian people have also believed that God uses the church as the theological safeguard to what should be believed in general and about the Bible in particular. After all, it is the community of believers—the church—who is responsible for handling God's revelation.

Since there are so many churches, it seems nearly impossible to discern those that could be considered true or orthodox. The concept of orthodoxy pertains to those beliefs, values, and practices representative of the historic or widely accepted views of the church. But as the church developed over the centuries, so did its beliefs, values, and practices. It would be incredible to think that there exists a single, untainted strand of Christianity that supersedes all other viewpoints.

Trying to prevent theology from spiraling out of control

Consequently, in this book I will explore the full Christian tradition by providing an ecumenical sketch of its beliefs, values, and practices as they developed in history. Because of the multiplicity of religious movements, denominations, and orders in Christianity, it is impossible to present every theological development. But we can describe in broad strokes some of the most formative theological developments in church history. This ecumenical approach does not seek church unity so much as it seeks a unity of understanding and appreciation for the varieties of church traditions. It intends to be inclusive of churches East and West, ancient and modern.

When some consensus over particular beliefs and practices was achieved in

church history, that consensus will be our focus. When no consensus was reached, a variety of viewpoints will be presented. I hope that this approach will be fair, as well as appreciative, of the variety of theological contributions made by Christians over the centuries.

Because this book is being written in the United States at the beginning of the millennium, it would be naïve to think that a great deal of concern will not be given to the interests of contemporary American perspectives on Christian theology. Such interests will be present in this book, but I hope that they will not detract from the at-

Christians trying to find consensus

tempt to present an ecumenical view of theology representative of the world-wide Christian church.

1.9 Conclusion

Whenever we think about God or any matters related to God, we are doing theology. That is, we are attempting to relate God to that which we believe, value, and eventually put into practice. We may be good at doing theology, or we may not. But the more intentional and knowledgeable we become in its practice, the better we will be at theology.

It is the purpose of this book to introduce theology to those largely un-schooled in the theology of Christianity. A breadth of theological issues will be presented, representing a comprehensive overview of how Christians have attempted to deal with them. Although the overview will be comprehensive, it cannot be in-depth in terms of the multitude of theological questions that could be raised. But it is hoped that the issues will be discussed in a way that is stimulating as well as fair to the variety of theological traditions representative of Christianity, regardless of whether it be East or West, ancient or modern. Readers are encouraged to read and decide for themselves with regard to the theological issues discussed. Even more, readers are encouraged to continue in their study of questions and ideas that are important to their understanding of God and God's relationship to them.

1.10 Questions for Further Reflection

1. What is the relationship between what you think, value, and believe (in theory) and what you say and do (in practice)? For example, how might belief in God affect what you say, where you go, what you do, how you spend your money?

2. When do you think theologically, that is, when do you most often consider God in your thinking? How important are your thoughts about God in what you say and do?

3. Can theological studies be spiritually harmful to people? Because some people consider Christian faith and reason to be in conflict, what liabilities are there in "faith seeking understanding" (Augustine)? What are the benefits?

4. How important is it for Christians to defend their faith, beliefs, and practices? What is their responsibility for explaining Christianity to others?

5. Which of the definitions of theology do you consider the most helpful? Why?

6. What is meant by an ecumenical approach to theology? What are the benefits and liabilities of such an approach?

1.11 Notes

1. Thomas C. Oden, *The Living God* (vol. 1 of *Systematic Theology;* San Francisco: Harper & Row, 1987), 5.

2. Francis Schüssler Fiorenza, "Systematic Theology: Task and Methods," in *Systematic Theology: Roman Catholic Perspectives* (ed. Francis Schüssler Fiorenza and John P. Galvin; 2 vols.; Minneapolis: Fortress, 1991), 1:5.

3. Ibid.

4. Paul Tillich, *Systematic Theology* (3 vols.; Chicago: University of Chicago Press, 1951), 1:3.

5. Augustine, *Tractates on the Gospel of John, 28–54* (trans. John W. Rettig; Fathers of the Church 88; Washington: Catholic University of America Press, 1993), 29.6.

6. Ibid. Cf. Philip Schaff, ed., *A Select Library of the Nicene and Post-Nicene Fathers of the Christian Church* (trans. R. G. MacMullen; 14 vols.; Grand Rapids: Eerdmans, 1979), 6:465, cf. 6:481.

7. Anselm, "Proslogion," in *Anselm of Canterbury: The Major Works* (ed. Brian Davies and G. R. Evans; Oxford World's Classics; New York: Oxford University Press, 1998), 87.

CHAPTER TWO

*Long ago God spoke to our ancestors in many and
various ways by the prophets, but in these last days he
has spoken to us by a Son, whom he appointed heir of
all things, through whom he also created the worlds.*
(Hebrews 1:1–2)

REVELATION

2.1 Introduction

When visiting the city of Joppa, the Apostle Peter one day climbed up on the roof of the house in which he was staying in order to pray (Acts 10:9–16). While praying, Peter went into a trance or deep sleep. He envisioned a large sheet lowered from heaven, which contained a variety of creatures, reptiles, and birds considered ritually impure according to Jewish law. Then Peter heard a voice saying that he should kill and eat what he saw. But Peter vehemently refused because he believed that Jewish law prevented him from eating anything considered profane or unclean. The vision appeared to Peter three times and suddenly disappeared.

Peter was greatly puzzled with regard to how he should interpret the vision. On the one hand, it was contrary to everything he knew, based upon the revelation of the Hebrew Bible and historic traditions. Such religious authorities were not to be taken lightly or ignored. Yet, circumstances that occurred after Peter's vision led him to modify his beliefs. Cornelius, a Gentile, converted to Christianity and had a vision of an angel who told him to speak with Peter. Peter, in turn, verified the authenticity of Cornelius' conversion, concluding that Gentiles, or non-Jews, should share in the salvation provided by Jesus. These experiences also helped Peter understand that which God revealed to him in the vision. Not only did Peter come to believe that all foods should be viewed as clean, he came to believe that God accepted all people without partiality.

Peter having a vision

The question of revelation or of conflicting revelations continues to be an issue today. Peter's puzzlement finally came to resolution, though it was a

> **God reveals much** to us. Some comes generally through the world in which we live. But such revelation needs more.
>
> God especially reveals things to us through Scripture, which tells us of God, love, righteous living, and salvation forevermore.

resolution that continued to be tested. What is our view of revelation? In particular, what is our view of how and when God reveals special truths to us about God and salvation?

2.2 What Is Revelation?

A common cartoon that we see in the comic papers is the picture of a bearded man walking down the street and carrying a sign that prophesies some divine revelation of gloom or doom. Of course, most of us look at such cartoons with amusement. But the idea of receiving a special revelation from God—regardless of whether it is for good or ill—is very sobering.

Revelation signifies a "revealing, unveiling, or uncovering" (Latin, *revelatio*). Revelation can be of a very general nature, a revealing or unveiling of any type of knowledge about the world and about ourselves. From a theological perspective, revelation refers to the revealing or unveiling of God and of other truths related to God.

Revelation represents a central part of the biblical message. From the beginning of biblical history, God reveals many things to people including specific knowledge of God. These revelations take place in a variety of ways. To some people, God speaks directly (Gen 2–3). Other times God reveals things indirectly through great events in history such as the exodus of the Hebrew people from Egypt (Exod 3:20; Deut 26:5–9), or the destruction of the Northern and Southern kingdoms at the hands of the various nations God used as instruments of punishment upon Israel and Judah (2 Kgs 17; 24–25; Isa 10:5–6; Hab 1:5–6).

Sometimes knowledge of the divine is gained through the natural world. Psalm 19:1 states, "The heavens are telling the glory of God; and the firmament proclaims his handiwork." This general revelation is available to everyone, but it does not necessarily give specific knowledge of God. So, more specific revelation is needed.

Most often, Scripture records God communicating to people through unusual methods. Those methods include:

- casting lots (Prov 16:33; Acts 1:21–26)

- divining stones (e.g., Urim and Thummim; see 1 Sam 28:6)

- deep sleep (Job 4:13; 33:15)

- dreams (Gen 37:1–11; Dan 2:19; 7:1; Matt 1:20; 2:13)

- visions (Isa 1:1; Dan 8:1)

- theophanies (Isa 6:1–5; Ezek 1:26, 28; Dan 7:9, 13, 22; Rev 4:1–5:14)

- angelic messengers (Luke 1:26–38; Acts 7:39; Gal 3:19)

In each instance, God reveals knowledge to people who then communicate it to others, especially those in the religious community. The community needs to discern the authenticity of revelation because it can be misunderstood or fraudulent for a variety of reasons. So the believing community needs to take responsibility in their acceptance of revelation from God.

In the New Testament, Jesus embodies the most complete self-disclosure of God to humanity (Heb 1:1–2). Through him, people learn more about God and salvation than had previously been revealed. Thus so much of theology is *christocentric*—that is, it focuses on Jesus. He became the lens through which other revelatory information is to be evaluated. Jesus serves as a corrective as well as illuminator of God's revelation to humanity.

Is God revealed through the casting of lots?

In time most Christians came to view Scripture as the most authoritative source for discerning God's revelation. Some consider it their only source of divine revelation, while others consider it one among other important sources. Regardless of how one views it, the Bible—its authority as well as its interpretation—remains one of the most important and thus one of the most highly debated topics of Christianity.

2.3 Understanding Revelation

2.3.1 General and Special Revelation

Over the centuries, Christians developed a theological distinction between two primary types of revelation. The first type is called *general revelation*, which signifies that knowledge available to all people at all times and places. This, of course, includes more than religious knowledge. But theologically speaking, general revelation pertains to that knowledge of the world that points beyond itself to God.

For example, Christianity possesses a long history of those who argue that God's existence is known through creation. Some argue that observation of the physical world and human history proves God's existence (Ps 19:1–2). Others argue that the existence of God is proven through the human conscience or an innate sense of deity (Rom 1:19–20).

General revelation has been a topic of great debate because knowledge of God determined by rational or empirical means alone is considered insufficiently certain or reliable. Our human powers of thinking and investigation are subject to a number of finite variables that give ambiguous knowledge of God and of things pertaining to God.

For this reason, *special revelation* from God is needed in order to supplement our finite human understanding. In Scripture, God was believed to communicate directly to people in a variety of ways. Eventually, Jesus was thought to provide the best revelation of God (Heb 1:1–4). But the nature and extent of divine revelation has progressively come under critical scrutiny by people concerned about how to discern truth about God, themselves, and the world. Thus, a variety of understandings of revelation have arisen in order to resolve questions dealing with the nature and extent of God's revelation.

A COMPARISON

General Revelation	Special Revelation
Available to all people	Available to a few people
Available at all times and places	Available at particular times and places
Intended for all people; they may discover it for themselves	Intended for all people; they must somehow be told
Declares God's greatness	Declares God's grace
Sufficient for condemnation	Sufficient for salvation
Biblical examples: Psalm 19:1–2; Romans 1:19–20	Biblical examples: 2 Timothy 3:16; 1 Peter 1:20; Hebrews 1:1–4[1]

2.3.2 Progressive Revelation

Progressive revelation signifies God's progressive revelation of truth to people. God does not reveal all truths to people at once. Instead, God gradually reveals aspects of God's divine nature as well as God's covenant relationships with people. The progressive nature of revelation especially pertains to Scripture and how later revelation is built on earlier revelation. The revelation of God and salvation through Jesus, for example, is described in the Bible as a *new covenant,* which reveals more fully the character of God and the ways in which God wants to relate with people (2 Cor 2:12–3:18; Gal 4:21–31).

Acknowledgment of the progressive nature of God's revelation, particularly God's special revelation, has several implications for Scripture. First, Christians need to be careful about how revelation as a whole is understood. To what degree may God still be revealing truth to us? What constitutes the most reliable source or sources of revelation? Second, Christians need to be careful about how they understand and interpret Scripture. To what degree are some portions of the Bible, presumably later ones, more reliable than other portions? How does one determine the degree to which later revelation complements or replaces prior revelation? The answers to such questions may have profound impact upon Christian beliefs, values, and practices.

2.4 Models of Revelation

Avery Dulles (1918–) is a Catholic cardinal and theologian who developed "models of revelation" in order to help us grasp the various ways that Christians understand God's revelation.[2] At times, models run the risk of oversimplifying complex ideas. But Dulles' models are helpful for an introductory study of revelation and for understanding how Christians articulate the ways in which God reveals truth to people. His work provides the following models.

Tinkering with theology

2.4.1 Revelation as Doctrine

The most common way of understanding revelation may be described as the model of revelation as doctrine. In this model, divine revelation is communicated objectively and authoritatively through the words of Holy Scripture. Doctrines are formulated in correspondence with propositions stated in the Bible. Since Scripture is understood as the inspired revelation of God, it provides sufficient information for determining all matters of Christian faith, value, and practice.

Great care must then be taken in the interpretation of the Bible and the subsequent development of doctrine. Some Christian traditions rely upon the interpretations of the church for determining proper doctrinal understandings. Both individual and corporate interpretation of the Bible is thought to be aided by the Holy Spirit, who gives illumination to those who seek to understand Scripture. Proper scriptural interpretation is thought to result in reliable Christian doctrine.

Does Christian doctrine come directly from Scripture?

This model of revelation as doctrine accepts the presence of general (or natural) revelation. But general revelation is of minor importance because it is insufficient for salvation. General revelation only pricks the conscience of people; it does not provide the way of salvation. The purpose of God's special revelation is to elicit saving faith through one's encounter with divine truth found in Scripture. Jesus embodies the pinnacle of truth, and it is response to his life and ministry that is especially crucial for salvation.

This revelation, however, is not available to people at all times and places. Instead it is revealed to particular people at particular times and places. Some call this the *scandal of particularity* because it suggests that eternal truth is discernable from temporal events. It is also scandalous because not all people seem to have equal access to it. Nevertheless, this model of revelation affirms that it is God's intention that particular people and events in history should be the *means* by which truth about God and salvation is communicated. This truth can be stated in biblically based propositions, for example, as found in the early doctrinal summaries of Christian belief such as the Nicene Creed. Doctrines elevated to the status of dogma represent those beliefs mandated for membership in a church or denomination.

> **THE TRUTH OF THE CHRISTIAN FAITH**
>
> Although the truth of the Christian faith surpasses the capacity of human nature, yet those things which reason has inherently in possession cannot be contrary to the Christian truth.
>
> THOMAS AQUINAS,
> SUMMA CONTRA GENTILES
> (13TH CENTURY)

Augustine is a prime example of one who viewed revelation as doctrine. He developed numerous interpretive principles and rules for properly interpreting the Bible. Certainly Augustine looked for the literal and historical meaning of Scripture. But he also looked for divine truths communicated through allegorical and typological meanings found in it. In addition, Augustine believed that spiritual purification was needed for the proper interpretation of Scripture. Our relationship with God, as well as our openness to the prompting of the Holy Spirit, is necessary for discerning God's revelation.

2.4.2 Revelation as Inner Experience

At the turn of the nineteenth century, Christians progressively doubted the reliability of the Bible as well as church tradition for discerning divine revelation. A view of revelation as inner experience emerged. The intuitive quality of inner experience became prominent; it was considered the only reliable knowledge available to an individual. In this regard, revelation corresponds to the self-disclosure of God by God's intimate presence within the inner spirit or mind of a human being. So, greater emphasis is placed upon the role of human intuition than is found when viewing revelation as doctrine. A person is thought to know God intuitively without the need of sensory organs, ordinary experience, or reason. The purpose of revelation is to impart both a sense of communion with God and an awareness of one's own spirituality.

Scripture remains important because it still contains the words of God. But it is intermingled with the human elements of myth and error. One may critically study the Bible in order to discern truth in it, but the apprehension of truth is dependent upon the personal illumination that an individual experiences. Truth does not come primarily through historical investigation because history only provides a mental image of human continuity. Instead, intuition supersedes other critical abilities to discern truth.

Friedrich Schleiermacher (1768–1834) believed that all people have a *feeling of absolute dependence* upon that which transcends personal existence. This inner experience signifies more than just a feeling or emotion. It represents a fundamental structure of personal existence that reveals primary religious truths related to God. The corporate comprehension of redemption experienced by the church represented the foundation for doctrinal formulations. Doctrine does not so much embody the summation of biblical teachings as the summation of the church's inner experience of God. Schleiermacher established this approach to theology because of growing distrust in revelation that comes from sources outside one's own experience. Doctrines were seen as secondary conceptions of more primary truths of religious experience and subsequently the former could be expressed in various ways.

Feeling of "absolute dependence"?

2.4.3 Revelation as Dialectical Presence

In the twentieth century, Christians increasingly grew reluctant to accept the propositions of the Bible as the basis of divine revelation. But they also distrusted optimism in human experience as the means to discern divine truth and live in authentic relationship with God. So there arose a more dynamic conception of divine revelation. God's self-disclosure was thought to occur in the moment people encountered the word of God as read or proclaimed in Scripture, a revelation facilitated by the Holy Spirit. The contents of the Bible do not represent the word of God but may *become* the word of God through the revelatory work of the Holy Spirit. God is dialectically present because divine disclosure occurs in the moment the person encounters Scripture. The words of the Bible do not themselves embody the words of God, but God uses Scripture as the means by which God chooses to encounter people.

The words of the Bible primarily represent the words of people that God uses as the means by which to reveal truths that transcend history. Scripture reveals that which is beyond history and our ability to discern truth historically. Only by faith can we know of God through a divine encounter. But it is an encounter that paradoxically occurs through our encounter with the Bible, and particularly its witness to Jesus. By faith we read and hear Scripture, and in those moments, the words of the Bible become the word of God to us by the work of the Holy Spirit, who facilitates our faith. Doctrines are dynamic rather than static because they develop in response to our encounter with the presence of God as we also encounter Scripture. But it is our encounter with God, rather than with unchanging doctrine, that is important for salvation.

Karl Barth (1886–1968) asserted that God initiates and fulfills divine self-disclosure without human effort. Although some scholars question whether the label of dialectic applies to the work of Barth, his theology reflects the dynamic nature of God's revelation. Revelation neither involves an objective doctrinal study of statically conceived biblical propositions nor does it involve the analysis of an inner experience of God. Instead it involves a personal encounter with God in the moment of faithful reflection upon the Bible. To Barth, only Jesus represents the "word of God" (John 1:1), though in a derivative—

The Twofold Word of God

albeit important—way the Bible also represents the word of God (Mark 7:13; Luke 8:11). In the event of our encounter with God, more is revealed than what the words of the Bible say. The words of Scripture, however, may paradoxically serve as the means to reveal existential meaning beyond its historical content.

2.4.4 Revelation as New Awareness

During the twentieth century there emerged an understanding of divine revelation as that which is discerned through a new awareness of personal transcendence and the power of self-transformation. Since we all are thought to share in divine creativity, we may tap into it by nurturing a heightened level of consciousness that transforms our perceptions as well as ourselves. The emphasis is not upon what God may do but upon what we may do through our growing participation in that which is divine.

Revelation as new awareness minimizes the historic understanding of Christianity, though it retains biblical ideas that are helpful for personal transcendence and self-transformation. The Bible is viewed as a human document. Its historicity is not important because truth is discerned by reason or a kind of mystical meditation. But Scripture still serves as a helpful paradigm for nurturing people in their divine creativity. Although traditional Christian doctrine must undergo reinterpretation, biblical ideas may provide helpful concepts, images, and stories for promoting personal transcendence and self-transformation.

Tillich sought common ground between theology and secular thought, for example, as found in psychology. He considered traditional Christianity to be limiting and instead sought a more universal foundation for one's existence. His emphasis upon *ultimate concern* reflected an attitude that transcended the limitations of historic Christian understanding. No theology can encompass the fullness of the divine. Thus Tillich argued that theology must always be reforming, which he described as the "Protestant principle." It reforms in accordance with a "method of correlation." This involves an analysis of the existential situation in which people find themselves in life. Then the task of theology is to demonstrate how the symbols of Christianity may answer the questions or solve the problems that arise.

2.4.5 Revelation as Historical

In the later half of the twentieth century there arose a renewed concern for viewing revelation as historical. This viewpoint rejects the historical unreliability of the biblical account of revelation. Instead, the Bible is thought to record adequately the great deeds of God in human history that reveal the nature and extent of God's saving disposition. Reason aids people in the critical and historical investigation of the Bible. Those who doubt the reliability of Scripture are thought to do so as a result of presuppositions that they bring to the text rather than through a truly inductive investigation of the text.

Revelation is inextricably bound up with history. Although God's self-disclosure is revealed indirectly through the totality of historical investigation, revelation is related to the continuity and particularity of history. The events of history, especially as found in the Bible, instill hope and trust in the God of history.

Wolfhart Pannenberg (1928–) considers both faith and knowledge to be rooted in history. Jesus was a historical person, and his life and ministry must be understood within its historical context. Thus, history must be studied critically without modern presuppositions that deny, by definition, the entering of God into history. However, history must be understood from an eschatological perspective, that is, from its endpoint. Pannenberg

History being drawn toward God

argues for a universal concept of history, so past and present religious truths must be understood within the context of an eschatological goal that draws all history toward God.

2.5 Revelation and Mystery

While Christians believe that God has revealed much to them in both general and special ways, much remains that is mystery. Christians are not embarrassed or sorry about the fact that mysteries and paradoxes permeate their theology. The Bible itself talks about the *mysteries* (Greek, *mysteria,* "hidden things") of the gospel (Eph 1:9; 3:3–5, 9; 6:19). It is not God's will that all things be revealed at this time (Deut 29:29; Job 11:7; Dan 12:9; 1 Cor 13:12; 1 John 3:2). Thus, Scripture warns us that complete revelation will not occur in this lifetime. In the meantime, sufficient revelation is available for all matters important for salvation and for living in accordance with God's will.

There are many reasons why God would not want everything revealed at this time. People are finite; they suffer from sin, ignorance, misery, and various types of bondage that limit their knowledge. Such limitations hinder their development as people as well as Christians. Yet, by the grace of God and God's various means of revelation, Christians may speak

How does one proclaim a mystery boldly?

meaningfully about God and matters related to God. Despite mysteries that exist in Scripture as well as life, Christians do not need to hold back in proclaiming that which they consider to be true and holy. They should not make their proc-lamations simplistically or without humility, but they should feel free to make them boldly!

2.6 Conclusion

All Christians accept that there is some form of revelation and that our reli-gious perspectives are dependent upon it. All accept that revelation is divinely provided, one way or another. Differences occur when the nature of revelation and how it is appropriated are discussed. But those differences do not lessen the priority of revelation for determining personal beliefs, values, and practices. Divine self-disclosure is integral to all of Christianity. Revelation—however it is understood—forms the Christian starting point of theological reflection.

The distinction between general and special revelation becomes clouded when we consider the various models of revelation. Some models place greater emphasis upon the need for special revelation, such as those in which revela-tion is conceived as as doctrinal, historical, or dialectical presence. Other mod-els, such as those in which revelation is conceived as inner experience or new awareness, allow for greater emphasis upon general revelation. Most Chris-tians accept that some degree of both special and general revelation come into play when reflecting from a theological perspective. It is not a matter of accept-ing either one view of revelation or another. Instead, it is more a matter of many views taken together, informing our understanding of revelation. One or more views may predominate; however, each view offers insight helpful for de-veloping a broad view of how God authoritatively communicates. So the issue of authority becomes important. Authority pertains to the degree to which any particular understanding of revelation affects people's beliefs, values, and practices. So it is to the issue of authority that we next turn in our discussion.

2.7 Questions for Further Reflection

1. To what degree can we know about God, given only general revelation, or, in other words, things we can discover for ourselves? To what degree do we need special revelation?

2. To what degree does special revelation provide propositional truth for the development of doctrine? How clear-cut is truth?

3. To what degree must we rely upon the more subjective aspects of an "inner experience" or "new awareness" for the development of Christian beliefs, values, and practices? Practically speaking, with how much sub-jectivity do we determine our beliefs, values, and practices?

4. What is the relationship between revelation and history? Can history pro-vide sufficient information about the God who transcends time and space?

5. To what degree does revelation represent a "dialectical presence"? How extensive is the paradox of finite humans having knowledge of an infinite God? Can people live with a paradoxical God?

2.8 Notes

1. H. Wayne House, *Charts of Christian Theology and Doctrine* (Grand Rapids: Zondervan, 1992), 38.

2. Avery Dulles, *Models of Revelation* (Garden City, N.Y.: Doubleday, 1983; repr., Maryknoll, N.Y.: Orbis, 1992).

CHAPTER THREE

*Now the eleven disciples went to Galilee, to the
mountain to which Jesus had directed them. When they
saw him, they worshiped him; but some doubted. And
Jesus came and said to them, "All authority in heaven
and on earth has been given to me."*
(Matthew 28:16–18)

AUTHORITY

3.1 Introduction

The Apostle Peter was recognized in the early church as the preeminent leader of the new Christian movement. Jesus had bestowed authority upon him, and Jesus' disciples, along with other Christians, deferred to Peter's leadership.

But when Peter visited the Christians in the city of Antioch, a problem arose (Gal 2:11–14). Earlier he had come to the recognition that God does not distinguish between Jews and Gentiles (Acts 10:10–35). So when Peter went to Antioch, he ate meals in fellowship with converted Gentiles. But this practice was frowned upon by a group of Christian Jews known as Judaizers who had a more conservative view of Jewish law. They pressured Peter into not eating with any Gentiles. Peter's example influenced other Jewish Christians, such as Barnabas, not to eat with any of the converted Gentiles.

Paul was aghast at the inconsistency of Peter's actions and rebuked him publicly. Peter had not only acknowledged earlier that God did not distinguish between Jews and Gentiles, he had given his support to Paul in ministry to the Gentiles. Yet Peter allowed himself to be persuaded by the prejudices of the Judaizers. So Paul publicly challenged the authority of Peter even though Peter was the preeminent leader of the church. But Paul believed that he argued on behalf of a higher truth of God's revelation that must confront Peter, despite the authority of his ecclesiastical leadership.

We all rely on authority, whether it involves a parent or spouse, teacher or employer, friend or government.

God's authority is supreme, yet God also gives us Scripture, minds, and other means for godly living and discernment.

3.2 What Is Authority?

All of us live under and rely upon authorities of one sort or another. As children we relied upon the authority of our parents or other caregivers in order to survive. When we entered school we relied upon the authority of our teachers in order to develop further our minds and social skills. Without the presence of knowledgeable authority figures, children would hardly be able to live and mature. Even as adults we rely upon the authority

Paul challenging Peter's authority!

of others more knowledgeable than ourselves in the areas of work, travel, investments, and so on. It is impossible for a single person to discover all that can be known without authoritative sources outside oneself.

Authority pertains to the right and power to command and be obeyed. God ultimately is the source of all authority, though in practice people live with a variety of authorities. In this world, God permits many to speak and act with authority. Sometimes the authority has to do with certain rights and privileges, and at other times it has to do with the authority to exert power.

Jesus exercised unique authority in his teachings and actions. In fact, people marveled that he taught and acted with such great authority in contrast to the scribes and Pharisees who appealed to outside sources for their authority (Matt 7:29; Mark 1:27). Jesus later bestowed authority and power upon the disciples to minister as he did, and they continued to do so long after Jesus' life and ministry (Matt 10:1; Mark 6:7; Luke 9:1; cf. Acts 1–2).

During the early development of the church, there arose a variety of competing sources of religious authority. Certainly the disciples continued to exert authority over the young church. But as the church grew and extended throughout several continents, the question of authority became more problematic. The authority of the Jerusalem church and of Peter and the disciples remained preeminent. But the Apostle Paul also grew in authority, and as we have already seen, it conflicted with the preeminent authority of Peter's ecclesiastical leadership.

3.3 Developments in Religious Authority

3.3.1 Ancient Church

Over time the center of church authority transferred from Jerusalem to Rome. The bishop of Rome increasingly became viewed as the first among the other bishops in the ancient church. After Christianity became legally and socially accepted under Emperor Constantine (280–337 C.E.), the ancient church tried to expand and consolidate its religious authority. This was accomplished in a variety of ways. But the most notable theological development occurred in the several councils called throughout the Roman Empire in order to establish orthodox standards of Christianity.

The Nicene Creed represents the firstfruit of the ecumenical councils held during the fourth century. The motivation behind the establishment of the creed had to do with the Arian controversy that argued Jesus was neither fully divine nor fully human but instead a semi-divine or angelic being. Thus the Nicene Creed served to confront Arian teachings as well as provide an authoritative summary of Christianity. The Nicene Creed affirmed both the humanity and divinity of Jesus.

How much authority should the pope have?

Later councils worked to establish, among other things, the canon of Scripture. Various writings from the ancient church were accepted as inspired and authoritative for matters of Christian beliefs, values, and practices. Although the Bible was considered to have apostolic authority, its acceptance was based upon the prior authority of the church to describe the nature of Scripture. This stance contained a tension that remained largely unchallenged until the time of the Protestant Reformation. Certainly other tensions arose during the interim, such as the conflict in authority that arose between the Western and Eastern churches. In 1056, the Western and Eastern Christian churches officially split to form what we today call the Catholic and Orthodox churches.

In the remainder of this chapter we will investigate how Christians throughout history viewed the concept of authority, particularly with regard to religious beliefs, values, and practices. It will not be an exhaustive study, but it will present typical views of religious authority. We will begin with the ancient church and map out some of the more prominent historical developments in how Christians understood theologically the nature and extent of religious authority.

3.3.2 Medieval Church

Despite the schism between the Catholic and Orthodox churches, both held similar views with regard to the nature and extent of religious authority. Religious authority primarily came through the church, which was chosen and empowered by the Holy Spirit to continue as God's representative on earth. Although ultimate authority comes from God, the church receives authority by God's proxy.

The church received the *deposit of faith,* which embodies the sum of revelation and tradition. The deposit of faith was attested to in Scripture (John 16:13). It was passed from the apostles to the succession of bishops, who had the responsibility of safeguarding and defining the body of teaching and commands entrusted to them by Jesus and preserved through the work of the Holy Spirit. The *magisterium* possesses this authoritative role committed to the church, manifesting the power to determine proper beliefs, values, and practices. After the schism between the Western and Eastern churches, both the Catholic and Orthodox churches considered themselves, respectively, to be the only true keepers of the apostolic succession of bishops to safeguard the deposit of faith.

Scripture is thought to represent the highest form of written revelation, but it was the church that accepted, preserved, and approved a *canon* (or standardized collection) of Scriptures. The church continues to serve as the greatest authority by which to understand properly the divine traditions contained in the Bible. Although the Bible is considered to be inspired by the Holy Spirit, its origin and continuation must be understood within the context of the church. So the authority of Scripture does not supersede that of the church and its historic traditions. Instead, it stands in mutual authority along with that of the church. The historic traditions of the church contained in its doctrine, teaching, and practice serve as necessary for determining all Christian matters. The religious hierarchy of the church is responsible for overseeing aspects of authority, jurisdiction, and sovereignty.

Does an assemblage of clergy create more authority?

When the Catholic and Orthodox churches divided, much of the schism had to do with the center point of religious authority, especially within the church. The Western church considered the bishop of Rome—the pope—the sovereign head of the visible church. The Eastern churches did not recognize the pope as the sovereign head of the church. Instead, the Eastern churches recognized the authority of regional bishops—Patriarchs—who honored the patriarchate of Constantinople as first among equals. In modern times, both Catholic and Orthodox churches continue to regard the church as critical in authoritatively determining matters of Christian faith and practice.

3.3.3 Protestant Reformation

The Protestant Reformation occurred in the context of sixteenth-century Europe. Martin Luther (1483–1546) was foremost among those who challenged the authority of the Roman Catholic Church, pope, and magisterium in favor of the primacy of scriptural authority. It was Luther's belief that the pope, along with the hierarchy of the Catholic Church, had abused his authority, forsaking the essentials of biblical teaching concerning salvation and other matters related to Christian life. So Luther sought to reform not only the abuses of the church but also the very structure of authority that made the abuses possible.

HISTORIC VIEWS OF RELIGIOUS AUTHORITY

Medieval Church and Church Authority
Church represents sovereign authority
Church oversees divine traditions (esp. Scripture) and historic traditions
of the church
Catholicism (e.g., Thomas Aquinas [ca. 1225–1274]), Orthodox churches

Reformation Church and Scriptural Authority
Primacy of "Scripture only" (*sola scriptura*)
Continental reformation churches (e.g., Martin Luther [1483–1546], John
Calvin [1509–1564])

Anglican Church and the Added Authority of Reason
Reason serves as the "mediator" (*via media*) between scriptural and
church authority
Church of England (e.g., Richard Hooker [1554–1600])

Deism and the Authority of Reason
Knowledge of God comes primarily through reason rather than revelation
(e.g., Herbert of Cherbury [1583–1648], Benjamin Franklin [1706–1790],
Thomas Jefferson [1743–1826])

Evangelical Revivals and Scripture, Tradition, Reason, and Experience
Primacy of scriptural authority, understood in light of tradition, reason,
and experience
Pietism (e.g., Philipp Jakob Spener [1635–1705]), Methodism (e.g., John
Wesley [1703–1791]), Great Awakening (e.g., Jonathan Edwards
[1703–1758])

Liberal Protestantism and the Authority of Experience
Primacy of experience in understanding Scripture (theology "from
below")
Liberal Protestantism (e.g., Friedrich Schleiermacher [1768–1834]; cf. Paul
Tillich [1886–1965])

Neo-Orthodoxy and the Reassertion of Scriptural Authority
Primacy of scriptural authority, understood dialectically
Separation of faith and reason (theology "from above")
Neo-Orthodoxy (e.g., Karl Barth [1886–1968])

Postmodernism and Non-foundational Theologies
Authority of a certain nature is questioned, due to the relativism of
culture and other influences
Theologies emphasize faith rather than rational or empirical foundations
of religious certainty

Luther argued that "Scripture alone" (Latin, *sola scriptura*) provided sufficient revelation for matters of Christian beliefs, values, and practices. Christians did not need to rely upon the authoritative proclamations of the church in order to interpret the Bible. Such proclamations were helpful, but they only possessed historic authority. Scripture, however, was considered divinely inspired, which was confirmed through the ongoing testimony of the Holy Spirit. Thus all individuals had the right and responsibility to interpret the Bible for themselves through the divine illumination available to them. One did not need the church for scriptural interpretation nor was the formal role of the church required for salvation. Instead, we are saved by God's grace alone when we respond in faith to the divine provision for salvation (Rom 3:21–30; Eph 2:8–9).

Luther on trial in church

John Calvin (1509–1564) was the most systematic theologian among the reformers, and his writings continue to be influential among many Protestants. Calvin agreed with the preeminent authority of the Bible and argued for its sole authority in matters of Christian beliefs, values, and practices. Neither Calvin nor Luther neglected the historic traditions of the church; they were thought to mirror Scripture. The patristic writings, along with the ecumenical creeds, were highly valued in leading contemporary Christians in their biblical interpretation. But the reformers reserved the right to read the Bible for themselves in establishing Christianity, particularly as formulated in the confessional statements of individual churches.

Luther and Calvin benefited from Renaissance and Humanist ideas that emphasized a revival of classical sources and values. They also emphasized an increased role that humans—individually and socially—play in developing the world beyond the church-centered culture of the Middle Ages. For example, Renaissance Humanists such as Desiderius Erasmus (ca. 1469–1536) promoted scholarship *ad fontes* (Latin for "to the sources"), which emphasized the study of Greek and Roman classics, including the Bible. Reexamination of original biblical texts by scholars such as Luther and Calvin supported their reformation of Christianity. From their perspective, Scripture declared itself to be the special revelation to which all Christians must give primary authority. Thus, Scripture must be the beginning and end of theological inquiry.

Calvin worked hard to establish the primacy of scriptural authority

3.3.4 Anglican Church

The continental Reformation, which took place on mainland Europe, influenced the Reformation that took place across the English Channel in England. But the Anglican Church (Church of England) developed differently than the Protestant churches in continental Europe. The Anglican Church wanted to avoid what were thought to be overreactions found on the continent. But they also wanted to break completely away from the Catholic Church. So the Anglican Church endeavored to develop a "middle way" (Latin, *via media*) between the Catholic and Protestant churches.

In terms of religious authority, the middle way of the Anglican Church led to the development of a new theological method. It mediated between the primacy of scriptural authority, on the one hand, and the historic traditions of the church, on the other hand. This way the Anglican Church sought to avoid the excessive tendencies found in both Catholic and Protestant churches.

In the seventeenth century, Richard Hooker articulated Anglican teachings about religious authority. Influenced by Reformed (Calvinist) churches, he rejected Puritan teachings in England. Such teachings were thought to have uplifted a literal reading of the Bible, considering unlawful anything not expressly contained in it. Rather, Hooker argued that both ecclesiastical and civil laws were subservient to natural law, which is an expression of God's supreme reason. Scripture, along with ecclesiastical and civil laws, must be understood in light of reason. Reason enables Christians to discern rightly between the words of the Bible and the historic traditions passed down by the church. The permanence of divine revelation did not preclude the need for development in particular beliefs. Thus Hooker articulated a view of religious authority that affirmed the primary authority of Scripture, while also asserting reason and tradition as genuine—albeit secondary—religious authorities.

Hooker's confidence in reason reflected a growing confidence in reason throughout the Western world. This confidence in reason eventually became known as the Enlightenment, or modern, era. Advocates of Enlightenment ideas increasingly questioned traditional beliefs, values, and practices that had been handed down to them through both religious and non-religious conventions. Instead, they put their trust primarily in reason and scientific method for uncovering truth. French philosopher René Descartes (1596–1650) is usually thought of as the founder of the Enlightenment, through his method of reasoning, known as Cartesianism. Descartes systematically doubted all traditional and religious knowledge he had been taught, and instead created his own basis of certainty, namely, the fact of his own self-conscious existence. He put forth the famous phrase, "I think, therefore I am." From this certitude, Descartes reasoned through intuition and deduction that God exists; however, traditional ideas about God may need revision.

3.3.5 Deism

Enlightenment ideas captured the attention of certain Christians who came to be known as deists. Deism signifies the belief that God created the world, complete with natural laws and other potentialities that enable it to run on its own. An analogy often used was that God created the world to run like a well-crafted clock. God does not actively participate in creation, however. Knowledge of God—the cosmic clockmaker—and right living can be achieved rationally through natural and scientific observation.

Early deistic ideas arose in seventeenth-century France, and the British deists such as Herbert of Cherbury (1583–1648), outlined five principles of deism that influenced Anglican Christianity. Deistic ideas were promoted in America through such notables as Benjamin Franklin (1706–1790), Thomas Jefferson (1743–1826), and Thomas Paine (1737–1809). Deists, especially in England, promoted a kind of natural religion and were the first to question critically the credibility of the Bible. Reason was, for the most part, sufficient for determining the best ways for Christians to live.

Did God create the world like a clock to run on its own?

3.3.6 Evangelical Revivals

During the seventeenth and eighteenth centuries, a variety of religious movements arose that sought to revive spiritually the established Protestant churches. Some refer to these movements as *evangelical* revivals because they sought to recapture the vital experience of the gospel—"good news"—of Scripture.

In continental Europe, Pietism developed during the seventeenth century in the effort to breathe spiritual life into a Lutheranism that had become scholastic, focusing on rational, doctrinal aspects of Christianity. Philipp Jakob Spener advocated proposals that helped to revive the living faith of the Lutheran church. For example, he established small group meetings in his home for the purpose of prayer and Bible study. Spener's proposals spread in renewal of the church throughout the world. The Pietist impulse today continues to encompass much of worldwide Christianity, even if it does not do so by name.

John Wesley (1703–1791) was influenced by Pietism in the emergence of the Methodist revivals in England. A growing emphasis upon the holiness of Christianity led Wesley to refer to experience—along with church tradition and reason—as genuine religious authorities in the proper interpretation of the Bible. Here Wesley built upon the view of religious authority prevalent in the Anglican Church. Scriptural authority was unique and

Wesley building upon Scripture

primary in theological reflection and in ministry. However, Wesley recognized that Christians had always functioned with an understanding of religious authority more complex than stated. Later, his integrative understanding of religious authority came to be known as the *Wesleyan quadrilateral.* The quadrilateral tries to articulate the interdependent relationship Wesley saw between the primacy of scriptural authority along with its integrative relationship with church history, critical thinking, and relevant experience.

In the American colonies, Jonathan Edwards helped to promote and articulate the character of revival that spread throughout the country. Known as the "Great Awakening," emphasis was placed upon the visible experience of conversion as evidence for its authenticity. Edwards sought to discourage excessive emotionalism, though, by distinguishing between healthy and unhealthy religious affections. He gave tremendous leadership to revival in America, and his writings continue to influence Christianity in the United States.

3.3.7 Liberal Protestantism

At the turn of the nineteenth century, Schleiermacher defended Christianity from its "cultured despisers" by appealing to inner religious experience. We have already investigated his view of revelation as inner experience (ch. 2). Schleiermacher made this defense within the context of the Enlightenment. The Enlightenment, as an intellectual movement in Western history, challenged traditional ideas, emphasizing the primacy of reason and strict scientific method. Religion, especially Christianity, was progressively challenged by the skepticism of the Enlightenment. So it was to the primacy of experience that Schleiermacher turned in order to defend Christianity in a way that was thought possible in light of skepticism.

Schleiermacher's approach to theology has sometimes been called theology "from below" because it starts with the particularity of human experience and understanding rather than an understanding thought to be specially revealed from God. Because of all the doubts cast upon scriptural as well as church authority, Schleiermacher argued that one needed to approach theology from the most reliable source available, namely one's own inner experience. The approach to Scripture one took involved inductive Bible study reflective of scientific method. In the contemporary world, it had become unreasonable to affirm the divine inspiration and trustworthiness of the Bible. Instead, one needed to let Scripture speak entirely for itself without presuppositions that prevented one from the critical historical study of it.

The emphasis upon the primary authority of experience led to a movement known as liberal protestantism, which has had influence far beyond that of Protestantism. Because liberal protestantism considered it necessary to be open to reformulations of Christian doctrine, a variety of theological viewpoints emerged. Tillich represents one variation with his understanding of revelation as new awareness. But other significant developments also occurred in the twentieth century. The following are a few related developments.

Process Theology

Process theology encompasses various religious developments dependent upon the process philosophy of Alfred North Whitehead (1861–1947). Whitehead was a scientist and philosopher who developed a view of the world in constant process, which he considered the most appropriate worldview based upon strict scientific investigation. In contrast to previous worldviews that conceived of everything in terms of "being," Whitehead conceived of reality in terms of "becoming." Theologians influenced by Whitehead reformulated Christianity in terms of process ideas. They thought that Christians, as well as Christian doctrine, were best understood as being in process. Even God is conceived of as being in process rather than such absolute and abstract terms as an eternal and immutable being.

This conception of God is sometimes known as *panentheism.* It involves the theological idea that God is in all things, and yet God retains a separate identity. God and the world are, in a sense, mutually dependent. It also means that God is not infinite but dependent upon people just as people are dependent upon God for the fulfillment of biblical principles of goodness and love. Process theology is thought to better explain the nature of an evolving world as well as the biblical view of God as participating with people in that process.

Liberation Theologies

Liberation theology arose in response to the various forms of oppression experienced by human beings. Theologians like Gustavo Gutiérrez (1928–), a Catholic priest, think that Christianity should be more proactive in dealing with the social, political, and economic struggles of the poor. The totality of God's redemption includes concern for these struggles as well as with those of a spiritual nature. The study of theology itself forms a secondary concern of Christians who should primarily be concerned with *praxis*—doing, action. For liberation theology the development of doctrine is only important to the degree that it facilitates God's call for the liberation of the oppressed, spiritually as well as physically. All theologies are, in fact, historically and culturally bound. They have no universal or doctrinal relevance beyond their own particular situations. So each community of faith must work together in order to develop its particular theological worldview.

A similar concern for racial liberation is occurring in the development of several ethnic theologies, such as black theology. James Cone (1938–) is representative of those who argue that God calls for an end to racial discrimination. Such liberation is considered inextricably bound up with the total redemption provided for by God for all who are impoverished spiritually as well as physically, culturally, and racially.

Who are the poor?

Feminist theology reflects the concern for gender liberation from the oppressive treatment of women that marginalizes if not actively discriminates against women. Theologians such as Mary Daly (1928–) and Rosemary Radford Ruether (1936–) have led the way in analyzing sexism within Christianity as well as in the general culture. They advocate ways of liberating people from their narrow prejudices against women in society as a whole and in the church.

Other liberationist theologies continue to arise. Among them are numbered womanist theologies that advocate liberation from the unique oppressions against women of color. Gay theologies advocate liberation from the oppressions against male homosexuals, and lesbian theologies advocate liberation from the oppressions against female homosexuals. In each case, particular experiences of oppression provide the starting point for developing theology "from below"—from the particularity of human experience and understanding.

3.3.8 Neo-Orthodoxy

Barth rejected the Liberal Protestant affirmation of any authority other than the Bible. In particular, he rejected the notion of natural theology—beliefs spawned from inner experience or any other type of general revelation. Instead, Barth thought that we must humbly submit ourselves to the revelation of God, specially revealed through Scripture.

Barth realized that we could no longer go back to a precritical understanding of the Bible. We had to acknowledge the fact that Scripture was written by people and that we could not with propositional certainty claim its divine inspiration. But we could acknowledge its non-propositional revelatory power. That is, the Bible does not reveal propositional truth so much as it serves to reveal God to us in a personal and intimate way. Paradoxically, God becomes self-disclosed to us through the event of reading or hearing Scripture. In that event, we encounter the very God of the universe. It is the personal encounter rather than the words of the Bible that is meaningful to our relationship with God.

Neither reason nor experience constitutes genuine religious authority for our Christian belief and practice. Only Scripture provides reliable truth, albeit in a paradoxical way whereby the words of the Bible become the words of God for us. Some have called this theology "from above" because of our humble acceptance of the words of Scripture as the words of God without becoming distracted with worldly concern for its reliability. Instead, we accept the Bible's reliability—as did the Reformers—based more thoroughly upon the inner testimony of the Holy Spirit.

3.3.9 **Postmodern Theology**

Some people refer to the contemporary world in which we live as postmodern. What is *postmodernism?* There is no consensus yet with regard to what postmodernism means. So it is a misnomer to speak of a postmodern theology per se. Instead, it is more appropriate to talk about a constellation of postmodern theologies, which share similar characteristics. Let us look at a number of those characteristics relevant to the subject of religious authority. To begin with, postmodernism rejects that which has historically constituted *modernism,* for example, historic confidence in reason, objective truth, and claims of universality. In some respects, postmodernism reflects Western concerns more than anything else, since it is a rejection of Enlightenment ideas. Yet, postmodern concerns apply throughout the world.

Postmodernism affirms practical reasoning rather than reasoning that claims universality based upon objective truth. Modernism tends to be optimistic with regard to the certitude people may have in the rational and empirical foundations of knowledge. In culture as a whole, the modern era had great confidence in science and technology—rather than traditional authorities—for discovering truth and happiness in life. Similarly, Christianity proclaimed its own confidence in certain fundamentals thought to provide rational and empirical foundations of religious knowledge. Christian *foundationalism* can appear in a number of ways. Catholicism believes in a synthesis of scriptural, magisterial, dogmatic, and systematic theology that provides certain truth. Protestants also believe in certain truth, usually based upon a view that the Bible does not err. Such a view argues that the truth of inerrant Scripture should appeal to any rational person. Of course, there are other variations of Protestant foundationalism, appealing to the certainty of particular experiences rather than Scripture alone.

In contrast to modernism and foundationalism, postmodernism argues that there are no certainties that can be proved rationally and empirically. Rather, truth is relative to the particular cultural context in which worldviews develop. It is subjective truth, which must be understood contextually rather than certainly. Consequently, worldviews must be understood as being *non-foundational,* that is, without rational and empirical foundations for being dogmatic to the exclusion of truths found in alternative worldviews. From a Christian perspective, a non-foundational view of theology requires a reappropriation of living by "faith, not by sight," that is, by rational and empirical certainty (2 Cor 5:7). It also recognizes the work of the Holy Spirit in the lives of both individuals and corporate groups—such as the church—in rightly understanding God and matters related to God.

How much of a foundation is necessary for building Christianity?

This does not mean that Christians cannot argue reasonably and persuasively for their beliefs, or that such beliefs become unbelievably subjective. However, they cannot argue dogmatically and simplistically, expecting others to be persuaded based upon unquestioned foundations of truth, based more upon rational and empirical verification rather than by faith.

Culture influences the affirmations people have, and it does violence—so to speak—when anyone claims universal truth that ignores, marginalizes, or discriminates against other views. Postmodernism is concerned about listening to all views, including views often overlooked due to the fact that they reflect minority or underrepresented points of view. Consequently, emphasis is placed more upon listening to the stories or narratives of other people, without allowing any particular narrative—or *metanarrative,* that is, a narrative claiming universality and exclusivity—to triumph over others to the point of excluding them. In a sense, one cannot help but speak with metanarratives if one is personally convinced of a particular worldview or religious worldview. But one may take care not to speak without humility, love, and tolerance for alternative views. The use of stories, images, music, and traditional resources as well as modern means presumably helps people develop a broader, healthier, and—from a Christian perspective—holier worldview. It also helps them develop greater sensitivity to the collective or communal dimensions of Christianity, in contrast to the more individualistic approach characteristic of modernism.

In order to overcome hegemonic conceptions of Christianity and the Bible, postmodernists have attempted deconstructions of church history. *Deconstructionism* attempts analyses that try to overcome the arbitrariness, manipulation, or bias that may have occurred in the writing and interpreting of the Bible as well as in the developments of the church. Such influences may have occurred due to the social, cultural, political, economic, religious, or gender dominance of certain views over others. Thus, postmodernists may undertake liberationist or feminist deconstructionism in order to evaluate the effects of educated/upper-class or male-oriented dominance upon Christianity and its development.

There is no single representative of postmodern theology. In fact, it is still not clear whether any contemporary theology will be known as postmodern long term. In the meantime, several theologies have been described as postmodern. James Fowler (1940–), a contemporary Protestant theologian, identifies four strategies for addressing postmodern issues. They include liberation and political theologies that engage postmodern experience directly at the point of suffering and theodicy; cosmological approaches that are concerned with a unified cosmology, grounding Christian doctrine in creation; hermeneutical approaches that appeal to classic Christian texts for their power and depth in addressing people from other times and contexts; and narrative-linguistic approaches that reject all universals and celebrate the locus of truth in particular, situated traditions.[1]

3.4 Conclusion

These views of authority portray only a few of the variations that exist among Christians. Just because the various viewpoints arose at different times in church history, it does not mean that they are any less prevalent or valid. On the contrary, since each view of authority arose, Christians have continued to affirm their particular understanding of religious authority. Certainly, modifications and nuanced understandings have arisen. But the viewpoints discussed continue to provide representative types of religious authority.

Each person and religious group must decide for themselves the authorities to which they appeal in determining their Christian beliefs and practices. No approach has a monopoly among Christians in church history. Each viewpoint has its own unique benefits, as well as liabilities, in terms of determining the heart of Christianity.

Regardless of one's viewpoint, however, one must delineate the relationship between the various religious authorities that at one time or another has included the Bible, tradition, reason, and experience. Even if one places primary emphasis upon Scripture, church tradition, or one of the others, one must still delineate the appropriate relationship between its religious authority and that of others. One may variously weigh the different types of religious authority, but one must also make explicit its nature in relationship to the other potential authorities.

3.5 Questions for Further Reflection

1. What is the nature of authority? What role does authority play in people's lives? What types of authority influence you?

2. What is the nature of religious authority? Who or what serve as religious authorities for you? Which authorities do you consider most relevant and reliable? Why?

3. Which view of religious authority presented in the chapter do you consider most persuasive? What are its benefits as well as liabilities?

4. To what degree do you find postmodernism a helpful way of describing the world today? To what degree do Christians need to address the concerns of postmodernism?

3.6 Notes

1. James W. Fowler, *Faithful Change: The Personal and Public Challenges of Postmodern Life* (Nashville: Abingdon, 1996), 179–90.

CHAPTER FOUR

All scripture is inspired by God and is useful for teaching, for reproof, for correction, and for training in righteousness, so that everyone who belongs to God may be proficient, equipped for every good work.
(2 Timothy 3:16–17)

SCRIPTURE

4.1 Introduction

The Bible tells of a personal letter of encouragement that the Apostle Paul writes to Timothy, a young colleague in ministry. After sharing about his own experience of persecution, Paul encourages Timothy by reminding the young colleague of his godly upbringing and of the instruction he received from the sacred writings, presumably the books Christians describe as the Old Testament. The early church understood them as pointing to Jesus and how salvation comes through faith in him, repentance, and baptism.

Paul continues to assure Timothy by affirming that all Scripture is inspired by God and is useful for teaching, reproof, correction, and training in righteousness (2 Tim 3:16). The purpose of Scripture is that everyone who belongs to God may become proficient, equipped for every good work, including Paul, Timothy, and everyone else.

Affirmation of the divine inspiration of Scripture forms a critical component of Christianity because it pertains to the belief that God somehow specially communicates to us through words that have been heard and preserved in writing. The nature and extent of that inspiration has, of course, been variously understood and applied during church history. Regardless of one's view of it, the Bible remains the distinctive reference point of Christian reflection. This is as true today as it was in the ancient church.

Is the Bible more than a book?

4.2 What Is Scripture?

Most religions of the world have sacred Scriptures. *Scripture* (or Scriptures) simply means "a writing." In a religious context, it refers to the sa-

> **Christians view Scripture** as special revelation, inspired by God and authoritative with regard to matters of belief, value, and practice.
>
> Scripture functions like a light that, aided by the Holy Spirit, guides people as they seek to love God and others with truth, compassion, and justice.

cred writings or book of any religion. In Christianity, Scripture refers to *the Bible,* which itself means "the book" or "the sacred book," and the two terms are used interchangeably in this book.

Christian Scripture does not give a comprehensive self-description of itself. The Bible actually developed over hundreds of years. It was written by kings, prophets, leaders, and eventually followers of Jesus. We will study a little about the development of the Bible. However, we will first look at some of the descriptions found in Scripture about the nature of God's words revealed and written for posterity.

4.2.1 Characteristics of Scripture

The Bible talks about "Scripture" or "Scriptures" (Matt 22:29; Luke 24:27, 45; John 2:22; 5:39; 7:42; 10:35; Acts 8:32; 17:11), but most of its characteristics are not described until after the lifetime of Jesus. Then, Scripture is described as being inspired by God, prophetic and sacred—the standard for beliefs, values, and practices (Acts 1:16; Gal 1:18; 1 Thess 2:13; 2 Tim 3:16–17; 2 Pet 1:20–21).

Prior to Jesus, the Hebrew (or Jewish) people were the ones chosen by God to receive special revelation about entering into covenant relationship with God (Gen 17:13; Exod 19:1–6; Deut 7:6; Ps 4:3). In their writings about God and their relationship to God, the "word" or "words" of God were considered sacred and eternal treasures given by God (Deut 11:18; Pss 19:8; 119:11; Isa 40:8). The words of God furnished both life and light, informing people how they were to be saved and how they were to live (Deut 8:3; Ps 119:105, 130; Prov 6:23). They included the promises as well as laws and commandments of God (Ps 119:47, 72, 82, 140; Prov 6:23). The words of God were considered powerful, at work in creation and judgment as well as giving life (Gen 1; Jer 5:14; 23:29; Ezek 37:7).

Similar views of the Hebrew Bible appear in writings after Jesus. Scripture is thought to be authoritative, inspired, and truthful in proclaiming the gospel—the good news of Jesus. These latter characteristics are so important to Christianity that they will be discussed at length later in this chapter.

God's words were written in many ways

4.2.2 Structure of Scripture

Christian Scripture traditionally consists of the Old and New Testaments. *Testament* has the meaning of a "covenant" (Latin, *testamentum*). The Old Testament refers to the Hebrew Bible, which is sacred to Judaism as well as Christianity. It was mainly written in the Hebrew language, with some Aramaic. The Old Testament is sometimes referred to as the First Testament because the New (or Second) Testament builds upon the former rather than replacing it. The Roman Catholic Church recognizes forty-six books in the Old Testament, while Protestants acknowledge only thirty-nine books. The difference is that Roman Catholics accept what are called the *deuterocanonical* books (Latin, "second canon")—books found in the Greek (Septuagint) translation of the Hebrew Bible but not in the original Hebrew text. Protestants sometimes call the additional books the *Apocrypha* (Greek, "hidden"). Hebrew Scripture has the same text as the Old Testament, though the books are listed in a different order.

With regard to the New Testament, both Roman Catholics and Protestants accept the same twenty-seven books. Christians distinguish between the Old and New Testaments in a similar way that they distinguish between the old and new covenants described in the Bible (Jer 31:31; 2 Cor 3:6; Gal 4:24–26).

4.2.3 Scripture as the Word of God

Christians often refer to Scripture as the "Word of God." There is biblical precedent for this. Throughout the Old Testament, there are numerous references to God speaking, either directly or indirectly, through the prophets (Exod 4:10–16; 34:27; Deut 18:18; Isa 8:1; 30:8–9; Jer 1:9; 30:1–2). In the New Testament, Paul talks about how the Jews had been privileged to be "entrusted with the oracles of God" (Rom 3:2). More specifically, Paul says, "We also constantly give thanks to God for this, that when you received the word of God that you heard from us, you accepted it not as a human word but as what it really is, God's word, which is also at work in you believers" (1 Thess 2:13). Clearly the words of Paul were spoken as if they were words of God, and so first-century Christians referred to sacred writings of Paul and other apostles as the word of God (Eph 6:17).

First-century Christians also referred to Jesus as the "Word of God." Most notably, John describes Jesus in dramatic fashion in the opening of his gospel account of the life of Jesus. He says, "In the beginning was the Word, and the Word was with God, and the Word was God" (John 1:1; cf. 1:14). Reference to Jesus as the *Word* (Greek, *logos*) represents a profound description of him as divine—the one involved with both creation and redemption (Pss 33:6; 107:19–20). On the one hand, it is most appropriate to refer to Jesus rather than to the Bible as the Word of God. Jesus is the living Word of God who is responsible for more or less everything about which Scripture speaks and that it represents. This is why some Christians want to refer only to Jesus, and not to the Bible as such, as the Word of God.

On the other hand, there is a biblical and historical precedent for speaking about Scripture as well as Jesus as the Word of God. Jesus spoke about his parables as the word of God (Luke 8:11), and he gave authority to his disciples to speak on his behalf, through the Holy Spirit, giving their apostolic pronouncements a derivative—albeit genuine—religious authority (Matt 16:19; 18:18; Luke 12:12; 1 Cor 2:13). Thus, the Bible powerfully represents God with us. Certainly we may continue to refer to Scripture as the word of God so long as we remember the true source of Scripture. While the Bible embodies the written word or words of God, Christians believe that Jesus is the true, living, and eternal Word of God, who divinely guarantees all that Scripture affirms.

4.3 Canon

"Canon" (Greek, *kanon*) means a "rule" or "measuring rod" by which ancient writings were identified as sacred writings. The Jews developed a canon of Scripture by rabbinical councils at the end of the first century, which early Christians later adopted. Christians developed their own canon that includes both the Old and New Testaments. With the exception of the Roman Catholic acceptance of the deuterocanonical books, Christians throughout church history have not modified the Old and New Testament canon.

The New Testament is made up of twenty-seven books, which include the gospel stories of Jesus as well as historical and prophetic books and letters written by early Christians. It was written primarily in the Greek language, with a small amount of Hebrew and Aramaic words transliterated into Greek. Most of the New Testament was thought to have been written during the first century, after the death of Jesus. However, general consensus about the canon did not occur until the end of the fourth century.

Wrong kind of canon?

4.3.1 History of Canonization

Although the canon of Christian Scripture has remained largely unchanged, it did not just plop down from heaven. Like people and nations, the Bible has a history. The books, letters, poetry, and other forms of literature were collected over time, and there was not always consensus with regard to what should be included in the canon. A number of purportedly first-century books and letters, for example, were not included as part of the Bible. This exclusion reflects the degree of scrutiny to which the ancient church went in canonizing sacred writings.

As the ancient church developed, copies of the Hebrew Bible and other writings of first-century Christians circulated throughout the Roman Empire. Various lists of sacred writings arose in Christian circles. However, no consensus arose for centuries, and there were no codified criteria for recognition of writings as canonical. Some criteria undoubtedly included the belief that writings were apostolic or had apostolic approval. Other criteria included belief in books containing Christ-honoring teaching and a history of spiritual contribution to the life and ministry of churches. To be sure, lists of most of the books of the New Testament arose early. However, it was not until the end of the fourth century that an ecclesiastical council codified the canon as we have it today at the Synod of Carthage (397). Such actions did not so much determine the canon as recognize what had progressively come to be accepted.

Is the canon open or closed?

Is the canon open or closed? In other words, would it be possible for God to reveal additional truth, or would it be possible to add to Scripture the words of ancient writings that may yet be found? Historically, most Christians have said that the canon is closed. The Bible is sufficient for salvation and all other matters pertaining to Christian beliefs, values, and practices. To be sure, God could do whatever God wants. However, advocates of a closed canon argue for the sufficiency of the Scripture that we have. On the other hand, Christians who argue for an open canon want to preserve the notion of God's dynamic, continuing interaction with humanity. Theoretically, at least, the canon of Scripture should be viewed as open. In practice, however, it would be difficult to reproduce the same kind of ecumenical conciliar work followed in the historic canonization of Scripture.

4.3.2 Transmission of Scripture

Old Testament Scripture was probably written on stone, clay, or leather, and New Testament Scripture was written primarily on papyrus. Over time, the Bible was meticulously copied on scrolls of leather and then on bound sheets of fine animal skins (vellum). In 1455, Bibles were first printed on Gutenberg's printing press. Today the Bible is printed on paper as well as recorded on tapes, discs, and computers.

The process of copying the Bible from one generation to the next is an important issue to Christians, who value the trustworthiness of the biblical record. A multitude of arguments (and counterarguments) have been used to affirm the care and precision copyists used in preserving every "jot and tittle" of Scripture (Matt 5:18, KJV). Jewish scribes were entrusted with making copies of the Hebrew Bible, and meticulous standards were used for preserving the accuracies of copies. Similar standards were used by medieval Christian monks and later transcribers of the biblical text. The accuracy of such copies was corroborated with the discovery in 1947 of the Dead Sea Scrolls, which contained the oldest known copies of the Old Testament, written as

Jewish and Christian copyists meticulously transcribed Scripture

early as the first century B.C.E. Of course, hundreds of copies of ancient biblical manuscripts exist, and scholars take great care in comparing and contrasting them, since hundreds of textual variations exist in the manuscripts.

Many translations of Scripture occurred throughout church history. In fact, the number of English translations has boomed over the past century. It lies beyond the scope of this book to talk about the variety of translations and paraphrases available today. Obviously, they vary in terms of translation principles, so people should take care in the particular Bible they choose to use for personal study and devotion. In addition, over the past two centuries, manuscripts have been discovered that seem to be more ancient than previous manuscripts used for earlier Bible translations such as the King James Version (1611). Since discrepancies often occur between ancient manuscripts, the oldest manuscripts are thought to provide more accurate copies of prior documents.

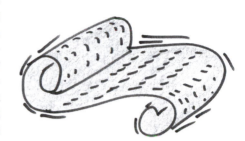

Ancient writings were written on scrolls

4.4 The Inspiration of Scripture

The notion of the divine inspiration of Scripture derives preeminently from the text of 2 Tim 3:16, which describes all Scripture as "inspired" by God—literally "God-breathed." Although the reference was undoubtedly intended to refer to the Hebrew Bible, Christians have applied the notion to the entire canon of Scripture. The inspiration of Scripture is supported by other verses that speak of its divine as well as human origin. For example, 2 Pet 1:20–21 affirms that neither Scripture nor its interpretation ever came by human will but by people moved by the Holy Spirit of God: "First of all you must understand this, that no prophecy of scripture is a matter of one's own interpretation, because no prophecy ever came by human will, but men and women moved by the Holy Spirit spoke from God." This affirmation of divine derivation probably included the writings of Paul, which are favorably mentioned later in the same book.

The ancient Christian church thought that God did more than inspire the original writing of the Bible. God's Holy Spirit was also at work in the communities that received, preserved, and transmitted the sacred writings. Likewise, the Holy Spirit of God was thought to be at work in the process of canonizing the writings and letters that gained authoritative status in the ancient church. The illuminating work of God was also thought of as being present in the ongoing process of the interpretation and application of Scripture.

How did God inspire the Bible?

For the most part, the divine inspiration of Scripture went unchallenged until the time of the Enlightenment, which challenged prior authorities. At this time a growing emphasis upon the inductive study of the Bible became important to those trusting less in theological and church traditions handed down to them. Instead, they placed increasing trust in their own critical skills of reason and scientific method to discover reliable truth, even in the study of the Bible. Some treated Scripture as an entirely human document, while others still tried to understand the Bible in light of its claim to divine inspiration. Over time, different viewpoints arose with regard to the nature of inspiration. Some placed greater emphasis upon the human dimension of biblical inspiration, while others responded with views that placed greater emphasis upon the divine dimension of biblical inspiration. The different viewpoints cannot be easily sorted into separate categories. Instead they can more easily be understood on a continuum between two poles, accenting either divine or human dimension of inspiration. We will review a few of them.

4.4.1 Accent on the Divine

The view of inspiration that most emphasizes the divine element may be described as that of *dictation*. This view argues that God dictated the very words of Scripture recorded by human authors or copyists. A mechanical view of inspiration occurs in this viewpoint, where the people involved serve a somewhat passive role, because the writers of the Bible represented God's faithful scribes. The frailties and imperfections of the human authors are set aside in the transmission of the revelation of God so that the Bible is seen to be without any errors. This view of inspiration is deductive in its approach to Scripture, using particular verses such as 2 Tim 3:16 as determinative for interpreting the nature and extent of God's inspiration in the writing of Scripture. It may use syllogistic logic in arguing its point. For example: If God is perfect, which the Bible suggests, and if Scripture is inspired by God, which the Bible also suggests, then Scripture must also be perfect in some meaningful sense of the word.

Did God dictate Scripture?

The verbal or plenary view of inspiration holds that all parts of Scripture are inspired, but it places more emphasis upon the human role of people in writing the Bible. For example, this approach places greater emphasis upon the literary and historical context in which biblical authors wrote. But even in this viewpoint, God so thoroughly guided the writing process that the very words of the authors are those that God intended them to write. Thus, the divine inspiration extends to every word written so that no part of Scripture is viewed as humanly flawed.

The attempt to recognize both the divine and human dimensions of Scripture is found in the *concursive* view of inspiration. This view holds that God simultaneously revealed truth while the human author(s) was moved to write. Thus the Bible can be studied from an almost incarnational perspective, whereby one views Scripture as being entirely inspired by God and entirely inspired by the people who wrote it. On the one hand, one can study the Bible as a document inspired by God. On the other hand, one can study it as one would study any human document. There is a paradox involved here that can only be resolved by faith. Despite the attempt to equally affirm both the divine and human elements of inspiration, the divine element is usually thought to vouchsafe the Bible from any significant degree of human error. But the possibility of human input, which is finite by nature and susceptible to sin, is recognized and considered in reflection upon matters of Christian beliefs, values, and practices.

4.4.2 Accent on the Human

As Christians increasingly used inductive Bible study method in accordance with scientific method, they acknowledged an increasing number of inconsistencies found in biblical accounts of history, geography, science, and other matters related to the text. This acknowledgment led some Christians to doubt the divine dimension of inspiration and instead viewed the Bible increasingly as a human document. We will review some of those who accent the humanness of Scripture.

In order to account for the variations in Scripture, some Christians developed views of biblical inspiration that represented only a portion of the Bible. These views have variously been described as *dynamic, partial,* or *degrees of* inspiration. They affirm that God inspired portions of the Bible or especially important ideas contained in it, but also that the human authors had freedom to write in accordance with the limitations of their particular place and time. The result is that contemporary interpreters must work to uncover the kernels of divine truth that Scripture reveals. Such interpretation involves a great deal more than discerning the clear and obvious meaning of the text. One would have to use a variety of historical and critical methods of biblical interpretation in order to evaluate the Bible. The need for this type of biblical interpretation would undoubtedly lead to a variety of interpretations, but such would be necessary if truly inductive methods of Bible study were employed.

Other Christians view the inspiration of Scripture as more *mystical* in orientation, involving some sort of divine illumination. Here human authors are thought to be intimately communing with God, where their normal powers of writing are heightened. No specific words of God are communicated to the authors. They must write on their own. Thus their writings are inspired, though the particulars of what they wrote are subject to the limitations of their finite humanness.

Finally, some Christians dispense with the notion of divine inspiration altogether, arguing that Scripture may possess a high degree of *intuition* or *natural* religious insight. Everyone must seek God through spiritual awareness that they develop with or without the help of the Bible. But the Bible signifies a historically significant reference point. It provides language, imagery, and religious stories—myths—that help people understand and open their lives for transformation in relationship to God as well as others.

4.5 The Truthfulness of Scripture

With the rise of historical and critical methods of scriptural interpretation, the truthfulness—the degree to which the Bible may be reliably regarded as true—has come under intense scrutiny. Of course, there will always be debate with regard to one's understanding of truth. Does truth only consist in those statements that correspond exactly to what exists, or does it consist in those statements that make sense when viewed in light of a coherent body of knowledge? In other words, does there need to be a one-to-one correspondence between a statement and verifiable facts, or should truth be viewed as that which presents the most coherent conception of reality? Certainly these questions go beyond the scope of this book, but they help us to realize the complex nature of talking about the truthfulness of Scripture.

Since the Bible is so central to Christianity, many views of its truthfulness have arisen. They range widely on a continuum, varying from inerrancy to errancy. Other views exist that try to nuance subtle distinctions between the two poles of debate. Sometimes, the same words used to describe the truthfulness of Scripture are defined differently by other views, so attentiveness needs to be used in understanding the particular meaning of terminology. Certainly the particular view a person adopts has tremendous impact upon how centrally the Bible influences the theological development of Christian beliefs, values, and practices. It also impacts how historically and critically biblical passages are interpreted and applied.

How accurate is the Bible?

4.5.1 Inerrancy

Those who argue for *inerrancy* place great emphasis upon divine inspiration and the factual truthfulness of Scripture. They take care to explain or harmonize apparent variations in Scripture with its divine inspiration and, consequently, its complete trustworthiness. The Roman Catholic Church has spoken of the inerrancy of Scripture along with that of the church's infallibility. The term has also been used by conservatively oriented Protestants in their affirmation of the inspiration and authority of Scripture. The most ardent supporters of biblical inerrancy maintain that the Bible does not err in any respect, including statements about history, geography, and science.

Those who argue for inerrancy deal with variations found in the Bible in a variety of ways. Some consider the evidence in support of Scripture and its divine inspiration to be so overwhelming that those apparent discrepancies are inconsequential and do not need to be explained. Apparent discrepancies are just that: apparent; they are not genuine discrepancies or errors.

Others take the apparent discrepancies more seriously. They argue that the Bible should be interpreted from the perspective of ancient rather than modern conceptions of truth, evaluating Scripture on its own terms. So modern biases are identified, critiqued, and eliminated from the examination of ancient biblical texts. Such interpretative procedures are considered more appropriate to the worldview characteristic of the original authors. For example, the "Chicago Statement on Biblical Inerrancy" states the following with regard to the truthfulness of Scripture:

> We deny that it is proper to evaluate Scripture according to standards of truth and error that are alien to its usage or purpose. We further deny that inerrancy is negated by Biblical phenomena such as a lack of modern technical precision, irregularities of grammar or spelling, observational descriptions of nature, the reporting of falsehoods, the use of hyperbole and round numbers, the topical arrangement of material, variant selections of material in parallel accounts, or the use of free citations.[1]

Sometimes conjectures are made to explain apparent discrepancies when data is not currently available in relationship to questions that arise about the truthfulness of Scripture. Archaeology, for example, has cast doubts upon the historical and geographical accuracy of the Bible. But archaeological discoveries have also provided dramatic evidence in support of the integrity of scriptural texts with regard to their historical and factual accuracy.

Usually attempts to harmonize apparent discrepancies rely upon the principle of divine inspiration, asserting that all discrepancies ultimately can be resolved based upon its divine origin. Conversely, attempts to diminish the divine inspiration of Scripture fail to provide an interpretation that does justice to the coherence of its claims to present God's self-revelation. Skeptical interpreters of the Bible may point out perplexing textual problems, but their skepticism produces its own problems when trying to make sense of texts that purport to speak for and about God.

There are variations in how inerrancy is understood. Some understand it as *complete, full, or absolute inerrancy,* pertaining to matters of history and science as well as Christian beliefs, values, and practices. Others understand inerrancy as limited to matters of Christian

---

WHAT CONSTITUTES AN ERROR?

- Biblical phenomena that lack modern technical precision?

- Irregularities of grammar or spelling?

- Observational descriptions of nature?

- The reporting of falsehoods?

- The use of hyperbole and round numbers?

- The topical arrangement of material?

- Variant selections of material in parallel accounts?

- Use of free citation?

theology, particularly that of salvation. In this understanding inerrancy does not apply to historical, geological, or other scientific matters. *Limited inerrancy* signifies the view that biblical errors, properly speaking, apply to theological matters rather than to matters of geology and history. Still others want to claim that the term only applies to an *inerrancy of purpose,* that is, that Scripture does not fail for the purposes for which God intended it to be written. Such a view might actually accept numerous errors in the Bible, but they are not errors that prevent God from saving people and for reliably guiding them in Christian living. This view allows for a great breadth of interpretation, relative to the soteriological purposes of Scripture.

4.5.2 Errancy

Those who view the Bible as being predominantly from human origin have little problem with seeing its finite qualities. Some refer to this as an *errantist* view. To such people the Bible consists of a variety of legends, myths, and other types of oral traditions that were handed down to later generations who collected, edited, and preserved them in accordance with their contemporary questions and concerns. For example, the early books of the Old Testament are often thought to be the compilation of numerous stories and writings from the ancient Hebrews. They were compiled sometime after the Jewish people had been conquered and exiled, near the midpoint of the first millennium before Jesus. These accounts are thought to contain numerous errors in history, geography, and science, which no amount of harmonization can resolve. Of course, the extent of the Bible's errancy can be thought to extend far beyond matters of history, geography, and science. It may extend to spiritual and theological errors as well.

Mistakes are unfortunate but not the end of the world

Even the more recent writings of the New Testament contain troublesome discrepancies. From the birth and resurrection narratives in the Gospels to the Lukan account of the early church in Acts, the textual inconsistencies lead to an errant view of the Bible. Rather than dodge the discomforting conclusion of an errant Bible, one should endeavor to formulate ways to conceive of Christianity that does justice to a realistic appraisal of sacred writing God provided.

The errantist view admits that discrepancies occur in the Bible, though the degree to which those problems are important depends in large part upon one's view of revelation. If revelation represents a type of inner experience (Schleiermacher), new awareness (Tillich), or even dialectical presence (Barth), then the presence of historical, geographical, scientific, and other errors may not strongly impact one's understanding of Christianity. Instead, divine inspiration is thought to occur through more intimate, spiritual encounters with God, and the factual reliability of the Bible does not necessarily challenge one's beliefs, values, and practices. God is not about the work of establishing propositions of absolute truth but of initiating saving relationships with people. One must trust in the ongoing work of God, rather than upon the Bible, to accomplish what is necessary with regard to divine self-revelation and salvation.

4.5.3 Infallibility

The term *infallibility* has long been used in the Roman Catholic tradition to describe the trustworthiness of both the church and Scripture. Although it can have the meaning of not erring, it suggests more the idea of neither misleading nor being misled. Thus neither the church nor Scripture was thought to mislead in its presentation of God and other theological matters. In Protestant churches, infallibility has been used to describe the Bible, since Protestantism historically has questioned the authority of the church and its leadership and traditions. So, rather than a lack of error, the term has taken on the meaning of the trustworthiness of the Bible in fulfilling the purposes for which God intended Scripture to be written.

What does one do with apparent errors?

Imprecision or errors contained in the Bible are thought to be allowable in relationship to the purposes for which God intended Scripture to be written. Thus they are compatible with the notion of God's inspiration of Scripture and its authoritativeness for matters of Christian beliefs, values, and practices. The Bible should be thought of as trustworthy—indeed truthful—in neither having misled nor in misleading people with regard to knowledge that we have of God in Scripture and of salvation and the associated way of life.

Certainly there is tension in affirming that sacred Scripture contains imprecision and errors. But since this is the sacred writing that God gave to humanity, it must be sufficient for God's purposes. An infallible Bible seems preferable, on the one hand, to forgoing the factual trustworthiness of Scripture, and on the other hand, to endless attempts at harmonizing all its apparent variations. Christians should accept the Bible God provided with its limitations just as they should accept the church—all true believers—with its obvious limitations, past and present. They should not try to turn it into something it is not, using human arguments that distract from the work of God's Holy Spirit in and through Scripture.

4.5.4 Indefectibility of the Church

Some Christians think that it is inappropriate to look at Scripture as the theological safeguard for Christianity. Catholic and Orthodox churches, after all, argue for the indefectibility of the church. In its broadest sense, *indefectibility* means freedom from defects. Historically, Catholic and Orthodox Christians argue that the church of Jesus will never cease to exist. Although there may be individuals and groups of individuals who, from time to time, are guilty of manifold defects, the church itself will continue to endure. It is the church, rather than the Bible, that safeguards the authority and veracity of God's truth in the world. Thus, the Catholic Church argues that the church's infallibility is inerrant in that it, like Scripture, will never cease to exist in representing God. Moreover, it is the responsibility of the church to interpret the Bible aright.

How indefectible is the church?

Some Protestants also argue for the indefectibility of the church. This argument places more emphasis upon the Holy Spirit's presence and authority working primarily in and through the church rather than the Bible. In this context the inerrancy or errancy of Scripture becomes less crucial. In fact, for some it becomes irrelevant and misleading. It is the ongoing presence and life of the church that safeguards in this world the authority and veracity of God's truth. Scripture forms an important part of the church's indefectibility. But it is the church, rather than the Bible, to which God wants believers to look in the founding and promoting of Christianity.

4.6 The Interpretation of Scripture

There are many reasons why people read the Bible. Some read it devotionally, and some read it aesthetically as literature. Christians, at some point, study it with greater care and intentionality with regard to its interpretation. Since most Christians view Scripture as the theological reference point for their beliefs, values, and practices, its right interpretation is very important. Usually such study occurs prayerfully. But it also includes the mind, which seeks to use all that may be of help in interpreting and applying the Bible.

There is a difference between reading Scripture in order to understand its plain and obvious sense, as the Protestant reformers advocated, and to understand it from a critical interpretive perspective. While many people may be content with a straightforward reading of Scripture, at some point many begin to read it critically. That is, we begin to analyze the Bible based upon more than what the text says but also upon that which can be known through sources of knowledge other than the text.

It lies beyond the scope of this book to present the history and variety of ways in which the Bible is studied and interpreted. But we can provide a brief survey of biblical *hermeneutics* (methods of interpretation) that introduces many of the ways in which the Bible is understood.

4.6.1 Fourfold Sense of Scripture

The early church developed several ways in which to interpret the biblical text. A grammatical and historical reading of Scripture, of course, represented the primary way in which Scripture was understood. A literal interpretation of the Bible was the crucial reference point for all biblical studies. But soon there arose a concern for an allegorical or symbolic interpretation of the text, particularly when Scripture was not easily understood. Allegorical interpretation represented the search for meaning that underlies a plain or literal reading of the biblical text, which requires greater deliberation on the part of an individual in interpreting the Bible.

During the Middle Ages, a fourfold method of interpretation developed. First, the literal sense of Scripture revealed its grammatical and historical meaning. Second, the *allegorical sense* revealed the hidden meaning of Scripture. Third, the *moral sense* of Scripture revealed how people should live. Fourth, the *anagogical sense* of Scripture revealed the heavenly or future meaning of a biblical text.

Is there hidden meaning behind the biblical text?

The Roman Catholic Church considers the church to be the authoritative interpreter of the Bible, since the canon of Scripture is derived from the pronouncements of historic church traditions. The Orthodox churches agree that the Bible should not be interpreted outside the church, but they see the authority of the church as that which is derived from Scripture rather than the authority of Scripture being derived from the church. The Protestant emphasis upon "Scripture alone" led to the interpretive principle that "Scripture is to be explained by Scripture" rather than by any church or church tradition. Thus, inductive methodology predominated Protestant approaches to the observation, interpretation, evaluation, and application of the Bible.

4.6.2 Interpretive Principles

Many principles of biblical interpretation exist, which serve to help people interpret the Bible inside and outside churches. *Induction* and *deduction,* of course, aid in the interpretive process, beginning with inductive study before moving on to making deductive pronouncements about its meaning. Every person and church has to decide how quickly they move from inductive study, which seeks to investigate all relevant data for understanding Scripture. Such investigation helps to raise the probability of truth claimed through deductive demonstration and explanation.

When interpreting the Bible, there are at least three additional principles helpful for understanding and using Scripture. First, there needs to be concern for the *literary context* of the biblical passages being studied. What insights do we gain from insights from grammatical and literary studies related to the biblical text? Second, there needs to be concern for the *historical context* of the biblical passages being studied. What insights do we gain from historical studies of what took place at the time the biblical text was written? Third, there needs to be concern for the *genre* of the biblical passages being studied. What insights do we gain from distinguishing between different types of literary writing used in the biblical text? What difference does it make, for example, if the genre of a text is historical, poetic, missive, parabolic, or apocalyptic? The question of genre may, in fact, be one of the most important determinations in biblical interpretation. This consideration of genre along with consideration of the literary and historical context of a biblical text is important for understanding and applying Scripture. Such considerations led to the development of a variety of methods of interpretation.

What principles best help us interpret Scripture?

4.6.3 Methods of Biblical Interpretation

Over the centuries a variety of research methodologies developed to interpret the Bible. They include many helpful perspectives in understanding the literary and historical contexts of passages as well as their genres. Rather than present them in the order of their development, we will simply present some of the more prevalent methods of interpretation employed by biblical scholars as they engage in the *historical critical method.* This method of reading the Bible attempts to identify the historical context of events, people, and culture that lie behind the biblical texts and out of which they emerged.

- *Textual criticism* attempts to identify the original form of the biblical text by collecting, ordering, and evaluating the thousands of manuscripts of Scripture.

- *Grammatical criticism* attempts to identify the particular meanings of words and sentence structures, using philological and linguistic studies of the biblical text.

- *Source criticism* attempts to identify the literary development of biblical texts by trying to discern distinct sources that make up the composite final text (for example, asking whether a single book is written by one author or many).

- *Form criticism* attempts to identify the particular literary form in which biblical texts were written (for example, narrative texts, parables).

- *Sociological criticism* attempts to identify particularly the social context in which the biblical text emerged, emphasizing the social dynamic in which Scripture originally functioned.

- *Tradition and form criticisms* attempt to identify the formal patterns that underlie a text, particularly the way oral traditions functioned in shaping a biblical text.

- *Redaction criticism* attempts to identify the point of view of a biblical author and changes made in the oral traditions reported in a finished work (for example, in the Gospels).

- *Canonical criticism* attempts to identify the meaning of the Bible found in the canon as a whole, since meaning can be found from those who canonized Scripture as well as from the original authors.

- *Literary criticism* attempts to read the final form of the biblical text as a whole, considering the literary methods and artistry employed by biblical authors (for example, wordplay, symbolism, metaphor, etc.).

There are other approaches to biblical interpretation, for example, comparative religions criticism, narrative criticism, structural criticism, genre criticism, audience criticism, and so on. Considering all of the interpretive approaches, we discover that there are many potentially helpful ways to understand and apply Scripture today.

4.7 Conclusion

The Bible remains the theological reference point for Christians today—the place to begin reflection upon God as well as other religious matters. Not all, of course, consider Scripture the same way. Some consider its revelatory powers essential for Christian beliefs, values, and practices. Others see it only as a reference point for further religious investigation. But all consider Scripture necessary for determining what it means to be Christian and for reflecting theologically upon God and all matters related to God.

Certainly people must decide for themselves what the Bible means to them in terms of its revelation of truth. Certainly every doctrine we investigate hereafter will one way or another find its roots in Scripture. Thus, it is impossible to escape the basic teachings of the Bible as the reference point for this introduction to theology.

As we study individual doctrines we will certainly look at what the Bible has to say. Scripture verses will be mentioned, but they will be presented in terms of historical critical debate. This is a book of theology rather than biblical hermeneutics. But the theology described will reflect the product of extensive studies of the Bible, undertaken by many Christians at many times and places in church history. Verses mentioned should not be understood as proof-texts or the final word on issues discussed. Rather, they represent classical references in Scripture to theological issues discussed. As such they will be more illustrative than demonstrative of Christian doctrine.

4.8 Questions for Further Reflection

1. Is it significant that the Bible developed over a long period of time, both in its writing and in its canonization? How so?

2. What does it mean to consider Scripture the "Word of God"?

3. What does it mean for Scripture to be inspired by God?

4. What are the effects of inspiration: Is the Bible inerrant? If not, then how truthful may we consider Scripture to be?

5. When people read the Bible, how important to them is it that Scripture be inspired or truthful? How important is it to you?

6. In what ways do you interpret Scripture? Which principles and methods of biblical interpretation do you think are the most useful to you, the church, or to others?

4.9 Notes

1. "The Chicago Statement on Biblical Inerrancy," International Council on Biblical Inerrancy, 1978, published in Carl F. H. Henry, *God, Revelation and Authority* (6 vols.; Waco, Tex.: Word, 1979), 4:211–19.

GOD

God said to Moses, "I am who I am." He said further, "Thus you shall say to the Israelites, 'I am has sent me to you.'" God also said to Moses, "Thus you shall say to the Israelites, 'The Lord, the God of your ancestors, the God of Abraham, the God of Isaac, and the God of Jacob, has sent me to you': This is my name forever, and this is my title for all generations."

(Exodus 3:14–15)

WHO IS GOD?

5.1 Introduction

One day, while tending sheep on Mt. Horeb, Moses came across an amazing sight. He saw a bush blazing with fire, yet without the bush itself being consumed. When Moses looked closer, God spoke to him from out of the burning bush. God told Moses that he had been chosen to lead the Israelites out of captivity in Egypt. In response, Moses asked what he should say to the people if they ask the name of the God who sent him. God responded by saying, "I am who I am" (Exod 3, esp. 3:14).

Now this name—"I am who I am"—may immediately bring a sense of awe, but to the casual reader of the Bible, this appellate makes little sense. Upon investigation the name does not immediately bring greater insight. For example, the name may also be translated "I am what I am," "I will be what I will be," or possibly "He causes to be."[1] It is not clear what function the phrase serves in naming God. On the one hand, it may be a reference to the perfections of God's being. On the other hand, it may be a reference to the presence and actions of God in historical affairs. Today, process theologians prefer the latter reading, asserting that God should not be understood in terms of perfection. Instead God should be understood in terms of process just as people and world history are in a process of becoming a yet undetermined—perhaps inconceivable—reality.

One thing is for sure, Moses was in awe of this God he encountered in the burning bush. Moses knew this to be the God who also claimed to be the God of his ancestors—the God of Abraham, Isaac, and Jacob. Moses also knew that this was a powerful, though perhaps unpredictable, deity.

God appeared as a burning bush that was not consumed

> **No one can find** a greater mystery than people's belief in God, yet one can hardly find a more pervasive belief. Sometimes conceiving of it as a human projection or emotional crutch, people unwisely consider theism facetious.
>
> Almighty and personal; majestic and good; holy and loving—it is impossible to summarize the totality of who God is. Yet, upon such conceptions Christians base their every belief, value, and practice.

Whether or not Moses perceived this God as the sole deity of the universe or merely one among many gods is a moot point. Certainly God remained an awesome God to Moses. Months and years after this encounter with God, Moses continued to be awed by the God named "I am." We may be no more successful than Moses in fathoming the depths of who God is, but it is to that purpose that we now turn our discussion.

5.2 What Is God Like?

God is the supreme being. Christian theism—beliefs about God—affirms that God is almighty, personal, and Creator of the universe. At the same time, Christians have tried to name and define God, and they have also wanted to claim that God is indefinable, at least by means of our finite human means. Still Christians have continually tried to articulate their understanding of God. Their attempts have primarily arisen due to their understanding of God as found in Scripture.

One's conception of God has far-reaching impact. How one conceives of God may influence how one lives life. From a Christian perspective, God should influence one's day-to-day life. But there is often a difference between theory and practice. One may claim to believe in God, and yet live without a sense of God's presence or involvement. On the other hand, one may live with a constant sense of God's presence and involvement, without being able to articulate it. Let us look at Scripture in order to let it begin to shape our understanding of God and learn to appreciate the far-reaching impact of that understanding, whether we are fully conscious of it or not.

5.2.1 Names of God

The Bible offers numerous names for God. In Genesis, specific names for God are given. In Gen 1, creation is described as the work of *Elohim* (Hebrew for "gods" or "God"). The name is plural, but it is frequently used in the Old Testament to name the one, true God of Israel (Gen 1:1; cf. Pss 42–83). The name Elohim is associated with the creative power of God as the originator of the universe. It is a synonym for *Yahweh* (Hebrew, "Lord"), used frequently throughout Scripture, and *Adonai* (Hebrew for "lord" or "lord and father"; cf. Gen 15:2; Exod 4:10). The names may reflect different understandings of God, or they may reflect different literary sources for the Genesis stories about God, creation, and the eventual calling of Abraham and the Israelite people.

The best known name for God in the Bible is Yahweh, which is a transliteration of the Hebrew consonantal form יהוה (YHWH)—the *tetragrammaton* (Greek for "four letters"). Early Hebrew had no vowels, so we can only guess at how the name was pronounced. Later Jews did not speak the name because they considered the name of God too holy to be uttered. The name Yahweh is used

Can I buy a vowel?

when describing the covenantal relationship between God and people, reflective of God's goodness, mercy, and grace. The name Yahweh appears more than 6,000 times in Scripture, including the "I am" reference in Exod 3:14–15.

In some translations the name Yahweh is rendered Jehovah; in others, it has simply been transliterated into JHVH. Variations of Yahweh (or Jehovah) occur in the Hebrew texts:

- Yahweh-*jireh* ("the lord will provide"; cf. Gen 22:8, 14)

- Yahweh-*mekkodishkem* ("the lord who sanctifies"; cf. Gen 31:12–13; Lev 20:8; 21:8; 22:32; Ezek 20:12)

- Yahweh-*nissi* ("the lord my banner"; cf. Exod 17:15)

- Yahweh-*raah* ("the lord my shepherd"; cf. Gen 48:15; Ps 23:1)

- Yahweh-*rapha* ("the lord who heals"; cf. Exod 15:26; Isa 30:26; Jer 3:22; 30:17)

- Yahweh-*shalom* ("may the lord send peace"; cf. Judg 6:24)

- Yahweh-*shammah* ("the lord is there"; cf. Ezek 48:35)

- Yahweh-*tsidkenu* ("the lord our righteousness"; cf. Jer 23:6; 33:16)

Other biblical names for God include God most high (Deut 32:8; 2 Sam 22:14; Dan 4:17); everlasting God (Isa 9:6; 40:28); Almighty (Job 11:7; 33:4; Ps 91:1); God Almighty (Gen 17:1; Exod 6:3; Ps 89:8); Lord Almighty (Isa 6:3; 45:13; 47:4; 48:2; 51:15; 54:5); Lord God Almighty (Amos 5:15; Rev 4:8; 19:6); Mighty One (Gen 49:24; Pss 45:3; 50:1; Isa 60:16; Matt 26:64); Lord God (Gen 2:4, 7, 22; 3:21, 23); and Rock (Gen 49:24; Deut 32:4; Pss 19:14; 92:15; Isa 26:4). In the New Testament, God is also related to Jesus and the Holy Spirit, which will be topics of later chapters.

The following names and descriptions of God originated in various places and cultural contexts, spanning hundreds of years. Evaluating them historically and critically is crucial for responsibly developing the Christian doctrine of God. However, one should not despair in terms of what, finally, can be said about God. Theological formulations may not always appear as nice and neat as one

Shakespeare asked, "What's in a name? That which we call a rose by any other word would smell as sweet"

may want, but sufficient information—revelation—is available for meaningfully speaking about God.

5.2.2 Descriptions of God

Scripture is filled with descriptions of God. Throughout the centuries Christians have tried to catalog the variety of characteristics attributed to God in the Bible. Others have added to those characteristics their individual perceptions of God developed through personal experience and reflection upon every source of knowledge they have of God. The following list presents frequently mentioned attributes of God suggested in Scripture. They are only suggested because how one interprets particular Bible passages may vary. The attributes are listed in alphabetical rather than a theological order:

- benevolent (Deut 7:7–8; John 3:16)

- compassionate (Deut 30:3; 2 Chr 36:15; Lam 3:32)

- constant (or immutable) (Ps 102:27; Mal 3:6; Jas 1:17)

- eternal (Gen 21:33; Ps 90:2)

- everywhere (or ubiquitous, omnipresent) (Deut 4:39; Ps 139:8; Prov 15:3; Isa 66:1)

- faithful (Num 23:19; Ps 89:2; 1 Thess 5:24)

- free (Ps 115:3)

- gentle (Ps 18:35; Isa 40:11; 42:3; 2 Cor 10:1)

- genuine (or real) (Jer 10:5–10; John 17:3)

- good/goodness (Exod 33:19; Pss 25:8; 145:9; Nah 1:7)

- gracious (Exod 34:6; Eph 1:5–8; Titus 2:11)

- holy (Exod 15:11; Isa 6:3; 1 Pet 1:16)

- impartial (Job 34:18–19; Matt 5:45; Acts 10:34–35; Rom 10:12)

- infinite (1 Kgs 8:27; Ps 145:3; Acts 17:24)

- just (Acts 10:34–35; Rom 2:11)

- knowing/knowledgeable (or all-knowing, omniscient) (Pss 139:1–4; 147:4–5; Matt 11:21)

- life (Exod 3:14; Jer 10:10; John 5:26)

- light (Ps 27:1; Isa 60:20; 1 John 1:5)

- love/loving (or all-loving) (Ps 103:17; Eph 2:4–5; 1 John 4:8, 10)

- merciful (Exod 3:7, 17; Ps 103:13; Matt 9:36)

- one (or a unity) (Deut 6:4; 1 Cor 8:6)

- patient (or forbearing) (Neh 9:30; Rom 2:4; 3:25)

- persistent (Ps 86:15; Rom 2:4; 9:22)

- personal (or personality) (Exod 3:14; Gen 3)

- powerful (or all-powerful, almighty, omnipotent) (Ps 115:3; Matt 19:26; Rev 19:6)

- present (or near, immanent) (Pss 16:8; 34:18; 145:18; Jer 23:23–24; Acts 17:27)

- righteous (Ps 19:7–9; Jer 9:24)

- sovereign (Eph 1:21)

- spirit/spiritual (or simple) (John 1:18; 4:24; 1 Tim 1:17; 6:15–16)

- truth/truthful (1 Sam 15:29; John 14:6; 17:3, 17, 19; Heb 6:18; Titus 1:2)

- unsearchable (or transcendent) (Job 5:9; 11:7; Eccl 3:11; Isa 40:28; 1 Cor 2:16)

- unseen (or invisible) (Exod 33:20; John 5:37; Col 1:15; 1 Tim 1:17)

- wise (Ps 104:24; Prov 3:19; Dan 2:20; Rom 11:33)

Hello, God, are you there?

This list of attributes could easily be continued because the Bible says so much about God. But this list provides a helpful summary of characteristics attributed to God in Scripture.

Of course, the list above presents those attributes that Christians traditionally mention in description of God. But they do not exhaust the characteristics listed in Scripture. Other attributes paint a different, albeit important, picture of God. These are attributes that do not always fit easily into one's theology, yet they are a part of the biblical portrayal of God. For example, God is described in the following ways:

- angry/anger (Exod 4:14; Deut 9:19–20; Judg 2:14)

- boastful (Job 1:8; 2:3)

- causing evil/disaster (1 Sam 16:14; 2 Sam 24:15–16; 1 Chr 21:15; Isa 45:7)

- changeable (2 Sam 24:15–16; 1 Chr 21:15; Jonah 3:10)

- arbitrary/capricious (Rom 9:13; cf. Mal 1:3)

- gambling (Job 1:8–12; 2:3–6)

- jealous (Exod 20:5; 34:14; Deut 4:24; Josh 24:19)

- repenting/regretting (Gen 6:6–7; Exod 32:12, 14; 1 Sam 15:11, 35; Jer 42:10)

- testing (Gen 3:1–7; 22:1; Deut 8:2; Job 1:8–12; 2:3–6)

- vengeful/wrathful (Deut 32:35; Ps 94:1; Rom 12:19)

- genocidal (Num 31:7; Deut 7:2; 13:15; 20:17; Josh 12:19–20; 1 Sam 15:3)

What are we to make of these unusual attributes of God? The worst thing to do would be to overlook them. But we should also not look at them without knowing the particular context in which they occur in the Bible. Likewise, we should not look at them without knowing the greater context of Scripture in which they occur. Bible verses such as the ones above remind us that our biblical interpretation should not be built upon proof-texts, that is, by establishing whole theologies based upon individual verses that are interpreted in a simplistic fashion. Instead we need to be cautious and take time in studying the Bible and in developing beliefs about God.

5.3 The Doctrine of God

The earliest consensual description of God occurs in the Nicene Creed. It presents a short statement about God:

> We believe in one God, the Father all-governing, creator of all things visible and invisible.[2]

How are we to understand this early doctrine of God? To begin with, it was a theological statement affirmed by the early church because of their belief in God's special revelation to humanity. The Nicene Creed is based upon scriptural teachings, though we need to remember that the canon of Scripture had not yet been recognized by an ecumenical council. More importantly, the statement about God was thought to conform to the deposit of faith—the sum of revelation and tradition passed down from the time of the apostles, maintained by the magisterium of the church.

It remained less clear to Christians in the ancient church whether God could truly be defined. Their understanding of God as transcendent—one beyond the limits of human understanding—presented a problem to their developing theology.

In chapter 2, several methods of discerning the attributes of God were discussed. The first and most important method pertained to the special revelation of God found in Scripture. But the ancient church also thought that there were other ways of discerning the attributes of God by means of general revelation. For example, it was thought that one could learn about God by means of reasoning from *causality*, arguing that God represented the first cause of all that exists. This method of inference was thought to be especially important for arguments later developed for the purpose of proving the existence of God.

A second method of reasoning that proved valuable to those arguing for the existence of God pertained to attempts to infer attributes of God *a priori*, that is, by deductively reflecting upon the very idea of God. This rationalistic approach to knowing God affirmed that reason alone leads one to the conclusion that God exists.

A third method of reasoning by means of general revelation pertained to that of arguing for the attributes of God by means of *negation.* If God transcends all that is finite, including that of finite human existence, then God must embody all that is not finite. In this way God was thought to represent the opposite of limitations found in the world and humanity.

**What is the best way
to think about God?**

A final method of reasoning pertained to that of arguing by means of *heightening,* or *eminence.* In this regard, God was thought to correspond to the highest manifestation of humanity's best qualities. God was the perfect representation of all that is known of the world and people.

All of these methods were used to evaluate and categorize beliefs about God. For example, doctrinal developments that ensued made distinctions between the nature and character of God. The nature of God constituted those attributes thought to be absolute and incommunicable references to the essence of who God is. These references pertained to the transcendent nature of God, which included attributes of self-existence, immensity, infinity, eternity, and so on. Such attributes were ultimately considered to be beyond human comprehension, yet essential to the Christian understanding of God.

The character of God was thought to be more easily comprehended because the attributes described were related to those possessed by people. Indeed, how could God communicate with people unless God used similar methods of communication and of relating? However, God possessed these attributes to a more perfect degree than people, and indeed in some ways God's attributes seem in opposition to those possessed by a people tainted by the effects of sin. The references pertaining to the character of God included attributes of benevolence, compassion, faithfulness, goodness, mercy, righteousness, justice, truthfulness, and so on.

Over the centuries, Christians have variously understood and grouped the attributes of God. But for the most part there has been a consensus of who God is. This does not mean, however, that there has not been sometimes wild debate over the nature and character of God. We will look at some of the more critical issues that arose in describing the supreme being.

5.4 Tensions in the Doctrine of God

Whenever one attempts to speak of the supreme being of the universe with less than absolute minds, troubles are bound to arise. The following represent some of the more intriguing tensions that have arisen when reflecting upon the attributes of God—attributes that have great significance in terms of the nature and extent of our relationship with God.

Certainly a degree of mystery continually exists in human attempts to conceptualize and speak about God. Such is to be expected. When considering the following tensions, one should not necessarily hope or even want to resolve them. Perhaps God wants to challenge people to think and mature as they deal with the following attributes. Sometimes it is the process of reflection that benefits people more than presumed conclusions.

5.4.1 Transcendence and Immanence

On the one hand, God is considered to be *transcendent*. Transcendence pertains to the degree to which God surpasses our finite human abilities to conceive and describe. But if God surpasses our ability to conceive and describe, how can we say anything about God? How *immanent* is God?

Søren Kierkegaard (1813–1855) wrestled with the concept of God's transcendence. He did not think that it was possible to comprehend the essence of God. Indeed, Kierkegaard thought that human reason was incapable of developing an objective system of doctrinal truths that could describe God. God was not an object to be studied but a being with whom one entered into a subjective relationship characterized by passion of faith rather than reasoning calculation. Kierkegaard described faith as leaps, though not as blind leaps, as some have suggested. According to him, truth that was important to the individual, that is, to the individual existence of a person, was not objective in nature. Rather, truth of an existential nature, pertaining to one's individual existence, was subjective in nature, reflecting the kind of subjectivity characteristic of a personal relationship. This existential view of a highly subjective personal relationship with God made it virtually impossible to communicate to other people, other subjects.

**Kierkegaard preparing
to make a leap of faith!**

On the other hand, there arose numerous conceptions of God that emphasized immanence. Immanence pertains to God being near, present, everywhere, ubiquitous, omnipresent. In what sense is God everywhere? Is God present with us everywhere as an "other"—present but distinct, as Kierkegaard thought? Or does God permeate all of creation as the Apostle Paul suggests in quoting a phrase attributed to the Cretan seer Epimenides: "In him [God] we live and move and have our being" (Acts 17:28). Certainly Paul did not advocate a pantheistic conception of God in which God is identical with the universe. Nor did Paul advocate a panentheistic conception of God in which everything in the universe is imbued with God, though God remains more than all there is. Still Christians have wondered about the degree to which God is present. Christian mystics, for example, have argued for more than communion with God. Instead, there occurs a union in which individuality is dissipated into the oneness of God.

In the history of Christianity, predominant emphasis has been placed upon the transcendent *otherness* of God. But that otherness has not been emphasized to the degree found in Kierkegaard. Instead Christians have preferred to live with the tension—the paradox—of a God who is utterly and wholly transcendent. Yet God is one who is near us and actively involved in events. Certainly God sustains the creation made by God and God communicates to those created by God. How that takes place remains one of the many mysteries of God, and attempts to avoid the mystery result in beliefs that stray from classical understandings of God.

5.4.2 Unchanging and Changing

In Scripture God is thought to be constant, *unchanging*—the same yesterday, today, and forever. This affirmation represents a great encouragement to Christians, knowing that they do not have to relate with a God who is *changeable* and, perhaps, unpredictable.

In the ancient church, the word *immutability* was used to describe the constancy of God's character. Mutability or change was not considered an appropriate attribute of God; changeability was considered an imperfection. It implied that God was somehow subject to limitations, as people are subject to limitations. Immutability, however, carried with it overtones of Greek philosophical conceptions that understood God as being impassive and uninvolved in the lives and events of people. Over the centuries the concept of an immutable or impassive God has contributed to feelings that God is neither active nor particularly concerned about people and their problems. This does not reflect the biblical concept of a God who is both concerned and active. In Scripture we find that God *wills* change, but this does not necessarily mean

Did God create the world like a clock and then take off?

that there occurs an essential change in God's character. Still some Christians held to a deistic understanding of God, conceiving the deity as one who created the world and then let it run on its own without any divine intervention because God is either unresponsive or incapable of personal response.

Christians have alternately struggled with the constancy of God—sometimes emphasizing the perfect changelessness of God and at other times emphasizing the dynamic interaction between God and people. Classical biblical exegetes in ancient and medieval churches wrestled with those biblical passages, for example, that speak of God as "repenting" (e.g., Gen 6:6–7; Exod 32:12, 14; 1 Sam 15:11, 35; Jer 42:10). Their conclusion was that neither God nor God's eternal plans in relationship to people change. Rather, anthropomorphic metaphors and analogies are used in order to describe how God interacts with a people whose lives and circumstances change. There is no imperfection in the constancy of God when God interacts with finite human beings in the midst of their own changeability and unreliability.

In recent years, process theologians have struggled more than anyone else with the constancy—or inconstancy—of God. They see the Christian concept of God's immutability as reflective of Greek philosophical ideas found in the work of thinkers such as Aristotle (384–322 B.C.E.) who distort the biblical concept of God. Process theologians see God's loving responsiveness toward humanity from the perspective of the essential process-oriented nature of God. How can God genuinely interact with people, after all, if there is not genuine change and growth in relationship with God? The notion of an immutable God promotes a static image that results in caricatures of God as being a cosmic moralist who is unchanging, passionless, and a controlling power that preserves the present order of existence rather than change it for good. Process theological conceptions of God have had special appeal to those concerned with the problem of evil. They conclude that God does not refuse to overturn evil due to a lack of love. Evil prevails not because of an almighty God who mysteriously permits it to continue, but because God, who is also in the process of combating evil, struggles against it just as people do.

5.5 Language about God

Often, tensions involved with the doctrine of God stem from the problem of language. It is difficult for people to speak of God because our language seems inadequate to name the supreme being of the universe. This is not a new problem. The Bible talks about the difficulty of finding and addressing God: "Can you find out the deep things of God? Can you find out the limit of the Almighty?" (Job 11:7). Throughout church history, Christians have been scrupulous about how they crafted their words.

Today people are very aware of the words they use to describe anyone or anything, especially God. Words can be powerful as well as clarifying in communicating Christian beliefs, values, and practices. They can also be misleading and flat-out wrong. So, it is important to take time to talk about the nature of language and, in particular, about religious language.

5.5.1 The Nature of Religious Language

In the ancient church, Christians recognized that all language of God is *analogical* or *symbolic* in nature. For example, when the Bible speaks of God as being powerful or merciful, Christians in the ancient church realized that an analogy was being drawn between a characteristic of who we are as people and what God is like. God, of course, is thought to be in eminent possession of such characteristics. We cannot know the perfect degree to which God possesses such characteristics, but we can learn about God because of the likeness between ourselves and God. We can know the divine attributes sufficiently to speak of God even though there remains a paradox in what we say, describing the one who cannot be described.

Over the centuries Christians continued to acknowledge the analogical nature of their references to God. Thomas Aquinas (ca. 1225–1274), for example, distinguished between analogies of proportion and those of proportionality.[3] The analogy of proportion refers to likenesses that parallel both God and people. God, of course, eminently possesses the characteristics of power and mercy, for example. The analogy of proportionality, on the other hand, refers to a likeness in relations. For example, spiritual sight is used as an analogy with our physical sight. In a sense, the analogy of proportion referred to quantitative analogies while the analogy of proportionality referred to qualitative analogies. Aquinas preferred the former use of the analogy of proportion in describing God.

What is the nature of religious language?

Those who disagreed with analogical approaches to language about God emphasized the transcendence, otherness, and unknowability of God. In contrast, they preferred the *apophatic* way (Greek, "denial") of talking about God, which emphasizes that human conceptions of God are incapable of conceptualizing God. Since no human analogies adequately conceptualize God, people must speak *via negativa* (Latin for "the negative way"), using statements about God that are accompanied by negations, saying what God is not. For example, God is described theologically as being *omnipotent* or all-powerful, since people are finite and limited in power. Omnipotence does not precisely describe the extent of God's power as much as it describes God's power as being beyond human abilities to comprehend and articulate. To be sure, there are many Bible verses that reinforce the sovereignty of God, though that word is not used. Rather, it was borrowed from Greek thought about the divine. This does not disqualify its usage, but it should make Christians cautious about how dogmatically they refer to the omnipotence of God.

Similar concerns pertained to such descriptions of God as *omnipresent* ("everywhere present"), *omniscient* ("knows all things"), and other "omni" characteristics. Again, there are Bible verses that reinforce the ubiquitous presence and all-surpassing knowledge of God. However, the use of terms not employed in the Bible may introduce conceptions of God dissimilar to the complexity and nuances of Scripture's descriptions of God.

Protestants preferred not to speak in terms of *analogy of being,* or analogies that utilized parallel likenesses and likenesses of relations. Instead, they spoke

**Like, God is . . . like . . .
you know . . . like . . .**

of the *analogy of faith,* which affirmed that the sense of Scripture served as the basis for interpreting unclear or ambiguous texts. The analogy of faith was especially helpful in clarifying the doctrine of God, since they placed greater emphasis upon the transcendence, otherness, and unknowability of God. Barth especially thought that the analogy of being, utilizing knowledge based upon general revelation, had nothing significant to offer Christians. Rather, their knowledge of God came entirely from the special revelation of God and the analogy of faith.

5.5.2 Verification of Religious Language

In the twentieth century, the use of any type of religious language—much less language about God—came under the intense scrutiny of the analytic philosophy of logical positivism. Logical positivism is a philosophy that does not think that metaphysical (or supernatural) statements about God and other religious matters are meaningful because they lack empirical verification. Its principle of verifiability requires that a statement is only meaningful if it can—at least in principle—be empirically verified. Since God is not thought of as an object that can be studied like other objects of science, religious language was considered wrong, irrelevant, or ignored altogether. The questions of a progressively secular and materialistic society challenged the meaningfulness of religious language that cannot scientifically test its statements in order to ascertain its truthfulness.

A variety of responses were given to the challenge of logical positivism and others who argued against the meaningfulness of religious language. Some rejected the relevance of the principle of verifiability and argued that relevance is not restricted to empirical or logical cognition. Indeed, the principle of verifiability cannot itself be verified, since it cannot be empirically verified. Rather, the meaningfulness of religious language transcends empirical or logical cognition. This view of religious language places meaning largely outside the realm of empirical experience and rational reflection, which suggests a more numinous, or spiritual, understanding of Christianity.

Another response was to accept the critique proffered by the principle of verifiability, but to also argue that the meaningfulness of religious language pertained to its effect upon the emotional,

**Is God like other objects
that can be studied?**

ethical, or existential well-being of people. This view of religious language sees the effect of Christianity upon people as more meaningful than its claims to truth.

Most responses to the principle of verifiability accepted its premise, but argued that people need to develop a broadened understanding of the empirical and logical basis of religious language. Some argued that the very nature of analogical nature of religious language requires empirical reality in order to make its hypothetical descriptions of God. All disciplines of knowledge require the use of analogical and hypothetical reasoning, so religious language should not be prohibited from making logical inferences about who God is.

Another argument for the meaningfulness of religious language comes from the fact that Christianity is a historical religion. So much of what it claims to be true is inextricably bound up with historical events such as the resurrection of Jesus Christ. Because historical findings can be falsified, that is, proven to be wrong, they can also be verified. Just because not all religious claims have yet been verified, there is no more reason to reject its meaningfulness than scientific or behavioral claims that have not yet been verified empirically.

A final argument for the empirical verifiability of Christianity is the experiential commitments of believers, especially those who gave their lives for the sake of Christianity since the time of the disciples. The presence of Christians may not prove that Christianity is true. But it does mean that Christianity embodies a genuine phenomenon with religious language that cannot be dismissed outright simply because a limited conception of empirical and logical verifiability is imposed upon it.

How are our words—any words—meaningful?

5.5.3 Male and Female Language about God

Increasingly Christians have become concerned about male-exclusive language used in reference to God. Overwhelmingly, biblical language about God is male, for example, references to God as Lord, King, and Father. However, Christians ask whether male-exclusive references to God relate to women today. Such questions are mistakenly viewed, sometimes, as thoroughly modern, "politically correct" questions totally devoid of biblical and historic credibility from a Christian perspective. However, this is a "red herring," that is, it introduces a subject into the discussion in order to distract people from the truth or the matter in question. It may well be that the modern women's movement has forced Christians to reexamine their understanding of the Bible and church history. But that does not negate their questions, especially since there is ample biblical and historical evidence for such discussion.

Scripture provides numerous descriptions of God (or allusions to God) that are female or are related to female attributes. Certainly they represent a minority of descriptions of God. They exist, however, and should be included in our conception of God. The following list mentions some of them:[4]

- female homemaker (Ps 123)
- baker woman (Matt 13:33; Luke 13:20–21)
- seamstress (Gen 3:21; Job 10:10–12)
- midwife (Ps 22:9)
- both mother and father (Isa 42:13–14; 63:15–16; Jer 31:20; Deut 32:18; 1 Thess 2:7, 11–12)
- master and mistress (Ps 123:2)
- comforting mother (Isa 66:12–13; Hos 11:1–4, 8–9; Luke 13:34; Rev 21:2–4)
- the godhead as a woman in the process of giving birth (Deut 32:18; Job 38:8, 28, 29; Isa 42:14, 16; John 3:3–7; 16:21–22; Acts 17:26, 28; Rom 8:22–23; Gal 4:19)
- womb of God (Job 38:8–9, 28–29; Isa 46:3–4)
- nursing (Num 11:11–14; Ps 34:8; Isa 49:15; 1 Pet 2:2–3)
- fierce mother bear (Prov 17:12; Hos 13:6–8)
- female pelican (Ps 102)
- mother eagle (Exod 19:4; Deut 32:11–12; Job 39:27–30)

What are we to do with these descriptions, allusions, analogies, and metaphors? Mostly, Christians have ignored them. However, more and more they are understood to contain important biblical information about God.

> God rejoiceth that he is our Mother . . . Our Kind Mother, our Gracious Mother, for that he would all wholly become our Mother in all things, he took the Ground of his Works full low and full mildly in the Maiden's womb.
>
> JULIAN OF NORWICH,
> REVELATIONS OF DIVINE LOVE
> (CA. 1393)

Historically, ancient Christians such as Gregory of Nazianzus (ca. 325–389) talked about the gender of God. He argued that God was beyond gender differentiation. God was personal, but the transcendent nature of God surpassed human descriptions. Besides, however God is conceived, both men and women are said to be created in the "image of God" (Gen 1:27).

During the Middle Ages, Christian mystics such as Julian of Norwich (1342–ca. 1416) spoke of "Christ as Mother."[5] Moreover, she went on to talk about God in terms of Father, Mother, spouse, and brother, as well as Savior. Although female language about God did not often occur in church history, it did occur and was recognized as an important contribution to Christian understanding of God and how Christians should communicate God to others.

Today Christians increasingly use female imagery to describe God, for example, as mother. Some go so far as to use "goddess" language in describing God, since such language is thought necessary for justly recognizing the feminine character of God. There are dangers in doing this, of course, since goddess language has no direct analogy or acceptance in Scripture.

Others try to avoid male language in reference to God by using no gender-specific nouns or pronouns. God is God, and one should refer to God and God's self (or "Godself"), without male or female specificity. There are dangers in doing this too, since it runs the risk of depersonalizing God. The depersonalization of God may be a greater risk to biblical and historic Christianity than the use of male language to describe God, due to the importance of God's personal nature and relationship with people.

Most Christians, however, continue to use male language in reference to God. Although they may be

Our Mother, who art in heaven . . . ?

sensitive to women's concerns, they use the language that they believe God chose to be revealed through the Bible. God chose to be revealed to particular people, at particular times, and in particular places. We may not think that such particularity adequately characterizes God's eternal power and divine nature, but it represents how God chose to be self-revealed. Thus, we must accept that God chose to be self-revealed, more or less, 2,000 years ago, to Hebrew people, in southwest Asia, using male language in reference to God. This *scandal of particularity* offends some and makes them think that God is less relevant because of the cultural, ethnic, and gender limitations of God's revelation. However, Christians have generally thought that universal truth can be conveyed even through particular people, times, and places. Male language does not negate the universality of Christianity to people today, regardless of their particular ethnic, cultural, gender, or linguistic background. It is also argued that male language shows respect to biblical language, honoring God's mode of self-revelation.

5.6 Conclusion

Christians believe in a supreme being. Not all Christians believe the same things about God, but their belief in one God persists despite continuing challenges to this belief.

Just as Scripture does not provide a uniform description of who God is, one should not expect that Christians will give a fixed description of God that is not open to a growing understanding of who God is. On the contrary, it is a strength of Christianity that it continues to mature in its understanding and communication of who God is.

As Christians develop in their intellectual understanding of who God is, there is always the expectation that they will also develop in their personal awareness and communion with God. Expectations with regard to this personal encounter with God also vary among Christians, but the belief that it will happen does not.

Our conception of God has a tremendous impact upon our lives both individually and corporately. If we view God as essentially loving, our ultimate concerns will be different than if we view God as essentially judgmental. A view of God as actively at work in the world will produce within our lives a much different way of viewing things than if we view God as uninvolved or only involved by means of persuasion. So how we conceive of God impacts more than our theology. It impacts how we as individuals live. It also impacts how we see ourselves in responsible relationship with the world in which we live.

5.7 Questions for Further Reflection

1. Statistically, most people believe in God. In what different ways do they conceive of God?

2. How extensively may someone's belief in God affect what they think, say, and do?

3. What three characteristics do you most appreciate about God? What three characteristics do you appreciate the least?

4. To what degree can we actually conceive of God? To what degree can and should we talk about God?

5. What do you think about the concern of those who argue we should use generic terms in reference to God? What are implications of your viewpoint?

6. How do you refer to God? What do you think about those who refer to God as mother? or as goddess?

5.8 Notes

1. See notes for Exod 3:13–15 in Bruce M. Metzger and Roland E. Murphy, eds., *The New Oxford Annotated Bible* (New Revised Standard Version; New York: Oxford University Press, 1991), 72–73.

2. "Nicene Creed," *Encyclopedia of Christianity* (ed. John Bowden; New York: Oxford University Press, 2005), 300. What is commonly known as the Nicene Creed, initially drafted at the Council of Nicaea (325), was in fact promulgated by the Council of Constantinople (381).

3. This distinction may be confusing today because what Aquinas described as the analogy of proportion is often referred to as the analogy of attribution and the analogy of proportionality is referred to as the analogy of proportion.

4. See Virginia Ramey Mollenkott, *The Divine Feminine: The Biblical Imagery of God as Female* (New York: Crossroad, 1987).

5. See Julian of Norwich, *Revelations of Divine Love* (trans. A. C. Spearing; new ed.; London: Penguin Classics, 1999), chs. 57–62.

CHAPTER SIX

Go therefore and make disciples of all nations, baptizing them in the name of the Father and of the Son and of the Holy Spirit. (Matthew 28:19)

THE TRINITY

6.1 Introduction

The night on which Jesus was arrested and later crucified, he shared a meal with his disciples, a meal that has come to be known as the "Last Supper." There, Jesus made a curious comment to his disciples. He said that after he was gone, God the Father would send the Holy Spirit to be their advocate—one who would teach and aid them in all they thought, said, and did (John 14:25–26).

It is not clear whether the disciples fully understood what Jesus was talking about at the Last Supper, but the general consensus is that they probably did not. But sometime thereafter the disciples exhibited an apparent contradiction in their references to God. On the one hand, they affirmed the age-old Jewish belief in monotheism, expressed in the traditional Hebrew prayer, the *Shema* (Hebrew for "hear"): "The Lord is our God, the Lord alone" (Deut 6:4). On the other hand, they progressively revered and worshipped Jesus—a practice unimaginable among Jews unless they truly thought of Jesus as divine. For example, the book of Matthew attributes the closing words of Jesus to the disciples as a kind of baptismal formula, which was later repeated by the disciples and early church. They baptized new converts "in the name of the Father and of the Son and of the Holy Spirit" (Matt 28:19).

Jesus' baptism: Father, Son, and Holy Spirit all present

Throughout the New Testament we discover a number of references to God that equally, yet distinctly, refer to God in a threefold fashion, including God the Father, God the Son, and God the Holy Spirit. The authors never seem to develop this apparent contradiction between the unity and diversity of their references to God in their writings.

Instead, the authors of the early Christian church were seemingly content to share that which they understood about God without exploring all the implications of their affirmations.

> **The Trinity tells us** who God is and is not, defying human reasons: One God in essence, yet mysteriously revealed as three persons.
>
> We do know that God the Father created all, and the Son atoned for our sins. The Holy Spirit sanctifies our lives, leading to many transformations.

6.2 What Is the Trinity?

The Trinity was one of the earliest doctrines to be defined by the ancient church. It was an attempt to communicate the mystery of God in a way that did justice to the descriptions of God revealed in Scripture. In particular, it attempted to do justice to the references to God as one essential deity yet also as three distinct persons. The doctrine of the Trinity may be defined as the belief in one God who exists in three persons who are equal yet distinct. This definition is not an attempt to explain God. On the contrary, the God of the Bible is ultimately transcendent and thus incapable of definition by means of finite human words. The God of Scripture surpasses our human abilities to describe, yet paradoxically reveals sufficient knowledge of God for our salvation. Rather than dispelling the mystery of who God is, the doctrine of the Trinity, in fact, preserves appropriately this mystery.

The doctrine of the Trinity tries to do justice to numerous passages of Scripture that communicate both the unity of God's existence and the threefold self-revelation of God to humanity. In particular, it speaks of both Jesus and the Holy Spirit, as discrete beings who still exhibit the essence of God. For example, the Bible ascribes the following divine attributes to Jesus and Holy Spirit, that are also ascribed to God the Father: the names of God, the attributes of God, the works of God, and worship that is due only God.[1] Recognition of these four biblical attributions to all three persons—Father, Son, and Holy Spirit—is remarkable. It distinguishes all three as being distinct, yet all three are attributed names, attributes, works, and worship due only to God.

FOUR ATTRIBUTIONS OF DIVINITY TO FATHER, SON, AND HOLY SPIRIT

- Divine names
- Divine attributes
- Divine works
- Worship

Specific biblical passages that include references to all three persons of the Trinity include the following texts. They do not exhaust biblical references to the Trinity, but they provide some of the clearest evidence:

- Jesus' baptism (Matt 3:16; cf. Mark 1:9–11; Luke 3:21–22; John 1:31–34)
- Jesus' baptismal formula of the so-called Great Commission (Matt 28:19)
- John's prologue and farewell discourses (John 14:26; 15:26)
- Paul's apostolic benediction (2 Cor 13:13)
- Paul's reference to the gifts (1 Cor 1:4–6)
- Paul's association of Father, Son, and Holy Spirit (Eph 2:18)
- Paul's reference to the "self-emptying" of Jesus (Greek, *kenosis*) (Phil 2:5–11)
- references to Father, Son, and Holy Spirit in John's letters (1 John 3–5, esp. 3:23–4:3)
- Jude's summary instruction (Jude 20, 21)
- John's salutation in the apocalypse (Rev 1:4–6)

Jesus' ardent prayer to God in the garden of Gethsemane

These passages do not prove the doctrine of the Trinity, but they illustrate the types of verses with which Christians in the ancient church struggled in order to determine their unique understanding of God. Their understanding, however, did not come easily or without controversy. In order to understand and appreciate the critical nature of the controversies experienced by the ancient church in formulating this doctrine (and their ongoing relevance for today), we need to spend some time reviewing what occurred.

6.3 The Development of the Doctrine

As the ancient Christian church grew and developed, there arose beliefs that were thought to be heresy. Originally, heresy (Greek, *hairesis*) simply meant another "choice" or "opinion." In time, other opinions were thought to be misleading and possibly perilous to Christian beliefs transmitted from the time of the apostolic church. Heretical beliefs were thought to address parts of biblical teaching, but not all of it. We will investigate examples of heresy in this chapter.

Decisions about the Trinitarian nature of God were not taken lightly. During the fourth century, Christianity had only recently been legalized and recognized as a viable religion in the Roman Empire. In addition to being difficult to understand, the doctrine of the Trinity was identified with vying social and political debates as well as biblical and ecclesiastical debates. Neither the church nor the canon of Scripture had congealed; many things were in flux. In this context, the doctrine of the Trinity slowly came to be accepted.

6.3.1 Arian Controversy

The Christian thinker Arius (ca. 256–336) posed the first great challenge to Christian conceptions of God in the ancient church. Arius advocated a *subordinationist* view of Jesus, that is, that Jesus is essentially subordinate to rather than equal to God. Arius did not think that biblical teaching, taken as a whole, justified the elevation of Jesus—a person, or a semi-divine person, at most—to a divinity. Instead Arius wanted to affirm what he considered to be the overarching theme of monotheism in Christianity.

At the Council of Nicea (325), Arius' views were rejected. In opposition to Arianism, Athanasius (ca. 296–373) championed what has come to be known as orthodox beliefs regarding a Trinitarian understanding of God. Athanasius argued that Jesus along with the Holy Spirit were genuinely divine, being of one essence or "the same substance" (Greek, *homoousios*) with God the Father. At the same time, they remained separate persons from one another. Thus the doctrine of the Trinity views God "undivided in divided persons." This theological conception of God is not easily—if ever—comprehended, but then what else might one expect from the transcendent God of creation?

Athanasius spent his entire life—sometimes persecuted for his views—arguing for this Trinitarian viewpoint. For example, he was able to bring about some unity of understanding through his discussion of key theological terms that had been misunderstood because theological debates were conducted in both Greek and Latin. Differences in meaning between similar Greek and Latin words used in debate needed to be clarified before there could be mutual understanding and acceptance of Trinitarian beliefs.

THE NICENE CREED

We believe in one God, the Father all-governing, creator of heaven and earth, of all things visible and invisible;

And in one Lord Jesus Christ, the only-begotten Son of God, begotten of the Father before all time, Light from Light, true God from true God, begotten not created, of the same essence as the Father, through whom all things came into being, who for us men and because of our salvation came down from heaven, and was incarnate by the Holy Spirit and the Virgin Mary and became human. He was crucified for us under Pontius Pilate, and suffered and was buried, and rose on the third day, according to the Scriptures, and ascended to heaven, and sits on the right hand of the Father, and will come again with glory to judge the living and the dead. His kingdom shall have no end.

And in the Holy Spirit, the Lord and life-giver, who proceeds from the Father, who is worshipped and glorified together with the Father and the Son, who spoke through the prophets; and in one, holy, catholic and apostolic Church. We look forward to the resurrection of the dead and life of the world to come. Amen.[2]

Other fourth-century advocates of orthodox Trinitarianism included Basil of Caesarea (a.k.a., Basil the Great, ca. 330–379), Gregory of Nyssa (ca. 335–394), Gregory of Nazianzus (329–389), and Augustine. The three former individuals are often referred to as the "Cappadocian fathers" because they were from Cappadocia in Asia Minor (modern day Turkey). The Cappadocians tended to place greater emphasis upon the diversity of the Trinity, while still affirming the unity of God. Their approach was more personal and dynamic in their holistic understanding of the Trinity, which became the dominant viewpoint of Eastern Christendom. Augustine, on the other hand, represented a more Western approach to understanding the Trinity. He began with the unity of God and understood the dynamic of the Trinity in ways that were more analytical and abstract. The combined work of the church fathers, however, contributed to a development in Trinitarian beliefs that finally led to the overturn of Arianism through the acceptance of the Nicene Creed at the Council of Constantinople of 381.

Although the Nicene Creed does not explicitly use the term "Trinity," its presence permeates the document. The threefold design logically presents Father, Son, and Holy Spirit. Each equally receives divine names and attributes, and they each do works that only God can do. The Nicene Creed reflects a classic articulation of the Trinity.

6.3.2 Non-Trinitarian Beliefs

Other non-Trinitarian views (heresies) arose. The various councils of the early church endeavored to refine Christian orthodoxy in ways that avoided problems perceived in heretical views. I already discussed the subordinationist tendencies in Arianism, so I will discuss some of the other challenges to early Christianity.

Monarchianism reflects the attempt to affirm monotheistic belief in God. It generally took two approaches to understanding God. The first view, sometimes referred to as *adoptionism* or *dynamic monarchianism*, affirmed that Jesus was a person upon whom the power of God rested and enabled him to achieve God's purposes. Thus Jesus represented God in amazing ways, but he in no way possessed essential union with God.

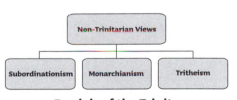

Denials of the Trinity

Those known as *modalist monarchians* affirmed that there is only one God, but that God's various appearances make it seem like there are multiple divine persons. But, in fact, there is only one divine being who is merely disclosed to people through different modes or names, functioning in different ways and times in relationship to people.

The early church regarded all of these monarchian beliefs, along with Arianism, as deficient because they failed to do justice to the fullness of the mystery of God revealed in the Bible. Although monarchians presented reasonable explanations of God, they failed to hold together the oneness of God as well as the diversity of God. The doctrine of the Trinity did not dispel all questions about the diversity of God, but it did address the variety of images of God portrayed in Scripture.

Some describe Father, Son, and Holy Spirit as three entirely different persons. It is tantamount to *tritheism*, affirming that all three persons of the Godhead are separate. This was not a common view within the early church. However, it continues to have adherents today, especially among those who think that all people may become gods, for example, Mormons. The Church of Jesus Christ of Latter-day Saints promotes Mormon theology, which thinks that latter-day revelation in the *Book of Mormon* supersedes the teachings of Scripture. Mormonism affirms that all people may progress eventually to salvation and, potentially, deification similar to that of the Father, Son, and Holy Spirit, who are separate divinities.

6.4 The Relevance of the Trinity

Many people object to the doctrine of the Trinity both inside and outside the church. Their reasons are many. First, the Trinity is too hard to understand and communicate to people. It doesn't preach! Second, the doctrine seems to be more philosophical in orientation than theological, perhaps owing more to the influence of Greek philosophy than to the Bible. This was a criticism leveled by Adolf von Harnack (1851–1930), a prominent church historian. Finally, some consider the Trinity to be irrelevant to contemporary people. Schleiermacher, for example, relegated it to an appendix of his theology.

Although the doctrine of the Trinity has been variously understood and appreciated throughout church history, it remains a cornerstone of orthodox Christian belief. Its relevance in this regard forms an important topic of discussion. I will review at least two general ways in which the doctrine of the Trinity proved relevant to the ancient church, as it does today.

6.4.1 Apologetic Relevance

Apologetics: Defending the faith!

The motivating force behind the conciliar development of the doctrine of the Trinity was the disputation with Arianism. Those who affirm the orthodoxy of Trinitarian beliefs still see the need for disputing viewpoints in opposition to the Nicene and other ecumenical creeds intended to safeguard a biblical understanding of God. Thus the doctrine of the Trinity serves an apologetic (or defensive) function in safeguarding the orthodox understanding of God.

This seems like a defensive or polemical reason for affirming the doctrine of the Trinity—a reason that seems to have less immediate concern for Christians today. Of course, one could debate how vulnerable the doctrine of the Trinity is. Views of God arise that continue to oppose the conclusions of the ecumenical councils, so certainly there will always be a need to defend the orthodox understanding of God. As such, there will always be a need for polemics—those who defend the boundaries of Christian beliefs. But certainly the more important relevance of the doctrine of the Trinity is its positive, constructive relevance.

6.4.2 Constructive Relevance

The early church considered the Trinity a useful concept for understanding the Bible and for setting the parameters of Christian belief about God. Historically, Christians found the doctrine of the Trinity to make more sense of difficult passages of Scripture that talk about Father, Son, and Holy Spirit. The Trinity helps to make explicit that which is contained implicitly in the Bible. It is a summing up of Scripture.

Trinity: Trying to organize Scripture

The doctrine of the Trinity also functioned as a key motivator in the organization of the church. Since the first ecumenical councils were called to articulate and defend a Trinitarian understanding of God, the church learned to develop its lines of communication and internal organization in order to cope with the pressing need to make a theological summary. In the long run, the Trinitarian controversies experienced by the early church strengthened it.

Most importantly, the doctrine of the Trinity served to set the parameter of the mystery of orthodox belief concerning God. Prior to the ecumenical councils, there had been no consensual understanding of Christian beliefs.

Afterwards, there had not only arisen a working understanding of God, there also arose helpful creeds that allowed Christians to articulate their basic beliefs. Creeds were especially important to the majority of Christians because so few of them were literate. The memorization and repetition of creeds provided a convenient way to communicate and inculcate the Christian faith along with catechetical aids that were developed.

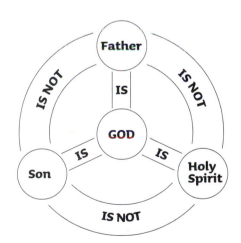

An ancient attempt to diagram the mystery of the Trinity

Certainly the doctrine of the Trinity separates it from other types of monotheism found in other religions. Just as the development of monotheistic beliefs formed a unique contribution to religious understanding in the world, the development of a Trinitarian understanding of monotheism formed a unique contribution to religious understanding in the world. Attempts to conceptualize and articulate the mystery of the Trinity remains a major distinguishing factor between Christianity and other religions in the world.

The Trinity has also provided ways in which to develop a comprehensive organization of Christian beliefs. It suggests the mystery as well as diversity of God's involvements with humanity. For example, it is indicative of the creative work of God the Father, the redemptive work of God the Son, and the sanctifying work of God the Holy Spirit.

THE TRINITY

Father	Creator, providential caregiver of the world, lawgiver, judge, promotes justice/resists injustice
Son	Savior of humanity, Lord, prophet, priest, present and coming king, brother/sibling, friend
Holy Spirit	Advocate, comforter, inspirer, intercessor, empowerer, sanctifier, gift-giver, giver of spiritual fruit

It is no wonder that numerous Christian theologies have been written in a Trinitarian format, dealing with theological issues pertaining to God the Father, God the Son, and God the Holy Spirit. This format helps to keep in creative balance the holistic dimension of Christian theology. God the Father is associated with creation, providential care for the world, giving the law, judging, and promoting justice as well as resisting injustice. God the Son is associated with being the Savior of humanity, Lord, prophet, priest, present and coming king, brother/sibling, and even friend. God the Holy Spirit is associated with being our comforter, advocate, intercessor, inspirer, empowerer, gift-giver, and giver of spiritual gifts. Although we associate certain characteristics with particular persons of the Trinity, all are thought to participate. Likewise, Christians and churches ought to reflect the variety of characteristics manifested in God, rather than focus narrowly on one person or work of God.

Praying in the name of the Creator, Redeemer, and Sanctifier

Christians sometimes use alternative ways of referring to the three persons of the Trinity. For example, people talk about God the Creator, Redeemer, and Sanctifier. The alternate naming of God has become especially popular among those who prefer to avoid the use of male-oriented language in reference to God, including Trinitarian references to God. Examples include: creator, savior, and sustainer; mother, child, and womb; and lover, beloved, and love. However, such usage needs to beware of the inclination to think of God in non-personal terms and of introducing new ideas about the Trinity not characteristic of the Bible.

With this in mind, there are several practical theological and ministerial implications to the doctrine of the Trinity. Christians do well to reflect upon their beliefs, values, and practices from a Trinitarian perspective. Those, for example, who focus more on the work of God the Father emphasize care for the world, society as a whole, and matters of justice and injustice. Those who focus more on the work of God the Son emphasize salvation, evangelism, and a personalized view of people's relationship with God. Those who focus more on the work of the Holy Spirit emphasize the dynamic presence of God to comfort and encourage as well as to empower believers with the fruit and gifts of the Holy Spirit. Focusing on all three persons of the Trinity and their divine works helps to remind people of the holistic ways God relates to people, the church, and to the earth itself. It also helps to remind everyone of the need for balance in how they reflect God's dynamic presence in their lives—how they participate in God.

> **PARTICIPATING IN THE TRINITY**
>
> You may ask, "If we cannot imagine a three-personal Being, what is the good of talking about Him?" Well, there isn't any good talking about Him. The thing that matters is being actually drawn into that three-personal life, and that may begin any time—tonight, if you like.
>
> C.S. LEWIS, MERE CHRISTIANITY (1943)

6.5 Contemporary Concerns

Over the centuries a variety of debates arose over the Trinity. Surprisingly most of the debate has involved variations on past controversies rather than new concerns. During the Reformation, a teaching called Socinianism arose that advocated a kind of monarchianism that later came to be known as Unitarianism. Unitarianism advocates belief in God as one person alone, reflecting the ongoing concern for the ancient monotheistic understanding of God.

In the twentieth century, Barth did much to renew interest in the doctrine of the Trinity through his focus upon it in his systematic theology. He was concerned, for example, that the ancient references to the three "persons" of the Trinity might be confused due to the contemporary understanding of "personality" that might erroneously lead people to an almost tritheistic understanding of God. Barth argued that God should be understood as one in personality or consciousness and three in ways of being. A similar viewpoint was asserted by Karl Rahner (1904–1984), who articulated the three-ness of God in terms of distinct manners of subsisting.

$$1 + 1 + 1 = 1$$

Does Trinitarian math add up?

In contrast, some Christians thought that Trinitarianism should be distinguished altogether from monotheism, which inherently tends toward monarchianism. For example, Jürgen Moltmann (1926–) asserts that the three-ness of God has been neglected in Western Christianity, and that there needs to be greater emphasis upon the diversity of God's activities. We should continue to talk about God as three persons because the unity of God should be understood in terms of a single being, albeit a being that is social in nature, wherein the personhood of God is determined by inter-subjective relationship.

Another debate has arisen over the relationship between the three persons of the Trinity: Is their relationship hierarchical, or is it egalitarian? This question has become especially important because of the rise of feminist concerns with regard to the Christian understanding of the relationship between men and women, possibly reflecting their createdness in God's image. Sometimes Christians interpret the Trinity as conveying an eternal hierarchy; sometimes they interpret the Trinity as conveying an eternal egalitarian relationship. Certainly the Bible seems to state things that suggest different works as well as relational differences. Yet, historically, the church has presented the creeds and the Trinity in terms of equality rather than hierarchy.

6.6 Conclusion

The Trinity remains a cornerstone of biblical, orthodox Christian belief. It may not easily be understood or, when understood, may be viewed with subtle differences. Yet it constitutes a distinctive belief of Christianity. It is not a doctrine of ancient relevance only, though it played a crucial role in the early development of the church. Today the Trinity continues to be a lively doctrine of Christian self-understanding and expression. The liveliness is in part due to the fact that Christians are again discovering the various ways in which the Trinity is relevant. It is relevant for biblical, historical, and theological studies. It is also relevant for the practical lives and ministries of Christians. Those who take the time to delve into the mystery of the Trinity and its present-day applications will discover the doctrine not to be a dry, abstract relic of the past but a suggestive, helpful concept.

6.7 Questions for Further Reflection

1. Why is the doctrine of the Trinity hard to understand? What could make it easier for people to understand? How can people think most constructively about the Trinity?

2. Why is the doctrine of the Trinity important for understanding and interpreting the Bible? Why is it difficult to discern the Trinity in Scripture?

3. Why is the doctrine of the Trinity important for understanding the historical development of Christianity? Why is the doctrine critical for understanding the organizational development of the ancient church?

4. How can the doctrine of the Trinity be of help to people today? How is it relevant to people individually? How is it relevant to the church and ministry?

6.8 Notes

1. Oden, *The Living God,* 195–201.
2. "Nicene Creed," *Encyclopedia of Christianity,* 300.

CHAPTER SEVEN

The heavens are telling the glory of God;
and the firmament proclaims his handiwork.
Day to day pours forth speech,
and night to night declares knowledge.
There is no speech, nor are there words;
their voice is not heard;
yet their voice goes out through all the earth,
and their words to the end of the world.
(Psalm 19:1–4)

KNOWING GOD

7.1 Introduction

Psalm 19 provides a marvelous hymn in honor of God as the Creator of the universe. In it the glory of God is thought to be manifested in the phenomena of the heavens. The psalmist David was jubilant in his praises to God and to the manifestations of God's power and benevolence. The proof of God's greatness was in the effects of divine creation. All one had to do was look at the world in which we live and the evidence of God's existence was thought to be inescapable. Elsewhere in the psalms David exclaims, "Fools say in their hearts, 'There is no God'" (Pss 14:1; 53:1). It was logically inconceivable to David that anyone could look at the beauty and orderliness of the world in which we live and not believe in God.

A similar view of the self-evidence of God's existence can be found in the writings of Paul to the Christian church in Rome. There Paul states, "Ever since the creation of the world his eternal power and divine nature, invisible though they are, have been understood and seen through the things he has made" (Rom 1:20a). Paul seemed to think that all people inferred God's existence through observation of the world in which we

Does God exist?

live, or that through conscience they instinctively knew of God's existence (Rom 2:14–16). There was no need to prove the existence of God. Of course, there was not the pervasive skepticism related to God's existence that later arose. Skepticism did progressively increase, which nowadays seems to be reaching a crescendo.

7.2 Does God Exist?

In Scripture the existence of God is barely questioned. God's existence is assumed. Only the fool was thought to question the existence of God. So there was not much of a need to defend or provide an apologetic for God's existence. Instead, there was the need to defend the supremacy of God among the many gods worshipped in the ancient Near East. The conflict over the worship of one God versus many gods and idols was ongoing. From the time of the Ten Commandments (Exod 20:1–17; Deut 5:6–21), which prohibited the worship of any God but Yahweh (Lord) and also prohibited idol worship, there was continued emphasis upon the one and only God.

During the time of the New Testament, belief in God continued to go largely unquestioned. Even in Athens—the center of Greek philosophy—Paul did not sense a need to defend God's existence. He instead pointed out an Athenian altar with the inscription, "To an unknown god," and tried to identify the person and characteristics of the one true God (Acts 17:16–34).

Do only fools not believe in God?

Certainly there were a number of things the early Christians had to defend in their new religious movement. In particular, emphasis was placed upon the resurrection and how the truthfulness of Christianity was inextricably bound up with its historicity (1 Cor 15). Early Christian apologetics defended Christianity against charges of atheism, but such charges arose mostly out of confusion over the type of God in which Christians believed. The best known arguments on behalf of the existence of God, however, did not arise until after the turn of the first millennium. These arguments relied primarily upon general revelation—knowledge naturally known to all people through rational reflection and observance of the world. Generally speaking, arguments for the existence of God can be divided into two groups: rational and empirical arguments.

Fools say in their heart that there is no God. Yet, committing one's life to anyone or anything other than God seems incredible.

Belief in God requires risk, but it is belief that is reasonable. It is no blind leap of faith; God makes everything more understandable.

7.3 Rational Arguments

Anselm was one of the most prominent thinkers to influence Christian theology after the time of Augustine. Anselm was unlike many previous Christians who relied primarily upon Scripture and other written authorities for the basis of belief. Instead he cultivated knowledge available through rational thought about God and matters related to God. Such knowledge was *a priori* ("that which precedes"), that is, knowledge that is prior to and independent of sense experience. Knowledge is ascertained primarily as a rational rather than empirical endeavor. Similar to Augustine, Anselm thought that reason was a precondition of faith. One could not reflect upon faith without assuming the reliability of one's thought processes. So Anselm endeavored to stretch the limit of our reasoning capabilities with regard to God.

One of Anselm's more systematic applications of rational thought had to do with the *ontological argument* for the existence of God. The ontological argument holds that God's existence is proved by reason because the Christian idea of God must logically be true. Anselm thought that God's existence is rationally self-evident. Reason does not usurp the need for special revelation; it facilitates and complements that which God revealed. Thus Anselm expected understanding to follow faith, and one of the ways in which this occurred was through arguing for the reasonableness of God's existence.

The ontological argument may be stated simply in terms of the following syllogism. Syllogistic argumentation begins with two premises:

> **PRAYER FOR KNOWLEDGE**
>
> Therefore, Lord, you who give knowledge of the faith, give me as much knowledge as you know to be fitting for me, because you are as we believe and that which we believe. And indeed we believe you are something greater than which cannot be thought. Or is there no such kind of thing, for "the fool said in his heart, 'there is no God'" (Ps. 13:1, 52:1)?
>
> ANSELM, PROSLOGION
> (11TH CENTURY)

First premise: God is that than which nothing greater can be conceived.

Second premise: That than which nothing greater can be conceived is existent (otherwise, it would be less than that than which nothing greater can be conceived).

Conclusion: God is existent (or God exists).

Of course, Anselm's argument was far more sophisticated than this summary. But it is the simplicity of the argument which, in part, has made its logic so persuasive throughout the centuries.

The following reflects a more elaborate as well as precise rendition of Anselm's ontological argument:

1. We believe that God is something than which nothing greater can be thought.

2. When an unbeliever hears this, it is understood, and what is understood exists in the mind.

3. But what exists in the mind and also in reality must be greater than what exists in the mind alone.

4. So that than which nothing greater can be thought cannot be that which exists only in the mind.

5. So that than which nothing greater can be thought must exist in the mind and in reality, too.

6. So God must exist in reality.[1]

According to Anselm, this argument demonstrates the *reasonableness* of the Christian belief in God's existence. To think otherwise is thought to be foolish—like the fool described by the psalmist.

7.4 Empirical Arguments

Aquinas also believed that belief in God's existence was a reasonable proposition. But he did not think that the existence of God was provable by rational argumentation alone. Aquinas did not think that we could rationally conceive of the essence of who God is, so we could not be sure of what was meant by Anselm's definition of God as that than which nothing greater can be conceived. But Aquinas did think that we could learn of God through the effects of God's work in creation.

Aquinas thought that human knowledge was derived primarily from empirical evidence found in the world. Such evidence was complementary to Christian faith. In fact, God's existence could be inferred through five arguments that utilize knowledge revealed from the natural world. Because these arguments are founded on sense experience, they are called *a posteriori* (Latin for "that which follows after" empirical evidence) arguments. Aquinas' five arguments may be sub-divided into two categories of argumentation. Cosmological arguments argue from observation of the cosmos (creation), and teleological arguments argue from observation of the *telos* (Greek for "end," "purpose") of the cosmos.

7.4.1 Cosmological Arguments

In observing the cosmos—the world, the universe—Aquinas made several observations. The first observation has to do with motion. Aquinas' argument from *motion* notes that everything is in motion. But motion is initiated by a "mover." Since Aquinas could not conceive of an infinite regress of motion, he held that at some point there must be a "prime mover." God must exist as the prime, unmoved mover of the universe.

Is God the prime mover of the universe?

The second argument from *causality* observes that everything is subject to causality. Everything that happens has a cause. But causality does not appear to regress infinitely. Therefore, there must be a first cause of all causality. God must exist as the first, uncaused cause of the universe.

The third argument from *contingency* observes that everything is dependent upon something else for its existence. Things that occur in the world are obviously all possible, but there is no necessary reason for their existence. But there must be some existence in the universe that is necessary. Therefore, God must exist as the only necessary, self-existent being.

The fourth argument from *degrees of being* observes that there appears to be a hierarchy of being in the world. Some things seem to be of greater and lesser degrees of perfection and imperfection. Therefore, God must exist as the highest perfection, the perfect being.

Empirical Observation	Attribute of God
Motion	Unmoved (prime) mover
Causality	Uncaused (first) cause
Contingency (possibility)	Self-existent (necessary) being
Degrees of being (perfection)	Perfect being
Design (order)	Designer (orderer)

7.4.2 Teleological Arguments

Aquinas' final argument from *design* observes that there is a sense of order and purposefulness in the universe. The design cannot be accounted for by chance alone. Instead there must be an intelligence that accounts for its order and purposefulness. God must exist as the designer of the universe. This argument is sometimes referred to as the *teleological argument*, since its argumentation is based upon there being a *telos*—order or purpose—for the universe.

Later Christians argued that the world functioned like a clock. But could a clock come into existence by chance? No. There had to be a clock maker—an intelligent being who created the clock, giving it both a sense of order and purpose.

Over time several variations of the teleological argument arose. Each variation argued for God's existence in order to account for an orderly aspect of the world. For example, some argued for the existence of God based upon the universal presence of *a moral conscience* in people. Others argued that the very orderliness of our *mental reasoning* makes little sense in a world of chance, devoid of an intelligent creator. Still others argued that *religious experience* confronts us with a reality that can only be explained by the existence of God.

Could a clock exist without a clock maker?

Schleiermacher held that our "feeling" of absolute dependence produces an inner experience of God or decision of faith that is not easily communicable in the usual cognitive, religious terms. Divine revelation of God's existence may come to us through the words of Scripture and tradition but not as objective words or propositional truths. It is not easy to determine either the nature of God or the nature of encounter a person has with God. But the personal encounter rather than the authority of a propositional view of revelation guarantees the existence of God.

Perhaps the best summary argument from a teleological perspective reflects that of *congruity*. The argument from congruity holds that theism is the most adequate hypothesis to account for the disparate aspects of our physical, mental, moral, and spiritual existence. It builds upon all the prior arguments, recognizing that each one contributes to a cumulative case in defense of the existence of God. The argument from congruity accepts the probabilistic nature of human knowledge, but then proceeds to argue that theism constitutes the most comprehensive way to account for the most disparate aspects of life.

7.5 Doubts about God's Existence

There have always been doubts about the existence of God. Otherwise, there would never have arisen so many ways to argue for God's existence. But skepticism about the existence of God increased greatly during the time of the Enlightenment. The Enlightenment was a time of increased confidence in people and their ability to discover truth through the powers of reason, observation, and experiment. Traditional beliefs and values, including religious beliefs and

**Does the world reflect a
God of order or chaos?**

values, were dismissed. In particular, David Hume (1711–1776) challenged the prevailing *a posteriori* arguments for God's existence. Hume argued that the world did not provide clear-cut evidence for the existence of God. On the contrary, he contended that the facts of reality could not be established beyond probabilities. So we can never have certain knowledge of God based upon empirical evidence.

Hume continued by saying that even if evidence could point to the existence of God, to what kind of God would it point? The world is filled with chaos, pain, and suffering, as well as order. If God is ultimately responsible for the world as we experience it, God would need to be conceived much differently from that of historic Christianity. For example, God might have been conceived as being primarily chaotic or evil, rather than orderly and good.

Following Hume's lead, Immanuel Kant (1724–1804) systematically rejected all arguments for the existence of God based upon a view of religion within the limits of reason alone. Kant argued that both the cosmological and teleological arguments for the existence of God relied upon the ontological argument. That is, at some point every argument for God's existence assumed a definition of God, which—by the very definition—claimed to describe reality transcendent of human knowledge. In the case of Anselm, God represented that-than-which-nothing-greater-can-be-conceived, and in the case of Aquinas, God represented the unmoved mover or first cause. These arguments assumed definitions that may be logically coherent but remained unverifiable through empirical means.

Kant did advocate the existence of God. But he advocated God's existence as a necessary assumption in order to make sense of the human moral conscience. Kant's *moral argument* for the existence of God holds that God, freedom, and immorality are necessary assumptions in order to vouchsafe the universal moral conscience present in all people. Kant was unaware, however, that this argument reflected a variation of the teleological argument because it intends to account for the apparent orderly presence of a moral conscience among people.

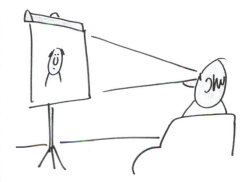

Is God a projection of our inner selves?

After Kant, there arose decidedly atheistic attacks upon Christian theism. Among them was the work of Ludwig Feuerbach (1804–1872), who argued that God corresponded to an illusion, a projection of people's highest human aspirations. However, as an illusion, belief in God prevented people from achieving their fullest potential. Karl Marx (1818–1883) considered religion to be a symptom of social and economic disorganization. Belief in God was also considered illusory, representing nothing more than an attempt to deal with human misery. Sigmund Freud (1856–1939) also considered God to be an illusion, a projection of the unconsciousness. Belief in God reflects nothing more than an unconscious attempt to deal with the fear and resentment caused by our human inability to cope with our psychological development.

7.6 Volitional Justifications for Belief in God

In a post-Enlightenment world, the possibility of speaking of God has been greatly diminished in the thoughts of critical scholarship. This skepticism is due, in part, to the denial of absolute authority. So Christians have increasingly turned to the volitional dimension of their religious belief in order to account for the existence of God. Some have argued, for example, that religious belief in God's existence is a matter of volition (the act of willing) rather than a matter of reason or experience.

Kierkegaard articulates perhaps the most passionate affirmation of the existence of God. According to Kierkegaard, religious beliefs could not be verified rationally or objectively in experience. In fact, the claims of Christianity appear absurd to individuals in the midst of their earthly existence. One can only accept God's existence, if at all, by a leap of faith. Faith occurs more like a passionate reflex of personal existence than a reflective act of the mind. Faith in God is a tremendous paradox to the mind. The lack of a rational or objective foundation for religion results in an existential understanding of religion, which is characteristically subjective and individualistic in nature. Thus Kierkegaard's existential view of religion has come to be known as *fideism* ("faith") because religious truth is founded on faith, rather than reason or experience.

In a similar way, Barth distrusted any attempts by means of general revelation to speak of God. Instead one must respond in faith alone to the revelation of God, which represents—paradoxically—the self-revelation of God through the medium of Scripture. Our acknowledgment or decision to believe in God is not the result of a rational decision based upon some type of objective or propositionally stated evidence. Rather, it is an existential act on a different, more significant level of religious decision than occurs on a merely conceptual or cognitive level of reflection. This view of faith precedes and controls the use of reason in theology. All other sources of knowledge must reinforce the knowledge of faith, which itself is based on presuppositions considered unverifiable by either reason or evidence.

Do theistic assumptions work better than atheistic assumptions?

William James (1842–1910) offered quite a different view of Christianity, but his convictions constitute yet another volitional justification for belief in God. James advanced *pragmatism* as a worldview that included the affirmation of God's existence. Pragmatism holds that truth is that which has practical value for a person's life. The truth of an idea is established through its ability to "work" on behalf of the individual. James affirmed the existence of God because it made a practical difference in his life. He further thought that theism "worked" for society as a whole. Belief in the existence of God was justified because of the decision that such a belief, though tentative and changing in nature, resulted in practical benefits for people.

7.7 Conclusion

Because of the ways in which society currently views arguments about divine reality, it may seem impossible to prove the existence of God. Such proof, however, may not be necessary since Christianity has always advocated the need for faith. That advocacy does not deny the need for reason or for a reasonable faith. It only denies that there is a proof for God's existence that is sufficient for convincing people of it.

Perhaps the best way to view arguments for the existence of God is not as *proof* of anything so much as a way for thinking about the *reasonableness* of Christian faith in God's existence. If someone has difficulty conceiving of the existence of God, various arguments for the existence of God provide ways for people to conceptualize and explain the reasonableness of that faith. No doubt various degrees of certainty will arise with regard to their belief. This is all right, so long as there remains some understanding of their belief in God's existence.

Thus arguments for the existence of God continue to serve a significant role in Christian thinking. They provide ways in which to better conceive of God and to explain the reasonableness of their beliefs.

7.8 Questions for Further Reflection

1. Do you believe in the existence of God? Why? How would you explain your belief?

2. Do arguments for God's existence actually prove God's existence? How effective are they in demonstrating the reasonableness of belief in God?

3. Which arguments for the existence of God do you find more convincing: ontological arguments? cosmological arguments? teleological arguments? volitional arguments?

4. What can be learned from those who either doubt God's existence, or actually supply arguments against the existence of God?

7.9 Notes

1. This represents a variation of the summary by G. R. Evans, *Anselm and Talking about God* (Oxford: Clarendon, 1978), 44.

CHAPTER EIGHT

O Lord, you have searched me and known me.
You know when I sit down and when I rise up;
you discern my thoughts from far away.
You search out my path and my lying down,
and are acquainted with all my ways.
Even before a word is on my tongue,
O Lord, you know it completely.
You hem me in, behind and before,
and lay your hand upon me.
Such knowledge is too wonderful for me;
it is so high that I cannot attain it. . . .
For it was you who formed my inward parts;
you knit me together in my mother's womb.
I praise you, for I am fearfully and
wonderfully made.
Wonderful are your works;
that I know very well.
(Psalm 139:1–6, 13–14)

THE WORKS OF GOD

8.1 Introduction

Psalm 139 is one of the more memorable psalms attributed to David. In it David breaks out in praise to God: "I praise you because I am fearfully and wonderfully made. Wonderful are your works" (Ps 139:14). Throughout many of the psalms—as well as throughout the Bible—God is praised for the many ways in which God works in the world and in the lives of people.

Psalm 139 serves primarily as a lament—a prayer for deliverance from personal enemies. There David describes several of the works of God. To begin with, God created the world. Only God was thought to have the power to create the universe, and only God had the power to protect David from his enemies. God is present throughout creation, searching and knowing every creature, every person, so that no secrets can be kept from God. God's knowledge surpasses that of the present. Indeed God possessed foreknowledge in the past of who we would become, and God possesses foreknowledge of the future. David was convinced that God would bring about justice and judgment upon the wicked, particularly upon his enemies. Until that time, however, David was further convinced that God would lead him in the way of righteousness.

The works of God are worthy of praise. Their enumeration may be surprising to many readers because of the diversity of ways in which God works. Such works are worthy of study because they reflect both the attributes of who God is and how great, good, and loving God's works are on behalf of people.

8.2 What Are the Works of God?

The work or works of God are the various ways in which God participates in physical and spiritual activity in order to achieve specific purposes. Although the *works* of God are thought of as being as unsearchable as the *attributes* of God, we may

What kinds of work does God do?

still discuss the works of God for the same reasons Christians argue that we may discuss the attributes of God. Usually the works of God represent the working out of the attributes of God—the actions that result from who God is. After all, the works of God are a reflection of the nature and character of God.

Because of the many ways the Bible describes the works of God, Christians over the centuries have grouped them into discreet categories for consideration. The categories are not intended to limit our understanding of the works of God, but to introduce the more significant aspects of God's ongoing involvement in our lives.

The works of God may be seen and studied separately, but they must never be seen and studied isolated from a holistic understanding of both who God is and how God acts. One should never, for example, reduce one's understanding of God based upon only one of the three persons of the Trinity. For the sake of study, one work of God must be studied before another work of God. But failing to keep in mind all of the works of God in the midst of studying one of them would result in a diminished and probably uninviting concept of who God is. We will begin by focusing on God as Creator, which forms both the chronological and logical starting point of discussing the works of God.

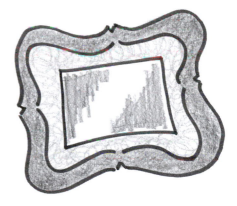

The works of God are a reflection of the nature and character of God

8.3 Creator

Scripture begins by talking about God creating the world: "In the beginning when God created the heavens and the earth" (Gen 1:1). The Nicene Creed begins by describing the work of God as that of "creator of heaven and earth, of

A throne is symbolic of God's sovereignty over creation

all things visible and invisible."[1] This statement is intended to affirm the supremacy of God's power and authority overall all that is.

God's sovereignty is almighty and universal (Exod 15:18; 2 Chr 20:6; Ps 24:10; 1 Tim 1:17; Rev 19:6). In reference to God's sovereignty, Scripture refers to God as King and to the throne of God as a symbol of sovereignty (Pss 45:6; 103:19; Isa 66:1; Matt 5:34; Rev 4:2; 20:11). That sovereignty extends to control over people, individually and collectively. All these references guarantee that God not only created the world, God is in charge of it.

In God's sovereignty and majesty, God is not thought to create out of any sense of incompleteness or need. Instead God freely created the world and creatures such as human beings out of love for the purpose of fellowship with God. Thus God's sovereignty over creation is manifested in love and justice and not in terms of power alone.

As Creator, God is thought to be the source of all that is. This is why God is described as the maker of all things visible and invisible. The ancient church did not have a view of the world as complex as the one we have today. So, in order to account for those aspects of reality which they considered unseen, they described God as the maker of all dimensions of the universe, including those which they could not understand or possibly begin to conceive. As such, God was thought to create "out of nothing" (Latin, *ex nihilo*). This affirmation of the early church was used in contrast to alternative views of divine creation. For example, the early Christians contrasted their view of God as Creator with that of Greek philosophers who thought of God as the one who forms the universe in accordance with "Ideas"—intelligible forms

Did God sculpt the world from already existing substances?

of reality upon which God patterned the universe, shaping eternal and perfect realities into reality of a temporal and imperfect nature. Plato (ca. 428/27–348/47 B.C.E.) advocated this philosophy, which was thought to be intuited by reason alone. God, in fact, represented more of a convenient myth for explaining the nature of the universe to the masses than for explaining its actual origin, which remained a mystery.

Ancient Christians distinguished their theistic view of God from that of *monism.* Monism states that all things in the universe are derived from and are equal to one ultimate source. A variation of monism is *emanationism,* which holds that the universe proceeds by necessity from the one ultimate source of the universe—God. This was a view of Neo-Platonic philosophy that had an influence upon Christians in the ancient church. Although early Christians believed that all things in the universe derived from one ultimate source, namely God, God was not identified with all that is. God represented a personal supreme being who created, but was not equal to, the creation. Conversely, creatures were thought to be dependent upon God, yet they were real and good because God had created them.

Christians also distinguished their view of God and God's work from that of *dualism.* According to dualism, there exist two equal yet distinct realities in the universe. From a theistic perspective, dualism affirms that there are two supreme beings. Presumably one supreme being is good and the other evil, both of whom are vying for control of the universe. This was a view of *Manichaeism,* which was a religious movement that had an influence upon Christians in the ancient church. Manichaeism was appealing because it provided a rational explanation for the existence of evil in the universe. Evil exists because there is an eternal conflict taking place between the two supreme beings in the universe vying for control.

Are good and evil in eternal conflict?

Certainly the work of God as Creator is a complex issue. It is complex in both understanding God and the nature of creation. We have only begun to talk about issues related to creation itself, and more will be discussed in the next chapter on Creation.

8.4 Providential Caregiver

Not only did God create the world, God cares for the world. God did not create the world and leave it to run on its own without further interaction between God and creation. *Providence* is the word Christians use to describe how God sustains, governs, and develops all aspects of creation in accordance with God's will. Thus God's sovereignty covers the preservation and enrichment of the world as well as its creation.

The extent of God's providence extends to the physical world, world history, and the lives of individuals. It is because of God that the physical world functions in orderly, recognizable ways (Job 5:10; Ps 65:9–10; Jer 10:13; Matt 6:26; Acts 14:17). People study nature and determine its laws. Such studies provide innumerable benefits scientifically, medically, technologically, and in other ways.

How does God care for the world?

God providentially cares for the development of events and circumstances in world history. This includes all people and nations (Job 12:23–24; Ps 22:28; Jer 27:5–6; Dan 2:21; 4:17; Acts 4:27–28; 17:25–27). In particular, God chose Israel to be the people through whom God provided special revelation about God, human beings, and how they may become reconciled temporally and eternally (Exod 6:7; Num 23:9; Deut 4:37; 2 Sam 7:23; Ps 135:4; Isa 43:1).

God's providential care extends to the individual lives of people. Christianity has always believed that God is intimately involved with our day-to-day lives as well as with our eternal well-being. The subject of God's providence is complex, and much has been written about it. In the chapter on Providence and Evil, we will unpack the topic further.

8.5 Lawgiver and Judge

God is a holy God, a God of righteousness (Gen 18:25; Exod 15:11; Ps 99:9; Rev 15:4). For this reason, God gave people laws to obey, most notably the Ten Commandments (Exod 20:1–17; Deut 5:6–21). These laws were given by God to Moses in order to regulate the covenant relationship God established with the people of Israel (Josh 8:31–32; 23:6; 2 Kgs 23:25). So God acts in ways that promote righteousness, including issues of justice (Ps 103:6; Zeph 3:5; John 5:30). The righteousness of God surpasses our ability not only to comprehend, but also to put into practice. But because God promotes righteousness, God also judges that which is unrighteous and unjust (Ps 96:13; Eccl 3:17; Heb 12:23).

People often dislike talking about judgment as one of the primary works of God. They would rather hear about God's love and mercy than about God's judgment and punishment. After all, do we not live in an enlightened world in which values—even religious values—are relative to genetic and environmental factors beyond our control? No doubt such factors exist today as they did at the time of the biblical authors, though we are more aware of them now and possibly more preoccupied with them. But Scripture still upholds the holy righteousness of God and how God judges impartially and will execute future punishment upon those who refuse to live in accordance with God's purposes. The judgment of God reflects God's opposition to sin and evil.

God gave laws to help people?

It is essential to understand and appreciate the judgment of God in order to know truly the person and works of God. There cannot be salvation without judgment, or mercy without justice. In order to uphold the moral character of creation, God must judge unrighteousness. If God was to be merciful to people for salvation and disregard all standards of righteousness, of what value would such standards be? They would be a sham. Yet to God they are not a sham. On the contrary, it is as important to God to uphold the moral character of creation as it is to save those who transgressed against it.

God knows the thoughts, words, and deeds of people, and God will hold them accountable. That does not mean that God will not be merciful to those who are saved, but it does mean that even those who are saved need to be careful about behaving in ways that are pleasing to God.

One should not talk long about the work of God as judge without also talking about God as Savior. The two works of God are inextricably bound up with one another. They are two sides of the same coin. Focusing on the judgment of God alone gives a truncated view of who God is and how God relates to us. This focus would make God seem like a legalistic enforcer of law who has no compassion for people. On the other hand, focusing on the mercy of God alone also gives a deficient view of who God is and how God relates toward us. This focus would make God seem like a doting, indulgent parent who does not care enough to train a child in the ways of God's righteousness.

Are there benefits as well as liabilities to judgment?

8.6 Savior

Central to the Christian message is salvation, full and free, which is graciously given by God to all who have faith in the atonement for sins provided by Jesus (John 3:16–17). Jesus is our Savior—our Redeemer—who embodies God's active involvement in the forgiveness of sins and reconciliation of people to God. Although the work of atonement is usually identified with the person and work of Jesus Christ, it is first and foremost to be understood as the work of God because Jesus reflects the personal work of the triune God in the world (Pss 27:1; 37:39; Isa 12:2; 25:9; Zech 3:17; 1 Tim 4:10).

Salvation constitutes more than the divine forgiveness of sins. Certainly God forgives the sins of humanity, but even more God wants reconciliation with people and a renewed relationship with them. God wants more from people than the confession of sins and sorrow over a broken relationship. God wants to join in fellowship in which people desire to love God and also their neighbors.

God's provisions for salvation form a major theme of all divine revelation to humanity so that, in a sense, all of history is salvation history. In it is revealed God's love and mercy as well as God's power and authority over sin and evil. God is progressively working out the regeneration of people and also that of the world. Most of God's actions, in fact, serve to fulfill the saving purposes of God.

The fullness of God's salvation has not yet been revealed. There is a sense in which the salvation of God is "already," though "not yet" fully, revealed (Heb 2:8). We live in an interim period in which God has already conquered the power of sin and evil, yet the fullness of God's kingdom has

God's kingdom: "already, not yet"

not arrived. This results in a tension that Christians experience, being "in" the world but not "of" the world. But this tension itself is thought by Christians to contribute to rather than detract from the saving purposes of God.

8.7 Sanctifier

The work of God as sanctifier points to the regenerative work of God's Holy Spirit in the world. Jesus made atonement for the sins of humanity through his death and resurrection on the cross. But it is the Holy Spirit who represents the personal work of the triune God here and now, enabling and empowering people both for their salvation and for fulfilling God's purposes for us in the world (Rom 15:16; 1 Pet 1:2).

Church catechisms refer to sanctification as one of the great headings for understanding the present, dynamic work of God's Holy Spirit. Sanctification refers to how God intends to bring believers into greater conformity with the likeness of God who is holy and righteous (John 17:17; 1 Cor 1:30; 2 Tim 2:21). God does not become the Savior of people without also wanting to become the Lord of their lives (Acts 2:36; 1 Cor 8:6; 12:3). The lordship of God's Holy Spirit refers to the enabling and empowering of believers to progressively act in ways that reflect God's love, holiness, righteousness, and justice.

God's sanctifying work is sometimes referred to as the sustaining work of God so that God is referred to as "sustainer." It is true that God sustains the world in its existence, preventing it from deteriorating or self-destructing altogether. (In a post nuclear age, it takes great faith to believe that people will not do something utterly foolish by blowing up the world.) Sustaining also means providing nourishment, support, and endurance. This sustenance means more than maintaining the status quo. Instead it leads to more growth and effectiveness in achieving the purposes of God.

God guides people's lives

The work of the Holy Spirit is manifested in a variety of ways. The Holy Spirit works, for example, to make believers holy, to develop disciplines of contemplation, to manifest spiritual power, to evangelize, and to work for social justice. The work of the Holy Spirit is ever new and often unexpected, perhaps in ways inconceivable to us now. The end or goal is wholeness for people, groups of people, and the world itself. How that end will be achieved is a matter of ongoing debate among Christians. But there is consensus that God intends history to reach an end that surpasses all ability on the part of people to comprehend.

Despite the fact that the kingdom of God has not yet been fully manifested in creation, God still intends to work for goodness and perfection—aspects of God's holiness. Such work reflects who God is. God would not work in ways contrary to divine nature, so it should not surprise us that God calls believers to ever greater tasks for ministering to all needs of people and of the created world itself.

8.8 Conclusion

The works of God have only been touched upon in this chapter. The fullness of those works will continue to be elaborated throughout this book. Virtually each chapter deals with yet another way in which God interacts with people in the world.

The works of God are a reflection of who God is. It is especially important to remember the works of God as Creator, judge, Savior, and sanctifier. These works do not encapsulate all of God's works, but they highlight the ongoing involvement by God in our lives. Christians have always believed that you cannot know who you are and where you are going—so to speak—without knowing the person and work of God.

If we think that our view of God and God's works is deficient, then we need to review and possibly revise that which we believe. Our beliefs have a tremendous impact upon our actions, so we would do well to reflect ever anew upon our concept of God so that we do not sell ourselves short. That includes our ideas about God. We should make sure that our concept of God is not too small, too incapable of helping us live in a complex world in need of a God great enough to deal with all its problems and concerns.

> **CONTEMPLATING THE WORKS OF GOD**
>
> Dangerous it were for the feeble brain of man to wade far into the doings of the Most High; whom although to know be life, and joy to make mention of his name, yet our soundest knowledge is to know that we know him not as indeed he is, neither can know him; and our safest eloquence concerning him is our silence, when we confess without confession that his glory is inexplicable, his greatness above our capacity and reach.
>
> RICHARD HOOKER,
> ECCLESIASTICAL POLITY
> (16TH CENTURY)

8.9 Questions for Further Reflection

1. How many ways do you think God works in and through your life: personally? in the church? in the world?

2. Why is it important to view God as Creator? How should we view God's creation?

3. Although God providentially cares for the world and for us, how does God work as sanctifier? In what ways does God's sanctifying work give us hope: individually? socially?

4. Why is it important to view God as a giver of law? How does God's judgment relate to people's ethical decisions? How does it relate to God as Savior?

5. What are other ways that God works?

8.10 Notes

1. "Nicene Creed," *Encyclopedia of Christianity,* 300.

CREATION

In the beginning when God created the heavens and the earth, the earth was a formless void and darkness covered the face of the deep, while a wind from God swept over the face of the waters. (Genesis 1:1–2)

CREATION

9.1 Introduction

In the letter to the Hebrews, it is said, "By faith we understand that the worlds were prepared by the word of God, so that what is seen was made from things that are not visible" (Heb 11:3). Christians have long believed that God created the world along with everything else in the universe. However, this affirmation rests upon faith because our human abilities to search into the origin of the universe are limited. Thus, faith constitutes an essential ingredient of Christians' view of the creation.

Throughout most of history, few Christians questioned the divine origin of the universe. Although alternative creation stories circulated among most cultures in the world, Christians continually rejected theories of creation that denied divine creativity. Certainly many, such as Nicolaus Copernicus (1473–1543) and Galileo Galilei (1564–1642), questioned the structure and order of creation, but there was little doubt that it had been put in place by God.

With the rise of evolutionary thinking during the nineteenth century, most notably through the work of Charles Darwin (1809–1882), views of the nature and origin of the universe began to change dramatically. Those changes increased throughout the twentieth century so that today the theory of evolution holds the dominant cultural view with regard to the origin and development of the world as well as biological life.

How have Christians responded to the challenges of evolutionary thinking? Some wholly rejected the discoveries of science, arguing that such evidence was unconvincing or irrelevant to the revelation of Scripture. Others accepted scientific evidence as complementary to Scripture and attempted to find ways to reconcile the two. To be sure, some rejected Christianity altogether because of their inability to reconcile adequately in their minds and hearts the sometimes conflicting assertions concerning the origin of the world and life itself. Too often, however, people are unaware of the sophistication as well as the diversity of the ways in which Christians over the centuries have attempted to view the origin and overall nature of divine creation.

9.2 What Is Creation?

Creation is all that God has brought into being. This affirmation can be found throughout the Bible from the first book, Genesis, which means "origin," through the New Testament. Although references to creation are surprisingly few in the Bible, the entire religious worldview of Scripture flows out of the belief that God is Creator of all that is. Throughout the Old Testament, biblical authors affirm God as Creator and the creation as a marvelous reflection of divine ordering (Neh 9:6; Pss 24:2; 102:25; 104:5; Isa 40:28; 48:13).

New Testament authors also affirmed belief in the creation of the world by God. But Jesus introduced the possibility of a new creation or recreation of a world that—like humanity—had become distorted. Paul spoke of how creation anthropomorphically longs to be set free from its bondage to decay (Rom 8:19–23).

Is the world longing to be set free from its bondage and decay?

9.2.1 Starting Point: Genesis

The first chapters of Genesis, however, contain the core of Christian beliefs concerning creation. There God ostensibly spoke and brought forth into creation all that exists in the universe in an orderly, purposeful fashion. The creation of humanity represented the pinnacle of God's creation.

Christian scholarship has distinguished between two apparently different accounts of creation found in Gen 1:1–2:4a and 2:4b–25. Historically, the two accounts were considered complementary rather than contradictory. The second, which is considered older, is referred to as the Yahwist account of creation because the preferred name for God is Yahweh. Here we are told in folkloric terms of the creation of human beings and the responsibilities they have in the world God created, a world that is to be treated with proper respect. People have responsibilities to the world, to the God who created the world, and to each other. More will be said about the nature and responsibilities of people in the subsequent chapter.

The first account is usually referred to as the priestly account of creation because its form reflects that of a poem or hymn written sometime near the sixth century B.C.E. Additionally, it is thought that Gen 1 was based upon a much older tradition of creation, reflective of other ancient Near Eastern creation stories. Biblical writers were thought to have drawn from other accounts of creation. The biblical story of creation, however, depicts God as creating in complete freedom. Creation does not occur as a dramatic conflict between God and another deity or primordial chaos as is found in other ancient mythology. Thus the monotheistic view of God characteristic of Jewish faith emerges from the first depictions of God as Creator.

9.2.2 Alternative Interpretations

People often think that asking critical or historical questions about the interpretation of Genesis is a modern phenomenon. Some think, for example, that before Darwin no one questioned a literalistic six-day interpretation of the biblical creation narrative. But this is simply not the case. In addition to questions about the two creation stories mentioned above, questions about the historicity of the book of Genesis in general were discussed by the early fathers of the church.

A number of patristic writers questioned inconsistencies in the creation story. A literal interpretation did not make sense. There were too many unanswerable questions about how creation occurred, the stories of Adam and Eve, Cain and Abel, Noah and the flood, and so on. In such instances, allegorical, spiritual, or moral interpretations of the biblical texts made more sense (ch. 4). Christians such as Origen (185–251) and Augustine accepted allegorical interpretations of Genesis, and they did not think that such readings damaged the trustworthiness of Scripture. Nor did they think that allegorical, spiritual, or moral interpretations of parts of the biblical text necessarily led people to disregard the trustworthiness of other texts. People have to be careful going about the task of interpretation on a verse-by-verse, chapter-by-chapter, book-by-book basis. But they do not need to sacrifice common sense for the sake of rationally and empirically untenable conclusions about the Bible.

9.3 The Development of the Doctrine of Creation

The Nicene Creed affirms that God, who governs all things, is the Creator of heaven and earth, and of all things visible and invisible. In this affirmation, the ancient church attempted to communicate that God was responsible for all that there is, including those aspects of life which were unseen or as yet unknown. This included references to heavenly as well as earthly realities, spiritual as

---

ALLEGORICAL INTERPRETATION OF CREATION

Now what man of intelligence will believe that the first and the second and the third day, and the evening and the morning existed without the sun and the moon and stars? And that the first day, if we may so call it, was even without a heaven (Gen. 1:5–13)? And who is so silly as to believe that God, after the manner of a farmer, "planted a paradise eastward of Eden," and set in it a visible and palpable "tree of life," of such a sort that anyone who tasted its fruit with his bodily teeth would gain life. . . . I do not think anyone will doubt that these are figurative expressions which indicate certain mysteries through a semblance of history and not through actual events. . . .
[T]he reader must endeavor to grasp the entire meaning, connecting by an intellectual process the account of what is literally impossible with the parts that are not impossible but are historically true, these being interpreted allegorically in common with the parts which, so far as the letter goes, did not happen at all. For our contention, with regard to the whole of divine scripture, is that it all has a spiritual meaning, but not all a bodily meaning; for the bodily meaning is often proved to be an impossibility.

ORIGEN, ON FIRST PRINCIPLES
(3D CENTURY)

> **God created all that is,** and cares for it far beyond our understanding. All God created is good.
>
> Despite sin and evil that occur, we should learn about and care for the world as we believe God would.

well as physical beings. Even angels were thought to be created by God as divine messengers or emissaries among people on earth.

9.3.1 Creation Out of Nothing

The creed tries to distinguish the Christian understanding of God's creativity from that of alternative views of creation held by others. The phrase "creation *ex nihilo*" (Latin, "out of nothing") arose as a way to emphasize the distinctive characteristics of Christian beliefs. God did not create the world from some kind of eternal, preexistent material that limited God's creativity. Instead, Christians denied that any source other than God was responsible for creation. Thus Christians rejected the views of dualism, monism, and emanationism.

The idea that God created out of nothing was thought to be implied both in Scripture and in the statements of the ecumenical creeds. The most explicit reference to it, however, appears in the Apocrypha. For example, 2 Macc 7:28 says that God did not create heaven or the earth "out of things that existed." The belief in creation out of nothing continues to persist throughout most of Christendom.

How did creation occur?

The ancient church distinguished between two stages of creation. The first stage consisted of God's creation of the substance from which the rest of creation was to be formed. The primary or unformed matter corresponded to that described in Gen 1:1–2. The second stage consisted of the shaping or imparting of form to matter. Here God molded the world into its variety of cosmic, geological, vegetative, and animal dimensions.

In affirming that God created out of nothing, Christians also affirmed that God did not create the world out of a sense of need or self-fulfillment. Instead creation was a free act of God that flowed out of the goodness and power of the divine will. God created the world with benevolent purposes in mind because people are to enjoy creation and have fellowship with God. These views were held by Christians in contrast to views of God as finite or evil.

Because God created everything and repeatedly described it as "good" (Gen 1), we are to view the whole of creation—including ourselves—as good. In contrast to competing views of the world, Christians denied that God's creation was either illusory or inherently evil. Creation remains dependent upon God, but that does not detract from the fact that it is real and good.

9.3.2 Time and Eternity

Just as God created the spatial dimension of the universe, God also created its temporal dimension. Augustine distinguished between time and eternity. He viewed time as a period or sequence of duration that consisted of a past, present, and future. Time, like space, was part of finite creation, and someday it, along with the rest of creation as we know it, will come to an end. Eternity, on the other hand, pertains to God, who is not limited by past, present, and future. Instead, eternity transcends time and is qualitatively and not just quantitatively different from time as we know it.

Following Augustine, Christians have traditionally conceived of time as linear in the sense that it is thought to have both a beginning and an end. It is not cyclical or transmigratory, as in some systems of thought. Because of the linear conception of time, events that occur in time may contribute unique and often significant information not accessible through reason or mystical experience. God, for example, discloses special revelation that is known no other way than through the medium of historical events. Consequently, the study of history is inextricably bound up with the study of theology because it is through events that occurred in particular places and times that God chose to be revealed.

A Christian view of time tends to be linear rather than cyclical

9.4 Creation and Evolution

Evolution is the continuous change that occurs from simple to more complex forms. Darwin developed his evolutionary theory after numerous empirical investigations. He theorized that evolutionary change occurred in the development of organic life and provided scientific evidence to support his hypothesis. Darwin dramatically impacted how modern people view the world in which we live. Certainly his work influenced a growing acceptance of evolutionary theory for multiple aspects of life. Today the dominant scientific views of the universe accept evolutionary theory as the best understanding of the development of life.

A variety of Christian viewpoints have arisen in response to evolutionary theory and its impact on our modern understanding of our world and its creation. Although it is difficult to do justice to the complexity of each viewpoint, we can provide a helpful summary of ways in which Christians have continued to affirm divine creation in a world dominated by evolutionary theory.

Broadly speaking, all such responses may be considered "creationist" because they affirm God as the Creator, rather than the evolutionary confluence of chance elements. Too often creationism has become identified narrowly with the notion of a six-day creation. This is unfortunate because often Christians attempt to reconcile faith in divine creation with scientific discoveries. Certainly creationism represents the most traditional Christian view, though there is no orthodox view per se. Evolutionary theory continues to develop, as have Christian views of creation.

9.4.1 Young-Earth Creationism

Young-earth creationism holds that the Bible provides a relatively accurate description of divine creation and that the world can be little older than six thousand years of age. This literalistic reading of Gen 1 possesses a long history of observance, going back to the ancient church. It is the result of a literal interpretation of the days of creation as twenty-four-hour periods in which God dramatically brought the universe into existence by word of command (Exod 20:11).

How did God make the earth?

Apparent discrepancies between this view and scientific evidence are resolved in several ways. One way, of course, is to say that science has nothing to do with Christian faith. But this response allows for no possibility of dialogue with science. Another way is to say that God created the world in a mature fashion, just as God created Adam and Eve not as infants but as mature adults. If the universe appears to be billions of years old, it is because God wanted us to view it that way. A final way of resolving apparent discrepancies occurs through what has come to be called *creation science.* Creation science is a variety of scientific investigation that attempts to provide scientific explanations for how the universe has come to appear to be quite old, when in fact it is quite young. The explanations largely involve theories involving significant atmospheric and geological catastrophes that must have occurred in the past.

Catastrophism is a scientific idea that many of earth's geological features formed as a result of past catastrophic activities, for example, floods, earthquakes, volcanoes, and meteors. Catastrophism contrasts with uniformitarianism, which is the idea that geological features are best understood through the processes of change at the same rates observed today. From the perspective of creation science, the biblical account of the flood—among other events—provides evidence for how the created world looks much older than it actually is. The same is true for fossil evidence of plants and animals.

Intelligent design is a contemporary idea that the world, especially the biological world, is too complex to be explained without postulating an intelligent designer. Living organisms are too complex and interconnected to have occurred by chance. The genetic evolution of the structures of living organisms by random changes is mathematically implausible. Belief in God and creationism are plausible mathematically and scientifically.

9.4.2 Old-Earth Creationism

Some Christians think the world is quite old and that an old-earth does not negate belief in creationism. Those who affirm *old-earth creationism* do not see an inherent conflict between Scripture and evolutionary theory, so they attempt to bring about reconciliation between the two. They study Gen 1 in order to see whether there are viable interpretations which allow for the apparent scientific fact that the universe is billions of years old. One interpretation is that there existed a tremendous "gap" in time between several of the first verses of Genesis. Millions or billions of years may have occurred before the first twenty-four-hour days of creation occurred. Another interpretation is that the Hebrew word for "day" may be understood as referring to more than a twenty-four-hour day. Instead, references to a day of creation may refer to an indefinite period of time in which millions or billions of years of God's creation may have occurred.

These views acknowledge that the universe might be quite old, but they do not generally view evolutionary theory as being directly applicable to the creation story. The progressive nature of God's creation may account for why scientists mistakenly suspect an evolutionary view of the universe. However, there is no necessary contradiction between their view of divine creation and a divine mechanism of creation that took an extended period of time.

Is the earth young, or is it old?

Old-earth creationism is more open to dialogue with science, and is willing to learn from scientific advances, such as those in geological and biological research. The progressive nature of the biblical account of creation is complemented by what scientific investigation of God's creation reveals.

9.4.3 Progressive Creationism

Progressive creationism contends that divine creation occurs *de novo* (Latin, "anew," "again")—the creation or supernatural transformation of existing life forms. From this perspective, God continues to create genuinely new "kinds" of plants, animals, and other creatures in the world (Gen 1:11–25). The new kinds of creatures, rather than constituting life forms that have merely evolved from previous forms, are unique creations not fashioned from preexistent materials. Some describe progressive creationism as microevolution because it affirms evolutionary change within various kinds of creatures. This contrasts with macroevolution, which affirms evolutionary change across all kinds of creatures. Certainly the emphasis is placed more upon the importance of God's new creative interventions than upon the developmental characteristics of evolution.

Thus people are thought to be an entirely new kind of creation. They were created uniquely in God's image and not fashioned from other kinds of creation. People should not be thought of as having evolved from a previous form of life. The spiritual and physical aspects of human beings represent new, unique creations by God.

In some respects, progressive creationism is compatible with both young-earth and old-earth creationism. In other respects it is not. What is important to point out is that more than one or two Christian perspectives on this topic exist. The views Christians hold tend to be more complex and varied than is often thought. There may be a much broader middle ground of viewpoints than is generally acknowledged.

9.4.4 Theistic Evolution

Theistic evolution reflects a view of divine creation that sees evolution as a part of God's creative purposes. God may have created originally with a *de novo* act and then permitted evolutionary processes of change. Not all elements of creation were created in their final forms; there is ongoing development within the created order. *De novo* creation may no longer occur, though God has the power to modify developments within evolution. From this perspective, evolution is not thought to be the mere product of chance occurrences in time and space. Instead it reflects God's creativity, directly and indirectly through the natural laws God created in the universe.

Sometimes Christians prefer to call theistic evolution something else because they do not want any association between creationism and evolution. For example, they may speak of their view as development in creation rather than theistic evolution, creative evolution, or evolutionary creation. However, the fact remains that evolutionary change is thought to be a part of God's creation rather than an alternative to it. People are still the culmination of God's creative purposes. They evolved from previous life forms, but this all reflects a part of God's plans for humanity. The occurrence of the image of God in people—the spiritual nature or soul—remains one of the many mysteries of God's creation.

Evolution may be part of God's creation

A variation of theistic evolution may be found in deism, which thinks that God created the universe and the laws of nature and then let them run on their own. God does not directly govern creation, nor does God intervene in it. Although God created all creation, particular developments occur on the basis of the laws of nature. This view of creation most fully embraces the sciences. Deists are convinced that God has given people the intellectual as well as spiritual wherewithal to live lives pleasing to themselves as well as to God. Thus, people should feel free to investigate the various geological and biological laws of nature. They will then gain greater understanding of evolution and other dynamics of geological and biological development.

9.4.5 Demythological Interpretation of Creation

Demythologization interprets the Bible as being primarily mythological in orientation. Advocates of this view believe that the purpose of Scripture is to speak existentially to our immediate spiritual needs, not to provide detailed historical and scientific information. Creation and our understanding of it are seen as mostly irrelevant to the spiritual concerns of our lives. Concern over issues of creation displays a temptation to turn away from more central issues related to the quality of our relationship with God.

Because there is more than one understanding of the nature of myth, it is difficult to come up with a comprehensive demythological interpretation of creation. In general, advocates of demythologization contend that just as our reasoning is incapable of successfully discerning the historical kernels of Scripture, it is incapable of determining scientifically the true origin of the universe and of biological life. Thus the debate over origins is moot—it will go on forever without any satisfactory resolution. Instead, we should turn our attention to the more immediate personal and spiritual needs that the Bible specifically addresses.

This view of creation is least interested in formulating an explanation or apologetic for the divine origin of things. More emphasis is placed upon the immediate situation of life. Issues of science, geology, and biology are interesting and important areas of investigation, but they are not as important as people's spiritual status in relationship to God.

Does the biblical creation story contain myth?

9.5 Creation and the Environment

In studying the doctrine of creation, there are issues of growing importance to Christians as well as to people in general. One such issue is the earth's environment—the physical context in which we live. What should be the Christian view of the environment? More specifically, what should be the Christian view of how to care for the world over which God gave people "dominion" (Gen 1:28)?

Environmentalism is a relatively modern concern for preserving the ecological balance of the world. Yet, environmental concerns should come as no surprise to Christians who, according to Scripture and church tradition, view the world in which they live as a part of God's creation. Because God created it as something good and something over which people are to have dominion, Christians should be responsible in terms of how they care for it. They should be as careful in caring for the physical well-being of the world as they are in attending to other people and creatures.

What are the implications of polluting God's good creation?

People in general have not always placed environmental concerns at the forefront of their personal and social agendas. Christians have not done any better. In fact, at times, they have done worse due to certain world-denying theologies that considered the earth and its resources something to be exploited rather than cultivated and developed. Even if the world is thought to come to an end soon, eschatologically speaking, we should not be dissuaded from positively valuing and caring for the good world God created.

Living in a post-nuclear age, Christians should be especially sensitive to the ease with which people could destroy the world. Even if we should be fortunate enough not to destroy ourselves, the fear and anxiety produced by the threat of nuclear holocaust has had an emotionally as well as spiritually damaging effect upon the world. Similar fears and anxieties have arisen due to the devastating amount of pollution and other environmentally destructive practices produced by contemporary technological societies—not to mention their real-life physical consequences. Concern for environmentalism seems to be an issue of tremendous import for self-preservation if for no other reasons.

How bad do things have to get before we care?

The goodness of creation—despite the presence of sin and evil in the world—constitutes the cornerstone of Christian environmental concerns. Concern for our ecology should not be seen as just another bit of ideological whim or political correctness. Instead it should be seen as a distinctively Christian concern, though the degree to which Christians are personally concerned and socially active on its behalf will inevitably vary. We, no less than God, should value and care for the ecological balance of the world, seeking to preserve it in ways that are conducive to our well-being as well as being well-pleasing to God.

9.6 Conclusion

Although creation has been variously understood by Christians over the centuries, there remains the affirmation that the universe was created by God. The universe did not occur by the chance interaction of physical laws and materials. Instead the universe was created by God. It is good and purposeful. Creation serves as the context in which God created people and wants to have fellowship with them.

Evolution is not a fell threat to Christianity. Although evolutionary ideas have challenged the Christian doctrine of creation, Christians have answered that challenge in a variety of ways. Some have responded by rejecting the relevance of evolution altogether, while others have adopted many evolutionary ideas in order to reformulate their understanding of theology. There are, however, more than one or two ways of viewing the doctrine of creation in light of evolution. Christians do not need to think that they have lost intellectual integrity in a modern scientific world. They believe in divine creation rather than in a strictly scientific worldview, though science is equally dependent upon belief, since definitive scientific proof related to the origins of the universe are not forthcoming.

The doctrine of creation challenges Christians to specific concrete actions with regard to their responsibilities in the world. To be sure, Christians need to provide a coherent view of the origin of things. They also need to treat the world in a way that reflects the goodness of God's creation and their responsibility to care for it. Concern for God needs to carry a corollary ecological concern for the world God created and for all of God's creatures.

9.7 Questions for Further Reflection

1. Why is it important to believe that God created the world? How does this belief affect our view of the world?

2. What is significant about the notion of God creating "out of nothing"?

3. How do Christians view time? What is its significance in contrast to other views of time?

4. What is the relationship between Christians' belief in creation and evolution? To what degree do you think they are compatible or incompatible?

5. With regard to different Christian views of creation, which views do you consider the most persuasive? Why? How essential are these views to Christianity?

6. How should Christians view environmentalism? To what extent are they responsible for caring for God's creation?

CHAPTER TEN

The Lord is my shepherd, I shall not want.
He makes me lie down in green pastures;
he leads me beside still waters; he restores my soul.
He leads me in right paths for his name's sake.
Even though I walk through the darkest valley,
I fear no evil; for you are with me;
your rod and your staff—they comfort me.
You prepare a table before me in the presence of my enemies;
you anoint my head with oil; my cup overflows.
Surely goodness and mercy shall follow me
all the days of my life,
and I shall dwell in the house of the Lord
my whole life long. (Psalm 23)

PROVIDENCE AND EVIL

10.1 Introduction

The book of Isaiah speaks of God as a loving parent who shapes and molds us into wonderful clay pottery that reflects the purposes of God. Isaiah 64:8 says, "O Lord, you are our Father; we are the clay, and you are our potter; we are all the work of your hand." This marvelous metaphor helps to give us a glimpse of the quality of care and purposes God has for people.

People often marvel at how potters shape and mold clay on a potter's wheel. From a seemingly insignificant lump of clay, a potter patiently works the clay into beautiful bowls, plates, cups, and other artwork. Some pieces take more time than others. Some take more work. The potter sometimes has to contend with the quality of the clay. But usually the potter can achieve the intended purpose for which the clay was chosen to be shaped and molded.

God shapes people as a sculptor shapes stone

God's care for the world and for its inhabitants is referred to as the providence of God. It has to do with more than just the care for creation. It also has to do with every aspect of its existence—its creation, its end or goal, and its fruition. All these things have to do with God's providence.

10.2 What Is Providence?

Providence generally represents God's sovereign care for creation. This care includes God's good creation of the world and people (Gen 1). It also includes God's ongoing involvement in preserving, guiding, and cooperating with creation—with the earth, with nature. God's providential care for creation includes a "foreseeing" or "forecaring," because God knew the implications of creation for both the world and the people who live in it before it was crafted (Gen 45:8; 50:20; Job 14:5; Ps 139:16; Matt 10:29–31; Rom 8:28). God orders events in creation, nature, and history so that God's ultimate purposes for creation will be fulfilled (Job 12:23–24; Ps 22:28; Jer 27:5–6; Dan 2:21; 4:17; Acts 4:27–28; 17:25–27).

In addition to creating the universe, God is thought to sustain, preserve, and uphold it (Pss 65:9–10; 147:8–9; Matt 6:26; Acts 14:17). But God does not permit things to occur without there being an ultimate purpose or end for creation. Moreover, God does not remain uninvolved in creation. God created the universe but then endeavored to work in cooperation with creation. The nature and extent of God's cooperation, however, raises a variety of issues that need to be discussed with regard to divine governance. We will deal with some of the more critical issues pertaining to Christian views of God's providential governance.

> **THE PROVIDENTIAL CARE OF GOD**
>
> The doctrine of providence deals with the history of created being as such, in the sense that in every respect and in its whole span this proceeds under the fatherly care of God the Creator.
>
> KARL BARTH, CHURCH DOGMATICS (1936)

10.2.1 Providence and Creation

Although nature forms a part of God's creation and is dependent upon God, to what degree does God govern nature? To what degree is nature independent of God's control? Some Christians have argued that because God is the supreme being who created the universe, all events of nature reflect God's direct will. But this view overlooks the independent character of God's creation. God created the world in accordance with certain natural laws by which it functions. These laws represent a part of God's *general providence* that permits the universe to function in independent, orderly ways. Natural laws are a part of God's creation, and they are discernible through scientific investigation.

Within the universe, there is a degree of necessity because it functions in relationship with natural law. Things function in accordance with natural laws.

Isaac Newton contemplating natural law

For example, when you drop something, it does not fall up. Natural law describes actions and events that occur in the physical universe, and laws of gravity explain some of those actions and events. Through scientific investigation, we can learn much about the world in which we live. What we learn can help us scientifically, medically, and technologically. It can even help us religiously as we care for the world, others, and ourselves.

There is also a degree of randomness that occurs in nature as we perceive it. Just as some things occur by necessity (natural laws), some things occur randomly. For example, rain occurs because of observable natural causes, but one cannot predict every cause at work at any given time. Randomness is a part of the created order of the universe. Some Christians have argued that randomness is a result of the fall of humanity and of creation (Gen 3), and that it was not a part of God's original good creation. This speculation is, however, to some extent moot because we have to deal with the world in which we live. As it is experienced at this point, we observe that the world functions with both necessity and randomness, and these qualities of nature are compatible with God's governance of nature. For example, when we flip a coin, we understand the physical mechanics that make it turn up heads or tails. We can even predict the probability of how often heads or tails might turn up after the toss of a coin. But in any given situation we cannot precisely predict whether a tossed coin will turn up heads or tails because the outcome occurs in a random fashion.

Does randomness have a place in God's creation?

It is possible for God to intervene in the governance of nature by acting in ways that seem contrary to the laws of nature as we understand them. These acts of *special providence* may include a vision, miracle, resurrection, and so on. Miracles, for example, are observable events that are dramatic in that they are inexplicable in terms of known natural laws. In fact, they may always be inexplicable given all that can be humanly known about nature.

In the post-Enlightenment world, Christians as well as non-Christians have become increasingly skeptical of the authenticity of special providence—of the miraculous. This includes contemporary as well as biblical accounts of miracles. Since miracles are no longer thought to occur, many consider the biblical accounts to be legendary or mythical. Legends and myths, of course, play significant roles in shaping communities such as those in the Bible. So the accounts of miracles are to be studied for their social and cultural functions but not as historical accounts.

Accounts of miracles and other acts of special providence, however, do occur in the Bible, and the consensus of church history is that the accounts, to a greater or lesser degree, are historical. This is especially true of the resurrection of Jesus, which represented the primary historical fact preached by the apostolic church in verifying the truth of Christianity.

It should be noted, however, that acts of special providence are uncommon even in the Bible. Time after time, people were amazed when such events occurred. Given the fact that Scripture covers the span of many hundreds of years, not many visions, miracles, or resurrections occur. When they do occur, they are often during brief, albeit religiously significant, periods in history. Most of the miracles recorded in the Bible occur around the time of the Israelite exodus from Egypt and conquest of Canaan, the time of Elijah and Elisha, and the time of Jesus and the disciples. These were critical periods in the revelation of God's saving purposes. Some Christians, such as C. S. Lewis (1898–1963), caution us that, while we are to avoid the skepticism of the Enlightenment, we should also avoid the presumptuousness of expecting God to constantly perform miracles. After all, the laws of nature were instituted with divine purposes in mind, and God does not lightly perform acts of special providence unless they contribute to the revelation of God's saving purposes for humanity.

10.2.2 Providence and Humanity

As with nature, God is thought to preserve, guide, and cooperate with people in caring for them. People are dependent upon God because God created them and provides for their ongoing existence. Likewise, God has a purpose or purposes for people and for their future. We may not always know the nature of those purposes, but we believe that God has a wonderful plan for everyone individually as well as collectively.

God also cooperates with people in bringing about God's purposes. People are dependent upon God, yet they are also independent. Their independence stems from the freedom given to them by God and also by the freedom afforded by living in a world structured according to natural laws. This freedom allows for incredible possibilities for human fulfillment, accomplishment, and relationship with—among others—God. But there are also tensions or problems that can and do arise. We will look at some of the more problematic areas in which people find themselves in God's creation.

How much of our lives is a matter of luck?

Providence and Fate

Fate is the idea that events are determined by forces over which there are no human controls. Sometimes fate is thought of in terms of the stars; other times it is thought of in terms of behaviorism or psychoanalytical theories. Usually fate is thought of as being controlled by a god or gods who predestine the events of the world.

From a Christian perspective, God is generally thought to foreknow all that happens so that, in an ultimate sense, God is sovereign over creation and the events of history. But if God is considered the primary cause of all that occurs, we must also consider numerous secondary causes that occur in the world. For example, we discussed the random as well as necessary characteristics of nature. Random events may occur in accordance with the laws of nature that have no direct relationship to divine causation. God may foreknow such events, but God does not preempt them. God's eternal providence is not thwarted. Rather, God permits events to occur in ways that we experience as fortune or chance. Like the toss of a coin discussed earlier, random events do occur in the lives of people, and that randomness is compatible with divine providence. Certainly it is thought that God could overrule any event caused by secondary causes. God could, for example, intervene in the world as an act of special providence. But for the most part God permits human lives and world events to unfold within the order God created.

Sin

Divine providence is also compatible with human freedom, and consequently with sin. The nature and extent of human freedom will be the topic of discussion in a later chapter. For now, it is enough to affirm that God ordained that human beings, though dependent upon God for their creation and preservation, still possess the freedom given to them by God at their creation. Because people are free, they are capable of a degree of self-determination, self-control, self-direction, and self-regulation. Freedom means that people can make their own choices, of their own volition.

This freedom is a tremendous gift from God, but it also carries tremendous responsibility and potential for disaster. If there was no potential for disastrous results due to human freedom, human choices would not truly be free. Human choice may, for example, result in sin. People may choose to do that which is contrary to God's purposes for them. In fact, because people have freedom of choice and may act in sinful ways, those actions may in turn have the effect of bad fortune on others. Ultimately, all sin and bad fortune is thought to be the result of evil. But how does evil fit into the Christian concept of divine providence?

10.3　Evil

Throughout church history, evil has been understood in a variety of ways. Simply put, evil signifies that which is morally bad or harmful. In Scripture, it is sometimes personified as Satan—the devil. Satan was an angelic creature who apparently rebelled against God and continues to lead spiritual opposition to God's purposes in the world.

In the early church, the most common way of understanding evil was developed by Augustine, who did not consider it to be a person, substance, or principle. Instead, evil consisted of a "privation of good"—that which distorts or ceases to be as God intended it. Neither Satan nor people were inherently evil because they were created by God, and God did not create evil. However, when any of God's creations exerted free will in opposition to the purposes of God, they acted in an evil fashion. So evil does not represent an eternal reality but a distortion or cessation of that which was good in its original state.

In time, Christians distinguished between two types of evil: moral and natural (physical). Moral evil pertains to free-will choices that are immoral based upon the righteousness of God and God's moral dictates. Natural evil pertains to physical events that are considered harmful, such as earthquakes, famine, and other natural disasters. Regardless of one's understanding of the nature and extent of evil, its presence seems problematic in consideration of God's providential care for the world.

Can we discern the source of evil?

10.3.1 Problem of Evil

The classic problem of evil predates considerations of theodicy by early Christians. Apparently the dilemma was formulated by Epicurus (341–270 B.C.E.) nearly three centuries before the birth of Jesus. Simply stated, the classic problem of evil may be stated in three propositions which, taken together, appear irreconcilable:

- God is all-powerful (almighty, omnipotent).
- God is all-loving (benevolent).
- Evil exists.

The following question arises: If God has the power and benevolence to prevent evil, then why does God not do so? Either God lacks the power to prevent evil or God lacks benevolence. But Christians did not want to deny either God's power or benevolence. Since they could not deny their experience of evil or, at least, the effects of evil, some explanation needed to be given.

10.3.2 Theodicy

Theodicy represents the justification of God's power and goodness in a world in which there is evil. Recent attempts to justify God have rejected the appropriateness of the three propositions of the classic problem of evil. Some, for example, have denied the almighty power of God. Thus evil exists because God lacks the power to prevent it from occurring. Process theologians argue that God's power is persuasive in nature rather than coercive, so God cannot coercively prevent evil but can only persuade people to work together

May evil actually be no-thing?

against evil. Some liberation and feminist theologians do not so much deny the almighty power of God as redefine it, for example, speaking about the power of God more in terms of compassionate enabling and empowering.

Other Christians have denied the benevolence of God, arguing in "protest" against God's willingness to permit such heinous events as the Holocaust during World War II. Less extreme views do not deny the benevolence of God but redefine it. They say that events such as the Holocaust represent a time of trial or perhaps punishment. God's willingness to share in the sufferings of humanity through Jesus, however, vindicates the benevolence of God.

The most common ways of justifying the power and benevolence of God also reflect the most ancient ways. In the early church, both Irenaeus (ca. 130–202) and Augustine would have considered the classic problem of evil to be inadequate for reflecting upon the problem of evil. Instead, it needs to be modified in order to take into consideration a broadened perspective of the work of God in human lives. Irenaeus, for example, argued that God permitted evil for the purpose of "soul-making." People were unable to grow in an environment where there were no potentially negative consequences for their actions. So God intentionally created an environment in which evil would inevitably occur in order that people might genuinely exercise their freedom and mature in the process.

May we put God on trial?

Augustine argued that evil was the result of free choices on the part of people, and it was not the direct will of God but the permissive will of God that allowed evil to occur. Augustine thought that it was more beneficial to people that they sinned—committing evil—and later received the divine benefit of salvation than to have never sinned at all. The benefit of eternal life in heaven, exemplified by the resurrection, would more than compensate for any evil, pain, or suffering experienced in this world.

10.4 God's Care for People

Although various theodicies may console the mind of Christians, they may not console their experiences of evil, pain, and suffering. The hurt, grief, and confusion do not easily go away even in the midst of helpful theological insights.

Some have said that we live in the best of all possible worlds, an appalling statement to anyone who has suffered, been hurt, or cried.

Indeed God cares for the world, but gives it and its human inhabitants independence. Despite people's rejection, God still cares, and for them God's Son—Jesus—died.

Thomas Oden provides some encouragement to those who are troubled about the presence of evil, pain, and suffering in the world. He suggests that God's relationship to us is best understood as a good parent who permits us the freedom to get ourselves into trouble, but who also works to hinder, overrule, and limit undue trouble. Oden draws upon classical exegetes in order to outline four levels or aspects of God's parenting people in the midst of their experiencing evil, pain, and suffering:[1]

- God guides and parents by *permitting* our freedom to play itself out, even if we play it out in the direction of our own and others' suffering.

- God parents us by *hindering,* and at times directly resisting, our ill-motivated actions.

- God parents us by *overruling* us when we are completely out of line.

- Finally, God parents wisely by *preventing* other forces from triumphing cheaply or tempting inordinately.

Are parents good or evil for teaching their kids to ride a bicycle?

10.5 Conclusion

The consensus of church history is that God indeed is the Creator of all that there is and that God continues to care for the world in preserving, guiding, and cooperating with it. Although there are various understandings of God's providential work, Christians seek to learn more and more about how to mature in their relationship to the divine and how their lives and the world might be transformed as a result.

How you view God has a tremendous impact upon your life. If you consider God to be the Creator of the universe and actively involved with people, you will be very attentive to the person and work of God. If you consider God to be other than classical conceptions, you will adjust your beliefs and practices so that they concur with your conception. If you consider God to be a caring parent, you will relate to God as good children would to their parent.

The works of God are a reflection of who God is. If we think that our view of God and God's works are deficient, then we need to review and revise that which we believe. Our beliefs have a tremendous impact upon our values and actions. So, we would do well to reflect seriously upon our concept of God so that we do not miss out on the fullness of who God is and who we may become with the help of God.

10.6 Questions for Further Reflection

1. What does it mean for God to care for the world? What does it mean for God to care for you?

2. To what extent does God control things? To what extent does God give nature freedom, a freedom manifested in a measure of randomness? To what extent does God give people freedom?

3. What is evil? Who is responsible for evil: Satan? people? God?

4. How is it possible to believe in a powerful and loving God in a world in which evil and sin exist?

10.7 Notes

1. Oden, *The Living God,* 300–302.

HUMANITY

CHAPTER ELEVEN

So God created humankind in his image,
in the image of God he created them;
male and female he created them.
God blessed them, and God said to them,
"Be fruitful and multiply, and fill the earth and subdue it;
and have dominion over the fish of the sea
and over the birds of the air
and over every living thing that moves upon the earth."
(Genesis 1:27–28)

THE IMAGE OF GOD

11.1 Introduction

The foundation upon which Christian beliefs about humanity begin is found in Genesis. Here, people are described as having been created in the *image of God* (Gen 1:27–28; 5:3; 9:6). They are differentiated in terms of gender—male and female. But both sexes are given the responsibility of reproducing and of exercising dominion over the world.

Soon after the biblical account of creation there occurs the account of human moral failure and the subsequent consequences of sin (Gen 3). This juxtaposition makes it difficult to distinguish theologically between those biblical ideas that pertain to people as God created them and to those that pertain to people distorted by sin. In this chapter we intend to study the nature of people as God intended them to be. In a subsequent chapter we will study the nature of sin and the effects of sin upon humanity.

When Jesus was born, it was thought that he—more than anyone else—authentically portrayed people as God intended them to be. Although examining Jesus raises as many questions as he provides answers related to what it means to be truly human, he still gives us invaluable insight into all that God wants people to be.

Scripture uplifts Jesus as a role model to be followed. In thoughts, words, and deeds Jesus provides an example (John 13:15; Rom 15:5; 2 Cor 10:1; Phil 2:5; Col 3:13). Jesus himself reminds people of the image of God in which all human beings are created. In his words and actions, he instructs and encourages us with regard to how people may again live lives pleasing to God and themselves.

The doctrine of humanity is frequently contested, in part because there has been so much written and investigated about human nature. It is also, in part, because we all have the ability to evaluate that which we read and study about human nature, based upon our own experience. This knowledge may help or hinder our investigation; it depends upon the individual. Certainly it is hoped that historic doctrines will help to shed light on what it means to be human both on a universal and individual level.

11.2 What Does It Mean to Be Human?

Scripture describes human nature in a variety of ways. First of all, people are depicted as creatures created by God. The Bible further describes God's human creations as real and good, albeit dependent upon the Creator.

Although the Bible is the starting point of our discussion, it will be supplemented by other insights. Scripture reveals invaluable knowledge about what it means to be human. Such knowledge is born out in our experience and in the evaluation, conceptualization, and application of that experience. Taken together, Christians believe the most important insights into humanity, individually and collectively, are attainable.

11.2.1 Origin of People

How people were created—how they originated—remains an issue of debate. Christian views depend in large part upon a prior view of creation (see ch. 9). One who believes that God created people in a fashion identical to the first chapters of Genesis will also hold that humanity came into existence with the creation of Adam and Eve. The determination of human nature, then, would involve the systematic investigation of Scripture.

Who were Adam and Eve?

However, if one believes that God created people in a more progressive or evolutionary fashion, however, the determination of human nature will involve a more subtle, albeit biblically oriented, approach to the subject. In either view of the origin of humanity, the determination of human nature can be informed by sources other than the Bible, resulting in a refined Christian anthropology.

11.2.2 Human Attributes

The most significant biblical reference to human attributes describes human beings—both men and women—as creatures made in the "image" and "likeness" of God (Gen 1:26). Scripture, however, does not inform us of what this distinction may mean. We are left with the responsibility of distilling from other biblical passages what it means to be created in God's image.

The Genesis passage certainly suggests important characteristics about the image of God. Genesis talks about the complexity of being human. Inner (personal) complexity, social complexity in relationship with others, and complexity in relationship with the created order define what it is to be human.[1] These complexities occur in a physical context, yet they also happen in a spiritual context, at least in terms of people's relationship with God. God told the people, among other things, to have dominion over creation, so there are also tasks that are important for their identity.

People are depicted as possessing a variety of attributes. It seems that people are, among other things, endowed with physical, rational, spiritual, moral, and social dimensions. These attributes can be found in the first chapters of Genesis as well as the rest of Scripture. First, people were created with physical bodies, reflective of the physical world in which they live. Second, people are thought to have a spiritual dimension sometimes referred to as "spirit" and sometimes as a "soul." Third, people have reasoning capabilities that far surpass that of animals. Fourth, people are considered to be morally obligated in their relationship with God as well as in relationship to other aspects of God's creation. Such an obligation implies that humanity possesses freedom of choice. Fifth, people are social beings because God created not one but multiple people. Altogether, these characteristics clearly distinguish people from the rest of God's creation.

What does it mean to be human?

Subsequent reflections upon these various dimensions of being human produced a variety of viewpoints with regard to developing a Christian anthropology. I will present key theological insights into what it means to be human, created in God's image.

11.3 Christian Anthropology

The ecumenical creeds did not focus primarily upon the development of a Christian anthropology—the study of people. Their focus on the nature of God, Jesus, and the Holy Spirit precluded extensive discussions of other doctrines. Thus, there is little consensus provided by the ancient church about human nature.

The creeds do, however, speak of the resurrection of the *body*. The resurrection will be discussed later, but what we will focus upon now is the fact that people have bodies. The creedal affirmation of the body may not seem all that important at first. What we know of the body is that it is finite and eventually needs resurrection. The concrete, physical dimension of our humanness is significant because many ancient as well as contemporary religions disregarded this aspect of being human. Instead emphases were placed upon the rational, spiritual, or moral dimensions of our humanness. But the physicality of our bodies is an important dimension of who we are, and Christians should not minimize its importance. Like Jesus, who placed great importance upon the physical health and well-being of people, Christians should not consider the physical dimension

Christians celebrate their physicality!

of their lives to be inferior to other dimensions. Physicality is inextricably bound up with other dimensions of humanness, temporally and eternally, due to the resurrection of human bodies (Acts 10:39–41; Rom 15:54).

Some Christians dismiss the importance of the physical dimensions of our humanness. Asceticism, for example, frequently surfaced as a way to tame the body. Ascetic practices were sometimes encouraged because of the identification of the body with the baser aspects of human nature, exacerbated by problems due to sin. However, asceticism led to extreme practices that denied the inherent goodness of our physical lives. Certainly self-control is virtuous, but not at the expense of a healthy view of our bodies. If we have a holy, healthy view of our physical bodies, we might take better care of that part of who we are.

To be sure, it is impossible to consider what it means to be human by only looking at what Scripture and church history have to say about people. Consideration should also be given to the physiological makeup of people. Likewise, we should reflect on the psychological, sociological, political, and other dimensions of human existence. The theological study of human beings should not diminish or exclude such considerations. On the contrary, Christians welcome such investigation. They also welcome what God has revealed through Scripture as it helps people gain greater insight about both their temporal and eternal lives. More will be said about the complexities of human existence in the next chapter. For now, we will return to insights found in the Bible and church history.

11.4 The Image of God

As Christian theology developed an understanding of the nature of humanity, emphasis was placed primarily on recognizing what it means that human beings are created in the *imago Dei* (Latin, "image of God"). Usually the image of God has been thought of in terms of the immaterial qualities that make people unique. On rare occasions, however, the image has also been thought of in physical or material terms.

On the one hand, the uniqueness of people being created in the image of God can be understood in a holistic way. People reflect the rational, spiritual, and moral attributes of God, though in a finite and limited

AFTER GOD'S OWN IMAGE

After God had made all other creatures, he created man male and female; formed the body of the man out of the dust of the ground, and the woman of the rib of the man, endued them with living, reasonable and immortal souls [this is man's constitution]; made them after his own image, in knowledge, righteousness and holiness [this is the image of God in man].

WESTMINSTER LARGER CATECHISM, ANSWER 17 (17TH CENTURY)

> **People were created** in the image of God. Both men and women were created the same way, reflecting God's personal and social characteristics.
>
> As such, men and women are blessed; they are called to be fruitful and have dominion over the world, caring for all as God cares for us.

way. On the other hand, particular human structures, functions, or relations may constitute the sum and substance of what it means to be created in the image of God. In church history, several attempts have been made to distill the essential image of God in humanity, though no one view has gained a consensus. Instead each view helps to give greater depth to our knowledge of who people are and how they may reflect God's image.

11.4.1 Structural View

A structural view of the image of God asserts that particular human attributes constitute the sum and substance of our likeness to God. These attributes include psychological, rational, volitional, and spiritual qualities in people. By possessing one or more of these qualities, people always reflect the image of God. Even if people sin, they still reflect the essential likeness of God.

Aquinas, for example, held that rationality represented the attribute that most reflected the image of God. Rationality also separated people from animals in the created order. A corollary to rationality was human volition. Our freedom of choice allowed people to function socially and morally. It made it possible to grow more into the likeness of God, for example, through the development of virtues.

Another structural view of the image of God envisions people having a spiritual dimension to their lives. In particular, people possess a soul. Although the presence of a soul has been variously understood by Christians over the centuries, its presence is thought to represent our essential likeness to God.

In what ways do we reflect God's image?

11.4.2 Functional View

A functional view of the image of God asserts that people reflect the likeness of God by what they do rather than by who they are in their structural makeup. For example, people reflect the image of God to the degree that they act in a moral, righteous fashion. This view posits that God created people to live in obedience to God's will. When people are disobedient, they no longer reflect the likeness of God. The image of God may not be totally absent, but our likeness to it is distorted. When people are obedient, they appropriately reflect the likeness of God and may grow in righteous godliness.

Another functional view of the image of God addresses humanity's dominion over creation. Genesis 1:26, 28 state that God created people to have "dominion" over all aspects of God's creation. Because this divine command occurs in conjunction with the description of people in the image of God, some Christians have asserted that we reflect the image of God to the degree to which we exercise appropriate dominion over the world. This dominion does not represent an authoritarian type of dominance but a responsible ethic of work and care for the world.

11.4.3 Relational View

A relational view of the image of God asserts that what is most significant about people is that God created them to be in relationship with one another. There is an important social dimension to what it means to be human. It also implies a moral responsibility toward the social reality of our lives and world. Who we are socially, in our relationship with others, is as important as who we are as individuals.

The most important relationship for people, of course, is our relationship with God. When we are not in a right relationship with God, we no longer reflect God's image. It is only when we are in an appropriate relationship with God that we truly reflect the likeness of God. This priority placed upon personal relationship with God is reminiscent of existential views of people and Christian belief.

VIEWS OF THE IMAGE OF GOD

Viewpoints	Characteristics	Examples
Structural view	Who people are	Physicality, psychology, rationality, volition, spirituality
Functional view	What people do	Morality, exercising dominion
Relational view	How people relate	Relations with God, self, and others

11.5 Human Freedom

All views of the image of God presume that people were created with freedom of choice. God created people in a way that their decisions would be self-determined. Decisions may be affected by influences outside that of human volition, but decisions are finally the responsibility of the individual. Outside influences cannot sufficiently account for what causes someone to think, speak, and act.

Some Christians think that freedom is the determinative feature of being created in God's image. All three views of the image of God, listed above, can be understood as involving human freedom. They involve volition structurally, functionally, and relationally. (Of course, they could be understood as involving rational and spiritual dimensions as well.) Certainly God is thought to be free. Thus, even if there are other ways in which people manifest the image and likeness of God, human freedom constitutes an essential component of being made in the image of God.

How free are people?

Human freedom becomes a more complex issue when viewed in light of sin. Although few Christians deny that people were created with freedom of choice, a great deal of diversity arose with regard to the nature and extent of human freedom after the influence of sin. The topic of human freedom under the influence of sin will be discussed at length in the chapter on God's Grace & Our Choice.

11.6 Original Righteousness

Before sin was thought to affect human nature, people were thought to possess "original righteousness." They were morally upright or, at least, innocent of sin (Gen 2). Christians such as Augustine thought that people were created with righteousness as a part of original human nature. Thus the inclination of people was to do that which fulfilled their inherently righteous nature. This did not guarantee that people would always act righteously, but such was their inclination. If people acted sinfully, their original righteousness would be lost or significantly distorted.

Aquinas considered righteousness to be a gift given to people after their creation. It was not inherent in their human nature. Instead it was endowed upon people only as a gracious favor from God. Such righteousness would also be lost or distorted if people sinned.

Irenaeus, on the other hand, thought that people were created with the potential for good and evil, and so were morally neutral. They did not necessarily possess original righteousness, only the potential for growing in righteousness. But if people had the potential to grow in righteousness, they also had the potential to sin and increase in their sins.

Pelagius (ca. 354–418) went further than Irenaeus by saying that people do not possess original righteousness. They only possess freedom. We should not speak in terms of either a righteous or sinful nature. Instead we should emphasize the freedom people possess and the naturally endowed potential they have to choose between good and evil.

11.7 Conclusion

In order for people to be holy and healthy, they need to have a balanced perspective of who they are—of how God intends for them to be. This is aided by Jesus, who more than anyone represented the model of humanity.

People are inherently valuable because they are created in the image of God. This image is probably more complex and far reaching than any one viewpoint can encapsulate. Instead there are numerous ways in which people reflect the image of God. But each viewpoint helps us to conceptualize the fullness of who we are as rational, spiritual beings, complete with moral as well as relational responsibilities toward ourselves, others, and also to God.

No doubt other ways exist in which people may, through the help of God, grow in conformity with the image and likeness of God. People are not to be content with who they are, particularly as their lives have been affected by sin. Reflections upon God's intentions for human beings give them a goal toward which to aim in their attempts to understand and fulfill themselves through right thought, speech, and action. By the grace of God, amazing things await those who believe and obey God.

11.8 Questions for Further Reflection

1. What does it mean to be human?

2. What does it mean to be created in the image of God? How should we honor the fact that people are created in God's image?

3. To what degree should other data be factored into our understanding of what it means to be human: physiologically? psychologically? socially? politically?

4. Which view of the image of God, if any, do you find most persuasive? Is a combination of views more persuasive?

5. To what degree does being created in God's image reflect relations with others? To what degree is it social as well as individual?

6. Why is belief in human freedom important? How does freedom reflect being created in the image of God?

11.9 Notes

1. See Charles Sherlock, *The Doctrine of Humanity* (Downers Grove, Ill.: InterVarsity, 1996), 29–48.

CHAPTER TWELVE

*What are human beings that you are mindful of them,
mortals that you care for them?*

*Yet you made them a little lower than God, and
crowned them with glory and honor.*

*You have given them dominion over the works of your
hands; you have put all things under their feet.*
(Psalm 8:4–6)

THE HUMAN PERSON

12.1 Introduction

In Ps 8:4–6, we find a hymn celebrating God's glory and the God-given dignity of people. Certainly the psalmist conveys a high opinion of people. They are, after all, not only created by God but created in such a way as to share in God's goodness. Glory and honor are to be attributed to people, and they are to have dominion over all of creation.

Although some consider it the height of pride for people to think so highly of themselves, it is a consistent teaching of Scripture that people hold a special place in God's creation. Both in their nature and in the rights and privileges God has given people, human beings epitomize the focus of God's purposes in the world. These rights and privileges also come with responsibilities. In order to achieve all the purposes for which God created people, they need to develop a mature sense of who they are and what God wants them to become.

Plato wrote several dialogues or stories that featured his teacher Socrates. In the *Apology*, Socrates says, "The life which is unexamined is not worth living."[1] Christians need to understand who they are in all their constituent parts. This process of

Self-examination is essential!

self-examination is aided by all that can be learned from the physical and behavioral sciences. Such knowledge is invaluable in learning about people. But Christians further believe that it is necessary to gain insight into the spiritual dimension of their personhood. Without this perspective no one will begin to significantly approach the fullness of who they are as people.

12.2 What Are the Parts of Personhood?

What are the primary attributes of personhood? How do we analyze ourselves, that is, what are the most significant constituent parts of being human? What are the most important parts that make up who we are?

These questions may only make sense in a Western context because of our propensity to analyze things and people by breaking them down into basic constituent parts. Scripture, on the other hand, tends not to look upon people as a composite of parts that may or may not easily be reconciled. They are individual beings who—in their totality—stand before God. Individuals in the Bible are presented as holistic beings who are certainly complex, but not essentially fragmented in their makeup.

Scripture sometimes speaks of people as having a dual nature, consisting of a body and soul. At other times the Bible speaks of people as having a body, soul, and spirit. These distinctions may seem unnecessary in terms of understanding the significance of human nature, but they reflect important theological distinctions made by Christians in church history. Let us look at some of the different viewpoints.

12.2.1 Dichotomy

A dichotomous view of human nature distinguishes primarily between a body and soul. Scripture sometimes makes this distinction as constituting the whole person (Matt 10:28; 1 Cor 5:3; 3 John 2). Elsewhere, the Bible distinguishes, at the very least, between a material (physical) dimension and immaterial (spiritual) dimension in people (Gen 2:7). No distinction is clearly made between the spirit and soul of a person because the words are sometimes used interchangeably (Matt 20:28; 27:50; John 12:27; 13:21).

It is argued that this view represents the most simple and obvious makeup of human nature. Our own experience easily distinguishes between the physical and spiritual, immaterial dimensions of our lives. This view is thought to lend itself best to self-understanding, personal growth, and holy living.

Is the soul separate from the body?

Catholicism cautions against theological formulations of human nature that draw too strict a dichotomy between the body and soul. This tendency toward dualistic thinking was historically considered an unfortunate legacy of Greek philosophy, which places great emphasis upon the spiritual dimension of the soul and little upon the physical dimension of the body. This body/soul split was thought to reflect an unbiblical and unhealthy dichotomy that negated both the integrity of human nature and the value of humanity's physical dimension.

> **People represent God's creation,** created in God's image, and thus they are essentially good, whole, and long for unity with everyone.
>
> People deserve respect, despite any difference: black or white, male or female, rich or poor. From God's perspective, we all are one.

12.2.2 Trichotomy

A trichotomous view of human nature distinguishes between a body, soul, and spirit. Here the body refers to the material (physical) dimension of human life. The soul refers to the immaterial part of human life that is natural, including the intellect and will. The spirit of a person, on the other hand, also refers to an immaterial part of human life that is spiritual, involving a life principle apart from the soul. Scripture, for example, sometimes distinguishes between the body, soul, and spirit in its description of people (Mark 12:30; 1 Cor 2:14; 3:4; 1 Thess 5:23). Hebrews 4:12 suggests that the human soul and spirit may be separated.

This view of people allows for a more complex understanding of the immaterial dimensions of human life. In particular, it distinguishes between the natural aspects of the immaterial part of human life and the spiritual aspects. A trichotomous view of human nature is also thought to enrich our understanding and actions in relationship to ourselves, others, and God.

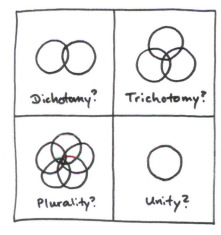

How many parts do we have?

12.2.3 Plurality and Unity

Some Christians argue that people are more complex than is expressed by the ancient categories contained in the Bible. The confusion caused by dichotomous and trichotomous views of human nature confirm that being human is more involved than either of the previous models conveys. Scripture, in fact, describes people in many more ways. It refers to the psychological, sociological, political, economic, and other dimensions of people. These factors must also be taken into consideration when reflecting upon who people are and how they are to live responsibly in relationship to themselves, others, and God.

This same plurality may be viewed—perhaps more appropriately—as a unity. If, in fact, Scripture makes no clear distinctions with regard to the constituent parts of humanity, perhaps we are better off thinking about people primarily as holistic beings. As such they should be thought of as a unity which may then be viewed from two, three, or a variety of ways. People should not be thought of discretely in terms of two, three, or more parts. Instead, they should be thought of as a unity—albeit a diverse unity—in the presence of God, as well as of themselves and others.

12.3 The Human Soul

A discussion of the constituent parts of human nature leads us to consider the human *soul*—the life principle of people (Gen 2:7). The Hebrews thought of

What and where is the soul?

the soul (Hebrew, *nephesh*) as the unifying description of people, who are living bodies. The idea of a soul has a long history that crosses many religious and philosophical lines. In ancient Greece, for example, the soul (Greek, *psyche*) was thought of as a disembodied spiritual entity, serving to animate and direct the body. It was sometimes thought of as immortal with the ability to transmigrate or reincarnate.

In Christian theology, the soul was sometimes associated with the human spirit and sometimes it was not. Either way, the soul was generally thought to constitute the essential life or self of a person. The soul is usually distinguished from the body because of its essentially immaterial nature, though the two aspects were not entirely unrelated. Sometimes, however, the soul is used in a more general sense in reference to the entire person, as today we would refer to the self. It is not so much that people *have* a soul as that they *are* a soul. As such, a person's soul may include the material and physical dimensions of life as well as the immaterial and spiritual dimensions. The holistic nature of the soul is reinforced by the biblical expectation of resurrection that includes people's bodies (Matt 2:20; Luke 21:19).

12.3.1 Origin of a Soul

The most common concept of the origin of the soul is the belief that God creates each individual soul. This viewpoint reflects a creationist view of the world in which God continues to create new life. Every person born constitutes a genuinely new person—a new soul. Generally, it is thought that God creates each new soul at conception. Although people procreate children through physical means, it is thought that only God enables the soul to come into existence.

In contrast to this creationist view, *traducianism* (from "shoot, sprout") asserts that the soul is transmitted from parents to their children. Traducianism holds that the soul, along with the body, is propagated by the parents, rather than the soul being created solely by God. Also known as *generationism,* this conception of the soul's origin better accounts for the transmission of sin—or a sinful nature—from parents to children. Today a growing number of Christians prefer a traducianist view in order to avoid overly spiritualized interpretations of human procreation and to avoid unnecessary confusion in conceptualizing the origin of individuals.

Although the origin of soul has not generally been a hot topic of debate, its discussion has resurfaced in contemporary debates about abortion and euthanasia. To some, the point of origin of the soul either contributes or detracts from a particular view related to the morality or immorality of such acts. For example, if a creationist view of the soul holds that God somehow implants a living soul into a fetus, it becomes important to determine at what point this occurs. Does it happen at the time of conception, at some stage of gestation, at the time of birth, or perhaps at some point after birth?

12.3.2 Immortality of Souls

Catholicism affirms the immortality of the soul—that the soul is immune to death. This affirmation comes primarily through biblical references suggesting the soul's immortality (Eccl 12:7; Matt 10:28). Further, biblical references to eternal life and eternal damnation point to the eternal nature of the human soul. Of course, from a Catholic perspective, the soul is thought of in terms of both its spiritual and immaterial dimensions, whereas resurrection is thought of in terms of the physical and material dimension. In addition to scriptural evidence, rational argumentation is offered in support of the soul's immortality. For example, everyone in the world possesses some form of a moral conscience and sense of ultimate accountability. This moral awareness would not occur without an eternal sense of right and wrong, which impacts human lives after death.

Most Protestants also affirm the immortality of the soul. Others, however, think of the soul's immortality as conditional. God may resurrect the souls of people, but they are not automatically immortal. Their immortality is conditional and requires resurrection, and there is little separation between the spiritual and physical dimensions of people's souls. When the Bible describes eternal life as a gift, it is expressed this way because a person's soul—holistically conceived—would not experience life after death without the addition of eternal life (John 3:16; 17:3; cf. Eph 2:8).

Historically, some Christians have not affirmed the immortality of the soul. When people die, every part of them, including their soul—however it is conceived—ceases to exist. Though this view is sometimes called "soul sleep," it is better described as "soul extinction" (Ps 13:3; Matt 9:24; 1 Cor 15:51). God may resurrect a soul for eternal life. God may also resurrect a soul for damnation, but not necessarily for eternity. Adventists, for example, believe that damnation is not eternal. Although people may be judged and condemned by God, their punishment is conditional—proportional to their degree of culpability. The ultimate end of those who reject God is *annihilationism,* or extinction of being.

12.4 Male and Female

Scripture describes both men and women as having been created in the image of God (Gen 1:27). All of God's commands to be fruitful and multiply, to

Both men and women are created in God's image!

fill and subdue the earth, and have dominion over it all pertain to both men and women (Gen 1:28).

Yet, throughout most of the Bible, as well as church history, there has occurred a patriarchal structure in most every relationship between men and women. Men have been viewed as having greater authority, responsibilities, and rights than women in family, church, and social settings.

This patriarchalism, however, has been strongly challenged by those who consider Scripture to be more conducive to an egalitarian interpretation of the relationships between men and women. Let us look at the various ways in which Christians have come to grips with this growing area of concern.

12.4.1 Patriarchal View

Historically, there existed a hierarchical structure in the Bible as well as in church history. Men were thought to have headship over women in the family, church, and society. In some instances, this hierarchical structure was thought of in terms of a strict chain of command.

Patriarchalism was thought to be a part of the order of creation. Since God created Adam first and subsequently created Eve from one of Adam's ribs,

Who is in charge?

there exists a priority of men over women in their various relationships (Gen 2:4b–25). This hierarchical structure is consistently repeated throughout Scripture, including references to how men should lead and how women should be submissive in the family (Eph 5:22; Col 3:18; 1 Pet 3:1–6), church (1 Cor 14:34), and society (Esth 1:20; Titus 2:3–5).

Today, those who affirm patriarchalism often try to temper the harshness with which this divinely ordained hierarchy has (at times) been implemented in the past. Instead they argue that the Bible continues to be progressive in advocating greater understanding and honor by men toward women. Jesus, for example, defied harsh patriarchal views of the first century in his positive valuation of women (Matt 27:55–56; Mark 7:24–30) and children (Matt 19:13–15). Scripture, after all, talks as much about the duty of men toward women as the duty of women toward men. Advocates of patriarchalism contend that within this context of a heightened regard for females, women will be able to experience more fully the fulfillment intended by God through submission in the family, church, and society.

12.4.2 Egalitarian View

Egalitarian views affirm the equality of men and women. God created men and women in the divine image, and both share equally in rights and privileges, as well as responsibilities in relationship to God.

There are several approaches taken, however, when Christians argue for this egalitarian point of view. Some take an exegetical approach, reinterpreting the Bible in ways overlooked or misunderstood in the past. Consider the following exegetical arguments put forth on behalf of an egalitarian point of view.

1. Scripture refers to women in positions of leadership, power, and authority, for example, Deborah (Judg 4–5), Esther (Esth 1–10), Priscilla (Acts 18:2–3; Rom 16:3–4), and four sisters who were prophets (Acts 21:9).

2. Patriarchalism is not consistently present in the Bible, for example, as when Paul speaks of the proper way women are to participate in church (1 Cor 11:4–5, 16) and later speaks of how women are to remain silent in church (1 Cor 14:33b–35).

3. Biblical references to the "headship" of men pertain to them as a "source" of life rather than as a social or church "authority" in a patriarchal arrangement (Eph 5:23; 1 Cor 11:3).

4. The subordination of women is a consequence of sin (Gen 3:16). Since we seek to overcome the other consequences of sin, for example, the pain of childbirth, toil of subsistence, and death (Gen 3:16–19), we should also seek to overcome the subordination of women.

5. Biblical principles promote equality (Gen 1:27/ 28; Gal 3:28) and reject any type of oppression (1 Pet 2:13–14, 18; 3:1). Just as Christians historically sought equality for both Jews and Gentiles (non-Jews), slaves and free people, we should seek equality for men and women.

No one portion of the Bible may in and of itself convince a person to overturn other portions that seem explicitly patriarchal in orientation. Some of the arguments, in fact, may seem to conflict rather than complement one another. But overall, the arguments provide exegetical evidence in support of an egalitarian point of view.

> **MALENESS AND FEMALENESS IN THE IMAGE OF GOD**
>
> [D]eeply rooted in Christian thought is an affirmation of the equivalence of maleness and femaleness in the image of God. This has never been denied, but it has tended to become obscured.
>
> ROSEMARY RADFORD RUETHER, SEXISM AND GOD-TALK (1983)

How equal should men and women be?

Other egalitarian views take a reconstructionist approach to Scripture that results in a thoroughgoing theological and exegetical reinterpretation of its teaching. This approach states that the Bible and its subsequent canonizers and interpreters were so patriarchal in their worldviews that they were incapable of viewing women in ways that are just. Therefore, it is necessary to reconstruct the Bible in a gender-free way, liberating women from patriarchalism.

12.5 Individuality and Community

Too often our understanding of the nature of humanity is conceived individually, without reference to the varieties of relationships and interconnectedness people have with other people, family relations, communities, institutions, cultures, and nations. People are social beings, and they cannot be fully understood only as individuals. They also have to be understood as communal beings with various interrelations. Such interrelations are inextricably bound up with who they are as people.

What role do others play in our self-awareness?

The social nature of people, in fact, reflects the social nature of the Trinity. Being created in God's image, which is Trinitarian, leads Christians more and more into recognition of the fact that social relations and community may have as much to do with personhood as with individual studies of people. It has long been known that an invaluable way of gaining self-awareness is by investigating the variety of relations people have (or have had) with parents, friends, school, work, church, and so on.

12.5.1 Roots of Individualism

In Western culture, a growing emphasis upon the individual and individualism occurred as far back as the Enlightenment, if not earlier in the Reformation. The Reformation placed greater emphasis upon the individual's relationship with God apart from the community of the church, and the Enlightenment placed even greater emphasis upon the individual's independence from outside influence and authority of any sort. Thereafter personhood was conceived more often from the perspective of an individual rather than that of an individual in relationship with others.

Eastern cultures, including Eastern Christian cultures, placed more emphasis on the relational and social dynamics of personhood, as well as Christendom. From a Western perspective, the Eastern emphasis may seem too extreme. After all, should there not be a balance between the individual and communal nature of humanity? There is, of course, not an either/or relationship between the two. Instead, there is a both/and relationship that needs to be incorporated when contemplating the nature of humanity.

12.5.2 One and the Many

People are not islands. This is as true spiritually and religiously as it is physically and civically. Christians need to develop their theology as well as their self-awareness in ways that reflect their interconnectedness with other people, family relations, communities, institutions, cultures, and nations. When such things are viewed individualistically, oversight may occur with regard to how they relate to other people, including their spouses, children, parents, and other significant others. One may also neglect social awareness and responsibilities for the communities, cultures, and nations in which one lives. This neglect can easily contribute to interpersonal insensitivity and the marginalization of others that can, in turn, lead to injustice, persecution, and violence. Although this may seem extreme, there are plenty of examples

Are Christians solitary islands unconnected from others?

of injustice in church history as well as world history to caution Christians against neglecting the social dynamics of their beliefs, values, and practices. Scripture is filled with the emphasis upon justice as well as love; the two go hand-in-hand. The neglect of societal, communal, and cultural dimensions of Christianity runs the risk of a truncated gospel and witness to the world.

The interrelatedness extends beyond relations with other people. It includes people's relations with institutions and other organizational constructs, whether they include churches, schools, businesses, clubs, philanthropies, or governments—national and international. These relations may have as much or more to do with understanding the nature of humanity as other considerations. It includes how people view law, politics, power, money, time, and other valuable resources. Certainly Christians cannot neglect the importance of their beliefs, values, and practices in connection with these institutional relations as with other personal relations. Issues of justice and love, accountability and empathy, judgment and mercy are as important in relationship to institutions as to individuals. It is naïve and dangerous not to include these considerations in developing Christian anthropology, ethics, and other doctrines.

12.6 Conclusion

Certainly there is more to being human than can be stated in a theological description of the image of God. No Christian anthropology is complete with only a theological look at personhood. But no anthropology is complete until it takes into consideration that humanity is created in God's image, which includes—if nothing else—the spiritual dimension of people. A holistic view of personhood requires consideration of the part (or parts) of the self that relates to God. God is the one ultimately responsible for the creation of people, as well as for the possibility of eternal life.

In understanding what it means to be human, it also helps to discern what the constituent parts of our personhood are. There is no consensus with regard to what it means to be human. Moreover, the more we learn about what it means to be human from physical and behavioral sciences, the more we may need to adapt our own conceptions. But at the heart of a Christian anthropology is the idea that there is a spiritual dimension of personhood. Regardless of whether we describe that dimension in terms of the human spirit or human soul, the spiritual dimension cannot be overlooked. It helps us to understand ourselves, and—more importantly—it helps us to come to grips with who we are in relationship to ourselves, others, and God.

It is vitally important for Christians to come to grips with what it means to be created male and female. Issues related to patriarchalism, feminism, liberationism, and egalitarianism are relatively recent in church history. Yet the implications of these discussions for how men and women treat one another have tremendous impact upon our lives personally, socially, and in the life of the church. If we are to avoid an uncritical and unredemptive preservation of the status quo, Christians face these questions squarely.

Finally, we must understand and appreciate the social as well as individual dimensions of personhood. We are not alone in the world, nor are we alone in the world with God. Investigating the social, filial, and communal dimensions of humanity is just as important as investigating people as individuals. There exists an important interdependence between people individually and corporately—an interdependence that includes God as well.

12.7 Questions for Further Reflection

1. Is it better to think of personhood in terms of unity or diversity? How should the different parts of people be analyzed? Which Christian view of the parts of personhood do you find most persuasive?

2. To what extent is Christian anthropology helped by the behavioral sciences: psychologically? sociologically? politically? economically?

3. What is the soul? How should we refer to people's souls?

4. What is the relationship between men and women? Should there be a patriarchal or egalitarian relationship between them? How do your views work out practically in marriage? church? society?

5. What do we learn about people from their interdependence with others? How important is the social and communal dimensions of life for understanding personhood?

12.8 Notes

1. Plato, *Apology,* in *Classics of Western Philosophy* (ed. Steven M. Cahn; 3d ed.; Indianapolis: Hackett, 1990), 54; cf. 41–56.

SIN

Now the serpent was more crafty than any other wild animal that the Lord God had made. He said to the woman, "Did God say, 'You shall not eat from any tree in the garden'?"

The woman said to the serpent, "We may eat of the fruit of the trees in the garden; but God said, 'You shall not eat of the fruit of the tree that is in the middle of the garden, nor shall you touch it, or you shall die.'"

But the serpent said to the woman, "You will not die; for God knows that when you eat of it your eyes will be opened, and you will be like God, knowing good and evil." (Genesis 3:1–5)

WHAT IS SIN?

13.1 Introduction

Most people are familiar with the story of Adam and Eve and of the serpent who tempted them to disobey God by eating the forbidden fruit (Gen 2:5–3:24). God had created Adam and Eve to live in the garden of Eden. There they could partake of everything but the fruit of the tree of the knowledge of good and evil. A serpent, however, tempted Eve to eat the forbidden fruit, which resulted in Eve giving some to Adam to eat. God, of course, discovered this transgression, cursed all who were involved, and banished Adam and Eve from the garden of Eden.

This story of the *fall* of humanity to sin is a classic story of love, betrayal, and tragic consequences. God created and loved Adam and Eve. They experienced an apparently idyllic life in the garden of Eden. God placed virtually no restrictions upon their lives, other than to avoid the tree of knowledge of good and evil.

A serpent appears on the scene and begins to cast doubt upon God's motives. It is not clear who the serpent is or from where the serpent came. The serpent has often been thought of as a wise, albeit deceptive, creature. There is also a hint of evil, supernatural power at work in God's creation. Be that as it may, the serpent beguiles Eve, who in turn gives the forbidden fruit to Adam, who becomes an accomplice to the transgression against God's prohibition.

Contemplating sin?

The consequences of their action—their sin—were calamitous. God cursed the serpent, condemning it to crawl and to be in enmity with people (Gen 3:14–15). God cursed Eve—and all women—to suffer pain in childbirth and to

> ### PARADISE LOST
>
> Of Man's first disobedience, and the fruit
>   Of that forbidden tree whose mortal taste
> Brought death into the World, and all our woe,
>   With loss of Eden.
>
> JOHN MILTON,
> PARADISE LOST (1667)

become subordinate to men (Gen 3:16). Likewise, God cursed Adam (Gen 3:17–18; Rom 5:12–21). God not only cursed Adam but the whole of humanity, and the very earth itself. Thereafter, people would have to toil on earth to provide for their needs, but, most significantly, they would eventually die. As a final act of punishment, God banished Adam and Eve from the garden of Eden (Gen 3:23–24).

The story of Adam and Eve and their fall from God's favor is a dramatic story that has mesmerized and influenced people for centuries. Although Christians are not in agreement about the identity of Adam and Eve, the story's influence persists in shaping personal and theological views of sin. Certainly there are a variety of ways in which Christians have interpreted the Bible's account of the fall of humanity. But each one—in its own way—always returns to the story of Adam and Eve in order to develop a doctrine of sin.

13.2 Understanding Sin

Sin basically signifies an offense against God. In Scripture, sin is understood in a variety of ways. Sin is disobedience to God (Gen 3:6), transgression of a law of God (1 John 3:4), or any unrighteousness (1 John 5:17). Our words can be considered sinful (Prov 10:19). So can our thoughts. Jesus said that sinful thoughts or intentions make us just as guilty of sin as the outward manifestation of our words and acts (Matt 5:22, 28). Even unbelief can be considered sin (Rom 14:23).

Sometimes sin is conceived not in terms of what is done but in terms of what is left undone. Neglecting to do that which is good is considered sin (Jas 4:17). Presumably the omission of good thoughts and words are equally worthy of guilt.

At other times sins were thought to be committed out of ignorance. People may have committed a sin according to the letter of the law so to speak, but they did not do it with evil intent. In these instances, Scripture still refers to such behavior as sinful, but allowances are made in light of them (Num 35:9–34; Josh 20).

> **God created people** in God's own image, and thus endowed people with great freedom and potential, which could be abused as well as used.
>
> People rejected God and continue to do so, which makes them liable to sin, alienation from God, and death, leaving people gravely lost and confused.

In sum, sin signifies any thought, word, or action that offends the righteousness of God or God's intentions for our lives. The extent of sin in our lives even includes our attitudes and dispositions. No part of our lives is thought to be exempt from the influence of sin.

The primary New Testament word for sin (Greek, *hamartia*) has the original meaning of "missing a target" or "failing to reach it." Sin is a deviation from God's will as well as character, implying that people in one way or another fail to achieve God's intentions for them. The historic development of the doctrine of sin has sometimes been referred to as *hamartiology*, though the term is seldom used anymore.

Have you missed the target?

13.2.1 Universality of Sin

Scripture affirms the universality of sin. All are sinful and fall short of the righteousness and glory of God (Gen 6:5; Isa 53:6; Rom 3:23; 5:12–14, 18–19). No one may say that they are without sin (1 Kgs 8:46; Prov 20:9; 1 John 1:8–10).

Often sin is conceived primarily in terms of personal sins, but sinfulness extends far beyond that of individual responsibility. Frequently in the Bible sin is conceived in terms of sins against groups of people and other societal sins (Gen 19:13; Exod 32–33; Lev 4:13–21; 25:28; Matt 11:20–24). Themes of justice and compassion for the poor and other dispossessed people in society represent continuous concerns in the Bible. There is no such thing as the privatization of sins.

Likewise, sins were thought to be committed by corporate groups of people as well as by individuals. The Hebrew nation, for example, along with the later kingdoms of Israel and Judah, were held guilty of corporate sins for which God held them responsible as a group (Josh 2:1). Thus, a corporate response to the presence of sin was as needful as an individual response.

13.2.2 Consequences of Sin

There occurred a number of consequences of sin. As already mentioned, the story of Adam and Eve described a number of specific curses against humanity. In addition to physical death, there occurred a separation between God and people that actually led to a kind of alienation. This alienation not only included an alienation between God and people, it also included an alienation from one's true self—as God intended us—and alienation from others. A spiritual blindness ensued, consisting of a hardness of heart, licentiousness, social injustice, and even violence. More than blindness, rebelliousness arose in people, especially rebelliousness toward God. This rebelliousness involves more than active aggression against God or transgressions against God's will. It also involves indifference to God and God's will, a form of passive aggression. The final result of sin is death of a spiritual as well as physical nature, which continues beyond this life into eternity.

Since all people are considered guilty of sin, this guilt changed the status of people before God. It signified a legal guilt or culpability for sin. It also signified a broken relationship with God, with others, and with oneself. Thus a general state of unhealthiness resulted which affected, in one way or another, every aspect of human existence. People are now in bondage to sin as if they are slaves to it (John 8:34; Rom 7:25). All aspects of their lives reflect orientations, outlooks, and actions tainted by sin.

13.2.3 Development of the Doctrine

The devil made me do it!

The ancient church was concerned about developing a proper understanding of sin. After all, sin signified the greatest barrier between people and God. Beyond the fact that all people were considered sinful, however, there occurred a number of different ways in which Christians conceived of sin. Much of the debate had to do with the origin of sin and its continuing effects upon people and their offspring.

In this chapter we will focus on the issue of the origin of sin. In the next chapter we will focus on theological understandings of the nature and extent of sin as they developed in church history. Certainly a discussion of the origin of sin is inextricably bound up with a more complete study of the nature and extent of sin. But we must begin with views of its origin.

13.3 The Origin of Sin

How did sin originate? That is, what is the source or cause of sin? Are people responsible for the origin of sin? Is some demonic power responsible for it? Or is God ultimately responsible for the origin of sin? These are questions that have perplexed Christians through the ages.

Is every person born guilty of their own original sin? Is every sin brand new? No one view of the origin of sin has gained consensual agreement, but distinct viewpoints have arisen.

13.3.1 Volitional View

Probably the most common Christian understanding of the origin of sin is the view that sin originated in free choices committed against God. From this perspective, people were thought to be righteous or at least morally neutral before sin occurred. But when people exercised their volition in ways that resulted in evil choices, sin occurred. These choices may have occurred in a variety of ways. For example, sin may have occurred as anxiety or as some betrayal of God, oneself or others, deviation or negligence from righteousness, disobedience toward God due to avarice, ingratitude, pride, rebelliousness, selfishness, sensuousness (appetites), and so on. But in each case, sinfulness occurred as a freely chosen thought, word, or action.

Augustine is the most prominent proponent of the volitional understanding of the origin of sin in the ancient church. He considered sin to be the result of pride or self-centeredness on the part of individuals. According to Augustine, sin does not constitute something in and of itself. Instead, sin consists of wrong choices. People choose to think, speak, and act in accordance with their own will rather than the will of God.

Decisions, decisions

From the volitional perspective, God permits people to commit sin. It is not the direct will of God for people to commit sin, but God permits them to exercise freedom of will. Although God foreknew that sin would occur, it is not God's primary will that sin should occur. God is prepared, however, to respond in an appropriate and saving way in response to the sin of humanity.

In the story of the fall of Adam and Eve, the presence of the serpent does not eliminate human responsibility for sin. People are still ultimately responsible for their decisions, despite the presence of outside influence or temptation. However, even considering the existence of an evil power in the world hostile to God—epitomized in the serpent, sometimes thought of as a reference to Satan—the origin of sin still comes down to a matter of the abuse of human freedom.

Although Scripture tells us even less about the origins of spiritual beings than it does of human beings, the evil or sin of Satan and demons would still have to be thought of in terms of the abuse of free will. If sin did not occur as a result of evil choices first made by Satan, then Satan would have to be viewed as an eternal presence of evil alongside that of a good God. But such a dualistic view has never been accepted in the history of the church. So, whether sin originated through Adam and Eve or Satan, it came about as a result of evil choices that were made.

13.3.2 Ignorance View

Augustine promoted his view of sin, in large part, in opposition to a view of sin propounded by Pelagius, whom Augustine accused of minimizing the depravity of sin. Although Pelagius left no writings with

Who is responsible for sin?

which we may adequately evaluate his theology, he was thought to view sin as ignorance. Thus sin is not the result of morally corrupt decisions but of an al-

most innocent ignorance on the part of people. On the cross, Jesus forgave those who crucified him, saying, "Father, forgive them; for they do not know what they are doing" (Luke 23:34; cf. Acts 7:60). Every person is born with relatively the same potential for living in righteous as well as unrighteous ways.

Those who view ignorance as the primary predicament of humanity emphasize a corresponding social predicament, namely the lack of education, including moral and spiritual training. In order for people to live righteous lives, they need moral illumination through appropriate education, mentoring, and other aids for nurturing righteousness.

In a post-evolutionary world, some Christians view sin as the natural result of people's animal nature. In trying to come to grips with conflict over survival instinct and cultural deprivation, people

Is there a problem?

naturally acted in ways that resulted in evil choices. As people evolve physically and culturally, they must also evolve morally and spiritually. This progressive understanding of human development, it is thought, represents the greatest hope for the future of humanity.

Other Christians conceive of sin primarily in societal rather than individual terms. This does not minimize the tragedy of sins and the effects of sins committed by individuals. But the core of the problem can be traced to social rather than individual sources. The social dimension becomes more important in conceiving both the origin and consequences of sin. Societal forces, more than anything else, explain the root of original sin, as well as continuing sins. All sins, in effect, are social sins. Thus, societal steps will need to be taken along with individual steps in overcoming sin.

13.3.3 Soul-making View

In a similar way, some Christians in the ancient church thought that God created people for the purpose of growing and developing into greater conformity with the image and likeness of God. Irenaeus, for example, thought that people were born with the potential for living in righteous as well as unrighteous ways. Unfortunately, all sinned due to evil choices. But the sin of humanity is a part of God's plans for their lives. God directly intended for people—past and present—to live in a context in which sin inevitably occurs. Only in the context of freedom, where wrong as well as right choices occur, do people learn to become responsible. Only in the context of freedom, where betrayal as well as love occur, do people learn to relate with others, including God, of their own volition.

This soul-making view of the origin of sin differs from the volitional view in that God is viewed as being more directly responsible for the origin of sin. Although people sinned due to their evil choices, God had created them in such a way that sin eventually occurs. Certainly this reflects a harsh way for God to refine people in their likeness to God. But it gives greater recognition to the intentional rather than unintentional explanation for how sin and evil could have occurred in a world created by God to be good. Like a parent, God introduced people to a challenging context in order for them to learn how to love and relate with God freely. It is better for them to endure temptation, pain, and suffering and then be redeemed from it than to have never experienced any challenges in life.

What is God trying to "cook up" with people?

An Irenaean-type theodicy has been thought by some to provide a more coherent view of how sin could fit into the ultimately beneficent plans of God for people and the world as a whole. Although God knew that life would be hard for people, a greater good could be achieved by having them endure sin and evil as well as pain and suffering.

13.3.4 Existential View

An existential view of sin involves the broken relationship between God and people that occurs when people respond in an inauthentic way to the trials, temptation, and anxiety they experience over the finitude of human existence. In the world, people are thought to experience a tremendous amount of anxiety (the anxiety of finiteness) because of their many limitations personally, socially, and spiritually.

Is stress a sin?

People experience themselves as being quite alienated in a world that often seems absurd to them from a rational perspective. An inauthentic response to the anxiety that results from a sense of finiteness and absurdity leads to endeavors to build a sense of security. The endeavor to build a sense of security often occurs at the expense of others and of a relationship with God. In a sense, a betrayal of God and of others occurs, and this betrayal of relationship constitutes sin. Human thoughts, words, and actions that occur independent of God and at the expense of others are considered sinful.

This contemporary view of sin emphasizes the interpersonal dimension of sin as betrayal rather than sin as breaking a rule. It does not exclude the notion of breaking a rule, but it places the idea of a personal relationship with God as most important in determining authentic human existence. Relationships rather than abstract rules or institutional laws constitute the most meaningful aspects of people's lives.

13.4 Conclusion

Sin represents a tragic yet real occurrence in the lives of people. No consensus about the origin of sin has been held by Christians in church history. But there is consensus about the fact that all people sin and that there are serious consequences that come about as a result of sin.

It is in opposition to sin and its effects that Christians struggle today. They struggle, of course, knowing that God was the first to struggle against sin, especially through the salvific person and works of Jesus. But people cannot begin to struggle against sin until they know a little about it, including its origin. From this starting point it will become easier to recognize and understand sin in the world. It will also become easier to struggle against it along with God, who leads in the struggle against sin and its consequences.

13.5 Questions for Further Reflection

1. What is sin? Why is the Christian view of sin important for understanding people?

2. What effects did sin have upon people? What effects did sin have upon the image of God in people?

3. What are consequences of sin for people individually? institutionally? socially?

4. Why did sin occur? By which view of the origin of sin are you most persuaded?

5. Why is it important for us not to neglect the doctrine of sin?

CHAPTER FOURTEEN

> *For the wrath of God is revealed from heaven against all ungodliness and wickedness of those who by their wickedness suppress the truth. For what can be known about God is plain to them, because God has shown it to them. Ever since the creation of the world his eternal power and divine nature, invisible though they are, have been understood and seen through the things he has made. So they are without excuse.*
> (Romans 1:18–20)

THE NATURE OF SIN

14.1 Introduction

Jeremiah describes the human heart—the self or soul of a person—as being deceitful above all things and desperately wicked. He says, "The heart is devious above all else; it is perverse—who can understand it?" (Jer 17:9). According to Jeremiah, the nature and extent of human sin extends beyond our understanding. Only God could possibly comprehend it and properly judge human beings.

Paul echoes a similar theme when he talks from personal experience about the presence and power of sin in the life of people and the struggle that occurs with it. He says:

> For I know that nothing good dwells within me, that is, in my flesh. I can will what is right, but I cannot do it. For I do not do the good I want, but the evil I do not want is what I do. Now if I do what I do not want, it is no longer I that do it, but sin that dwells within me. (Rom 7:18–20)

What are the "wages" of sin?

The struggle with sin has tragic consequences for this life. It influences us personally. It influences us in relationship to others, and it influences us in relationship to God. The effects of sin also have tragic consequences for the life to come. Paul talks about the consequences or "wages" of sin as death—death which results in eternal damnation (Rom 6:23).

The reality of sin and of God's judgment upon sin are harsh and difficult Christian concepts to comprehend and accept. This is especially true in a world that progressively wants to downplay the inherent evil in people and the variety of influences upon their lives in ways that excuse people from moral culpability. After all, how can people be held responsible for their thoughts, words, and actions when taking into consideration the genetic, environmental, and social challenges that put people at an unfair disadvantage? We live in a society that more and more looks down upon concepts of sin and guilt and instead looks toward psychological, sociological, political, and economic reasons for ill behavior.

Still, Christians affirm the biblical concept of sin—as it is variously understood—as being at the core of human problems. Sin may not be the direct cause of every problem that people have. But somewhere near the core of every problem, sin incites and exacerbates our human situation. Moreover, the unwillingness or inability to deal with sin has eternal consequences that many find difficult—if not inconceivable—to deal with on their own. For this reason, in order to begin to deal with the problems related to sin, we need to investigate further ways in which Christians have attempted to develop their understandings of the nature and extent of sin.

14.2 Perspectives on Sin

What is the nature or core characteristic of sin? Having discussed the origin of sin in the last chapter, we already discovered some of the sources of what Christians considered to be at the core of sin—a volitional offense against God, oneself, and others; ignorance of righteousness; and betrayal of personal relationships. Scripture, however, describes so many aspects of sin that it seems impractical to distill the core of sin. Nonetheless, Christians have attempted to determine the primary problem of sin, if for no other reason than the need to inform and preach about the problem of sin. While no one view may capture the totality of sin, taken together the various views provide insight into the complexity as well as evil bound up with the reality of sin.

The following summary lists many of the ways Christians in church history have understood the essential character of sin, whether committed by commission or omission. The core vices should not be thought of as unrelated to one another. On the contrary, they overlap and exacerbate one another:

- anxiety: Luke 12:25–26; Phil 4:6

- avarice (covetousness): Exod 20:17; Mic 2:2; Heb 13:5

- betrayal: Matt 10:21; 24:10–13; Luke 22:22; John 13:21

- deception: Rom 7:11; 2 Tim 3:13; Titus 3:3; Heb 13:3

> **Sin affects individuals,** society, and the world as a whole, contributing to alienation, ignorance, oppression, and persecution.
>
> Sin affects our relationship with God; our estrangement distorts how we relate to God, ourselves, and others, leading to many types of destruction.

- disobedience: 1 Sam 12:15; Eph 5:6; 2 Thess 1:8

- idolatry: Exod 20:4; Lev 26:1; Deut 11:16; 1 John 5:21

- ignorance: Lev 5:17; Acts 3:17; 1 Tim 1:13

- ingratitude: Deut 32:6; Rom 1:21

- negligence: Neh 9:35; Matt 7:26; Jas 4:17

- pride (vainglory): Prov 16:18; 21:4; 1 John 2:16

- rebelliousness (active and passive): Deut 9:24; 1 Sam 15:23; Isa 30:1; Ezek 2:3

- selfishness (self-centeredness): Matt 25:31–46; 1 Cor 10:24; Phil 2:4

- sensuousness (appetites, e.g., anger, envy, gluttony, lust, sloth): Prov 6:23–26; Matt 5:28; Col 3:5

In Western Christendom, these ways of understanding sin were usually conceived in legal or juridical terms. The sinner was thought to be a criminal—a breaker of God's laws. So, if sin was conceived in legal terms, the accused was to be brought to trial before God in a courtroom where God served as judge, made a judgment, and then pronounced condemnation or acquittal on the accused.

In Eastern Christendom, however, the tendency has been to view sin more in terms of an immature child or of a sick person who has a disease. God, in turn, is viewed more in terms of a great physician who provides therapeutic treatment for that which ails people. Salvation, in turn, is understood in terms of healing and wholeness as well as pardon and rehabilitation.

As the doctrine of sin continued to develop in church history, several significant distinctions or contrasts arose in order to understand more fully the nature of sin. We will look at a number of the more prominent differentiations that arose.

14.2.1 Mortal and Venial Sin

In trying to analyze sin, Catholics distinguished between *mortal* and *venial sins*. Mortal sins result in spiritual death, while venial sins weaken the spiritual well-being of a person. Thus mortal (grave, deadly) sins reflect a more serious understanding of sin as intentional opposition to God. Mortal sins are thought to be offenses against God and God's laws in a way that is freely chosen with full knowledge that one is transgressing a matter of serious import (Matt 23:33; 1 Cor 6:9–10; Gal 5:19–21; 1 John 5:16; contrast Matt 6:12; Luke 11:4; 1 John 1:8–9).

Since the time of the Medieval church, references have been made to seven "capital" or "deadly" sins. They include pride (vainglory), avarice (covetousness), lust, gluttony, anger, envy, and sloth. Although these embody sinful tendencies more than mortal sins per se, the seven capital sins reflect intentionality in opposition to God. For example, the theft of something extremely valuable for the sake of pride or avarice would be considered a mortal sin, in contrast to the theft of a trinket for the sake of economic survival. Both would be considered sins, but the prior act would be considered to be more serious, having spiritual as well as temporal consequences—spiritual death and separation from God's graces.

A venial sin signifies an offense against God and God's laws in ways that reflect certain mitigating circumstances, especially in that it is not committed in direct opposition to the love and will of God. For example, a person may sin out of ignorance or because of some limitation placed upon their volition. Although the distinction between venial and mortal sins may not always seem clear-cut, the emphasis largely rests on the sinful intentionality of a person's thoughts, words, or deeds. If certain behaviors reflect intentional rebelliousness—active or passive—against God, they are considered mortal sins. If certain behaviors do not reflect intentional rebelliousness but rather imperfect knowledge or volition, they are considered venial sins. Such sins still have destructive effects upon one's spiritual well-being, but God does not count them as having mortal ramifications for eternal life.

Is my sin venial or mortal?

Protestants do not generally make a distinction between venial and mortal sins. There is recognition of varying degrees of sinfulness, but distinctions such as venial and mortal are avoided lest someone become complacent in thinking that all their sins are of a venial rather than mortal character. After conversion, however, some Protestants like Wesley thought that the purification of sin that took place in the life of a believer primarily had to do with "sin properly socalled," that is, willful transgressions against known laws of God. This distinction reflects a concern for the intentional dimension of mortal sins rather than for the relatively unintentional dimension of venial sins.

14.2.2 Pardonable and Unpardonable Sin

All sins in this temporal life are considered pardonable or forgivable by God. At no time have people sinned so greatly or strayed so far from God that God would turn away from them. Scripture repeatedly speaks of God's patience and compassion in not wanting anyone to perish from sin in this life or in the life to come (Isa 48:9; Rom 9:22; 1 Pet 3:9). People, rather than God, prevent reconciliation with one another.

At times in church history, however, some have thought that particular sins were so horrific, so rebellious against God's Holy Spirit that they were considered unpardonable. This was in part due to an account in the Gospels about an unpardonable or eternal sin of blasphemy against the Holy Spirit (Matt 12:31–32; Mark 3:28–29; Luke 12:10). The account, however, seems to be a reference to the intentional and persistent rejection of salvation offered through God's Holy Spirit. Such impenitence, if it continues throughout a person's life, will lead to eternal separation from God because of the unwillingness to turn from sin. Ongoing rebelliousness may, in fact, result in a hardness of heart—a recalcitrance—that reduces a person's ability to recognize and repent from sin (Prov 28:14; Rom 2:5; Heb 13:3).

14.2.3 Objective and Subjective Views of Sin

In articulating the doctrine of sin, Christians have vacillated between conceptions that focus on the objective, legal dimension of sin and those that focus on the subjective, personal dimension of sin. On the objectivist end of the continuum, Calvin conceived of sin primarily in terms of transgressions against the objectively stated moral laws of God. He not only considered the breaking of divine laws to be sinful, he forbade anything not explicitly permitted in the Bible. Calvin was not a legalist in the sense that he accepted that meritorious works could earn salvation apart from the saving grace of God. On the contrary, he strongly affirmed salvation by grace through faith. But his view of sin tended to depersonalize sin, emphasizing penal tendencies in his theology.

A more rationalistic example can be found in Kant's view of religion within the limits of reason alone. Kant argued that people should live in accordance with the moral imperative. The moral imperative states that people should act rationally in ways that are universally understandable and binding. Reason dictates how people ought to act in every situation, or else they are guilty of sin.

In contrast to the perceived tendencies toward objectifying sin and the laws or imperatives that determine sin, some Christians advocated a more subjective, personal perspective. Sin involves more than the breaking of divine laws or imperatives; it involves the betrayal of a relationship—of God. Kierkegaard, for example, emphasized sin more as betrayal than as legal transgression. Of course, the nature of betrayal is more subjective than the breaking of a divine law or imperative. Such subjectivism, though, runs the risk of relativizing the concept of sin.

While every view of sin undoubtedly lies more toward one end of the objective-subjective continuum than another, we would do well to avoid going to extremes. Although there exists an undeniable personal and therefore subjectivist element in all decision-making, the objectivist element of a holy God who reveals righteousness to humanity cannot be overlooked. Instead views of sin need to incorporate both elements in the attempt to determine the most appropriate understanding of the nature of sin.

Is sin the breaking of a law, or is it betrayal?

14.2.4 Personal and Social Sin

Debate among Christians sometimes occurs with regard to the personal and social dimensions of sin. While issues such as oppression and injustice appear throughout the Bible, the tendency to view sin in personal rather than social terms pervaded much of church history. But as social consciousness grew, Christians became progressively aware of the fact that institutions or any groups of people are just as capable of sinning as individuals. Such sins include corporate opinions, words, actions, policies, and other social structures that are unfair or hurtful—sinful—toward individuals or groups of individuals.

The American theologian Reinhold Niebuhr (1892–1971) argued that institutions are incapable of acting as morally as individuals. This occurs for a variety of reasons. For example, people act irresponsibly and subsequently blame an institution or institutional red tape for corporate decisions that they, as individuals, would not make. This immorality is just as likely found in churches as other institutions because churches—by virtue of their institutional makeup—find it difficult to act as morally as individuals are capable of acting.

Don't all sins have a social impact?

Some Christians argue that sin should primarily be conceived in social terms. Sins of inequality, injustice, and so on are fundamental evils that plague humanity and in turn permeate the rest of life. No sin is committed in isolation. All sins have a social impact; everything is interrelated. Sins against God and others impact our lives personally, just as so-called personal sins have a social impact. So, if sin is conceived of primarily in social terms, the solutions to sin should also be thought of in social terms. The focus upon sins of a more personal nature reflects a naïve, self-centered perspective which diminishes a more complete conception of sin in social terms. The focus upon sins as essentially social in nature helps to take care of widespread injustices affecting people, which in turn helps people deal with struggles of a more personal nature.

Viewed socially, sin is essentially an abuse of power. Power, of course, can be abused in many ways. It can involve abuse against another person, or against groups of persons. Abuse of power can appear in every dimension of life: race, gender, culture, language differences, nationality, sexual preference, and religious differences. Abuse involves any type of violence against another: verbal, emotional, physical, sexual, economic, political, and so on. Violence is not limited to physical violence; it can occur through the marginalization of others, bias, discrimination, insults, and persecution—non-physical as well as physical persecution. Contemporary Christians, as well as society in general, are becoming increasingly aware of the types of abuse that occur in relationships, marriages, families, social relations, politics, institutions, and even international relations that include terrorism, militarism, conquest, and occupation. Sin becomes especially pronounced when it is understood as injustice toward others. Scripture, of course, is deeply concerned about fighting such injustice and promoting justice (Isa 58:6; Jer 22:13; Hos 10:13). Too often in church history, Christians have been negligent in their awareness of and advocacy on behalf of those who suffer abuse of one sort or another. In this respect they have failed to challenge evil and sin in all its manifestations.

14.3 The Extent of Sin

Throughout church history the effects of one generation's sin upon another have been a matter of concern. We have already discussed the universality of sin and also some of the effects or consequences of sin upon people—consequences for both present and future lives. Sin not only is thought to affect the relationship between people and God, it corrupts people's very existence—their thoughts, their words, and their actions. It corrupts the relationship between people with others, individually and socially. It is even thought to corrupt the physical world in which we live.

In light of these consequences, one of the questions increasingly asked by Christians pertained to the relationship between the sins of one generation and those of the next generation. For example, Christians were concerned about how the origin of sin affected those people who followed and how the pervasiveness of sin continued from one generation to another.

> **TEMPTATION OF POWER**
>
> What makes the temptation of power so seemingly irresistible? Maybe it is that power offers an easy substitute for the hard task of love. It seems easier to be God than to love God, easier to control people than to love people, easier to own life than to love life. Jesus asks, "Do you love me?" We ask, "Can we sit at your right hand and your left hand in your Kingdom?" (Mt. 20:21). . . . We have been tempted to replace love with power.
>
> HENRI NOUWEN, "MORNINGS WITH HENRI J. M. NOUWEN"

14.3.1 Typological View

Christians in the ancient church thought of Adam and Eve as historical people. But they often thought of them as more. Adam, for example, was seen in the New Testament as a *type*—a historical person who symbolizes certain truths. Adam is described as being typical of each person's guilt through sin (Rom 5:12–19). Every person is thought to be guilty of personal sins just as Adam was guilty of his own sins (Isa 43:27–28; 1 Cor 15:21). The original or primal sin of Adam is not necessarily thought to carry attendant guilt for future generations of people. References to Adam's first sin—the fall—merely symbolized the fact that all people sin and thus are incapable of saving themselves from the consequences of sin.

This typological view of sin does not consider sin or the guilt of sin as something transmitted from one person to the next, for example, from parents to children. Nevertheless, the sins of our ancestors have an irreparable effect upon us. The effects are real; they involve more than just a bad example. The sins of our ancestors resulted in a distortion of our character as well as in the very character of the world in which we live. The moral and spiritual sin of prior generations—along with the divine judgment upon it—cannot help but have a dramatic and often tragic impact upon all who follow. Thus people find themselves at a disadvantage in terms of their inability to live righteous lives. There is not, however, thought to be a direct transmission of sin or guilt of primal sin that occurs between people. Since neither Scripture nor experience provides a ready explanation concerning the concept of a sinful nature inherited by a new generation from its sinful ancestors, no attempt is made to penetrate the mystery of why all people sin. It is enough to acknowledge the universality of sin and the culpability of individuals for the sins they commit.

Not my type?

Later Christians who questioned the historicity of Adam and Eve still found typological significance in the account of Adam recorded in the Bible. Adam, along with Eve, symbolizes the fact that all people sin and thus they are deserving of the consequences of their personal sins. A typological view allowed for traditional emphases upon the universality of sin and its consequences, without having to be locked into a particular view of sin as inherited from sinful ancestors.

14.3.2 Pelagian View

Pelagianism argues that the only effect Adam's sin had upon subsequent people was that of a bad example. Regardless of whether Adam is conceived in historical or non-historical terms, there occurred no direct influence upon the subsequent sins of people. Instead people are thought to be born innocent of sin as well as any guilt of previous sin. Each person is capable of living their lives in a way that is righteous or unrighteous. Everyone must learn to live responsibly, avoiding thoughts, words, and actions that fall prey to the poor role models provided by Adam and other ancestors.

Certainly Pelagianism does not consider a righteous life something easy to achieve. On the contrary, it requires prudent and courageous dedication on the part of an individual. But this view is optimistic with regard to the potential God had created in people to live holy and healthy lives.

Continued emphasis upon the moral and spiritual corruption of people might, in fact, have a negative effect upon people. Rather than bringing them to an appropriate repentance, a preoccupation with sin might discourage people from the dedication needed to live righteous lives that are pleasing to God, as well as themselves.

14.3.3 Traditional View

The most common way Christians have viewed the nature and extent of human sin is encapsulated in the doctrine of *original sin.* This doctrine argues that the primal sin of Adam had corporate consequences for the entire human race. Because of Adam's (original) sin people are all born sinners even before they personally behave in sinful ways. Not only are people thought to be born guilty of sin, their human nature became corrupt. People now possess a sinful nature inherited by birth from sinful ancestors.

Augustine championed the doctrine of original sin, primarily in contrast to Pelagian views. Augustine thought that, because of Adam's original sin, people inherited a sin nature, which made them as guilty of sin as Adam. There remained in people no native ability to save themselves much less approach the possibility of living a righteous life. Here sin is thought to be imputed, that is, people are born with a sinful nature, which is an attribute they inherited from their forebears. Augustine actually speculated that the guilt of original sin was somehow passed down to children because of lust present during sexual intercourse.

To my children, I leave all my sin and guilt . . .

Although this idea of Augustine was not accepted, his understanding of inherited sin impacted subsequent developments in the doctrine of sin.

Bondage of the Will and Total Depravity

Catholics affirm original sin as the consequence of the fall of Adam and Eve. All people are born with the guilt of that first sin and thus suffer from its consequences. The consequences include death, of course, and also *concupiscence.* Concupiscence signifies a sinful disposition—a sinful nature—in which the lower appetites of the sensuous part of humanity overturn the rational and volitional parts, which were themselves distorted as a result of the fall. It is not quite the same as original sin, but it refers to the distorted condition of human appetites that was a result of original sin. Concupiscence, in its turn, produces such things as pride, ingratitude, rebelliousness, and disobedience toward God.

Luther spoke of a *bondage of the will,* which refers to the controlling or enslaving effect of the sin nature that people inherit at birth. Sin is thought to have a kind of power over people that affect the entire personality and character of a person. No one is exempt from this sin nature that results from original sin. It is as if people have now become incapable of doing anything but sin. Although some good impulses may remain in people, all thoughts, words, and actions are thought to lack good motives.

In a similar way, Calvin thought that the corrupting effects of sin were so pervasive that people should be thought of in terms of *total depravity.* Total depravity holds that every aspect of people becomes corrupted. This corruption includes the physical, psychological, rational, and social dimensions of human life, as well as the moral and spiritual dimensions. Nothing in this life can overturn the corrupting influences of original sin.

Transmission of Original Sin

Because sin was thought to be inherited from ancestors, a question arose concerning the way in which sin was inherited from one generation to the next. This question was especially critical for those who held to the doctrine of original sin because they thought that both the guilt of sin and a sin nature were inherited by a new generation from the original ancestors, resulting in eternal damnation.

Developments in the doctrine of original sin understood the transmission of sin in at least two ways. The *solidarity view* of original sin holds that sin is imputed to people because they are actual descendants of Adam and Eve. The guilt of their original sin continues to be transmitted by birth to later generations.

The *federal headship view* of original sin holds that Adam acts as a representative on behalf of the rest of the human race. Sin is imputed to people because of the original sin of Adam. He both represented and is representative of all humanity.

14.4 The Sin of Innocents

Another question that arose pertains to the sin of innocents—those who are born and die as infants. Are they damned, having been born with the inherited guilt of original sin? Will innocents be damned for eternity in addition to having experienced an untimely death, preventing them from having a chance to make moral and spiritual decisions for themselves? These questions were especially critical for those who affirmed the doctrine of original sin because of their belief in inherited sin and guilt of sin. But the questions are also relevant to the other views concerned about the extent of sin because in each instance there remains the belief that everyone born experiences disadvantages that incline them toward sin.

No completely satisfactory answer has been given to this question, at least not to the satisfaction of parents who have children who die in infancy. But a variety of viewpoints arose in order to begin to respond to this difficult question. Catholics, for example, hold that the baptism of infants removes the imputed guilt of original sin. This removal does not change the essentially distorted, concupiscent character of an infant's sinful nature. But it does absolve them from eternal damnation due to the inherited guilt of sin.

Protestants who continue to baptize infants often hold a similar view related to the spiritual protection of innocents provided by the sacrament. However, as Protestants progressively moved away from the practice of infant baptism, there arose several ways in which to view the original sin and guilt of innocents. Those Protestants who held a strong view of predestination considered the salvation of people to be a matter decided before anyone was born, so the eternal life of an infant was not precluded because of an untimely death. Other Protestants appealed to passages that seemed to guarantee special consideration for the salvation of innocents (Matt 18:14; 19:14; Mark 10:14–16; Luke 18:16). For example, when the infant child of David died, he said that the child would not return to him but he—David—would someday go to be with the child (2 Sam 12:22–23). Although this may be a simple reference to David's affirmation of his own mortality, it has been conceived as a special mercy for innocents.

An innocent may, of course, include more than infant children. It may include children who have not reached what some Christians call an *age of accountability.* Sometimes children are not thought to be accountable or responsible for the morality of their actions until they reach a certain age. Catholics refer to it as the *age of reason,* when a child is considered capable of determining right from wrong, accountable for moral decisions, and able to take on religious obligations. Some consider the age of seven through the time of puberty (near the teenage years) as the age of reason or accountability, in which children become responsible for their actions. Then they may go through confirmation and other religious rites of passage.

How can you blame me?

Some Christians do not believe that God holds all people equally accountable for sin. For example, people who are mentally, emotionally, or in some other way incapable or incapacitated for one reason or another are not considered equally accountable for sins as others in mature possession of their mental and volitional faculties. This principle brings to mind the earlier distinction made between mortal and venial sins—sins of a more intentional nature versus those of a less intentional nature. Although this concession introduces another subjective element into determining the nature and extent of sin, it is considered necessary and reflective of God's mercy and grace.

14.5 Sin, Ignorance, Misery, and Bondage

Sin is generally considered the main predicament people face in life. Sin and its effects are complex, of course, including natural and supernatural dimensions. However, sin is not the sole predicament people face. Indeed, people experience a variety of problems due to ignorance, misery, and bondage, to say the least. Of course, one could argue that ignorance, misery, and bondage are direct or indirect results of sin. Likewise, they may directly or indirectly cause sin. However, the unique yet widespread problems of ignorance, misery, and bondage deserve consideration alongside sin.

What holds you in bondage?

Not all ignorance is due to sin; people are ignorant because they are finite beings who are limited in their intellectual, emotional, and other human characteristics. Not all misery is due to sin; people experience misery due to their susceptibility to accidents, disease, and other misfortunes. Not all bondage is due to sin;

people may be subject to demonic bondage or oppression, and they may be subject to other types of bondage. People may be subject to various addictive habits, involving bondage to alcohol, drugs, eating, sex, gambling, and other vices.

In determining the problem or problems people experience, Christians realize that sin is not necessarily (and certainly not simplistically) the source of every problem. Problems in relationships may be due more to the need for training in communication than to sin on the part of one or more parties. Problems in meeting obligations may be due more to unfortunate pain and suffering than to sin. Problems of addiction may also not be the result of sin but the result of undeserved genetic or childhood habits.

Although Christians are concerned about sin, they are also concerned about the variety of ways that people find themselves challenged, buffeted, and defeated. Like Jesus, Christians seek to respond and minister to the holistic needs that they and others experience. With the grace of God, they are confident that sin and other problems in life can be overcome.

14.6 Conclusion

Sin certainly constitutes the key problem of human existence, as well as the key problem with which God is concerned in relating with people. Sin is that which disrupts our relationship with God, others, ourselves, and the world in which we live.

The complexity of our understanding of sin may always surpass our ability to comprehend it fully. It so thoroughly fills and affects our lives. Christians, however, contribute a great deal to our understanding of the underlying spiritual problem of human life. Certainly a theological understanding of sin does not resolve all human problems. People still need to learn about and master the psychological, sociological, political, and economic dimensions of life. But without attention given to the spiritual dimension, especially that of sin, it will be impossible to know ourselves fully and to discover how to overcome those things that hurt us individually and corporately.

The extent of the effects of sin can be overwhelming. They disrupt and distort every part of our lives, and there seems to be little human hope of averting the ongoing effects of sin in the world. Moreover, there seems to be little human hope of averting future effects of sin in life after death.

It is extremely fortunate that sin does not represent the final word Christians have to offer people. On the contrary, despite its horrific impact upon people and society, a realistic confrontation with sin brings us back to God—to consideration of people's only hope for sufficiently overcoming the effects of sin. It is to the divine provision for overcoming sin that we now turn our attention.

14.7 Questions for Further Reflection

1. What is the nature of sin? How would you describe it: legal, personal, social, institutional?

2. Do you find the distinction between venial and mortal sin to be helpful? In what way may it be unhelpful?

3. What is the difference between an objective and subjective view of sin? Why is the distinction helpful?

4. In what ways is sin social? In what ways does sin represent abuses of power? May social sins be greater than so-called personal sins?

5. How is sin passed on from generation to generation, if at all? What are the implications of your views for infants? What are the implications for others who may not have reached an age of accountability?

6. Is sin the sole predicament people face? How does sin relate to ignorance? misery? bondage? How should Christians respond to these problems?

JESUS CHRIST

Once when Jesus was praying alone, with only the disciples near him, he asked them, "Who do the crowds say that I am?" They answered, "John the Baptist; but others, Elijah; and still others, that one of the ancient prophets has arisen." He said to them, "But who do you say that I am?" Peter answered, "The Messiah of God." (Luke 9:18–20)

WHO IS JESUS CHRIST?

15.1 Introduction

The Synoptic Gospels—Matthew, Mark, and Luke—tell of Jesus and his disciples sailing across the Sea of Galilee (Matt 8:18, 23–27; Mark 4:35–41; Luke 8:22–25).[1] While sailing, a great windstorm arose and the disciples were terrified. But Jesus had fallen asleep. So the disciples woke Jesus in desperation, telling him about the situation and asking for help. Immediately Jesus spoke, and both the storm and wind became calm. Jesus then asked his disciples why they were afraid and why they had so little faith. The disciples, on the other hand, were dumbfounded. Basically, they kept asking themselves, "Who is this guy?" Not only had Jesus amazed them with his spiritual insights and teachings, Jesus performed miraculous feats of power and authority over the world of nature.

Jesus asleep in the storm?

The Gospels recount the ongoing attempts on the part of the disciples and others to figure out who Jesus was. There occurred a growing awareness of who he was, but divisions arose over the identity of Jesus. The disciples progressively came to the conclusion that Jesus was the Christ—the Messiah—literally, "the anointed one," chosen by God as the one to bring redemption and liberation (Matt 16:16; Mark 8:29; Luke 9:20; cf. John 6:69). But even their assurance of this conclusion wavered, and the disciples—along with the others—continued to work out in their own minds and hearts the identity of Jesus and the implications of his identity for them.

Throughout church history, people have continued to work out in their own minds and hearts the identity of Jesus and the implications of his identity for

How can one appropriately portray Jesus?

them. A great deal of consensus was reached in the ancient church, and Christians wrote in the creeds what they considered to be the essential affirmations about Jesus. But questions about Jesus continue to this day.

In this chapter we will look at the person of Jesus—the most critical person for understanding Christianity. The word "Christian," in fact, means a follower of Christ or one who believes in him. In particular, we will look at Jesus in his historical context as described in the New Testament.

The ability to reconstruct a truly historical portrait of Jesus has been highly contested. Although it is impossible to discuss all of the historical critical questions involved with exegetical studies of the person of Jesus, we will summarize the main issues raised by ancient as well as contemporary Christians. We will do this by looking at various aspects of the biblical account of Jesus' life, death, and resurrection.

15.2 Who Is Jesus?

It is difficult to discuss who Jesus was (or is) because of the many ways Christians have viewed Jesus over the centuries. Such views have increased over the past two centuries due to debates over how Christians should approach the study of Jesus. For example, should Christology—the "study of Christ"—begin with an inductive approach to the study of the Bible? Or, should Christology begin with a deductive approach that permits historic or contemporary understandings of Scripture to inform our understanding of Jesus?

Certainly every attempt to understand Scripture begins with an inductive approach. Having inductively investigated the Bible as a whole, one then attempts to draw general conclusions that help to explain less clear aspects of biblical teachings. So, all biblical interpretation utilizes both inductive and deductive reasoning. The question is not whether one can or cannot be completely objective in investigating the person of Jesus. Instead, it has to do with critically coming to terms with the presuppositions people bring to their study. Often the study of people's hermeneutical presuppositions—more than anything else—may tell us about the conclusions they will arrive at in the interpretation of Scripture.

> **Jesus, described as the Christ,** the chosen one of God, was born, lived, and died for the sake of our salvation.
>
> Jesus did more than die; he also resurrected, which guarantees all his teachings, and our heavenly celebration!

Everyone brings certain presuppositions to their investigation of the Bible. Most claim that they want to let Scripture speak for itself. But when the Bible is thought to say many different things, a look at the interpreter's presuppositions may reveal a great deal. For example, those who consider Scripture to be divinely inspired expect a high degree of accuracy in recounting the historicity of the life and identity of Jesus. On the other hand, those who consider Scripture to be more human than divinely inspired expect less accuracy related to the historical accounts of Jesus. Some contemporary interpreters, for example, find very little (if any) that provides a truly historical account of Jesus untainted by the preaching and concerns of the early Christians.

What presuppositions do we bring to understanding Jesus?

Another tension present in our attempts to understand Jesus stems from whether we should determine who he was based on what was said about him or what he did. Gospel statements about who he was might be unduly tainted by opinions held about him by the early church, which may not necessarily correspond to Jesus' self-perception. On the other hand, an investigation of what he did may not necessarily communicate the fullness of who he was without the help of those who attempted to describe him.

This is why several ongoing tensions exist among Christians who study the life and identity of Jesus with regard to the historical reliability and proper interpretation of the biblical accounts of him. Given this caveat, however, we will proceed by looking at classical theological concerns about Jesus. As we review these concerns, we will provide a spectrum of interpretations about the life and identity of Jesus.

Since this book is an introduction to theology, it is impossible to provide an in-depth study of the history of scriptural interpretation, particularly as it pertains to Jesus. So we will turn to the most common ways in which Christians historically have come to view the theological significance of Jesus' life. This will be viewed, of course, in light of the critical interpretive tensions mentioned above pertaining to the historical reliability of Scripture. At the end of this chapter, we will summarize some of the developments in biblical interpretation related to the so-called search for the historical Jesus.

15.3 The Birth of Jesus

Traditionally, Jesus was thought to have been born in Bethlehem in a rather humble fashion. Most people are aware of the story of the nativity, which means "birth": Jesus was laid in a manger, and his birth was announced by angels and witnessed by neighboring shepherds and magi from the east.

**Most people are aware of
the Christmas story**

Significant in the story was the fact that Jesus did not have a natural birth. Instead, Jesus was thought to be born of a virgin maid named Mary. Mary had been informed by an angel that she would miraculously give birth to a son, conceived by God's Holy Spirit rather than by a human father. The infant was to be named Jesus, which means "Yahweh saves."

15.3.1 Virgin Birth

Christians throughout the centuries have considered Jesus' virgin birth to be of tremendous theological significance. It distinguishes Jesus from other people and for the unique mission he was to fulfill. In particular, the birth was thought to signify the incarnate nature of Jesus—that he was fully divine as well as fully human. The mystery of Jesus' incarnate nature constitutes one of the major affirmations of the ecumenical creeds. The incarnation and its theological significance will be taken up in the next chapter. Presently we will focus more upon aspects of Jesus' birth and life. The story of Jesus' conception, birth, and early life appear in only two of the gospels—Matthew and Luke (Matt 1:18–25; Luke 1:26–38; 2:1–7). The events of the two stories complement one another, though the details vary. Together, Matthew and Luke provide the best known details of Jesus' early life.

One of the questions that arose with regard to Jesus' virgin birth pertained to the presence of original sin, since people are thought to have inherited sin in some way. If, despite being conceived by the Holy Spirit, Jesus had a human mother, how did he avoid the effects of inherited sin? Historically, Christians have believed that Jesus was not culpable of original sin. Usually this has been resolved by the fact that Jesus was conceived in a miraculous way that absolved him from the effects of inherited sin. But this view makes it seem like Jesus did not struggle against the same type of sin nature that the rest of humanity inherits. Others have resolved the issue by saying that Jesus was born with original sin but that it did not affect him as it affects others. But this view makes original sin seem less significant, especially in accounting for the pervasive and ruinous presence of sin in others.

Recent interpreters of the Bible have strongly questioned the historicity of the virgin birth. Because the virgin birth plays a relatively minor and somewhat ambiguous role in both Scripture and earliest church tradition, it is thought that the story merely represents a mythic addition to stories about Jesus. Besides, the notion of a virgin birth is an affront to modern people and is thus considered an obstacle to true Christian faith.

In response to challenges, Christians have responded in a variety of ways. Some have resolutely affirmed the historicity of the virgin birth, arguing that it is essential to the incarnation. Others have argued that the virgin birth is not necessary for the incarnation, but that it is true. Still others have argued that the virgin birth was possible, but that it is theologically dispensable, since it does not contribute anything directly to the saving purposes of Scripture.

15.3.2 Mariology

Catholics resolve the problem of Jesus and original sin by stating that Mary was herself immaculately conceived in such a way that sin was not later passed on to Jesus. Mary was a perfected person, created by God, who cooperated magnificently in people's redemption as the "mother of God." Catholics further believe in the perpetual virginity of Mary, since Jesus was thought to pass through the wall of her uterus rather than being born through the normal birth canal. This preternatural birth contributed to her spiritual and sexual purity. Later in life Mary was not thought to have died. Instead, Catholics believe in the assumption of Mary, that is, that her body and soul were assumed into heaven, where she reigns like a queen.

Madonna and child

Catholic theology about Mary (*Mariology*) is quite extensive. She is honored—not worshipped—in the church with religious feasts, devotions, and special titles. Few other people have been honored as extensively as Mary in hymns, songs, poetry, sculpture, painting, and literature.

Protestants have a high regard for Mary, but they do not honor her to the same extent as Catholics. For example, Protestants speak only of the virginal conception of Jesus and not of Mary's perpetual virginity. According to Protestants, after Jesus' natural birth, Mary consummated her marriage with Joseph and had other children. God's choice of Mary as Jesus' mother was a tremendous honor for her and for womanhood in the redemptive process. But honor should not extend beyond that of honoring Mary's faithful obedience to the will of God.

15.4 The Early Life of Jesus

Little is known about the life of Jesus other than what occurred during the approximate three years of his public ministry, which is recorded primarily in the Gospels. He was circumcised as an infant in accordance with Jewish law (Luke 2:21), lived an indeterminate amount of time in Egypt in order to escape persecution from Herod (Matt 2:13–15), and later returned to Palestine in order to live in the small city of Nazareth in the region of Galilee (Matt 2:19–23; cf. Luke 2:39).

Jesus as a boy

When he was twelve years of age, Jesus strayed for several days from his parents (Luke 2:41–52). On their return home to Galilee from a visit to the temple in Jerusalem, Joseph and Mary found that Jesus was missing. After a period of time searching for him, they found Jesus conversing with priests in the temple.

15.5 The Adult Life of Jesus

Aside from a few incidents from his youth, most of our information about Jesus relates to his adult life and ministry. Jesus was a popular preacher, teacher, and healer. Around the age of thirty, Jesus gathered a group of disciples and traveled throughout first-century Palestine (modern-day Israel and the Palestinian Territories) telling people about the imminent kingdom of God and how all should repent of their sins, have faith in God for their salvation, be baptized, and follow him in love for God and for their neighbors (Matt 4:12–17; Mark 1:14–15; Luke 4:14–15). Jesus lived a simple life. He taught almost anywhere, frequently using parables, which perplexed those who heard him (Matt 7; 9; 13; 18; 20; 22; 25; Mark 2; 4; 12; 13; Luke 5; 6; 8; 10–21). But the people were delighted and excited about how he healed the sick, cast out demons, and performed other miracles (e.g., Matt 8:1–9:8; Mark 1:21–34; Luke 4:31–44; John 2:1–12; 4:43–45).

We cannot discuss every aspect of Jesus' adult life and ministry. So we will focus upon some of the events and aspects of his life that have prompted important theological considerations throughout church history. Other considerations have to do with the very human aspect of Jesus' life, yet with the understanding that Jesus embodied far more than just another human being.

15.5.1 Baptism of Jesus

Early in his ministry, Jesus went to his cousin John the Baptist in order to be baptized (Matt 13:3; Mark 1:9; Luke 3:21). At first John refused to baptize Jesus because John thought that his cousin should be the one to be baptizing him. But Jesus recognized the spiritual leadership of John and wanted to identify with those who responded to John's call to repentance.

After Jesus was baptized, the Gospels recount that God's Holy Spirit descended upon him like a dove and a heavenly voice said, "You are my Son, the Beloved; with you I am well pleased" (Mark 1:11). This event reflects a sense of awareness and obedience on the part of Jesus with regard to a divine purpose he was to fulfill.

15.5.2 Temptations of Jesus

Early in his ministry, the Bible tells us that Jesus experienced temptations. Temptations are the enticement to evil or sin. Sometimes temptations prove the character of people by testing them, such as Job (Job 1–2), but they also entice people to the point of transgression and betrayal. Jesus had to resist devilish temptations that would benefit him but prevent him from fulfilling his mission.

Jesus demonstrated such resistance during a dramatic confrontation with Satan (Matt 4:1–11; Mark 1:12–13; Luke 4:1–13). Jesus resisted temptation, quoting Scripture in refusing to give into sin. The story implies that Jesus' temptations were real. His resistance was not easy, though the nature and extent of his temptation is not elaborated. Some commentators have questioned the realistic possibility of Jesus succumbing to temptation. However, the Bible suggests that genuine struggle occurred. It may well be that Jesus' temptations exceeded those experienced by others, because Jesus continually resisted temptation, whereas others do not.

Was Jesus tempted by a cookie jar?

15.5.3 Sinlessness of Jesus

Did Jesus sin? Could Jesus sin? Christians and non-Christians have often asked such questions. Scripture affirms that God sympathizes with our weaknesses and proclivity to give in to temptation because Jesus had "been tested as we are, yet without sin" (Heb 4:15). But the affirmation of Jesus' sinlessness does not answer all our questions. Some Christians argue that Jesus could not sin because of their belief in Jesus' inherent divinity. Others argue that the significance of Jesus' sinlessness was not in the fact that he *could* not sin but in the fact that he *did* not sin. Still others argue that Jesus' sinlessness has more to do with the avoidance of flagrant acts of misconduct than the avoidance of anxiety or other sinful expressions of human corruptibility.

Although we may never resolve this debate, it seems that Scripture wants to affirm that Jesus' sinlessness was necessitated morally, that is, it came as the result of his free choice. His sinlessness was not necessitated by a divine nature foreign to or overpowering his humanity. Jesus' sinlessness, however one understands it, resulted from his submission to the teachings of Scripture and the power of God's Spirit in resisting temptation. Jesus lived a Spirit-led life, and it had been God's Spirit that led Jesus into the wilderness, where Satan tempted him (Matt 4:1, 11; Mark 1:12; Luke 4:1, 14). It was the same Spirit who aided Jesus.

15.5.4 Ministry of Jesus

Jesus was not trained to be a priest, but he exhibited extensive knowledge of the Hebrew Bible, displayed wisdom about spiritual and moral matters, and preached and taught effectively throughout Palestine. Those whom Jesus chose as disciples were also not trained for the priesthood. So Jesus' ministry was very much a popular, grassroots type movement that largely occurred outside organized Jewish religion.

Although Jesus generally tried to avoid drawing public attention to himself and his ministry, it became difficult for him to stay out of the limelight as his ministry gained a reputation (e.g., Matt 4:23–25; Mark 1:32–34; Luke 12:1). Multitudes of people came to see and hear him, and many also came to be healed. Using his own words to describe his ministry to the disciples of John the Baptist, Jesus said, "the blind receive their sight, the lame walk, the lepers are cleansed, the deaf hear, the dead are raised, and the poor have good news brought to them" (Matt 11:5).

Both by word of mouth and, no doubt, by exaggerations of the already miraculous proportions of his ministry, Jesus was a religious phenomenon that could escape few people's attention. More and more people came to hear and speak with him, including those who were in authority. When confrontations occurred, it most often happened between Jesus and the leaders, who had responsibility for religious worship, theological scholarship, and political authority in conjunction with the reigning Roman government. In time, Jesus was considered a threat to the various institutions of Palestine. The perceived threat of Jesus to institutional structures of the country contributed to his eventual death.

15.5.5 Teachings of Jesus

Jesus taught about many things during his life and ministry. It would be difficult to summarize everything he addressed in his teaching and preaching. The main focus had to do with the kingdom of God and God's sovereign rule in the world (Matt 6:33; Mark 1:15; Luke 6:20; cf. kingdom of heaven: Matt 3:2; 4:17; 5:3). Sometimes Jesus spoke about how God's kingdom had already arrived (Luke 10:9; 17:21), but the *fullness* of God's kingdom had not yet arrived (Luke 13:29; 22:18). This "already, not yet" aspect of Jesus' teaching occurs other places in the Bible, reinforcing the feeling that people live a liminal existence— "betwixt and between" earth and heaven, present and future, faith and certainty. This sense of liminality increased due to Jesus' teaching in parables, which often had to do with encouraging the reign of God in our lives.

Jesus' parables represented some of the most profound as well as confounding aspects of his preaching and teaching. Parables are stories told to convey spiritual, moral, or common sense lessons. They may include proverbs, riddles, allegories, metaphors, similitudes, or narratives. As such, parables are not self-explanatory, and they often needed additional input from Jesus (Matt 13:10–23; Mark 4:10–20; Luke 8:9). Jesus' parables instructed people about morality as well as salvation and challenged people to reflect upon their values and practices, especially as they related to God. Most of Jesus' parables referred to the kingdom or reign of God. They told of what the kingdom of God is like and how people should live as a part of it. Although God's kingdom has not yet fully arrived, people may already live in accordance with its rules and principles.

Jesus seemed to rely upon indirect communication in order to communicate spiritual truths. But he clearly taught on issues related to salvation. Jesus repeatedly proclaimed the "good news" (gospel) about salvation and reconciliation with God that came through faith, repentance, and the willingness to follow him. Likewise, Jesus warned people of the possible consequences of judgment, damnation, and hell. He was especially critical of religious leaders who were hypocritical in their professional as well as private lives. In contrast, Jesus was particularly welcoming of those who humbly listened to and received his teachings. There was no one who seemed too lowly or needy for Jesus to reach out with words and actions that served to encourage and heal as well as to save.

15.5.6 Limitations of Jesus

Jesus experienced the limitations of human existence that others experience. Jesus grew from childhood to adulthood. He grew weary, hungry, thirsty, and sleepy. Troubling to some, Jesus did not have all knowledge while ministering with the disciples. On several occasions, Jesus acknowledged he did not know certain things, for example, the timing of the end of the age—the time of Jesus' return "with great power and glory" (Mark 13:26; cf. Luke 8:45). About this event Jesus said, "But about that day or hour no one knows, neither the angels in heaven, nor the Son, but only the Father" (Mark 13:32).

Although Jesus admitted ignorance about a number of things, he was well acquainted with sorrow, grief, tears, distress, and agitation. For example, Jesus agonized while praying in the garden of Gethsemane on the night he was betrayed for crucifixion (Matt 26:30–46; Mark 14:32–42; Luke 22:39–46; cf. Matt 26:37; 27:46; Mark 5:30; Luke 2:40; 4:2; 8:8, 23; 9:58; 24:39; John 7:27; 12:44). Luke reports, "In his anguish he prayed more earnestly, and his sweat became like great drops of blood falling down on the ground" (Luke 22:44). Although not all ancient manuscripts contain this verse, it highlights the genuine limitations of Jesus' humanity—his authentic experience of the limitations people experience, including the experience of death.

> **VULNERABILITY OF GOD**
>
> God may thunder His commands from Mount Sinai and men may fear, yet remain at heart exactly as they were before. But let a man once see his God down in the arena as a Man—suffering, tempted, sweating, and agonized, finally dying a criminal's death—and he is a hard man indeed who is untouched.
>
> J. B. PHILLIPS, YOUR GOD IS TOO SMALL (1952)

15.5.7 Miracles of Jesus

Many of the miracles of Jesus are well known. For example, Jesus turned water into wine (John 2:1–11), walked on water (Matt 14:22–33; Mark 6:45–52; John 6:15–21), and fed over five thousand people from only a handful of fish and bread (Matt 15:32–39; Mark 6:30–44; Luke 9:10–17; John 6:1–13). Jesus also cast out demons, healed the sick, resuscitated people back to life, and performed miracles over nature.[2] These miraculous signs and wonders caused Jesus to become so popular that he could only extricate himself from crowds of people with great difficulty (Matt 4:23–25; Luke 4:42–44). When challenged by his detractors, Jesus sometimes referred to the miracles that

Remember Jesus feeding 5,000 with five loaves and two fish?

attended his life and ministry as confirmation of his prophetic and divine mission (Matt 11:4; John 10:25, 38).

People have questioned the nature of Jesus' miracles as well as the miracles that occurred in other parts of the Bible. Many theories about miracles exist, though we will not examine them in this book. Generally, miracles are thought to represent an extraordinary achievement or event that exceeds natural agency, which attests to a divine power that transcends ordinary human or natural power. A miracle does not necessarily signify something contrary to nature; we may not yet know enough about how nature works. But a miracle signifies that God supervened in a way for which we can account. Like us, Jesus relied upon the power of God for the performance of miracles, since he lived his life in submission to God's Spirit working in and through him (Matt 12:28; Luke 4:14; cf. Acts 10:38).

Although Jesus performed many miracles, he tended to downplay them or actually ask others not to mention them (e.g., Mark 1:35–45; Luke 5:12–16). The occurrence of miracles certainly attracted people's attention, but they did not constitute the most important part of Jesus' good news. In fact, Jesus went so far as to chastise some who sought after signs and wonders. For example, he said, "An evil and adulterous generation asks for a sign, but no sign will be given to it except the sign of the prophet Jonah," namely, "the proclamation of Jonah" (Matt 12:39, 41; cf. Matt 16:1; 24:3; Mark 8:11). Jesus considered it more important that his followers respond to him in repentance and faith than pursue miraculous signs and wonders.

Over the centuries, Christians have gloried in the accounts of miracles in the Bible and in ongoing reports of miracles. However, Christians have also recognized the limitations in focusing too much upon them. For example, Christians recognize that Jesus did not focus all that much upon miracles. They also realize that miraculous powers may occur that are not of divine origin, perhaps through some secret art or by demonic activity (Exod 7:11, 22; 8:7; Matt 7:22; 24:24; 2 Thess 2:9).

Since the Enlightenment, some Christians have argued, using rational and scientific evidence, that miraculous occurrences are naturally explicable. Others have demythologized miracles altogether. Most Christians believe in miracles. But beliefs vary widely with regard to the frequency and significance of miracles. It does Christians no good if their faithfulness reduces to a simplistic credulity that endangers them and others. Miracles and those who claim to perform signs and wonders can, after all, be deceptive, manipulative, and demonic. So prudence and temperance are needed when considering and promoting miracles. Christians should be neither presumptuous nor pessimistic with regard to their beliefs about miracles.

15.5.8 Jesus' Spiritual Warfare

Scripture provides numerous examples of Jesus encountering Satan, casting out demons, and praying fervently against demonic influences, especially against believers. Like the previous discussion of miracles, the Bible presents these phenomena as real and vitally important for our theological consideration (e.g., Matt 4:10; 8:28–34; Mark 5:1–20; Luke 8:26–39; 10:18). Sometimes Christians refer to Jesus' encounters with Satan and demons as *spiritual warfare,* which involves prayer for supernatural conflicts that occur, and possibly exorcism. This warfare must be continued by believers today.

Christians disagree with regard to how involved they should become in spiritual warfare. Clearly, the degree to which people believe in demonic beings and their involvement in the world influences the extent to which they become involved in spiritual warfare. On the one hand, Christians who believe that angels and demons are currently engaged in war with one another pray tenaciously for divine victory in the spiritual realm. On the other hand, Christians who believe that angels and demons play a relatively minor role in our day-to-day lives may also pray tenaciously, but their prayers are not likely to be focused on the battle between supernatural beings. Instead, they pray for the human and social forces that buffet our lives. Regardless of people's particular views, God provides sufficient grace and spiritual armor to overcome any spiritual warfare we might experience in life (1 John 3:8; cf. Eph 6:10–17).

15.6 The Suffering and Death of Jesus

Just as Jesus genuinely experienced the limitations and temptations common to people, Jesus genuinely suffered and died. Jesus' sufferings were real, but he suffered for a purpose. Repeatedly Jesus claimed that God intended for him to sacrifice his life on behalf of humanity. Jesus did it as a voluntary act of love and obedience to God for the sake of others. He did not deserve to die, for, as we have seen, the Bible describes Jesus as being innocent of sin and, thus, undeserving of death. However, God permitted Jesus to endure humiliation, suffering, and death in order that a greater good—a greater purpose—might occur.

Christians consider the death of Jesus important despite its apparent injustice, because his death represents God's ultimate identification with the plight of human life, namely, that all die. His crucifixion reminds us of the humiliation and pain associated with his death. Yet, Christians believe that his death is not the end of the story. It is the beginning of a greater story, and the cross that once symbolized an ignominious death and defeat now embodies the blessed hope of Christians.

15.7 The Resurrection of Jesus

Throughout church history, the crux of so much Christian belief depended upon the actual, historical resurrection of Jesus. Although questions have increasingly been raised with regard to the authenticity of the resurrection,

Christians hold steadfast in their beliefs about the resurrection of Jesus and of his subsequent ascension to and session in heaven. Jesus' activities and influence did not cease with his death; they increased.

Historically and theologically, the resurrection lies at the center of Christian beliefs, values, and practices. The Apostle Paul said, "For I decided to know nothing among you except Jesus Christ, and him crucified" (1 Cor 2:2), implying that Jesus' death and resurrection were at the core of his ministry and the early church. Today the resurrection continues to be at the core of Christianity.

15.7.1 The Reality of Jesus' Resurrection

Since the beginning, Christians realized the preposterousness of their claim to the resurrection of Jesus. Paul understood this when he said, "we proclaim Christ crucified, a stumbling block to Jews and foolishness to Gentiles" (1 Cor 1:23). Elsewhere, Paul puts it more bluntly, saying that all Christian beliefs, values, and practices relate inextricably to the actual, historical resurrection of Jesus. In response to those who doubted Jesus' resurrection, Paul said:

> If Christ has not been raised, your faith is futile and you are still in your sins. Then those also who have died in Christ have perished. If for this life only we have hoped in Christ, we are of all people most to be pitied. (1 Cor 15:17–19)

From the time of the first century, Christians realized that belief in Jesus' resurrection had to be more than a superstition, exaggeration, or wishful thinking in explanation of the events surrounding his life and death. Even Jesus knew, before the crucifixion, that a case needed to be made for the possibility or probability of resurrection. For example, when arguing with a group of skeptical religious leaders known as Sadducees, Jesus said:

> You are wrong, because you know neither the scriptures nor the power of God. . . . And as for the resurrection of the dead, have you not read what was said to you by God, "I am the God of Abraham, the God of Isaac, and the God of Jacob"? He is God not of the dead, but of the living. (Matt 22:29, 31–32)

Who moved the stone?

So, when the gospel writers wrote their accounts of Jesus, they provided numerous proofs of his death as well as his resurrection. They described how Jesus died on the cross, was tested for certainty of death, was embalmed, entombed, and guarded by Roman soldiers for three days (Matt 27:57–66; Mark 15:42–47; Luke 23:50–56; John 19:31–42).

Regardless of the evidence, people may not believe in the resurrection. Yet, Christians often argue that belief in Jesus' resurrection does not represent belief in just any historical event. For example, it matters little whether people believe or do not believe that George Washington chopped down a cherry tree as a boy. However, it matters a great deal if people believe or do not believe in Jesus' resurrection and, correspondingly, their own resurrection. It constitutes a historical decision that demands a verdict.[3]

15.7.2 Ascension and Governance of Jesus

After Jesus spent time with the disciples and others following the resurrection, the Bible tells us that he visibly rose up into the air in ascension to heaven. The rising signifies the transcendent nature of eternal life. The physical departure was important to the early Christians because it explained his departure from the world, despite the fact that Jesus resurrected from the dead (Mark 16:19; Luke 24:51). After Jesus ascended, the book of Acts reports that two angels appeared, saying that Jesus would visibly return someday to the world (Acts 1:11; cf. Matt 24:27–39). The hope of Jesus' second "coming" (Greek, *parousia*) is a major theme of Christian belief throughout church history.

Christians believe that Jesus, having ascended to heaven, rules with divine authority. In Scripture, this governance (session) is depicted by describing Jesus sitting on the right hand of God, signifying his oneness with the Godhead (Mark 16:19; Luke 22:69). Jesus does not cease being involved in the lives of people; he increases his involvement through divine rule. Although the fullness of Jesus' governance has not yet occurred, his rule is sufficient for fulfilling people's salvation.

15.8 The Search for the Historical Jesus

Throughout church history, Christians have sought to discover the most historically correct interpretation of the Bible, especially with regard to the person and work of Jesus. Early debates about the historicity of the gospel stories occurred between the Alexandrian and Antiochene schools of biblical interpretation. Such debates occurred before the canon of Scripture was formally adopted near the end of the fourth century. The Alexandrians often employed *allegorical* and *mystical* expositions of the Bible, whereas the Antiochene school employed a more literal and historical method. During the Middle Ages, both types of biblical interpretation were employed along with *tropological* (moral sense) and *anagogical* (mystical or eschatological sense) interpretations of Scripture.

The Protestant Reformation tended to emphasize the literal and historical method of interpreting Scripture, but over time Protestants became increasingly critical in their historical interpretations. In the wake of the Enlightenment, interpreters increasingly questioned the historical accuracy of

How do you study Scripture?

the Bible and, in due course, its divine inspiration. So-called higher criticism studied the literary structure of Scripture, the authorship of books in the Bible, and probable dates for their writing. Tradition criticism critically studied the oral traditions on which much of the Bible was based, and form criticism studied the various literary forms in which the biblical text evolved. Such studies were then correlated with the Bible's "setting in life" (*Sitz im Leben*), analyzing the situation in which the words of Scripture were spoken, remembered, written, and arranged by the author or redactor of a book of the Bible. Given the increased historical-critical attention given to Scripture, a growing number of questions and concerns arose with regard to the accuracy of Scripture. Although interpreters had been able to live with the inherent tensions in Scripture for centuries, they no longer assumed the Bible's accuracy.

During the eighteenth century, English deists advocated that the Bible should be interpreted primarily as a human document for which human reason alone was sufficient for interpretation. Interpreting the Bible primarily as a human document led the way for the rise of historical-critical methodology in the nineteenth century. For example, H. S. Reimarus (1694–1768) was the first to question seriously the historicity of the gospel accounts of Jesus. David Strauss (1808–1874) argued that Jesus could only be understood when we recognize that his followers romanticized their accounts of Jesus' life and ministry. Adolf von Harnack thought that interpreters of Jesus needed to free themselves from the doctrinal developments of church history (e.g., Trinity, incarnation) in order to uncover the "historic kernels" of Scripture. Martin Kähler (1835–1912) distinguished between scientific history (*Historie*) and theologically interpreted history (*Geschichte*), arguing that we need to distinguish between that which was true and that which represented possible embellishments by Jesus' followers—a difficult but necessary task.

15.8.1 Critique of the Search for the Historical Jesus

Bible scholars in search of the historical Jesus

At the turn of the twentieth century, Albert Schweitzer (1875–1965) wrote *The Quest of the Historical Jesus*, which chronicled the rise of historical and critical interpretations of the Bible.[4] However, Schweitzer argued that the historical kernels interpreters found in the Bible revealed more about their own modern biases than about conclusive historical investigation. For example, when interpreters questioned the historicity of miracles in the Bible, was their skepticism based upon the biblical evidence or upon their modern assumptions that miracles do not occur? In other words, how much did their interpretive biases affect the way they interpreted the Bible?

Debate has continued throughout the twentieth and twenty-first centuries over the ability of interpreters to bring resolution to historical questions and concerns about the historical accuracy of the Bible. Some have wondered whether the debates serve any meaningful purpose for Christians.

15.8.2 Demythologization

During the twentieth century, Rudolf Bultmann (1884–1976) argued that debates over historical minutiae were endless, and they were misleading. Bultmann believed that Christian faith should be clearly distinguished from historical issues. We should read the stories, myths, and symbols of the Bible existentially, rather than historically, allowing God to encounter us as we read Scripture. The kerygma—preaching or teaching—of Scripture provides the event in which God may be revealed to us, as well as our salvation.

Bultmann argued that we must *demythologize* the Bible, deemphasizing its historical elements and instead uplifting its existential elements. This process uplifts the personal dimension of Christianity, diminishing its historical underpinning. For example, Bultmann demythologized the religious or "mythical" worldview of the Bible, including references to heaven and hell, and angels and demons. Instead, the stories of the Bible should be interpreted in parable-like fashion, helping people understand their existential lives and relationships to themselves, others, and God.

Some Christians consider the present deconstructionist movement to be an expression of demythologization. *Deconstructionism* denies that language has transcendental meaning. For example, people—limited by the finitude of their human knowledge—cannot know and, thus, cannot express anything meaningful about metaphysical reality, that is, transcendent reality. This is especially true of speech about God. Thus religious language is meaningless with regard to talking about God and matters related to God. We are left, instead, with arbitrariness and bias involved in the writing and interpretation of biblical texts. A deconstructionist approach to theology considers traditional talk about God as "dead"—reminiscent of the "death of God" theologies. Christians who advocate a deconstructionist approach to the Bible and theology call for a more radical kind of faith when we encounter the one who engages us beyond words yet requires a response. It is our response that is religiously meaningful rather than the words we use to describe it.

15.8.3 Hermeneutical Circle

Debates continue with regard to the historical and theological accuracy of the Bible in general and of the gospel accounts of Jesus in particular. Such debates may never end. The arguments seem to ebb and flow between optimism and pessimism with regard to the degree of accuracy found in Scripture. For example, some like Ernst Käsemann (1906–1997) argue that we do not give the biblical authors sufficient respect for their religious sophistication and for the trustworthiness of what they wrote about Jesus and other miraculous events. Still others, like participants in the Jesus Seminar—a long-term study of the historical reliability of Scripture—continue to challenge its trustworthiness. After all, most scholars acknowledge that the Gospels were written decades after the life of Jesus. The Greek language in which the Gospels were written is itself largely a translation of Jesus' original words, which were mostly spoken in the language of Aramaic.

Can one be caught in a hermeneutical circle?

Christians value the study of the Bible, and they try their best to interpret it well. One of the best insights that has arisen in biblical studies is recognition that interpreters need to become more self-aware of their own input in the interpretive process. Some people call this self-awareness a hermeneutical circle, in which exegetes interpret their own cultural context and religious biases, as well as those of Scripture. By becoming more self-critical of their own historical and critical interpretations of the Bible, it is hoped that ongoing efforts will become more accurate as well as applicable.

15.9 Conclusion

The study of the life, death, and resurrection of Jesus is a major focus of Christian theology. Being Christian demands it, since "Christ-ian" means being "like Christ." Yet, these studies cannot help but have an impact upon people, regardless of whether they are Christians. Jesus is perhaps the most influential person in world history, and seems to demand some type of response. That response may be intellectual, but—more often than not—people find themselves responding to Jesus spiritually, morally, and actively.

Starting with the life of Jesus, we raise a number of issues that need further study. In the following chapters, we will investigate some of the most critical ones with which people struggled throughout church history. Such issues continue to be of critical importance for us today.

15.10 Questions for Further Reflection

1. Do you believe in the virgin birth of Jesus? How important is such belief for one's salvation or for living a Christian life?

2. How important is it for us to think about the human aspect of Jesus? What does it mean for him to become hungry, to grow tired and perhaps irritable? What are implications of the fact that Jesus did not himself claim to know everything?

3. Did Jesus not sin? In what way do you think it is possible—or necessary—for Christians to affirm that Jesus did not sin?

4. Do you believe in miracles? Do you believe in angels and demons? Why? What difference does it make for your life?

5. How reliable do you consider the gospel accounts of the life, death, and resurrection of Jesus? Do you believe in the resurrection? Why?

6. What biases or presuppositions do you bring to the interpretation of Scripture? To what degree do people's beliefs in God—or the lack thereof—influence their interpretations? How important is it to be self-critical of one's interpretations of Scripture?

15.11 Notes

1. The Synoptic Gospels are the first three books of the New Testament: Matthew, Mark, and Luke. Although each gospel is unique, the Synoptic Gospels tend to present historical accounts of Jesus in similar ways.

2. For example: 1) exorcisms: Matt 8:28; 9:32; 12:22; Mark 1:26; 5:1; Luke 4:35; 8:26; 11:14; 2) healings: Matt 8:3, 5, 14; 9:2, 20, 27; 12:10; 17:14; 20:30; Mark 1:31, 41; 2:3; 3:1; 5:25; 7:23; 9:26; Luke 4:38; 5:13, 18; 6:6; 7:2; 8:43; 9:37; 13:11; 14:2; 17:12; 22:51; John 4:46; 5:5; 9:1, 3) resuscitations: Matt 9:18; Mark 5:42; Luke 7:11; 8:41; John 5:5, 11; and 4) miracles over nature: Matt 8:26; 21:19; Mark 4:39; Luke 8:24; John 21:6.

3. See Josh McDowell, *Evidence That Demands a Verdict: Historical Evidences for the Christian Faith* (2 vols.; Nashville: Thomas Nelson, 1999).

4. Albert Schweitzer, *The Quest of the Historical Jesus: A Critical Study of Its Progress from Reimarus to Wrede* (trans. W. Montgomery; 1910; repr., New York: Macmillan, 1968).

CHAPTER SIXTEEN

In the beginning was the Word, and the Word was with God, and the Word was God. He was in the beginning with God. All things came into being through him, and without him not one thing came into being. What has come into being in him was life, and the life was the light of all people. (John 1:1–4)

THE INCARNATION

16.1 Introduction

The followers of Jesus had difficulty trying to determine exactly who he was. The Apostle Peter, at one point, declared that Jesus was the Messiah—the anointed one of God—which constituted a pivotal point in the Synoptic Gospel accounts of Jesus (Matt 16:13–23; cf. Mark 8:27–33; Luke 9:18–22). The followers of Jesus knew he was more than a prophet, but it remained unclear with regard to knowing fully who he was. Throughout the Synoptic Gospels, the disciples tried to come to terms with what it meant for Jesus to be the Messiah. Usually they spoke of him as "Jesus" and only with reserve did they refer to him as the "Messiah" or, in Greek, "Christ."

The Apostle Paul became a Christian soon after Jesus' death, resurrection, and ascension. Although he claimed to have had a dramatic, personal encounter with Jesus at the time of his conversion, Paul's knowledge of Jesus mostly came after the fact. Interestingly, his references to Jesus have a loftier connotation, since he usually refers to him as "Christ" or "Christ Jesus" rather than "Jesus" or "Jesus Christ." It seems that Paul had fewer problems accepting the divine aspects of Jesus' life and ministry than the human aspects, whereas the disciples had fewer problems accepting his human aspects.

The Gospel of John is thought to have been written after the other gospels, and it provides more of a theological than historical presentation of Jesus. So, John seems less concerned about

Peter contemplating "Jesus, the Christ," and Paul contemplating "the Christ, Jesus"

chronology than about rightly presenting the person of Jesus, the Christ. John begins his gospel in dramatic style:

> In the beginning was the Word, and the Word was with God, and the Word was God. . . . And the Word became flesh and lived among us, and we have seen his glory, the glory as of a father's only son, full of grace and truth. (John 1:1, 14)

John makes it very clear that he considered Jesus—the Word—God. Truly Jesus was "Emmanuel," which means "God is with us" (Matt 1:23). But how could it be that John—a Jew, with a long tradition of monotheism and intolerance of idolatry—considered Jesus to be divine? This was not an easy concept for John or the early Christians. It was left up to later generations of Christians to struggle with what it meant for Jesus to be the "Word was God," more specifically that the "Word became flesh and lived among us." As Christians developed numerically and conceptually, the nature of Jesus became a primary focus of debate. Various views were put forth. Although debate has never fully ended, the doctrine of the incarnation became the consensual and thus orthodox view of Jesus' nature.

16.2 What Is the Incarnation?

Generally speaking, an incarnation means to embody, especially to embody in flesh. Early Christians eventually formulated the belief that Jesus was God incarnate—fully divine and fully human. This belief, however, did not arise without considerable debate and opposing points of view that significantly divided the ancient church.

Ultimately speaking, the incarnation of Jesus is a mystery. This, of course, should not surprise anyone because Christians were trying to understand the nature of God—the one who ultimately transcends our human abilities to understand and describe. Nevertheless, because of the belief that God became progressively revealed to us, Jesus was thought to be the greatest revelation of God to date. The Apostle John, for example, said, "It is God the only Son, who is close to the Father's heart, who has made him known" (John 1:18), and, "Whoever has seen me has seen the Father" (John 14:9). Jesus repeatedly communicated to his followers that he embodied the greatest revelation of God, but that revelation was not without mystery.

In the ancient church, it was as difficult for some to affirm the divinity of Jesus as it was for others to affirm his humanity. Surprisingly, that balance is as difficult for many Christians today as it was almost two thousand years ago. Despite regular temptations to resolve the mystery of the incarnation, the church tenaciously held

Christians are keepers of the mystery of Jesus Christ

> **Jesus is both human** and divine, fully one and fully the other; this is a mystery, which Christians have accepted.
>
> Jesus' humanity assures us that he understands our hopes and fears; Jesus' divinity assures us of all else God has promised.

on to the tension even though it made it difficult to defend the faith, as well as teach it from generation to generation.

Many Christians like to use the word "paradox" to describe the mystery of the incarnation because of how Jesus is described as being fully divine and fully human. It is not logical to describe Jesus as being fully divine and fully human, yet alternative explanations failed to do justice to Jesus. After all, the doctrine of the incarnation did not arise primarily as a result of idle theological speculation or of Greek philosophy imposing itself upon Christians, though these critiques are often made by opponents of the doctrine. Ancient Christians certainly speculated theologically and were influenced by Greek philosophy. But the doctrine of the incarnation arises primarily as an attempt to make sense of biblical teaching. The official canon of Scripture did not arise until the fourth century, and it was during the fourth century that most of the debate about the incarnation gave rise to the first ecumenical creed.

16.3 The Development of the Doctrine

In the fourth century, the Roman Empire finally accepted Christianity as a religion. Soon Christians openly discussed and developed their beliefs in ways previously prohibited. Although a growing consensus regarding basic Christian beliefs existed, the new freedom permitted a variety of alternative beliefs to arise. Such views were considered heretical, which originally meant only that such beliefs were different. In time, these beliefs were considered a threat to the Christian consensus.

Arianism (see discussion in ch. 6) was the first alternative belief that significantly challenged the consensus of the Christian church. Arius believed that Jesus was not God—he was not the same substance or essence of God. Jesus may have been the greatest being created by God, even greater than the angels. But he was human, not divine. This explanation made sense to many people, and Arianism increased in popularity. In response to a variety of concerns raised by the popularity of Arianism, Constantine called an ecumenical council, inviting the main church leaders from around the known world in order to discuss a variety of religious issues. At the Council of Nicea (325), Arius' beliefs were rejected, and a consensus among Christians

	Divine	Angelic	Human
Arianism		Jesus	
Monarchianism	Jesus		
Adoptionism			Jesus

Venn diagrams: Arianism, Monarchianism, and Adoptionism[1]

began to develop explicitly in the words of the Nicene Creed. Although Arianism provided a reasonable perspective, it was not thought to do justice to the words of Scripture, particularly the affirmation of both the full divinity of Jesus and his full humanity. Straying too far one way or another introduced non-biblical and theologically suspect beliefs, as we shall see.

Debate about Jesus continued during the time of the ancient church. The doctrine of the incarnation received formal definition at the Council of Chalcedon (451). The creed described Jesus as being "truly God and truly man"—consubstantial, or co-essential, with God as well as with humanity.[2] For example, in affirming the genuineness of his divine nature, Jesus was not thought to be "of like substance" (Greek, *homoiousios*) with God. Instead, Jesus was thought to be "of the same substance" (Greek, *homousios*) with God. In summary, the Chalcedonian definition did not intend to resolve the mystery of the incarnation as much as it intended to set the parameters of discussion.

In affirming the doctrine of the incarnation, alternative beliefs were rejected. For example, the following table summarizes a number of beliefs considered inadequate—heretical—for one reason or another. Their rejection often had to do with the fact that Christians were clearer about what they rejected than what they affirmed, since the essence of the incarnation remained a mystery.[3]

Interestingly, most of the so-called heresies rejected or diminished the significance of Jesus' humanity. Ebionism, on the other hand, primarily rejected or diminished the significance of Jesus' divinity. Over the centuries, numerous views of Jesus arose that, from the perspective of orthodoxy established by the ecumenical creeds, were considered questionable and a threat to biblical belief.

Most so-called variations reflect the overemphasis of either the divinity or humanity of Jesus. Over the past several centuries, the tendency increasingly emphasized Jesus' humanity, downplaying his divinity. This humanization of Jesus has appealed to people both inside and outside the church. It is easier for people to understand Jesus' humanity than his possible divinity. After all, it is easier to think of Jesus as a great moralist than to think of him as God. But non-orthodox views do not hold in tension what the ancient Christians considered essential to our understanding of Jesus, namely, that he was fully divine and fully human. Although it made Christian beliefs in Jesus excruciatingly paradoxical, Christians believed it was more truthful to Scripture to reject views that tended to be reductionistic in their attempts to make more logical their views of

> **SELF-REVEALING OF THE WORD**
>
> The Self-revealing of the Word is in every dimension—above, in creation; below, in the Incarnation; in the depth, in Hades; in the breadth, throughout the world. All things have been filled with the knowledge of God.
>
> ATHANASIUS, ON THE INCARNATION (4TH CENTURY)

Jesus. Only in an ongoing struggle with the doctrine of the incarnation will we be able to reflect humbly as well as appreciatively upon all that God accomplished through Jesus.

CHRISTOLOGICAL HERESIES

Name	Adherents	Beliefs	Problem
Ebionism	Ascetic Jewish Christians (ca. first century)	Jesus was only a human on whom the Holy Spirit descended at Jesus' baptism (Matt 3:16)	Ebionism disregards Jesus' divine nature, making him merely human—a created being.
Docetism	Gnostics (ca. first century)	Jesus was exclusively divine and merely appeared human, since physicality is evil.	Docetism disregards Jesus' human nature, giving God only the appearance of being human
Apollinarianism	Apollinarius (ca. 310–390)	In the incarnation Jesus received a new soul (or psyche)—the divine Logos, displacing his human soul or psyche.	Apollinarianism disregards the full humanity of Jesus Christ, advocating the dominance of God's will over the person of Jesus.
Nestorianism	Nestorius (ca. 351–451)	There were two separate persons in the incarnate Christ; Jesus *bore* God rather than becoming or being God.	Nestorianism denies that there can be two natures—divine and human—in one person, holding that Jesus exists as two persons rather than a unified whole.
Eutychianism	Eutyches (ca. 375–454)	After God became united with the person of Jesus, only the divine nature ruled his life.	Eutychianism diminishes and, for that reason, rejects the full humanity of Christ. God dominates Jesus' humanity.

16.4 Why Did God Become Human?

Why did God become human? What purpose did it serve for God to become incarnate? During the eleventh century, this question intrigued Anselm, and he undertook the writing of a book entitled *Cur Deus Homo* (*Why God Became Human*). Too often people think that God became human in Jesus for the purpose of salvation. This is, in fact, true. But Jesus came to do much more. The following provides a summary of reasons why God became human.[4]

16.4.1 To Reveal God to Humanity

Jesus represents the best revelation of God that we have because only in Jesus did God become incarnate. Jesus claimed that he made God known (John 1:18), and that if you had seen him, you had seen God (John 14:7–11). Christians believe that Jesus gives us the most accurate representation of the person and work of God. However, Jesus did not give a full or complete representation of God. No Christian would say that the fullness of God has been revealed. God transcends our finite human ability to understand, much less communicate. Nevertheless, no Christian would try to conceptualize God without making Jesus the decisive portrayal of God.

Jesus contemplating himself

16.4.2 To Provide an Empathetic High Priest

The book of Hebrews encourages believers by talking about how Jesus functions on our behalf as a high priest. For some, this image might make Jesus seem austere and unapproachable, especially since the notion of a high priest is alien to contemporary culture. On the contrary, the book of Hebrews argues that we should be encouraged and bold in approaching God because Jesus—our intercessor—can empathize with our humanness, based upon how he lived as a human (Heb 4:14–16). Although Jesus may not have succumbed to all the pitfalls of being human, he understands us and therefore has tremendous compassion for us. Believers may feel confident both in finding mercy for their sins and in finding gracious help for their every need.

16.4.3 To Model the Fullness of Human Life

Christians believe that our current human situation is marred by the fall of humanity into sin and the consequences that sin involves (chs. 13–14). When God became incarnate in Jesus, we saw what human life could be like without all the pitfalls of sin (1 Pet 2:21). Thus Jesus becomes our model after whom to pattern our lives, knowing that he gives believers—those who abide in God's presence—hope that their lives can become better (1 John 2:6). Remember that Christians do not believe that Jesus had unfair advantage in living his life, due to his incarnate nature; Jesus lived by the power of God's Holy Spirit, rather than by his inherent divine power (Acts 10:38). In life, Jesus humbled himself—emptying himself of his divine rights in order to fulfill all aspects of our salvation (Phil 2:5–11). This "emptying" (Greek, *kenosis*) is a crucial part of pointing out the genuineness of Jesus' humanity. As a result, Christians may look to Jesus as a genuine role model for how we are to live our lives, allowing God to work in and through us.

The "cruciality" of the cross

16.4.4 To Provide a Substitute Sacrifice

Most people think the reason God became incarnate in Jesus was to provide a substitute sacrifice or atonement on behalf of sinful humanity, which deserves death as a just punishment for their sins. This, in fact, he did, and because of Jesus' life, death, and resurrection, people have a means of being reconciled with God. Jesus vicariously represented all of humanity on the cross, dying as a ransom for our sins (Mark 10:45; 2 Cor 5:21; 1 Pet 2:24). Although he did not himself deserve to die as a punishment for sins, Jesus provided a substitute sacrifice adequate for redeeming all the sins of humanity (Heb 10:1–10). This sacrifice serves as a foundation for our later discussion of the nature and extent of Christian views of the atonement.

16.4.5 To Bind Up Demonic Powers

God became incarnate in Jesus in order to bind up and destroy the demonic powers at work in the world (1 John 3:8). The final victory of God has not yet occurred, yet Christians believe that Jesus' life, death, and resurrection provided victory over the power of Satan, demons, or whomever or whatever else confronts believers. Of course, Christians differ to the degree to which demonic powers are at work in the world. Nevertheless, they have confidence that believers must no longer submit to the evil influence of such powers. Christians who emphasize spiritual warfare do not believe that they need to fear the power of Satan and demons to possess them, though until the end times they may continue to find themselves spiritually oppressed. On the other hand, Christians who demythologize Satan and demons do not believe that they need fear the demonic powers of people in the world, manifested in institutional and social evils as well as evils that are more personal and individual in nature (Rom 8:38; Eph 6:12).

16.4.6 To Serve as a Just and Final Judge

People often fear a sense of judgment. Regardless of whether that fear is justified, Christians argue that God became incarnate in order for Jesus to serve as a fair, as well as empathetic, judge of humanity (John 5:22–27). This does not mean that believers need to fear judgment from God. On the contrary, Christians should realize that their salvation depends upon what God has done for us in Jesus rather than upon what they have done or left undone. Salvation has to do with repenting and responding in faith to Jesus. According to Jesus, such people have already "passed from death to life" (John 5:24). They may experience an earthly death, but they have been promised eternal life because of Jesus' atonement for our sins. Thus Christians do not fear final judgment because at that time they will receive fully the free gift of salvation.

16.5 Contemporary Christological Concerns

Debate about the person and work of Jesus continues today. However, the types of debate that occurred during much of Christian history differ somewhat from those that took place during the earliest centuries of the church. The ancient church seemed to struggle with views that challenged Jesus' humanity. Too many people wanted to emphasize his divinity, minimizing the genuineness of Jesus' humanity. As a result, the ecumenical councils often worked hard to uplift Jesus' humanity as well as his divinity.

During the past two centuries, the struggle has had more to do with Jesus' divinity. With a growing number of interpreters approaching the Bible as a predominantly humanly rather than divinely inspired book, the humanness and, especially, the finitude of Jesus became an issue. For example, if we focus on Jesus' humanity and avoid speculation about his divine spiritual or metaphysical nature, the meaningfulness of Jesus' human life and human ministry appear quite different. The portrait we are left with is of a very human, vulnerable person who may have struggled more than we realize with temptations and failures, and it raises the question of whether Jesus was all that confident in who he was and what God had called him to do. Some find this vulnerability to be very encouraging for people today, but it appears quite different from the orthodox view of Jesus as fully divine as well as fully human.

16.5.1 Liberation Concerns

Christians concerned about issues of liberation see a more human Jesus, empathetic with regard to the social, economic, and political problems people face today. A more human Jesus provides better encouragement to those who face marginalization, oppression, and persecution due to their poverty, ethnicity, nationality, or other cultural differences. Consideration of Jesus from a liberationist perspective reminds us of the Jesus often ignored: the Jesus who forcibly overturned tables of small business people outside the temple (Matt 21:12–27; Mark 11:15–19; Luke 19:45–46; John 2:13–17); the Jesus who condemned the religious leaders of the day (Matt 23:13–36; Luke 11:37–12:1); and the Jesus who even challenged the political leaders of his day, Jewish as well as Roman (Luke 23:1–12).

16.5.2 Feminist Concerns

Feminist theologians question whether a male savior can save women as well as men. Can a male sufficiently empathize with the needs of women in order to save them from the prejudice, injustice, and violence they experience? Conservative responses argue that it is a scandal of particularity that Jesus was born a particular gender, at a particular time, and in a particular place. Being a first-century Jew does not make Jesus any less relevant to non-Jewish, twentieth-century people. Others say that God honored women as well as men in the plan of salvation because it took a woman—Mary—along with a man—Jesus—for the incarnation to occur. This logic may appeal to those who specially venerate Mary, for example, Catholics. However, less conservative responses continue to question the relevance of a male savior for contemporary women. They argue that if we want to shed the sexism underlying historic views of the incarnation a re-imaging of Jesus needs to occur, as well as a re-imaging of God and the Trinity. Since Scripture offers female illustrations for God and for Jesus' teachings, as well as male illustrations, there needs to be more concerted effort in drawing out both gendered aspects of God in Christian beliefs, values, and practices.

Can a male savior help female people?

16.5.3 Uniqueness of Jesus

If people question the divinity of Jesus, especially in light of their growing awareness of the variety of cultural and religious expressions around the world, then people may eventually question the uniqueness of Jesus. Perhaps Christians should not be so exclusive in their claims to presenting Jesus as the way, the truth, and the life (John 14:6). In fact, a growing number of Christians challenge an exclusive approach to salvation, arguing that Christians should seek to understand and appreciate other religious expressions rather than evangelize them. Exclusivity in religion often employs a rhetoric that is unloving and may lead to violence toward others. A humble and inclusive spirit should characterize Christians' interaction with unorthodox as well as non-Christian viewpoints. Moreover, those who want to maintain the uniqueness of Jesus—as the way, the truth, and the life—need to become more aware and sensitive to how they interact with those from non-traditional expressions of Christianity or of non-Christian religions.

16.6 Conclusion

Historically, Christians have emphasized the importance of viewing Jesus as both fully divine and fully human. They have emphasized this doctrine of the incarnation, rather than settling for explanations that made the person of Jesus more understandable. Instead, Christians argued for the need to say that Jesus was both divine and human, and that the minimization of either characteristic diminishes biblical as well as doctrinal beliefs of the church. Even if people do not like the terminology of incarnation, they need to come up with some other expression that summarizes the same belief.

Christians often refer to the incarnation when speaking of their beliefs, values, and practices. The incarnation symbolizes how so many Christian practices, rituals, and ministries manifest both divine and human characteristics. Although there is no exact parallel with the doctrine of the incarnation of Christ, Christians often speak of their actions as incarnational, reflecting their human and yet divine character because God works in and through their lives. Likewise, the actions of a church, denomination, or religious movement may be referred to as a present incarnation of God's activities in the world today. The incarnational phraseology reminds Christians that they are not alone spiritually in how they speak and act.

16.7 Questions for Further Reflection

1. What does it mean to think of Jesus as being fully human and fully divine? Perhaps it would be better to think of what problems would arise, if we only thought of Jesus as being divine? Or, if we only thought of Jesus as being human?

2. Can you think of contemporary viewpoints of Jesus that reflect the heretical views of the ancient church? Why are such viewpoints sometimes referred to as heresies and the groups that hold them cults? Is such terminology warranted?

3. Reflecting upon why God became human, what reasons do you find most provocative? What reasons impress you the most personally?

4. In what ways do you think Christians act incarnationally? In what ways do you think that the church acts incarnationally?

16.8 Notes

1. Venn diagrams are often used in mathematics to illustrate the possible relationships between various groups of things. In this chart the solid circles represent Jesus as fully or essentially partaking of the represented attribute, while dotted circles represent Jesus as only partially or apparently partaking of the attribute. Thus Monarchianism represents Jesus as fully divine but only partially or apparently human.

2. "The Definition of Chalcedon," in Henry Bettenson and Chris Maunder, eds., *Documents of the Christian Church* (3d ed.; Oxford: Oxford University Press, 1999), 56.

3. This chart is an adaptation of that of House, *Charts*, 53–54.

4. The following discussion comes from Thomas Oden's summary of Anselm's *Cur Deus Homo* in *The Word of Life* (vol. 2 of *Systematic Theology;* San Francisco: Harper & Row, 1989), 102–5.

CHAPTER SEVENTEEN

If I am not doing the works of my Father, then do not believe me. But if I do them, even though you do not believe me, believe the works, so that you may know and understand that the Father is in me and I am in the Father. (John 10:37–38)

THE WORKS OF JESUS CHRIST

17.1 Introduction

The Apostle John tells the story of the time Jesus and the disciples met a man blind from birth. His disciples asked him, "Rabbi, who sinned, this man or his parents, that he was born blind?" (John 9:2). In response, Jesus turned the conversation away from causation, saying that neither the blind man nor his parents were the cause of the blindness. More specifically, sin was not the cause of the blindness. Instead, Jesus focused on how the man's blindness was an opportunity for God's work to be accomplished. He said, "We must work the works of him who sent me" (John 9:4). Jesus then made mud made with his own saliva and put it on the blind man's eyes. He then told the man to go and wash in a nearby pool. The blindness vanished.

Jesus ministered to others

In talking to the disciples, Jesus wanted to make it clear that he had a variety of works that God wanted him to accomplish. Likewise, the disciples had works that God wanted them to accomplish. God wanted to work in and through all of their lives, looking to Jesus as "the light of the world" (John 9:5).

Jesus performed many miraculous works. At one point, he appealed to such works in order to validate his divine endorsement: "If I am not doing the works of my Father, then do not believe me. But if I do them, even though you do not believe me, believe the works, so that you may know and understand that the Father is in me and I am in the Father" (John 10:37–38).

At the end of his gospel account, John said, "But there are also many other things that Jesus did; if every one of them were written down, I suppose that the world itself could not contain the books that would be written" (John 21:25). Actually, John may have come quite close to being right, since so many books have been written about Jesus!

How many books have been written about Jesus?

What happened to that blind man Jesus healed after he got lost in the crowd? Once the man had regained his sight, he, ironically, was unable to find Jesus. When the Pharisees found him, they interrogated the man and his parents about the healing and why it had occurred on the Sabbath, a breach of Sabbath laws according to the Pharisees. They wanted to discredit Jesus, but the healed man was unwilling to alter the truth of his story, implying that God's work was more important than any religious traditions. Consequently, the Pharisees denounced the man and drove him away.

Jesus found the man, encouraged him, and asked the man to believe in him (John 9:35–41). The man responded with spiritual insight by worshipping Jesus! The Pharisees stood nearby in stark contrast to the healed man, because they were blind to the person and work of Jesus. Recognizing their proud refusal to acknowledge him, Jesus told the Pharisees that their spiritual blindness demonstrated their continued bondage to sin.

17.2 The Names and Titles of Jesus

The names and titles given to Jesus in Scripture present a wide and diverse set of descriptions. Taken at face value, the names and titles of Jesus can be confusing. For example, some names and titles imply Jesus' humanity. His name was Jesus (Matt 1:21); he was referred to as the "Son of Man"—a technical term (Matt 8:20; 11:18); and Jesus was described as the son of Abraham (Matt 1:1). Moreover, Jesus was repeatedly called a man (John 1:30; 4:9; 10:38). On the other hand, some names and titles imply Jesus' divinity. He was called Immanuel (Matt 1:22), Lord (Matt 7:21; Luke 1:43), God (John 1:1; 2 Pet 1:1), "I am" (John 8:58, which reflects the divine name given in Exod 3:14; this includes a claim to pre-existence and oneness with God; see John 10:30–33), and Alpha and Omega (Rev 22:13). The names and titles by themselves do

> **During his lifetime,** Jesus preached and ministered to others, physically as well as spiritually, acting alternately as prophet, priest, and king.
>
> Jesus secured our salvation through his life, death, and resurrection. Someday he will come again, and fully bring his kingdom.

not provide precise clarity with regard to the person and work of Jesus—the Christ, the prophesied Messiah.

The doctrine of the incarnation (see discussion in ch. 16) became the ancient church's summary of the person and work of Jesus. Without intending to explain everything pertaining to Jesus, the incarnation set the parameters of the mystery of Christian beliefs. Once the ecumenical councils set those parameters with regard to Jesus, it became easier to understand what the Bible had to say about him, his ministry, and salvation.

World Heavyweight Messiah?

Of course, there have always been Christians who questioned the orthodox view of the incarnation. We studied some of them in the last chapter, and we noted that some Christians continue to challenge the doctrine of the incarnation today. So we must recognize that it remains a contested concept. Nevertheless, the overwhelming majority of Christians throughout church history have accepted the incarnation as a necessary assumption in understanding and appreciating the works of Jesus.

In summarizing the works of Jesus, Christians sometimes talk about the *estates* of Jesus and his *offices.* The estates pertain to the humbling of Jesus in becoming incarnate and to the exaltation of Jesus in his resurrection, ascension, and heavenly governance. The offices pertain to the primary ways in which Jesus fulfilled the works that God ordained for him on earth. Although these categories are not commonly known, they represent helpful ways of summarizing a variety of Jesus' works.

17.3 The Estates of Jesus Christ

The estates of Jesus generally refer to the "ascent" and "descent" that characterize the works of Jesus in Scripture, being both humbled and exalted. Such a description of Jesus' work is found in Phil 2:5–11 (cf. Heb 2:5–18). Jesus experienced humiliation in the fact that, despite his divinity, he was born, lived, suffered, and died. All people, of course, experience similar things. However, Jesus was thought to have humbled himself because he was God, who otherwise would not have had to experience human existence. This humiliation makes sense in light of the doctrine of the incarnation. Only as we understand that Jesus was the God-human, involving the theandric union (Greek, *theos,* "god" + *andros,* "man") of two natures in one person, can we appreciate what the Bible says about the humility of God in Jesus.

The Apostle Paul talks about how Jesus took the form of a slave or servant:

> Let the same mind be in you that was in Christ Jesus,
> who, though he was in the form of God,
> did not regard equality with God
> as something to be *exploited,*
> but *emptied himself,*

taking the form of a slave,
being born in human likeness.
And being found in human form,
he humbled himself
and became obedient to the point of death—
even death on a cross. (Phil 2:5–8, italics added)

Presumably, Jesus "emptied" himself (Greek, *kenoō,* related to the Greek noun *kenōsis,* "an emptying") of his divine prerogatives and authority, taking the form of a slave or servant. This "descent" oc-curred in order to achieve the work of salvation, among other things, through Jesus' life, death, and resurrection. God—rather than people—took the self-sacrificial steps necessary for providing reconciliation between people and God.

In response to his humiliation, God exalted Jesus. This "ascent" reinstated his divine preroga-tives and authority, signifying the completion of God's plans for salvation and for the eventual consummation of God's kingdom. The imagery of cross and death never encompasses the entirety of God's relationship with the world. Eventually God, through Jesus, overcomes the world and its problems (John 16:33).

Jesus "emptying" himself of his divinity?

The idea of *kenosis* strongly emphasizes the hu-manity of Jesus. However, many have questioned exactly what Jesus emptied himself of. For ex-ample, did Jesus empty himself of all his divine at-tributes, some divine attributes, or divine consciousness? Or, did Jesus retain his divine attributes but choose not to use them? Although Christians continue to question the precise meaning of *kenosis,* historic thought about the incarna-tion refuses to become too specific in trying to answer questions related to the mystery of Jesus' divine and human nature in one person.

17.4 The Offices of Jesus Christ

Jesus accomplished many works on behalf of God for the sake of humanity. One cannot easily categorize all of them. In order to simplify them, Christians often talk about the works of Jesus with regard to how he prophetically re-vealed God's will, mediated between God and people in a priestly fashion, and proclaimed and embodied God's kingly reign on earth. We will study what it means for Jesus to have worked as a prophet, priest, and king.

17.4.1 Prophet

The role of prophet had a profound impact on the religious life of Judaism. Throughout the Old Testament, prophets announced the words of God to the

> **While on earth,** Jesus did so much to provide a model for how to live our lives.
>
> As prophet, priest, and king, Jesus made other provisions by which people live abundant lives, based on truth and not on lies.

Hebrew people. Prophets served as intermediaries between God and people, challenging the latter to respond to God's concern for matters of truth and justice. Sometimes prophets served as the conscience of the Hebrews, and other times prophets predicted future events that could not otherwise be known.

Jesus served a prophetic role in his life and ministry. People acknowledged his work as a prophet (Matt 21:11, 46; Mark 6:15; Luke 7:16; 24:19; John 6:14; 7:40). Jesus proclaimed the good news, of course, and he also challenged the ongoing sinfulness of people and their hard-heartedness against God, especially pointing out the hypocrisy of religious leaders. Jesus acknowledged himself as being a prophet, representing the fulfillment of former prophets (Luke 4:16–30; 24:13–35; cf. Matt 13:57–58; 17:12). In fact, he was superior to the prophets because Jesus was more than a human prophet. He was God speaking, as the book of Hebrews says:

Are there modern-day prophets?

Long ago God spoke to our ancestors in many and various ways by the prophets, but in these last days he has spoken to us by a Son, whom he appointed heir of all things, through whom he also created the worlds. He is the reflection of God's glory and the exact imprint of God's very being, and he sustains all things by his powerful word. (Heb 1:1–3)

Prophecy and prophethood have been important Christian traditions throughout church history. Those who speak out prophetically are often thought to speak out against the status quo, however that status quo may look. For example, Francis of Assisi (1182–1226) spoke out against the materialism of the church and its dearth of spirituality; Martin Luther spoke out against the abuses of ecclesiastical power of the Roman Catholic Church; and Martin Luther King Jr. (1929–1968) spoke out against the civil injustices of racism.

17.4.2 Priest

Jesus' work as a priest differed from that of a prophet. Prophets tend to function outside the status quo of religious beliefs and institutions. Priests, on the other hand, tend to function inside them, promoting the formal worship of

God, and teaching and disciplining members of a temple, synagogue, or church. Although Jesus was not an official representative of Jewish religion, he certainly functioned in numerous priestly ways.

The book of Hebrews tells us a great deal about Jesus' priesthood. Jesus is a high priest superior to all previous high priests in the Hebrew lineage of Levi (Heb 4:14–7:28). He served as the mediator of reconciliation between God and people (Heb 2:17). Jesus was a sympathetic high priest, one who could thoroughly relate to the complexities of people's lives, yet remain sinless, affirming his superiority to the Levitical priesthood (Heb 4:14–15; 5:5; 7:26; 8:1).

The book of Hebrews uses the analogy of Jesus serving after the order of Melchizedek—an ancient priest who was thought to represent an eternal priesthood superior to the provisional and temporary priesthood of the Levites (Heb 5:1–25; cf. Gen 14:17–24). As our high priest, Jesus continues to mediate and intercede on our behalf with regard to all that holds us in sin, ignorance, bondage, and misery.

Christians no longer have high priests who function as they did in the Bible. Yet, there continue to be men and women who function in a priestly fashion in the church. Some churches have highly developed hierarchies of priests or ministers, and other churches believe in a priesthood of all believers—that everyone functions in priestly ways. We will discuss the various understandings of priesthood in the chapter on ministry (ch. 25). However, it is the case that people

Jesus' priestly works aided people

who continue to function as priests or ministers do so in a changed relationship to God. No longer do they need to offer the Levitical sacrifices on behalf of the sins of humanity. Instead, they oversee a new covenant relationship with God, because of the superiority of Jesus' sacrifice on the cross (Heb 8:1–10:39).

17.4.3 King

Throughout the Old Testament, there appear prophecies of a messiah—a savior, from the throne of David, a righteous branch—who would establish a government with order, justice, judgment, and peace (Isa 9:7; 32:1; Jer 23:5). Some Jews at the time of Jesus expected a political messiah. In fact, some of Jesus' disciples may have expected the same. However, the kingdom Jesus established represented the beginning of a course of action that would not be complete until the eschaton—the end times.

During his life, some recognized Jesus as the "King of Israel" (John 1:49; cf. Matt 2:2; 21:5). Indeed, Jesus performed miracles, healed the sick, cast out demons, and forgave sins as examples of his power and authority over all. Nothing had power and authority over him, except that which God permitted.

Only by choice did Jesus suffer as other people suffer. Then, his suffering came for a divine, salvific purpose.

Ironically, if not somewhat sardonically, Pilate, who was the Roman governor of Judea, ordered an inscription to be placed on the cross on which Jesus was crucified. It read: "Jesus of Nazareth, the King of the Jews" (John 19:19).

Jesus' miracles reflect his kingly works

Soon after Jesus' life, death, and resurrection, he was referred to as "the blessed and only Sovereign, the King of kings and Lord of lords" (1 Tim 6:15; cf. Rev 1:5; 17:14; 19:16). Although the fullness of his kingdom has not yet arrived, Jesus already reigns with grace and power in the lives of people (1 Cor 15:24–25).

The biblical imagery of kingship has had its ups and downs over the centuries. Over time, the representation of Jesus as a king became less relevant in a world in which kings played more dubious, ceremonial, and mythical roles. Likewise, the male imagery of a king has not been accessible to everyone in an era concerned about gender equality and inclusive language. Still, the notion of Jesus' king-like rule over the universe continues to be important to Christians, despite the provincialism of kingdom terminology (Phil 2:9–11; Col 2:9–10). Belief in Jesus' ultimate sovereignty continues to be a major affirmation of Christianity.

17.5 The Atonement

The word *atonement* comes from an old English term for "at-one-ment"—reconciliation between God and people. It appears in the King James translation of the Bible (1611). The terminology eventually dropped out of biblical translations but not out of theological explanations for what Jesus accomplished on the cross in reconciling the relationship between God and sinful humanity. Thus, the doctrine of the atonement articulates Christian beliefs about the provisions God made for our salvation, specifically through the work Jesus accomplished.

In the previous chapter, we discussed several reasons why Christians believe that God became human. The most conspicuous reason that God became human was to provide a means by which God saves people. However, what exactly did God accomplish through Jesus' life, death, and resurrection? That has been a matter of debate throughout the centuries. For example, to what degree did Jesus' physical death and resurrection provide an objective requirement for our salvation? This question emphasizes what God has done on our behalf. Yet, to what degree does our salvation require a subjective response of faith or repentance? This question emphasizes what we are to do in response to God.

A variety of views of the atonement arose throughout church history, and they can be categorized several ways. We will look at four general ways in which the

> **From what has God atoned,** through the work of Jesus Christ? God saved us from sin and all its atrocious effects.
>
> God continues to save us from ignorance and misery, and from all that binds us in life, so that we may be cleansed from all defects.

different views of the atonement may be summarized. Thomas Oden provides a helpful summary of these historic doctrines of the atonement, using key motifs for describing the divine provisions for salvation.[1] The motifs reflect the victor or dramatic motif, exchange or satisfaction motif, exemplar or moral influence motif, and the rector or moral governance motif.

There is no consensus in church history with regard to the particular understanding of how people receive salvation. Yet, the topic remains so important that Christians repeatedly try to conceptualize and communicate it. This endeavor benefits believers as well as those who do not yet believe. The variety of views, of course, stems from the variety of words and ideas contained in the Bible with regard to the atonement. Over the centuries, Christians have interpreted Scripture in the context of their own cultural understanding and concern. The result has been a rich, albeit sometimes confusing, doctrine. Each view, however, intends to present the best way in which to think about the atonement.

17.5.1 Victor or Dramatic Motif

The victor or dramatic motif reflects passages in Scripture that emphasize the complete bondage people experience in life and their inability to extricate themselves from the curses of sin. People are in bondage as if they are spiritual prisoners, and only Jesus can attain victory over all that enslaves them. He accomplishes this by giving his life as an appropriate ransom to free humanity (Mark 10:45). People are "bought with a price," which only God can pay through the suffering and death of Jesus (1 Cor 6:20). Only a dramatic sacrifice on the cross could save people from all that bound them in life.

Over the centuries, Christians understood this metaphor in a variety of ways. They considered the primary human predicament to be a matter of a bound will. People were in bondage to demonic captivity, and thus the ransom was paid to Satan. Others thought that people were in captivity to the to curse of sin, and perhaps a kind of ransom was paid to God, not that God needed a price per se in order to forgive people their sin. Today, people are thought to be in bondage to many things: money, power, drugs, sex, gambling, food, illness, poverty, discrimination, dehumanization, militarization, persecution, and so on. It seems as if our

Is the devil holding people captive?

bondage is becoming more complex and debilitating than we imagined in the past. It may also be, however, that it is our awareness of our bondage that makes it seem so oppressive.

In church history, Irenaeus and the "Cappadocian fathers"—Basil of Caesarea, Gregory of Nyssa, and Gregory of Nazianzus—argued that Jesus was victorious over that which held people in bondage. Over the centuries, Christians picked up on the theme of Jesus as victor—Christus Victor. The Lutheran theologian Gustaf Aulén (1879–1978) emphasized a modified ransom theory of the atonement, emphasizing a kind of cosmic victory over the power of sin and evil.[2]

17.5.2 Exchange or Satisfaction Motif

The exchange or satisfaction motif reflects passages in Scripture that emphasize the importance of the law, and how it is obeyed and fulfilled. People sin because of their transgressions against God's will, especially as God revealed it through various commandments and laws to guide people's lives. All have sinned, and God judged the result of their sin to be death (Gen 3:19; Rom 3:23; 6:23). Jesus counters this dilemma by doing what people could not, by obeying and fulfilling the law as God intended. Alluding to the original human—Adam—the Apostle Paul says, "For just as by the one man's disobedience the many were made sinners, so by the one man's obedience the many will be made righteous" (Rom 5:19). By dying on the cross, Jesus satisfied all requirements for salvation in exchanging himself for humanity and taking upon himself the just punishment of sin. The New Testament speaks of this substitutionary atonement as a sacrifice (Gal 3:13; Eph 5:2; Heb 2:9; 1 Pet 3:18), freeing us from sin by providing an acceptable substitute (Rom 3:25; 1 John 2:2; 4:10). Jesus' vicarious atonement provides the means by which people may be saved.

Sin represents the prime predicament that people experience. Because of their willful rebellion or passive indifference to God, people sinned and lost their relationship with God. Yet, they alone cannot restore their relationship, saving themselves from the punishment of their sins. Only God can provide the means by which they can be saved. Jesus serves as the voluntary and innocent sacrifice, who suffers in place of people so that they by grace through faith might receive the free gift of salvation.

Does sin dishonor God?

Anselm spoke of Jesus as having satisfied the honor of God, which had been offended due to the sins of humanity. Living during the time of the Middle Ages, Anselm interpreted Scripture in light of his feudalistic context. Jesus achieved divine satisfaction through his penitential sacrifice. During the Protestant Reformation, reformers like Calvin shifted emphasis away from appeasing God's honor to appeasing God's wrath, emphasizing that divine justice required a substitute for the penalty God exacted upon sinful humanity. Although some consider the notion of divine wrath to be incompatible with a loving God, wrath seems appropriate for a God who is both holy and righteous, as well as loving and merciful. After all, the requirement for a substitute is ultimately fulfilled by God rather than humanity.

17.5.3 Exemplar or Moral Influence Motif

The exemplar or moral influence motif reflects passages in the New Testament that emphasize the role model Jesus provided for people to follow. Jesus often told his followers that in order to be true followers they had to "deny themselves and take up their cross and follow" him (Matt 16:24). Eventually, God would "repay everyone for what has been done" (Matt 16:27). So it is important for people's salvation as well as for their day-to-day lives that they act obediently in response to Jesus' words and actions. Jesus said, "For I have set you an example, that you also should do as I have done to you. . . . If you know these things, you are blessed if you do them" (John 13:15, 17; cf. 1 Pet 2:21). This blessing reflects true Christlikeness, which is relevant for salvation.

This view of the atonement considers ignorance to be a primary human predicament. Because of human finitude, people need Jesus as the light to guide them into the truth of God's way for salvation. Christian discipleship and education help people overcome limits in their hearts, minds, and spirits. People are created in God's image, and that image becomes distorted due to the sin and evil of the world. However, Jesus helps to lead people into their full potential for love and service to God as well as to others. Thus, there is optimism to the degree to which God inspires people to accomplish their potential personally and socially. The strength of the moral influence view of the atonement comes from its emphasis upon the subjective response of people to the person and work of Jesus. God demonstrated love toward humanity in sending Jesus, and in turn God wants us to respond in love toward God and others.

During the Middle Ages, the French theologian Peter Abelard (1079–1142/23) rejected the pessimistic views of human nature held by the Catholic Church. No original sin destroyed the image of God in people, and so people should be optimistic to the degree to which they can fulfill their potential. Some relate Abelard to Pelagius, who thought that people possessed so much potential that they were responsible for their salvation. Of course, this overstates his belief, and that of Abelard, because God ultimately provides all that is necessary for living according to God's will. During the nineteenth century, Schleiermacher emphasized the moral example and influence of Jesus. Schleiermacher also resisted teaching about original sin. He thought it distracted people from their God-given potential to grow into conformity with the likeness of Jesus. People should learn to live responsibly, acting in loving and moral ways toward others as well as toward God.

Abelard was concerned about people's ignorance

17.5.4 Rector or Moral Governance Motif

The rector or moral governance motif reflects passages in the New Testament that emphasize how God provides salvation through executive clemency in order to overcome the sin and misery people experience. God did not require a wrathful or penal death sentence in order to save humanity; God, who is loving, could forgive people at any time without a blood sacrifice (Heb 10:4–10). However, God did not want to forgive humanity without upholding the righteousness and justice of God's laws, of God's moral realm. So, to uphold that moral realm, Jesus suffered on the cross in order to affirm that God's grace is not cheap. Jesus voluntarily suffered punishment on behalf of humanity, but not as their legal or penal substitute. Because Jesus was an innocent substitute, he died in order to affirm that God's laws are still in effect, even though God could save humanity without the requirement of the cross. Nowhere in Scripture does it say that Jesus was punished on the cross, but it repeatedly says that he suffered for our sake (Luke 9:22; Acts 3:18; 26:23; 1 Pet 1:11; 3:18). Instead, Jesus died in order to affirm that, although we are saved by God's clemency, God still wants us to uphold the importance of the moral realm and of living in obedience to it (1 Pet 2:21; 4:1).

Hugo Grotius (1583–1645) viewed God as ruler (rector) of the moral order of the universe, placing emphasis on the righteous governance of God. Grotius did not place emphasis upon God's need for satisfaction but on the need to maintain morality and justice. So, Jesus suffered on behalf of humanity in order to provide a substitute sufficient to affirm God's righteous governance. Believers should act responsibly in matters of morality and justice. This emphasis upon responsible Christian living appealed to the Arminian and Wesleyan traditions of the church.

Recently, the various expressions of liberation theology advocate God's concern for morality and justice, especially in the public expression of Christianity. Latin American liberation theology focuses on the misery the poor experience due to social, political, and economic injustice, as well as to the spiritual oppression of sin. Ethnic liberation theologies, such as black theology, focus on the misery people experience due to racism; feminist theologies focus on the misery due to sexism; and so on. These theologies emphasize that Christianity should be as much a public expression of God's holiness and love as a private expression, as much social as spiritual.

THAT MORTALS MIGHT GAIN ETERNITY

He took upon Him the flesh in which we have sinned, that by wearing our flesh He might forgive sins; a flesh which He shares with us by wearing it, not by sinning in it. He blotted out through death the sentence of death, that by a new creation of our race in Himself He might sweep away the penalty appointed by the former Law. . . . For Scripture had foretold that He who is God should die; that the victory and triumph of them that trust in Him lay in the fact that He, who is immortal and cannot be overcome by death, was to die that mortals might gain eternity.

HILARY, ON THE TRINITY (4TH CENTURY)

17.5.5 Summary of Atonement Motifs

More theories of the atonement exist. However, the ones mentioned above provide a broad biblical and historical summary of the doctrine. Since no consensus arose in church history, we may best approach the various doctrines of the atonement as a mosaic that provides ways in which Christians may conceptualize what Jesus did for humanity. No one way is sufficient for communicating the fullness of what Jesus provided on the cross both for salvation and for how believers should model their lives after him.

17.6 Conclusion

The works of Jesus are many, and they are crucial for the Christian understanding of salvation, for their beliefs and values, and for how they live their lives. Certainly Christianity throughout the centuries has been christocentric. That is, Jesus is central to understanding Christianity, interpreting the Bible, and applying Christian teachings to day-to-day lives, to the church and its ministries, and to the world at large.

In looking at the works of Jesus, it becomes easier to know what it means to live Christlike lives. In his works, Jesus provided for so many of the needs of humanity, showing concern for every dimension of their lives. Throughout church history, Christians have sought to know better and model better the works of Jesus.

17.7 Questions for Further Reflection

1. Why is Jesus' humiliation as important as his exaltation, especially with regard to the salvation of humanity?

2. In what ways did Jesus function prophetically? In what ways have Christians spoken prophetically throughout church history? In what ways do Christians speak prophetically today? In what ways should they speak prophetically, outside as well as inside the church?

3. How can we best appreciate the ways in which Jesus functioned in a priestly role? How can Christians best function today in similar roles?

4. What does it mean to say that Jesus is the "King of kings and Lord of lords"? What practical difference does it make in people's lives today?

5. Which view of the atonement impresses you the most? How can we learn from other views of the atonement?

6. What does it mean for Christians to be christocentric?

17.8 Notes

1. Oden, *The Word of Life,* 344–428.
2. Gustaf Aulén, *Christus Victor* (trans. A. G. Herber; Eugene, Ore.: Wipf & Stock, 2003).

THE HOLY SPIRIT

And I will ask the Father, and he will give you another Advocate, to be with you forever. This is the Spirit of truth, whom the world cannot receive, because it neither sees him nor knows him. You know him, because he abides with you, and he will be in you.

(John 14:16–17)

WHO IS THE HOLY SPIRIT?

18.1 Introduction

During his ministry, Jesus knew that religious leaders plotted to kill him. One way or another, Jesus realized that he could not remain with his disciples forever. For that reason he spent an increased amount of time alone with them. John recounts a time of intimacy, as Jesus prepared and encouraged the disciples for hard times ahead. He told them how they should relate to him, to one another, and to the world. He began this time with the disciples by saying:

> Do not let your hearts be troubled. Believe in God, believe also in me. In my Father's house there are many dwelling places. If it were not so, would I have told you that I go to prepare a place for you? (John 14:1–2; cf. John 14–17)

Jesus emphasized that he would not always be physically present with his disciples. He taught them how they should believe, hope, and love others. For example, they were to learn about God through the person, words, and works of Jesus. However, such teachings were not enough. Jesus assured the disciples that he would always be with them; he would not leave them orphaned. The spirit of his life and teachings would remain. Jesus had something—or, to be more precise, someone—that would be present with them more intimately than Jesus could ever be. He told them of a *paraclētos,* a Greek title variously translated as "advocate, comforter, helper, counselor, strengthener, supporter, adviser, or ally." This advocate would be intimately present with them forever. Jesus went on to describe the Holy Spirit in the following way:

> And I will ask the Father, and he will give you another Advocate, to be with you forever. This is the Spirit of truth, whom the world cannot receive, because it neither sees him nor knows him. You know him, because he abides with you, and he will be in you. (John 14:16–17)

The Holy Spirit represents the constant presence of God

Who was this advocate? How could this advocate be "in" them as well as "with" them? Jesus names the Holy Spirit as the one who will be the helper, whom God will send in the name of Jesus. The Holy Spirit "will teach you everything, and remind you of all that I [Jesus] have said to you" (John 14:26).

The person and work of the Holy Spirit provide essential clues to understanding Christianity and particularly its present relevance. Today, the Holy Spirit primarily serves as the one who represents "God with us." It is the Holy Spirit who works in and through the lives of people—Christians and non-Christians. If we want to know about God, it is through the person and work of the Holy Spirit that God's will is revealed and accomplished. Clearly, the Holy Spirit constitutes another mysterious, yet essential, aspect of Christianity. Consequently, if we want to know about God and matters related to God, we need to become acquainted with the Holy Spirit—the third person of the Trinity.

18.2 The Holy Spirit as Spirit

Christians refer to the Holy Spirit as the third person of the Trinity, being fully divine and fully personal. We briefly studied the Holy Spirit in an earlier chapter on the doctrine of the Trinity (ch. 6). In this chapter we will focus on the person and work of the Holy Spirit in greater depth.

Although Scripture tells us much about the Holy Spirit, the study of the Holy Spirit represents—in many ways—an exercise in theological imagination. We have to use our imagination, for example, because the Holy Spirit is "spirit"—a reality that people find difficult to understand and appreciate. God is spirit (John 4:24), so it should come as little surprise that the Holy Spirit is spirit, which the name itself signifies. Yet, the spiritual dimension of our lives continues to mystify as well as enthrall people.

Non-Christians as well as Christians have a fascination with the spiritual dimension of their lives. Some seek it zealously; others avoid it with equal zeal. Most, unfortunately, treat it with benign neglect. Nevertheless, people continue to find themselves both fascinated and drawn to the spiritual dimension—to spirituality, whether in thought, conversation, literature, or some other form.

> **The Holy Spirit** is the most mysterious personage of the Trinity, yet the most intimate divine presence.
>
> It is the Holy Spirit who now makes God's intimacy, power, and love known to us in their fullness.

Such fascination seems intrinsically mysterious, since spirituality—even our own spirituality—is not easy for us to comprehend, much less communicate. So it comes as little surprise that we find our discussion of the Holy Spirit enshrouded in mystery. In talking about the Holy Spirit, however, we should avoid indulging our imagination too much.

Michael Green (1930–) is a contemporary Pentecostal who warns us about misconceptions related to the Holy Spirit for which we should be on our guard.[1] First, Green warns us about those who consider the Holy Spirit to be so unknowable that nothing meaningful can be said. The unknowability of the Holy Spirit can also make us phobic, leaving nothing to talk about and nothing to learn about the third person of the Trinity. Second, we should beware of domesticating the Holy Spirit, limiting the Spirit's relationship to us to institutions and forms that people control rather than God. For example, we may think about the Holy Spirit only in terms of liturgy, or perhaps of charismatic power. Third, we should avoid undue emphasis upon the experience of the Holy Spirit at the expense of critical thinking. Experientially, one can become narrowly focused upon the spiritual gifts, which distracts a person from crucial insights about the holistic works of the Holy Spirit. This is why we need to begin our discussion of the Holy Spirit by focusing on that which is found in Scripture and church tradition.

What mistakes do people make in how they understand the Holy Spirit?

18.3 The Holy Spirit in Scripture

Throughout the Old Testament we find references to the Spirit of God. The Hebrew word for spirit is *ruach,* which is a feminine noun normally translated as "breath," "wind," or "spirit," depending upon the context. References in the Old Testament to the Spirit of God imply the presence and various works of God. However, like the doctrine of the Trinity, the Old Testament does not clearly distinguish the Spirit of God as anything or anyone other than a reference to the one true God. The Old Testament contains passages that speak of God's Spirit as a separate agent from the Lord, but no one anticipated the doctrine of the Trinity. From the vantage point of the New Testament, one can read the person and work of the Holy Spirit into the Old Testament, for example, at creation (Gen 1:26) and in the inspiration of prophecy (2 Pet 1:21). However, not until the writings of the New Testament do we clearly see the Holy Spirit individually identified. There the Greek word for spirit is *pneuma,* a neuter noun normally translated as "spirit." The adjective "holy" is added, resulting in the name "Holy Spirit."

New Testament reveals the person and work of the Holy Spirit progressively. The first references to the Holy Spirit seem to occur in the words of John the

**The Holy Spirit descended
on Jesus like a dove**

Baptist—the prophet of the Messiah. For example, John baptized with water, but he claimed that "one who is more powerful" would baptize "with the Holy Spirit and fire" (Matt 3:11). After John baptized Jesus in the Jordan River, the Holy Spirit descended "like a dove," as God the Father spoke audibly, stating his approval of Jesus as his son (Matt 3:16; cf. Matt 3:11–17; Mark 1:9–11; Luke 3:21–22; John 1:31–34). Christians often refer to the baptism of Jesus as one of the most significant statements of the Trinity, as well as of the individuality of the Holy Spirit.

After Jesus' baptism, the Bible interestingly talks about how the Holy Spirit guided and ministered to Jesus. Jesus was anointed by the Spirit (Acts 10:38), led and guided by the Spirit (Matt 4:1; Luke 2:27), and empowered by the Spirit (Matt 12:28; Luke 4:14). Scripture even says that Jesus was "full of the Holy Spirit" (Luke 4:1; cf. 4:14). Thus, the Holy Spirit represented an active presence in the life and ministry of Jesus. As with Jesus, the Holy Spirit represents an active presence in our lives.

Scripture provides many names for the Holy Spirit, reflecting the various attributes and works of the Holy Spirit:

- Holy Spirit (Luke 11:13; John 20:22)

- Advocate (helper, counselor, or comforter—John 14:16, 26)

- Spirit of truth (John 14:17)

- Spirit of holiness (Rom 1:4)

- Spirit of life (Rom 8:2)

- Spirit of adoption (Rom 8:15)

- Spirit of God (1 Cor 2:11)

- Spirit that is from God (1 Cor 2:12)

- The Lord, the Spirit (2 Cor 3:18)

- Spirit of faith (2 Cor 4:13)

- Eternal Spirit (Heb 9:14)

- Spirit of grace (Heb 10:29)

- Holy One (1 John 2:20)

Each name reflects a work of the Holy Spirit as well as an attribute. Such names will help us unfold the church's beliefs about the Holy Spirit.

Not readily apparent in the above names is the personal character of the Holy Spirit. Too often people today think of spirit (or spirituality) in impersonal as well as immaterial ways, yet Jesus refers to the Holy Spirit in personal terms. Although the Greek word for "Spirit" is the neuter noun *pneuma,* translators generally choose the masculine pronoun "he/him" to refer to the Spirit in order to convey the Spirit's personal nature. The Greek text, which normally uses the neuter pronoun to refer to the Spirit, does occasionally use masculine pronouns as well (John 14:26; 15:26; 16:7, 8).

Historically, Christians have referred to the Holy Spirit with male specific language, though it is understood that God ultimately transcends the distinction between male and female. Overall, Christians consider it more important to retain the personal character of the Holy Spirit than to allow the third person of the Trinity to diminish into an impersonal and immanent religious force. After all, the Holy Spirit represents the ongoing presence of Jesus—a person (John 16:13–15). It is as if Jesus continues to be with us. The Holy Spirit is Christ's spirit working in and through the life of believers. Thus, our understanding of the Holy Spirit relates interdependently with our understanding of Jesus.

The Holy Spirit is like looking at Jesus

18.4 The Development of the Doctrine

18.4.1 Early Churches

The Holy Spirit appears in the writings of the early church. However, not much effort was given to developing doctrines of the Holy Spirit. Those efforts would arise when alternative opinions (heresies) began to surface in attempts to explain biblical and other Christian references to the Holy Spirit.

Early "rules of faith" and, eventually, creeds developed in response to beliefs considered dangerously heretical. The earliest creedal concerns had to do with the person and work of Jesus, but indirectly Christians also needed to determine his relationship to God the Father and God the Holy Spirit. As a result, the Nicene Creed contains three main sections that deal with God the Father, Son, and Holy Spirit.

Nicene Creed

In particular, the Nicene Creed provides insight into both the person and works of the Holy Spirit. In fact, it says more about God the Spirit than it says about God the Father! Observe what the Nicene Creed says about Christians' belief in the Holy Spirit:

> And [I believe] in the Holy Spirit, the Lord and life-giver, who proceeds from the Father, who is worshipped and glorified together with the Father and the Son, who spoke through the prophets.[2]

Here the key works of the Holy Spirit, according to the early church, become apparent. First, Christians believed in the Holy Spirit, who was mentioned as the third person of the Trinity alongside God the Father, and God the Son. So, the work of the Holy Spirit represents the work of God.

Second, the Holy Spirit is personal—the Lord, and the work of the Holy Spirit involves a personal relationship with people (see section 3 above). The Holy Spirit is not merely a power or the impersonal "it" of some historic attempts to present a more inclusive concept of God. These terms run the risk, however, of conceptualizing the Holy Spirit as other than a person—other than a personal God working in and through people. Although there is virtue in avoiding male-exclusive language with reference to the Holy Spirit, we still have the "scandal of particularity" with regard to the specifics of how God, including the Holy Spirit, was revealed in Scripture.

What can we learn about the Holy Spirit in the earliest creeds?

Third, with regard to lordship, the Holy Spirit is the person who most immediately represents the presence and power of God in our lives. The extent of the Holy Spirit's lordship extends to the Spirit's role as the giver of life. No doubt such life is primarily understood as eternal life; however, it also refers to Christians' belief in the presence of God, the Holy Spirit, at creation, as well as at other significant times in salvation history.

Fourth, references to the Holy Spirit proceeding from the Father and the Son reflect the early church's attempt to claim that the Holy Spirit was not created, as people or angels were created. Instead the Holy Spirit processes, which signifies a unique relationship to God, just as the Son was uniquely referred to as begotten by God—not made. The concept of "procession" comes from the Greek and Latin words for "emanating" from another. This does not reflect emanationist philosophy, which sees all of reality emanating (by necessity) from one central principle of perfect being. However, the early church used the concept of procession to affirm the Holy Spirit's similarity in essence with the divine being, without losing personal distinctiveness. Thus, the work of the Holy Spirit reflects the distinctive character of Jesus as well as that of God.

Fifth, the Holy Spirit is to be worshipped and glorified, along with the Father and the Son. The Holy Spirit is no less divine than the other persons of the Trinity, so the Holy Spirit inspires as well as receives worship.

Sixth, the Holy Spirit spoke by the prophets. That is, past prophets prophesied—spoke on behalf of God—through the Holy Spirit. More specifically, the words of Scripture were thought to be inspired primarily through the work of the Holy Spirit. Second Peter 1:20–21 says, "First of all you must understand this, that no prophecy of Scripture is a matter of one's own interpretation, because no prophecy ever came by human will, but men and women moved by the Holy Spirit spoke from God."

In sum, the Nicene Creed provides a marvelous starting point for understanding the work, as well as the person, of the Holy Spirit. The ancient creeds as a whole did not exhaust the early church's view of the Holy Spirit, but they do provide a reliable starting point for further inquiry.

Apostles' Creed

Many Christians are more familiar with the Apostles' Creed than they are the Nicene Creed. The Apostles' Creed is shorter, so that is in part why it became more popular in church usage. Although the Apostles' Creed was thought to be based upon the most ancient of apostolic teaching, it was not formally adopted by churches until the eighth century. Interestingly, the Apostles' Creed says virtually nothing about the Holy Spirit, except for the fact that there is a Holy Spirit. Observe:

> I believe in the Holy Spirit.[3]

That is it! Although the Apostles' Creed is overall shorter than the Nicene Creed, it is significant that the attention given to the Holy Spirit dramatically decreased during the fourth through the eighth centuries. No doubt, this reflects a diminished amount of attention given to both the person and work of the Holy Spirit!

How fully did the disciples know the Holy Spirit?

Montanism

During the development of the early church, one notable proponent of the Holy Spirit was labeled a heretic, possibly becoming a symbol of Christian uncertainty and apprehension about the Holy Spirit. Montanus (ca. mid-second century) prophesied that a special outpouring of the Holy Spirit would result in a speedy return of the "Heavenly Jerusalem" to earth. These apocalyptic pronouncements came with ecstatic emphases, visions, and trances, which required an ascetic life in anticipation of God's return. Tertullian (ca. 155–230) adopted Montanist ideas and championed the pneumatics, or spirit-filled Christians, vis-à-vis, established church Christians.

In response to Montanism, ecclesiastical synods and the bishop of Rome formally condemned Montanist beliefs, casting aspersions upon dramatic expressions of the Holy Spirit. In fact, Montanism included the first religious views condemned as heretical by ancient churches. Thereafter, Christians seemed to expect the work of the Holy Spirit in ways that are more conventional.

Does the Holy Spirit communicate through a trance?

For example, they thought the Holy Spirit worked through the development of virtues and the spiritual disciplines.

18.4.2 Medieval Churches

The creedal reference to the Holy Spirit in the Nicene Creed became a point of controversy between the Eastern and Western churches. The Western churches, led by the Roman bishop—the pope—added a phrase to the Nicene Creed without the consent of the Eastern churches. The phrase is known as the *filioque,* which is Latin for "and the Son" or "and from the Son." It can be found in the following creedal statement: "We believe . . . in the Holy Spirit, the Lord and life-giver, who proceeds from the Father [and the Son]."[4] The latter phrase was added in order to affirm the equality of the Trinitarian relationship between God the Father, Son, and Holy Spirit. It was thought that the reference to the Holy Spirit proceeding from the Father only gave undue prominence to God the Father, diminishing the Son. Although the churches influenced by Rome had reasonable theological reasons for wanting to make the change, they did so without ecumenical consent. For this reason, the *filioque* became a theological point of contention at the schism between what became the Roman Catholic Church and the Orthodox churches in 1054.

The person of the Holy Spirit was important to both the Catholic and Orthodox churches. The Holy Spirit played an important role in Christian spirituality for both the clergy and laity, though in different ways. But in every instance, it was the Holy Spirit that was involved with empowering virtue and other saintly practices to which God calls believers.

18.4.3 Protestant Reformation Churches

The Protestant Reformers did not question the person of the Holy Spirit. They accepted the ancient creedal formulas of the Holy Spirit. The Protestant Reformers also saw the Holy Spirit at work, though they largely saw the work of the Holy Spirit in terms of guaranteeing the inspiration and authority of Scripture. The Holy Spirit not only inspired Scripture; the internal testimony (witness) of the Holy Spirit testified to the present trustworthiness and relevance of biblical teaching.

During the Enlightenment or modern era, an increased amount of attention focused upon the Holy Spirit. Christians did not question the person of the Holy Spirit, though they did question the particular work or works of the Holy Spirit. Over time, a variety of views arose, which will be studied in the next chapter. However, the historic consensus of the person of the Holy Spirit remained largely intact.

Does the Holy Spirit tell us nothing more than what we find in Scripture?

As the Enlightenment progressed, Christians increasingly became skeptical of what could be known about God. The Protestant Reformers questioned the authority of the church, but Christians also came to doubt the trustworthiness of the Bible. Some philosophers like Kant severely questioned the limits of reason with regard to religious reflection, leaving many wondering to what authority they could turn. Christians like Schleiermacher appealed to experience as the starting point in determining Christian beliefs, values, and practices. Although Schleiermacher did not intend to abolish historic Christianity, he did think it needed modification. For example, he dismissed belief in the Trinity, thinking that such views were incompatible with reason and experience. Instead, Schleiermacher considered references to the Holy Spirit to be general references to the spiritual presence and work of God.

18.4.4 Post-Reformation Churches

As Protestantism developed, a variety of views arose with regard to the works of the Holy Spirit. For example, George Fox (1624–1691) emphasized the present and active work of the Holy Spirit through what he called the "inner light." The inner light existed in everyone; it was "that of God in everyone." Fox taught that believers should be attentive to the presence of God's Spirit, which guided them with regard to the truths and will of God as well as in their relations and activism on behalf of others. The inner light could give assurance of salvation as well as inner knowledge. Of course, Fox was so thoroughly knowledgeable of Scripture that he did not see these ideas in opposition to each other. However, the Society of Friends (Quakers), who followed Fox's leadership, sometimes took his teachings into mystical directions undreamed of by Fox.

The Pietist movement, headed by the German Lutheran Philipp Jakob Spener (1635–1705), also emphasized the experiential dimension of God's presence primarily in the Holy Spirit. Spener experienced Christianity very personally and inwardly, and he encouraged others to experience the same thing. He preached, taught, and organized small devotional groups (Latin, *collegia pietatis,* "schools of piety") in order to promote heartfelt religion. Pietism had widespread influence, for example, on British Methodism.

Wesley founded Methodism with an emphasis upon evangelism, social concern, and holy living. Wesley appreciated the Pietist emphasis upon devotional groups, and he expanded them dramatically, emphasizing a greater degree of spiritual accountability. Wesley believed that the Holy Spirit was a dynamic agent of change, personally as well as socially. The Holy Spirit worked a variety of ways in people, through their consciences as well as through various instituted and prudential means of grace. Wesley thought that believers have the privilege of experiencing a second work of grace, subsequent to conversion, which leads to one's

---

TESTIMONY OF THE SPIRIT

The testimony of the Spirit is that alone by which the true knowledge of God hath been, is and can be only revealed.

THE CHIEF PRINCIPLES OF THE CHRISTIAN RELIGION AS PROFESSED BY THE PEOPLE CALLED THE QUAKERS, II (1678)

We should be careful about all views of the Holy Spirit

entire sanctification. He considered this to be a specific work of the Holy Spirit, which some described as "Holy Spirit baptism."

Schleiermacher challenged historic beliefs about the Holy Spirit. Instead of thinking about the Holy Spirit in a personal, Trinitarian way, he thought about the Holy Spirit as the spirit of the community of believers, rather than as God. Schleiermacher considered the Holy Spirit the "being of God" in the church, that is, believers in the church reflecting upon their sense of absolute dependence upon God. His beliefs tended toward a unitarian conception of God, encouraging others to downplay the person and work of the Holy Spirit as well as the divinity of Jesus.

18.4.5 Contemporary Churches

The twentieth century experienced a dramatic focus upon the Holy Spirit through the rise of the Pentecostal movement. Pentecostalism emphasizes the empowerment of the Holy Spirit in the lives of believers through Holy Spirit baptism. The movement interpreted Holy Spirit baptism as an outpouring of divine grace, subsequent to conversion, which bestowed spiritual gifts on believers. Speaking in tongues was generally considered the physical evidence of Holy Spirit baptism. The gifts of the Holy Spirit were then used in ministry for the church. Early representatives of Pentecostalism include Charles Fox Parham (1873–1929) and William J. Seymour (1870–1922). Seymour oversaw the "Azusa Street Revival," which inspired Pentecostal beliefs and practices around the world. In addition to speaking in tongues, Pentecostals also emphasized "signs and wonders," healing, and spiritual warfare. Pentecostal churches and denominations began to develop, primarily because they were not accepted by existing denominations. They had no choice but to develop independently.

How enthusiastic does God want us to be?

In the 1960s, an increasing number of Christians in existing denominations began to manifest the various gifts of the Holy Spirit, including speaking in tongues. For example, the Episcopal priest Dennis Bennett (1917–1999) and the Catholic priest David Du Plessis (1905–1987) spoke in tongues, yet remained within their respective denominations. No longer was it necessary to separate in order to manifest all the gifts of the Holy Spirit. The growing emphasis upon the Holy Spirit's bestowal of such gifts to all believers became known as the "charismatic movement." The charismatic movement, which emphasizes all the gifts of the Holy Spirit, considers speaking in tongues as one of the gifts that evidence Holy Spirit baptism. This dynamic view of the Holy Spirit progressively influenced Christianity worldwide. Some estimate that at the beginning of the twenty-first century more than half of all Christians considered themselves to be Pentecostal or charismatic.

Christians began to reconsider their beliefs about the person and works of the Holy Spirit. Whether the Pentecostal movement directly or indirectly influenced them, an increased amount of attention was directed toward developing the doctrine of the Holy Spirit. As a result, a variety of theological issues has arisen with regard to the person and works of the Holy Spirit.

18.5 Contemporary Concerns

The Trinity continues to be a topic of debate today, and the resurgence of emphasis upon the Holy Spirit drives the debate further. With regard to the Holy Spirit, an increasing approach is to reduce the Holy Spirit to a "power" or "relationship" rather than an individual "person" of the Trinity. For example, the Holy Spirit represents the power or love that binds God the Father and Jesus, or God with people. In both instances, the Holy Spirit loses individuality and personality. It resolves some of the intellectual problems related to the Trinity; it seems easier to refer to the Holy Spirit merely as God's Spirit rather than a separate center of consciousness. However, this approach to the Holy Spirit seems reductionistic, diminishing the repeated references to the Spirit as distinguished from God the Father and God the Son. Although church history has not always focused much attention on the doctrine of the Holy Spirit, the Holy Spirit has traditionally been referred to as a person—the third person of the Trinity. Changing views on the Holy Spirit would have an equally significant change upon views of the Trinity, which represents one of the most distinctive—albeit controversial—beliefs of historic Christianity.

Feminist Christians have raised another question about the Holy Spirit, wondering about the appropriateness of referring to the Spirit with male pronouns. Why do Bibles refer to the Holy Spirit as "him" when the Hebrew word for Spirit (*ruach*) is female and the Greek word for Spirit (*pneuma*) is neuter? Why do we not refer to the Spirit as "she," or, at least, "it"? Are not the biblical and subsequent theological and church references to the

Is the Holy Spirit: a) male, b) female, c) none of the above?

Holy Spirit a reflection of male-oriented interpretation, which marginalizes women and their concerns? In response, some Christians refer to the Holy Spirit using inclusive rather than male exclusive language. Of course, this response needs to make extra effort to preserve the personal understanding of the Holy Spirit.

Another debate has to do with whether the Holy Spirit and, for that matter, Jesus have a subservient relationship to God the Father in the Trinity. Such debate was increased by those who argue for hierarchical relationships permeating the whole of creation, reflective of a hierarchy of relationship within the very nature of the Trinity. Jesus, for example, while he lived on earth, repeatedly spoke of his reverence and obedience to God the Father. Is not the Holy Spirit similarly subservient to God the Father? As discussed in the chapter on the Trinity (ch. 6), such debates have occurred throughout church history. Although exceptions have arisen, the consensus of Christians has been to affirm the mutuality and interdependence of the three persons of the Trinity rather than hierarchy. Hierarchy indeed occurs in God's creation, but it is not pervasive.

18.6 Conclusion

The Holy Spirit is the immediate representative of God in our lives. Individual Christians and, indeed, churches may not always place explicit attention upon the person and works of the Holy Spirit. Since Pentecost (Acts 2:1–13), it is the Holy Spirit who is present in and who works through people. The Holy Spirit is divine—the third person of the Trinity, and thus the Holy Spirit is as personal as God the Father and Son.

Do Christians pray to the Holy Spirit? Certainly prayers, even in the Bible, are made in the name of the Father, Son, and Holy Spirit. When Christians pray to God, they pray to the Holy Spirit as much as to the Father and Son, even though specific names are not used. Most prayers in Scripture are made to God the Father, although some are made to Jesus, the Son. Consequently, explicit names used in prayers are usually to God the Father, but prayers never exclude the Son and Holy Spirit.

Pentecostalism revived Christian emphasis on the person and works of the Holy Spirit. Every Christian tradition has rethought and reemphasized the Holy Spirit. As a result, a greater understanding and appreciation of the Holy Spirit, as well as openness to the Spirit's work, arose. Although not all agree with regard to the nature and extent of the works of the Holy Spirit, all agree about the centrality of the Holy Spirit in every aspect of Christian beliefs, values, and practices.

18.7 Questions for Further Reflection

1. Who is the Holy Spirit? Who is the Holy Spirit in relationship to God the Father? and God the Son?

2. Why is it important to emphasize the personal nature of the Holy Spirit? What happens if the Holy Spirit is not considered personal?

3. What is the Holy Spirit like? In what ways is the Holy Spirit like Jesus?

4. How should we regard feminist Christian concerns about the language we use in reference to God? the Holy Spirit?

5. To whom do you pray? What does it mean to pray to God in light of the discussion of the Holy Spirit?

18.8 Notes

1. Michael Green, *I Believe in the Holy Spirit* (rev. ed.; Grand Rapids: Eerdmans, 1989), 11–15.

2. "Nicene Creed," *Encyclopedia of Christianity,* 300.

3. "Apostles' Creed," *Encyclopedia of Christianity,* 300.

4. "Nicene Creed," *Encyclopedia of Christianity,* 300; cf. 305. This version includes the *filioque,* "and the Son," which is still confessed by many, but not all, Christians in Western Christendom. The *filioque* remains a point of contention between Orthodox churches and those who affirm the Western creed.

CHAPTER NINETEEN

To each is given the manifestation of the Spirit for the common good. To one is given through the Spirit the utterance of wisdom, and to another the utterance of knowledge according to the same Spirit, to another faith by the same Spirit, to another gifts of healing by the one Spirit, to another the working of miracles, to another prophecy, to another the discernment of spirits, to another various kinds of tongues, to another the interpretation of tongues. All these are activated by one and the same Spirit, who allots to each one individually just as the Spirit chooses.
(1 Corinthians 12:7–11)

THE WORKS OF THE SPIRIT

19.1 Introduction

After Jesus died, resurrected, and ascended into heaven, Luke—the author of Acts—records that the disciples and other believers gathered in Jerusalem. On the day of Pentecost, they experienced the promised arrival of the Holy Spirit in a dramatic way. In Jewish tradition, Pentecost commemorated the giving of the Law, seven weeks after Passover. However, Luke gives Pentecost a brand new meaning:

When the day of Pentecost had come, they were all together in one place. And suddenly from heaven there came a sound like the rush of a violent wind, and it filled the entire house where they were sitting. Divided tongues, as of fire, appeared among them, and a tongue rested on each of them. All of them were filled with the Holy Spirit and began to speak in other languages, as the Spirit gave them ability. (Acts 2:1–4)

The gift of the Holy Spirit

Following this dramatic experience of the Holy Spirit, Jesus' followers began to speak in ways that everyone understood. They communicated regardless of different ethnic, cultural, or national backgrounds, coming from Parthia, Media, Elam, Mesopotamia, Judea, Cappadocia, Pontus, Asia, Phrygia, Pamphylia, Egypt, Libya, Cyrene, Rome, Crete, and Arabia. The people were truly amazed, though some thought Jesus' followers were drunk, due to the unexpected nature of their speech.

Peter responded by preaching to them about Jesus as well as the Holy Spirit, and about how Jesus provided for their salvation. From his perspective, all that happened constituted a fulfillment of Old Testament prophecy. Quoting the book of Joel, Peter said:

> In the last days it will be, God declares, that I will pour out my Spirit upon all flesh, and your sons and your daughters shall prophesy, and your young men shall see visions, and your old men shall dream dreams. (Acts 2:17, citing Joel 2:28)

Peter continued by specifying how Jesus lived, died, and resurrected. Having been exalted in heaven, the Holy Spirit then visibly and audibly arrived to those who believed in Jesus.

In response to Peter's preaching, the people asked what they should do. He said, "Repent, and be baptized every one of you in the name of Jesus Christ so that your sins may be forgiven; and you will receive the gift of the Holy Spirit" (Acts 2:38). Luke records that on the day of Pentecost about three thousand people converted and "devoted themselves to the apostles' teaching and fellowship, to the breaking of bread and the prayers" (Acts 2:42).

How does the Holy Spirit work in our lives?

What happened at Pentecost? What do we make of the physical phenomena reported—a rushing wind? the appearance of fire? the unexpected speech? What do we make of the spiritual phenomena reported—an infilling, gifting, or baptism of the Holy Spirit? boldness to speak and preach? thousands of converts? To be sure, biblical interpreters have disagreed with regard to what happened. Yet, what happened seems pivotal for the church and the ongoing development of Christianity, theologically as well as historically. Let us turn to the works of the Holy Spirit in order to understand further how God has worked and continues to work in the world.

19.2 The Biblical Background

We discussed the biblical names of the Holy Spirit in the previous chapter. The names of the Holy Spirit reflect the various attributes as well as works of the divine Spirit. Although it is unclear whether writers of the Old Testament recognized the Holy Spirit to be individually at work, the New Testament writers see the works of the Holy Spirit continuously throughout history. For example, the Holy Spirit works in creation, providence, and ministry. Old Testament references to the Spirit of God at work in anointing and empowering believers reflect the person and work of the Holy Spirit. Certainly, the New Testament identifies the divine Spirit as the one who inspired prophets and

What does the Holy Spirit do?

biblical writers prior to the coming of Jesus (2 Pet 1:20–21), as well as other works of God.

The New Testament uses a variety of types or symbols for talking about the works of the Holy Spirit. It includes the divine Spirit as a descending dove, purging fire, invisible wind, and cleansing water (Matt 3:16; Luke 3:15–18; John 3:5–8; 1 John 5:6–8). Prior to the time of Pentecost, the Holy Spirit seemed to appear and act only intermittently in the lives of people. The divine Spirit seemed to be present always with Jesus, however. It was not until after Pentecost that the Holy Spirit was thought to be present and active with everyone.

Scripture gives a surprising number of ways in which the Holy Spirit works. No historic categories encapsulate the fullness of the works of the divine Spirit. The following list summarizes some of the ways the Holy Spirit works in the lives of people. The Holy Spirit:

- Reveals God and Jesus: John 14:26; 16:13; Eph 3:2–6; 1 Tim 3:16; 4:1

- Calls people to salvation: John 14:26; 16:13; Eph 3:2–6; 1 Tim 4:1

- Gives life: John 6:63; Rom 8:11; 2 Cor 3:6; 1 Pet 3:18

- Reconciles people with God: John 3:5–8; Rom 6:3–11; 7:4–6; 8:9–11; 1 Cor 6:17–19; 12:12–13; Gal 3:14, 26–29; Eph 2:1–10; 4:3–16; Titus 3:4–7

- Regenerates: John 3:3–8; 6:63; Titus 3:5

- Indwells: John 14:17; Rom 8:9, 11; 1 Cor 12:13

- Fills believers: Eph 5:18; cf. Acts 4:8, 31; 6:3; 9:17; 11:24; 13:9

- Empowers: Rom 8:13; Gal 5:17–18, 22–23

- Baptizes: Matt 3:11; Mark 1:8; Luke 3:16; 1 Cor 12:13

- Assures of salvation: Rom 8:12–17; 2 Cor 1:22; Gal 4:6; Eph 1:13; 4:30; 1 John 3:24; 4:13; 5:7

- Teaches: John 14:26; 16:13; 1 John 2:20, 27

- Guides: John 14:17; 16:13; Gal 5:16, 25; cf. Acts 8:29; 13:2; 15:7–9; 16:6; Rom 8:14

- Sanctifies: 2 Cor 3:18; Gal 5:16–25; Jude 20–21

- Comforts: John 14–16

- Aids in prayer: Rom 8:26–27

- Gives fruit: Gal 5:22–23

- Gives gifts: Rom 12:3–13; 1 Cor 12; Eph 4:7–16; 1 Pet 4:10–11

The Holy Spirit works for the collective as well as individual good of people, especially in and through the church. The Holy Spirit inspires and serves the church in a variety of ways. They include the following:

- Inspires prophets: Neh 9:30; 2 Pet 1:20–21
- Inspires Scripture: Acts 1:16; 2 Pet 1:20–21; Rev 14:13
- Creates community and unity: Rom 5:5; 8:23; 2 Cor 5:5; Eph 1:14; 2:18; 4:30; 1 John 1:3; 3:1–10, 24
- Helps in church and pastoral decisions: Acts 15:28
- Calls to service and ministry: Acts 8:29; 13:2; 16:6–10

Although these lists are not exhaustive, they give us a glimpse of the importance of the Holy Spirit for understanding the present, dynamic relationship of "God with us." In a sense, the Holy Spirit embodies the ongoing presence of Jesus in our lives and in the world. Jesus never left us because—indeed—he is more present with us than ever, since Jesus is present in the Holy Spirit at all times and in all places.

> **Although the Holy Spirit** works like the wind, the Holy Spirit gives the gift of salvation forever.
>
> Thereafter the Holy Spirit continues to work for our comfort, encouragement, guidance, and power.

19.3 The Holy Spirit at Work

The works of the Holy Spirit are not limited to the individual. Certainly the Holy Spirit works in individuals, calling them to salvation and empowering them in various ways. The Holy Spirit also works communally in the lives of churches, enabling believers for the Christian life and for ministry. Indeed, the Holy Spirit is thought to work throughout the world. Providentially the Holy Spirit is present everywhere, acting for the benefit of people individually and collectively, inside and outside the church. The works of the Holy Spirit are interrelated with the works of God the Father and Jesus. They complement rather than contradict or upstage one another. This interrelatedness reflects the "economy" of God, that is, the interrelatedness (or interpenetration) of the three persons in the one triune God. It also reflects how each person of the Trinity works in ways that wonderfully complement all the ways God works in and through the lives of people.

19.3.1 The Holy Spirit and Scripture

Scripture describes the words of prophets as inspired by the Holy Spirit (2 Pet 1:20–21): "First of all you must understand this, that no prophecy of

Scripture is a matter of one's own interpretation, because no prophecy ever came by human will, but men and women moved by the Holy Spirit spoke from God." This verse reflects Christians' belief that the Holy Spirit not only inspires prophetic utterances, the Spirit divinely breathed (Gk., *theopneustos*, lit. "God-breathed"; 2 Tim 3:16–17) the words of Scripture, which the Nicene Creed affirms.

Among the many gifts of the Holy Spirit, discussed later in this chapter, prophecy is most often listed among spiritual gifts. This is significant because of the importance Christians place upon the word or words of God, which are spoken, written, and experienced. Prophecy, which includes both forth-telling and fore-telling God's words, constitutes a preeminent part of God's self-revelation and self-disclosure. Moreover, prophecy continued to have importance in church history, impressing upon us the ongoing presence and works of the Holy Spirit.

How much does the Holy Spirit aid the interpretation of Scripture?

In addition to inspiring Scripture, the Holy Spirit aids people in understanding it. The Holy Spirit continues to aid people in all matters related to understanding or discerning truth (John 14:26; 16:13; 1 Cor 2:13). The Holy Spirit aids people in discerning the spirits (1 Cor 2:14; 12:10; 1 John 4:1–3), whether events that occur and decisions we make are of God or not. Prayer is a primary way in which people commune with the divine.

In addition to prayer, the Bible serves as the divinely inspired guide to which believers have most often turned for discerning their beliefs, values, and practices. Traditions of the church may aid believers in decision-making, whether they pertain to individual or church matters. Of course, care needs to be used in terms of which church tradition or traditions believers use. Nevertheless, they provide a wealth of wisdom, as relevant today as when they began. Traditions of the church also aid believers in determining matters of importance in the world outside the church.

Rational thinking aids people in discernment. God-given minds allow them to think logically and thoroughly in ways that help in making decisions. Personal experience, insight gained from scientific and behavioral scientific investigation, and other resources in life may aid people in their biblical interpretation as well as Christian reflections. Finally, circumstances may sometimes aid people in discerning God's will for their lives and for the well-being of others, individually and socially.

19.3.2 The Holy Spirit and Pentecost

Pentecost was a pivotal point in church history. In fact, some consider it the beginning of the church. After Jesus ascended to heaven, the disciples were promised that the Holy Spirit would soon come upon them. One day many of

Jesus' followers, including the twelve disciples, experienced the Holy Spirit in a dramatic way. In Acts 2:1–4, people from many nations who heard the followers of Jesus speaking in tongues (or in some way they could all understand) were amazed at what they heard. Luke recounts how thousands of people converted to "the Way" (Acts 9:2; 19:23; 22:4), which became the church—all true believers in the gospel of Jesus. When people repented in response to the gospel message, Peter said, "you will receive the gift of the Holy Spirit. For the promise is for you, for your children, and for all who are far away, everyone whom the Lord our God calls to him" (Acts 2:38–39). Here the gift pertains to the new life in Jesus, and the universal call for salvation is apparent from the beginning of the church. Later in Acts, a plurality of gifts is discussed. But from the beginning, Pentecost dramatically inaugurated the growth and development of the early church.

What happened at Pentecost?

However, were the events of Pentecost associated only with the inauguration of the church? Did it represent an ongoing model of how believers are to experience the Holy Spirit? In particular, how are we to understand the speaking in tongues that apparently took place at the time of Pentecost?

Some think that Pentecost was a onetime event, that involved the pervasive coming of the Holy Spirit and the beginning of the church. The speaking in tongues that occurred was not necessarily a universal event, which all believers are to experience. Indeed, special gifts of speaking in tongues and prophecy ceased after the first century (1 Cor 13:8). This cessationist view considers speaking in tongues, interpretation of tongues, and other "signs and wonders" to be a part of how God's Spirit worked in the past. Now the Holy Spirit works differently—eminently through the teachings of Scripture.

Others think that what amazed people was not that the followers of Jesus spoke in foreign or, perhaps, angelic tongues. Instead, they all spoke in Greek, the international language. Since people who heard the followers of Jesus were from all around the world, they did not expect local people to speak in a way universally understood. As a result, they were amazed. Still others think that the followers spoke in divinely given tongues or languages, not anything that could be humanly known.

Speaking in tongues may have involved known, foreign languages so that others might understand them; it may have involved an angelic tongue, which only those filled with the Holy Spirit might speak or interpret. Speaking in tongues, along with other so-called gifts of the Holy Spirit, appears throughout the New Testament. These gifts have become a topic of concern, especially today as there has been a marked increase in accounts of Pentecostal and charismatic phenomena.

Since all the followers of Jesus spoke in tongues, might not the events of Pentecost constitute a privilege for all true believers? Should all speak in tongues and manifest one or more of the apparent gifts of the Holy Spirit? What of those who think that these dramatic gifts of the Spirit ceased? Are all such phenomena since Pentecost due to psychological misperceptions, or even demonic activity? It is to these and related questions that we now turn.

19.4 The Holy Spirit and the Christian Life

Jesus notably spoke of the Holy Spirit as the *Paraclete*, from the Greek word *paraklētos,* "an advocate." The root of this word connotes the idea of being "called to the side of people." Intimate and ever present, the Holy Spirit serves to comfort, encourage, and serve as our advocate, interceding on our behalf, guiding us to truth, and empowering our lives with divine grace.

It is not possible to discuss at length all the ways the Holy Spirit works in and through the lives of believers, the church, and the world. However, some aspects are particularly noteworthy. We will focus on the fruit, charisms, and gifts of the Holy Spirit.

19.4.1 Fruit of the Spirit

In addition to the gift of the Holy Spirit, Christians are also thought to receive the fruit of the Holy Spirit. The gift of the Holy Spirit refers to salvation (Acts 2:38; Eph 2:8–9). The fruit of the Holy Spirit is usually thought of in terms of the various character qualities or virtues of God.

Paul talks about various fruits of the Spirit. The list he gives is impressive, but it should not be considered exhaustive. In his discussion of the subject, Paul describes both vices and virtues, which was a practice common in the Greco-Roman world. However, he talks about them in terms of the liberty believers have through salvation. It is a freedom to serve and enjoy God, and to do so without self-indulgence (Gal 5:13–18). Such freedom will not come without struggle and the ongoing need for God's grace, but Paul is confident that believers who "live by the Spirit" may avoid vice and experience the various fruits of the Spirit: "love, joy, peace, patience, kindness, generosity, faithfulness, gentleness, and self-control" (Gal 5:16–23, esp. 16, 22–23). These fruits or virtues are in store for those who endeavor to live the Christian life in ongoing relationship with God's Holy Spirit.

What are the fruits of the Spirit?

19.4.2 Blessings of the Spirit

Since the time of the first-century church, Christians talk about the charismata or charisms (Greek, *charismata,* "gifts of grace"), which are gifts of grace given by the Holy Spirit. The words "charismata" and "charisms" can be used interchangeably, for example, in Catholicism. However, the charismata—or, more specifically, gifts of the Holy Spirit (1 Cor 12:4–11, 14–15)—are often thought of in quite specific terms, while charisms are thought of more generally in terms of the variety of ways God works graciously in the lives of believers. We will talk more about the gifts of the Holy Spirit in the next section, and we will focus more on charisms here.

Catholics and others in the Anglican tradition talk about the charisms that believers exhibit in life. On the one hand, believers receive the charism (gift) of salvation, and on the other hand, they receive and exercise other charisms that, among other things, build up the Christian community. Such charisms can vary widely, since all that believers say and do function graciously in relationship to others. For example, someone may be an especially insightful preacher, administrator, counselor, spiritual director, or compassionate server of those in need. All such services of love may be described as a charism that believers exercise for the benefit of others.

The expression of love, of course, is considered the greatest virtue (1 Cor 13:13) and the fulfillment of Jesus' greatest command—the command to love God with one's whole heart, soul, mind, and strength, and to love one's neighbor as oneself (Matt 22:34–40; Mark 12:28–34; Luke 10:25–28). Charisms—gifts of the Holy Spirit—and the divine favor, grace, and power they represent must always be understood in relationship to God's love and God's will for believers to exhibit love as well as faith and hope. The priority of love supersedes all discussion of the fruit, charisms, and gifts of the Holy Spirit.

19.5 The Gifts of the Holy Spirit

The gifts of the Holy Spirit are thought to be abilities and qualities that enable believers to build up the church and to minister the variety of people's needs, spiritual and physical, individual and social. The gifts of the Holy Spirit function to glorify God (1 Pet 4:11), build up the body of believers (1 Cor 12:7), and equip them for ministry (2 Cor 10:3–4). Scripture mentions these gifts but does not systematically elaborate them. As a result, opinions differ about the nature and function of the gifts of the Holy Spirit.

The gifts (plural) should be distinguished from the gift (singular) of the Holy Spirit, which describes salvation. Likewise, the gifts should be distinguished from the fruit of the Spirit (Gal 5:22–23). Nor should the gifts be reduced to human abilities, qualities, or capabilities. Although they overlap, spiritual gifts and human powers are to be distinguished.

Some Christians do not think that there are gifts given specifically by the Holy Spirit. Scripture may list various gifts as descriptions of the variety of ways believers minister rather than prescriptions of specific giftings. The fact that references to the gifts mention different sets of gifts provides reason not to think of them as unusual endowments of the Holy Spirit. From this perspective, references to the gifts of the Holy Spirit have more to do with the multiplicity of ways God

What are the gifts of the Holy Spirit?

works in and through the lives of believers. As such, so-called gifts may have more to do with charisms, broadly conceived, than discrete abilities, qualities, or capabilities empowered by the Holy Spirit.

Since the rise of Pentecostalism, Christians increasingly focused upon the gifts of the Holy Spirit. Since gifts were thought to be specifically given to believers, it became important for them to discover their gifts, use them, and discover further ways to expand upon their contribution to the kingdom of God. Since gifts are thought to be divinely given and not humanly developed, people should not presume to claim any particular gifts. Yet, God may call people to certain tasks in response to their gifts.

19.5.1 Number of Spiritual Gifts

Early church discussions of the gifts did not specify a particular number of gifts. Indeed Augustine thought there may be an unlimited number of gifts. Any specific empowerment of the Holy Spirit might be considered a spiritual gift, and this understanding reflects the idea that spiritual gifts are charisms.

Aquinas grouped the spiritual gifts in terms of those concerning knowledge, speech, and miracles. Sometimes Christians distinguish between gifts that are ordinary, reflective of the day-to-day lives of believers, and those that are extraordinary, reflective of miraculous ways God works in and through believers. A common Pentecostal division of gifts lists the nine found in 1 Cor 12:4–11. The division is made between gifts of utterance (gifts of tongues, interpretation of tongues, and prophecy), gifts of action (gifts of healing, miracles, and faith), and gifts of knowledge (gifts of knowledge, wisdom, and discernment).[1] To this division of gifts could be added others, for example, a division between gifts of witness, community, and service, or between ordinary gifts—enabling and serving gifts—and extraordinary (or dramatic) gifts, including miracles, speaking in tongues, and so on.

Below is a list of four biblical passages that talk about spiritual gifts.[2] Some Christians have shortened the list. However, others have added to it anything from exorcism (Acts 5:16; 8:6–7) to singing in a church choir (though affirming the latter as a spiritual gift has more to do with imagination than biblical precedence).

19.5.2 Extraordinary Spiritual Gifts

It lies beyond the scope of this book to discuss each spiritual gift. But some gifts of the Holy Spirit have been more unusual and dramatic than others. It is in this sense that I call them extraordinary (also known as sign gifts). They are not necessarily better or more essential to Christians and the church. In fact, Paul usually tries to relativize the various gifts, emphasizing the interdependence of the gifts for the common good (1 Cor 12:4–11).

We will discuss two sets of spiritual gifts that seem to be closely related to each other. First, prophecy represents a starting point of God's revelation to people, and discerning God's word or words is very important. Second, speaking in tongues represents one of the more famous (or infamous) manifestations of

GIFTS OF THE SPIRIT

Rom 12:6–8	1 Cor 12:4–11	1 Cor 12:28	Eph 4:11
Prophecy	Prophecy	Prophecy	Prophecy
Teaching		Teaching	Teaching
Serving			
Exhortation			
Giving			
Giving Aid			
Compassion			
	Healing	Healing	
	Working miracles	Working miracles	
	Tongues	Tongues	
	Interpretation of tongues	Interpretation of tongues	
	Wisdom		
	Knowledge		
	Faith		
	Discernment		
		Apostleship	Apostleship
		Helps	
		Administration	
			Evangelism

the gifts of the Holy Spirit, and thus deserves our attention along with its interpretation.

Prophecy and Discernment

Throughout the Bible, God made revelations to people by means of prophets—those people chosen by God to speak on behalf of God. Prophecy connotes words spoken on behalf of God, communicating divine knowledge and will for a particular place, time, and people. Although people seem most intrigued by the prophetic prospect of predicting the future, most of Scripture informs people of what God wants them to know and act upon now.

Prophetic utterances were thought to be inspired by the Holy Spirit (2 Pet 1:20–21). Unusual methods were associated with prophecy, for example, visions and dreams. Yet, God revealed God's self, salvation, and related matters by such methods.

Prophecy is also described as a gift of the Holy Spirit (Rom 12:6; 1 Cor 12:10; 14:22). Instructions are given to respect and test prophetic utterances in order to discern if they are from God (1 Thess 5:20–21). Thus it is important to think of the gift of discernment (1 Cor 12:10) in relationship to prophecy.

Scripture is filled with prophets who challenged the status quo

Indeed believers have both the right and responsibility of discerning the spirit or divine origin and truth of prophetic claims, lest they be misled. Of course, all people are expected to exercise discernment. Although some believers may be specifically gifted to discern God's truth, justice, and love, all believers are expected to be discerning and to mature in discernment. Likewise, believers are called to exhibit many of the gifts, regardless of particular gifts believers are thought to have. All are to exercise faith; all are to exercise service; all are to exercise discernment. To the measure God has given individual ability, they are responsible.

Biblical exhortations to discernment are as applicable to groups of believers as they are to individuals. Although God often chooses individuals to speak prophetically and exercise discernment, it is as important for believers collectively to do so as well. This is especially true for churches. Churches need to speak prophetically and to discern wisely how they determine their beliefs, values, and practices. They should never permit individuals to claim sole access to God and knowing God's will. Churches have the right and responsibility to discern the spirit or divine origin and truth of prophetic claims, lest they be misled as much as individuals may be misled.

Prophetic speech may lead to prophetic protest!

Today individual preachers and teachers are thought to manifest the gift of prophecy, and prophetic claims may pertain to more than matters of conversion. Many claim (or are recognized) to speak prophetically about many matters that reflect God's will. Historically, Christians spoke prophetically for the sake of justice, condemning such injustices as slavery, racism, and other wrongs committed against the poor, marginalized, or persecuted. Of course, Christians have been equally guilty of contributions to such injustices, often claiming to speak prophetically or biblically on their behalf. For this reason, prophecy should never occur without discernment, lest the claim to divine authority be abused. But discerning Christians—and churches—should not be fearful of prophetically pronouncing that which they believe God has prompted within them.

Tongues and Interpretation

After the rise of Pentecostalism, speaking in tongues flourished among Christians of all churches, denominations, and nations around the world. Its pervasiveness is as startling as its paucity prior to the twentieth century. What are we to think of speaking in tongues, and correspondingly of how to interpret it?

There are at least four ways to define speaking in tongues. First, speaking in tongues may be a known (or human) language, which may be understood by anyone familiar with it. This definition interprets Pentecost by saying that the people from the many nations were amazed to understand what the followers of Jesus were saying in their own languages (Acts 2:4–13). Second, speaking in tongues may be an unknown (or angelic) language, which would require the divine gift of interpretation, as well as speaking in tongues. This definition reflects the words of Paul, when he talks about speaking "in the tongues of mortals and of angels" (1 Cor 13:1). Third, speaking in tongues may be demonically rather than divinely inspired, which might be a view held by those who think that all the gifts of the Holy Spirit ceased after the apostolic era in the first century. This definition would be highly suspicious of any speaking in tongues and might consider it a matter of spiritual warfare. Fourth, speaking in tongues may be a psychological manifestation in a person rather than a divine gift. Of course, one could interpret the gift of tongues as indirectly due to the work of the Holy Spirit rather than directly to the Spirit's work. But when one thinks of speaking in tongues more (or altogether) in human terms, rather than divine terms, the distinctiveness of the spiritual gift diminishes.

Pentecostals initially thought of speaking in tongues as something more than a gift of the Holy Spirit. It represented the physical evidence of Holy Spirit baptism—a crisis experience subsequent to conversion, when a believer receives power (or fire)—the fullness of the Holy Spirit. Some considered speaking in tongues a third work of the Holy Spirit, subsequent to conversion and entire sanctification (or moral cleansing). Others considered it a second work, which may or may not include entire sanctification. But subsequent to conversion, God through the Holy Spirit gave believers the privilege of greater spiritual power.

This experience subsequent to conversion has sometimes been described as baptism by, in, of, or with the Holy Spirit. Despite debate over the particular preposition used, Pentecostals considered Holy Spirit baptism a special privilege and opportunity to live and minister more effectively. Sometimes Pentecostals consider speaking in tongues the initial, physical evidence of Holy Spirit baptism, while others consider it one of several evidences.

Is the widespread enthusiasm of Pentecostalism the work of the Holy Spirit?

Holy Spirit baptism may be evidenced in other ways, especially in the variety of gifts of the Spirit.

Are the utterances of one speaking in tongues words *from God to people?* If so, there needs to be interpretation, either by the person who speaks in tongues or by someone else. On the other hand, is speaking in tongues better understood as words or prayers *from people to God?* If it is understood as prayers, listeners would not expect an interpretation to include a word or words from God to people, especially if it occurs with the phraseology of prophecy. Of course, speaking in tongues may be thought to include either words from God to people, or words or prayers from people to God. That would make interpretation all the more crucial.

Public speaking in tongues can be a rich part of church worship. It can also be the cause of great consternation and divisiveness, either out of ignorance or an understanding of tongues-speaking at variance with others. Most churches that recognize and encourage speaking in tongues usually have developed guidelines for when, how, and by whom speaking in tongues is permitted. For that matter, churches that do not recognize or encourage speaking in tongues also have guidelines. It is important for the leadership in a church to clarify and communicate such guidelines if they are to positively handle public speaking in tongues.

First Corinthians 14 has much to say about speaking in tongues in public; however, people interpret it differently. For example, 1 Cor 14:40 states that churches should do all things "decently and in order." But what is decent for one church may be indecent to another, and what is orderly for one church may be disorderly to another. Members of a church or denomination need to decide how they understand and oversee speaking in tongues.

Some Christians think of speaking in tongues as more a private prayer language than a public part of worship. Of course, it may be considered both. As a private prayer language, individuals are thought to "pray with the spirit" and "pray with the mind also" (1 Cor 14:15). In the context of 1 Cor 14, some consider speaking in tongues an eminent way of relating spiritually with God, whether it be in a private or public context. It is noteworthy that Paul claimed to "speak in tongues more than all of you" (1 Cor 14:18).

What does it mean to be baptized by the Holy Spirit?

19.6 The Baptism of the Holy Spirit

Baptism, generally speaking, is an act of initiation, usually by use of water. Holy Spirit baptism refers to that which John the Baptist promised would accompany the ministry of Jesus (Matt 3:11; Mark 1:8; Luke 3:16). When did it occur? It occurred, at least, at Pentecost. Luke understood the events of Pentecost as the fulfillment of Joel 2:28–32 (see Acts 2:16–21). But was Holy Spirit baptism an event that happened once for all, or is it representative of ongoing events in the lives of believers?

Historically, salvation was not thought of as a single event. To be sure, one's conversion may occur at a particular point in time, regardless of one's consciousness of it. However, salvation was thought of more in terms of a single complex event. It began at the initiation of God's grace; it continued and developed throughout the life of a believer; and it ended with glory in heaven. However, in this life, in what discreet ways did the Holy Spirit work in and through the lives of believers? Are there multiple stages in which people relate with the Holy Spirit?

19.6.1 One Stage or Two Stages?

It is somewhat arbitrary to think of salvation in terms of one or two stages. Certainly the many bountiful ways that Christians believe God works in their lives defies reductionistic categorizations. Yet, there seem to be general categories that are useful in the beginning, at least, to look at the ways in which the Holy Spirit works or is present in believers. Historically, Christians sometimes used initiation and confirmation language in talking about salvation. For example, Catholics talked about multiple sacramental stages of baptism and confirmation. They also talked about the heightened stages of moral, ministerial, and mystical communion possible in the lives of totally consecrated believers. Some Protestants had similar views; however, emphasis more often than not was placed on the instantaneous nature of salvation, due to the decisive nature of salvation by grace through faith. References to Holy Spirit baptism had to do only with conversion rather than with the pursuit of a heightened stage of spirituality.

Some Protestants talked about a second identifiable activity of the Holy Spirit, subsequent to conversion. Wesley, for example, talked about the empowerment of the Holy Spirit available to believers, whereby they may be increasingly cleansed through faith and repentance from remaining sin in their lives. Entire sanctification represented that point, subsequent to conversion, when believers totally consecrate their lives to God. By the grace of the Holy Spirit, they are empowered to love God with their whole heart, soul, mind, and strength, and to love their neighbors as themselves. Although Wesley did not refer to entire sanctification as Holy Spirit baptism, he permitted his followers to do so in describing the experience of the Holy Spirit subsequent to conversion (Acts 8:14–17). This second stage

> **CAUSE OF ALL HOLINESS**
>
> I believe the infinite and eternal Spirit of God, equal with the Father and the Son, to be not only perfectly holy in himself, but the immediate cause of all holiness in us: enlightening our understandings, rectifying our wills and affections, renewing our natures, uniting our persons to Christ, assuring us of the adoption of sons, leading us in our actions, purifying and sanctifying our souls and bodies to a full and eternal enjoyment of God.
>
> JOHN WESLEY, "A LETTER TO A ROMAN CATHOLIC" (1749)

of Christianity was thought to be present in the lives of first-century Christians (see Acts 2; 8; 10; 19; 22).

Pentecostalism emerged out of the Wesleyan and Holiness emphases upon the work of the Holy Spirit, subsequent to conversion. When believers spoke in tongues, such experiences were thought possibly to represent a third work of God—of Holy Spirit fire! Over time, entire sanctification and empowerment with the gifts were identified with Holy Spirit baptism, or baptism in, with, or by the Holy Spirit. Some Pentecostals make a distinction between baptism *by* the Holy Spirit, which describes initiation into salvation, and baptism *in* or *with* the Holy Spirit, which describes empowerment and the fullness of the Holy Spirit. Scriptural references to the workings of the Holy Spirit in Acts suggested distinct activity in the lives of believers quite different from that of conversion. Often such workings were accompanied by speaking in tongues along with other cleansing (Acts 10:44–48; 19:5–6; cf. 2:1–4). There seemed to be, at least, two stages of workings by the Holy Spirit in the lives of totally consecrated believers.

19.6.2 Fullness of the Spirit

Believers thought to have experienced a second stage of divine grace are sometimes described as having experienced the fullness of the Holy Spirit. It refers to the Spirit's presence and control of the total life of a believer. In the Bible there are a number of instances when believers are described as being full of the Holy Spirit. For example, being full of the Holy Spirit may generally refer to the controlling disposition of believers (Luke 4:1; Acts 7:55). It may also refer to sudden inspiration (Luke 1:41, 67).

Scripture does not speak specifically about the fullness of the Holy Spirit, so some caution should be taken in how the phrase is used. At times, believers who claim the fullness of the Holy Spirit also claim a spiritual superiority that becomes judgmental of others who have not had similar experiences. Of course, spiritual superiority is not new. It has arisen among a variety of Christian traditions at different times throughout church history, usually with destructive effects. References to the fullness of the Holy Spirit should be used to encourage and challenge rather than judge others.

Is the spiritual glass half empty or half full?

19.7 Conclusion

The Holy Spirit embodies the most immediate presence of God and of God's involvement in people's lives. Theologically, prominence given to the Holy Spirit constitutes an essential doctrine for the day-to-day practices of Christians as well as for what they believe and value. Historically, Christians have not always focused adequately on either the person or works of the Holy Spirit. But they have neglected to do so to their detriment. Understanding the Holy Spirit goes a long way toward maintaining the vitality as well as content of Christianity.

Emphasis on the Holy Spirit reminds people of the ongoing presence and involvement of God in the world to reveal truth as well as salvation. The Holy Spirit calls, regenerates, baptizes, indwells, assures, comforts, intercedes, advocates, aids in prayer, empowers, teaches, guides, and sanctifies. Without this understanding, people—Christians, in particular—may overemphasize the works of God the Father, focusing more on issues of creation, providence, law, justice, and judgment. Of course, these issues are essential to Christian understanding. However, they need to be balanced with the works of the Holy Spirit. Likewise, there may also occur an overemphasis upon the works of God the Son—Jesus. Such works are, again, critical. They have to do with providing salvation, serving as a role model, being a friend as well as brother, empathizing with people, and so on. There is overlap between the works of all three persons of the Trinity; it could not be otherwise. But attention to the Holy Spirit focuses so critically on the immediate, dynamic relationship people may have with God. Whether it be through initiating salvation, or enabling the fruit, charisms, and gifts, the works of the Holy Spirit are essential to Christian beliefs, values, and practices.

19.8 Questions for Further Reflection

1. How important is the Holy Spirit in the lives of people today? in believers?

2. What are the most important ways you think the Holy Spirit works?

3. What is the relationship between the Holy Spirit and Scripture?

4. How do you distinguish between the gift and gifts of the Holy Spirit?

5. What do you think about Pentecostalism and its emphasis upon all the gifts of the Holy Spirit? What do you think about the more extraordinary gifts of the Holy Spirit?

6. What is your understanding of Holy Spirit baptism? What are implications of your understanding?

19.9 Notes

1. Green, *I Believe,* 195–248.
2. Kenneth C. Kinghorn, *Gifts of the Spirit* (Nashville: Abingdon, 1976), 38.

SALVATION

CHAPTER TWENTY

*Then I heard the voice of the Lord saying, "Whom shall
I send, and who will go for us?" And I said, "Here am
I; send me!" And he said, "Go and say to this people:
'Keep listening, but do not comprehend;
keep looking, but do not understand.'
Make the mind of this people dull, and stop their ears,
and shut their eyes,
so that they may not look with their eyes,
and listen with their ears,
and comprehend with their minds,
and turn and be healed.'"* (Isaiah 6:8–10)

GOD'S GRACE & OUR CHOICE

20.1 Introduction

The book of Isaiah recounts the story and visions of the Prophet Isaiah, who willingly responds to God's call to prophesy to a nation on the verge of being conquered and sent into foreign captivity. Isaiah's prophecies to the Israelite people relate to their social, political, and spiritual lives. The promises in Isaiah include references to future events, which extend far beyond the conquest and captivity to an "anointed" ruler, perhaps a messiah, who will graciously bring redemption to Israel. In the meantime, the Israelites were to heed the warnings and exhortations in preparation for the events to come.

When God asks, "Whom shall I send, and who will go for us?" Isaiah enthusiastically responds, "Here am I; send me!" (Isa 6:8). Isaiah's eagerness stands in stark contrast to Moses, Jeremiah, and Jonah, who reticently responded to the call of God (Exod 3:11; Jer 1:6; Jonah 1:3). However, the words God immediately wants Isaiah to speak prophetically are puzzling. They are words that seem intended more for "hardening the hearts" of people, dulling their ears and eyes, than for bringing about understanding, repentance, and healing (Isa 6:9–10). The so-called hardening of hearts gave rise to difference of opinion among Christians, spanning back to the first century. The significance of the words was not just for Isaiah's place

Are people hard-hearted?

and time. Writers of the New Testament reiterate their significance after the time of Isaiah.

Five times, writers in the New Testament paraphrase or allude to the Isaiah passage quoted above. Yet, their understanding of the passage varied. All recognized the gracious ways in which God works in and through the lives of people, including their salvation. Some references place more emphasis on what God does in and through the lives of people, and some references place more emphasis on what people are responsible for regarding their salvation. The former pertains more to what God foreordains or predestines with regard to people's salvation, and the latter pertains more to how people are responsible to accept or reject the salvation that God foreordained.

For example, the Gospels of Mark and Luke place more emphasis on what God does in and through people's lives (Mark 4:10–12; Luke 8:9–10). In both instances, the Isaiah passage appears in reference to the parables Jesus taught. Apparently, the parables hide rather than reveal truth outside Jesus' network of disciples. Like the words God directed Isaiah to prophesy to Israel, Jesus selectively revealed truth to others.

The Gospel of John stands somewhat as a transitional statement between God's divine initiation of salvation and people's response to accept or reject it (John 12:37–43). In reference to signs Jesus performed, John described their unbelief as a fulfillment of Isa 6:10: "He [God] has blinded their eyes and hardened their heart, so that they might not look with their eyes, and understand with their hearts and turn—and I would heal them" (John 12:40). Yet, John also states that some chose to believe in Jesus but would not confess it publicly "for fear that they would be put out of the synagogue" (John 12:42). Here, personal responsibility appears prominently in explaining the apparent hardness of people's hearts.

The Gospel of Matthew and the Acts of the Apostles clearly place more responsibility on people, at least for their failure to respond freely to God's gracious provision for redemption. Matthew speaks about Jesus' use of parables, and he paraphrases Isaiah differently than Mark and Luke. Matthew reports Isaiah as having said:

> You will indeed listen, but never understand, and you will indeed look, but never perceive. For this people's heart has grown dull, and their ears are hard of hearing, and they have shut their eyes; so that they might not look with their eyes, and listen with their ears, and understand with their heart and turn—and I would heal them. (Matt 13:14–15)

Luke in the Acts of the Apostles offers a similar interpretation to that of Matthew (Acts 28:25–27). Luke reports the following paraphrase by Paul, regarding why people reject God. Paul said, "For this people's heart has grown dull, and their ears are hard of hearing, and they have shut their eyes" (Acts 28:27). Ironically, the Gospel of Luke offers a different view of Isaiah than what Luke reports Paul having said (Luke 8:9–10).

What are we to make of these passages? It is not surprising that in church history a variety of views arose in trying to understand the relationship between divine initiation and human initiation—individually or collectively—in salvation. This is not to say that the Bible is inconsistent or, worse, self-contradictory. It is to say that the Bible contains a more complex and, yes, mysterious view of the relationship between divine and human roles in salvation, which is not always admitted by Christian scholars, pastors, and laity. Nevertheless, the Bible contains sufficient information for people to come to salvation and to have a mature understanding of these important dynamics. They are important not only for salvation; they are important for all of life. Just as Christians need to discern the responsibility of God and themselves for salvation, they also need to discern the responsibility of God and themselves for all aspects of their day-to-day lives. Let us begin discussion of the doctrine of salvation by investigating various Christian views of the relationship between God's initiation of salvation and people's response to it.

God or me? God and me? God alone?

20.2 The Biblical Background

When talking about the nature of God's role and people's role in salvation, we must remember that, ultimately, only God knows for sure how it is accomplished in the lives of people. Since we are talking about the work of a transcendent God in finite people, there remain certain mysteries, which we may not comprehend in this life. This certainly is true of predestination and human freedom, which are the terms that will be used in this section for talking about God's role (divine initiation) and people's role (human response). People intuitively experience a sense of responsibility, yet they know there exist numerous limitations on their freedom. How free are they? How responsible are they? What role does God play in initiating, enabling, and completing their salvation? Christians believe that God has revealed sufficient information for them to develop their beliefs, values, and practices about salvation and matters related to it. They may not be able to devise exact analyses, but they know enough to understand salvation, as well as how to live lives that are pleasing to God and satisfying to themselves.

It is sometimes difficult to understand different interpretations of Scripture because Christians with different viewpoints use the same verses to substantiate their beliefs, values, and practices. With regard to issues related to God's grace, predestination, and human freedom, numerous verses could be used. Let me list a few, for example, that suggest the sovereignty of God and of divine predestination, which emphasize the control God asserts over the lives and salvation of people. From this perspective, God is thought to ordain specifically or meticulously what occurs. Here are examples:[1]

> For surely I know the plans I have for you, says the Lord, plans for your welfare and not for harm, to give you a future with hope. (Jer 29:11)

> You did not choose me but I chose you. And I appointed you to go and bear fruit, fruit that will last, so that the Father will give you whatever you ask him in my name. (John 15:16)

> For those whom he foreknew he also predestined to be conformed to the image of his Son, in order that he might be the firstborn within a large family. (Rom 8:29)

> Blessed be the God and Father of our Lord Jesus Christ, who has blessed us in Christ with every spiritual blessing in the heavenly places, just as he chose us in Christ before the foundation of the world to be holy and blameless before him in love. (Eph 1:3–4)

On the other hand, a number of biblical passages suggest general divine sovereignty in a way compatible with human freedom. From this perspective, God is thought to be sovereign, but within that sovereignty, God permits a measure of freedom by which people may choose to accept or reject God's gracious offer of salvation. Here are examples:[2]

> Now if you are unwilling to serve the Lord, choose this day whom you will serve, whether the gods your ancestors served in the region beyond the River or the gods of the Amorites in whose land you are living; but as for me and my household, we will serve the Lord. (Josh 24:15)

> For God so loved the world that he gave his only Son, so that everyone who believes in him may not perish but may have eternal life. (John 3:16)

> For those whom he foreknew he also predestined to be conformed to the image of his Son, in order that he might be the firstborn within a large family. (Rom 8:29)

> For freedom Christ has set us free. Stand firm, therefore, and do not submit again to a yoke of slavery. (Gal 5:1)

Notice that at least one of the same Scripture passages appears in both lists. That is because scriptural passages are sometimes interpreted differently, and it will be important for us to investigate why that occurs.

20.2.1 Key Terms

In order to discuss the topics related to the divine initiation of salvation and people's response to it, we need to begin with some simple definitions. In particular, we will look at the terms of grace, predestination, and human freedom. *Grace* signifies God's dealing with humanity in undeserved ways. It involves unmerited favor from God to people, and it involves God's empowerment of people. Most notably, grace signifies a gift of God's love and goodness toward people. However, it involves more than divine favor; it also involves divine empowerment for people to be and do as God wants.

Predestination signifies God's decision in choosing who will be saved and who will be damned. Of course, divine predestination may involve God's decisions for more than the eternal destiny of the saved. In the context of this chapter, however, emphasis will be placed mostly upon understanding God's role in people's salvation. Related to predestination are the terms election and repro-bation. *Election* refers to God's decision in choosing people or groups of people for salvation or service on God's behalf. *Reprobation* refers to God's decision in choosing people or groups of people for damnation.

Human freedom represents the concept that people—to a significant degree—freely determine their own be-havior and that no external causal factors can adequately account for their actions. Differences arise, of course, with regard to what degree of freedom people possess. In the course of our discussion, we will study various ways in which Christians have understood human freedom. Understandably, there exist a number of factors that affect human decision-making: spiritual and physical, emotional and intellectual, nature and nurture, and so on. Note that the term *human freedom* is used instead of *free will* because Christians sometimes oppose the latter term, as it suggests humanism or a purely philosophical view which focuses on human potential rather than God.

Decisions, decisions!

In the context of this book, human freedom and free will are comparable terms because in each case freedom results from God's divine provision rather than from some human or evolutionary potentiality. It is still by God's grace that people have the wherewithal to choose, always within the prerogative of God.

20.2.2 Gift and Task

Christians agree that God provides salvation as a *gift*. It is a matter of grace; it is not something people earn (Eph 2:8–9). It comes at the initiation of God.

Likewise, Christians agree that salvation involves a response or *task* for which people are respon-sible, though they differ with regard to the degree to which they are responsible. All Christians ex-pect that people play some role in salvation, and great care is taken to comprehend the divine and human dynamics that occur. This is an important question, since what Christians believe in theory about their role in salvation may have a dramatic impact upon the practice of their lives and their relationships to others. What people believe im-pacts their values and their actions, personally and socially, inside and outside the church.

Salvation as both gift and task?

The precise relationship between salvation as a gift and salvation as a task is, of course, a mystery. Those who emphasize salva-tion as a gift warn against those views that run the risk of seeing salvation as something that can be earned or merited by people. On the other hand, those who emphasize the necessity of human responsibility warn against those views that run the risk of making human thoughts, words, and actions irrelevant to salvation. Based upon what we have seen so far in the Bible, it may be that God never intended to provide precise answers to certain questions people may ask about salvation. It may be that God, like a loving parent, wants us to grow as we reflect upon the question of divine and human prerogative in salvation. Instead of answering us, God challenges us to grow up as we consider the many dynamics of faith, hope, and love for God, for ourselves, and for others. Although there remain differences in degree, Christians agree that some measure of divine and human responsibility exists for salvation. It is both a gift and a task.

20.2.3 Related Terms

Foreordination is God rendering certain an event before it occurs in time. God's foreordination is sometimes known as the "decrees of God," which cannot be thwarted. Those Christian views that emphasize the sovereignty of God argue that God's decrees, like God's grace, are irresistible. In the book of Romans Paul says:

> We know that all things work together for good for those who love God, who are called according to his purpose. For those whom he foreknew he also predestined to be conformed to the image of his Son, in order that he might be the firstborn within a large family. And those whom he predestined he also called; and those whom he called he also justified; and those whom he justified he also glorified. (Rom 8:28–30)

This passage suggests that God foreordains all that happens. If God foreknows the future, it is because God's knowledge coincides with God's decrees.

Another key term is *foreknowledge.* Understanding foreknowledge in relationship to God is tricky because God is thought to exist in eternity, without restrictions upon knowledge of time as people experience it in their finitude. Basically, foreknowledge signifies God's prescience or foresight concerning future events in the lives of people. Many Christians emphasize the importance of foreknowledge for their view of predestination and human freedom, arguing that God predestines based upon what he knows in advance. Somehow God bases decisions about salvation on foreknown information about people and their decisions rather than solely on factors within God. Regardless of a person's final view, the relationship between divine foreknowledge and foreordination signifies a key element of the discussion.

20.3 Historical Development

The relationship between divine predestination and human freedom came to prominence in Augustine's response to Pelagius' view of salvation. It is difficult to determine precisely what Pelagius believed, since we have no existent writings from him. All we know comes from references made about Pelagius in the voluminous writings of Augustine. Regardless of Augustine's precision in stating the views of Pelagius, the parameters of debate as defined by Augustine's writings continued to be used by Christians throughout church history.

20.3.1 Pelagianism

Pelagianism affirms that people are born essentially good. Because they are created in God's image as part of God's good creation, they are free to do what is necessary for salvation. Their innate goodness, established by God's grace, enables people to live good lives pleasing to God. Ignorance, more than sin, prevents people from making right choices. Therefore, churches need to educate and nurture Christians in ways that please God as well as themselves. They have the primary responsibility for helping people achieve the God-given potential they receive.

In the eighteenth century, deists advocated a similar understanding of humanity and its relationship to God and creation. According to deistic teachings, reason was the primary way God wants people to learn about God and about what is important for living righteous lives. The Enlightenment undoubtedly encouraged deistic beliefs, reinforcing a growing individualism and optimism about the God-given powers people have to solve the problems of life, both individually and socially. Early founders of the United States had deistic beliefs, including such leaders as Thomas Jefferson and Benjamin Franklin. Reference to God in the Declaration of Independence is to "Nature's God"—an un-mysterious creator of the world. Like a clock maker, God created the world and left it to run on its own. The task of people is to use their minds and other human potentialities for experiencing God's creation to its fullest. One's mind, rather than prayer, is the best way for discerning matters of religious import.

Is the world a giant clock?
Is God the clock maker?

20.3.2 Semi-Pelagianism

In addition to Pelagianism, Augustine objected to the more moderate variations of Pelagius' beliefs known as semi-Pelagianism. The semi-Pelagianists generally emphasized both the grace of God and the freedom of people to work cooperatively for salvation. God brings an offer of salvation; however, humans must take the initiative to receive salvation. Salvation requires the grace of God, but people are able to approach God for salvation. Augustinians did not consider salvation as such a team effort; salvation is totally by the grace of God, given only to the elect.

In church history, John Cassian (ca. 365–433) and Abelard are identified as advocates of semi-Pelagianism. This label identifies them with heresy, since Pelagianism was considered a heresy by an early church council. Indeed, throughout church history the epithet of Pelagianism has been used indiscriminately against anyone thought to put too much emphasis upon people's responsibility for salvation, vis-à-vis God's responsibility. However, one should always be careful in labeling someone as Pelagian or even semi-Pelagian.

Interestingly, one could describe other religious traditions of the world as semi-Pelagian in the sense that responsibility is often placed largely at the feet of people for their salvation, enlightenment, or self-actualization. In fact, Christians sometimes make this distinction in contrasting Christianity with other religions. Although many religious traditions speak of redemption and salvation, people are responsible for initiating it. Christianity, on the other hand, places the onus of salvation on God. It is God and God's grace, rather than human effort or merit, which ultimately secures eternal life.

20.3.3 Augustinianism

In contrast to Pelagianism and its variations, Augustine argued that due to sin people were utterly incapable of doing anything for their salvation. People are totally depraved, in bondage to sin. Correspondingly, salvation is utterly due to the grace of God. People do nothing to merit redemption from their sin. Although Augustine did not consider people totally passive with respect to salvation, he did not think they contributed anything toward meriting it. People are to have faith, hope, and love, but if these are to be genuine, they must be generated by God's grace rather than by anything humans may do.

Augustine believed in human freedom. In fact, he considered sin to be the result of the abuse of freedom God originally gave people, particularly as found in the Genesis story of Adam and Eve (Gen 3). The primal fall of humanity prominently figures in Augustine's understanding of predestination and human freedom. Evil itself lacks being, since God did not create evil. Instead, evil arose due to people's depraved choices. Thereafter, people have been incapable of any good and are irreparably dependent on God for salvation. Due to the grace of God, some, rather than none, will receive eternal life.

According to Augustine, God foreknows the future because, from our perspective, God foreordains it. There is no distinction made chronologically between the decrees of God, God's knowledge of them, and events that occur. Since God is all-powerful and all-knowing, God both plans and enacts all that God wills for the world, for people, and for their salvation.

Reformation Theology

Throughout church history, many followed Augustine's lead in emphasizing how salvation is a gift and in de-emphasizing the role of humanity in order to avoid any hint of works-righteousness, that is, salvation by good works. The Protestant reformers Luther and Calvin, in particular, championed Augustinian ideas with regard to the sovereignty of God and the extent of divine initiation for salvation in contrast to human response. For example, Calvin placed so much emphasis on divine predestination that he developed a doctrine known as *double predestination.* Double predestination holds that God, before the creation of the world, decreed who would be saved (elect) and who would be damned (reprobate). Such decrees were not dependent on any foreknown faith, merit, or virtue on the part of the elect, or the lack thereof on the part of the reprobate. How God determined who would be saved and who would be damned was a mystery which Christians must accept rather than question. Not until people met God would they fully understand and appreciate God's love and justice.

Augustine did not use the language of double predestination, but he substantively established it. Augustine affirmed the sovereignty of God so much that life and death, salvation and damnation, were due to the decrees of God. Luther also did not use the language of double predestination, and so followers of Luther have argued that he affirmed *single predestination*: God predetermines who is saved, but the origin of sin and eternal damnation of people remains a mystery. Be that as it may, both Augustine and Luther considered God, who is sovereign, to be in complete control of all that happens. Calvin, however, considered double predestination to be the logical conclusion to the Bible's teachings on the all-powerful nature of God. He did not think that, from the perspective of systematic theology, Christians should shirk the sterner conclusions of divine revelation as found in Scripture.

Compatibilistic Freedom

Did Calvin deny human freedom? No, he affirmed it because human responsibility occurs in Scripture. However, Calvin held to what some call a *compatibilistic* view of human freedom. From his perspective, people have freedom to do that which God elects them to do. Thus, people are only free when they think, speak, and act in ways compatible with how God created them and decreed their lives to be. This view of human freedom connotes what some would call meticulous predestination, where everything that happens in life reflects God's direct will. Although God's permissive will may allow for freedom not directly ordered by God, God's perfect will for people and the world cannot be thwarted.

Philosophically, Augustinian views are sometimes referred to as *determinism,* since everything that happens seems to be determined by God, that is, by a power other than that of people or nature. Philosophical terms sometimes cloud rather than clarify theological discussions, since they bring a variety of concerns not immediately commensurate with understanding biblical and historic Christianity. Still, the terminology is related to that used by Christian theologians, so some connections are needful, if not helpful.

Although some Christians use deterministic terminology to describe their beliefs, none of them are truly deterministic in the sense that people are like automatons or robots without any freedom at all. Likewise, no Christians are really indeterministic or voluntaristic in their views of human freedom, since no one has utter freedom to determine the circumstances of their lives. In a sense, all Christians affirm some degree of synergism, which sustains a measure of cooperation between people, God, and other potential factors in decision-making. That is, there is some measure of gift and task involved with their understanding. Historically, Augustinians would be appalled at being called synergistic because it detracts from the sovereignty of God. God alone provides salvation! Yet, in affirming God's predestination as well as human freedom—

however the latter is conceived—there exists the notion of cooperation, even if the cooperation is considered essentially a mystery that no one fully comprehends. The idea of synergism captures the element of gift and task, particularly in relationship to people's salvation. Although Augustinians would put immeasurably greater emphasis upon divine initiation for salvation, they would not negate altogether the response—the task—on the part of people. Thus, compatibilistic freedom acknowledges a role on the part of people for their salvation, even though God sovereignly governs all that happens.

How much do God and people cooperate?

20.3.4 Semi-Augustinianism

Semi-Augustinianism is the view that God provides grace to all people, which enables them freely to accept or reject God's offer of salvation. Divine grace works in people's lives prior to their decisions; it is called prevenient grace. In a sense, God's grace enables people's decisions—beginning, continuing, and bringing such decisions to fruition for people's salvation. In all instances, God initiates people's movement toward salvation, so in no way do people earn or merit redemption. Nevertheless, God wants people to accept salvation freely. Their faith involves a human response, even if the precise explanation for it remains as mysterious as other aspects of God and God's relations with people.

Semi-Augustinianism is not a term with which most Christians are familiar. This is due, in part, to the tendency among Christians historically to lump all discussion of divine initiative and human response into two broad categories. People seem to contrast Augustinianism and Pelagianism. However, just as semi-Pelagianism offers a moderate view of Pelagianism, semi-Augustinianism offers a moderate view of Augustinianism. In fact, it can be argued that semi-Augustinianism is the most predominant view of predestination and human freedom throughout church history and today.

Development of Semi-Augustinianism

The ancient church benefited from most of Augustine's views. One of the exceptions was his view of predestination and human freedom. Although Augustine still exerted influence upon these topics, most Christians retained a concern for acknowledging human responsibility for salvation as well as for living a Christian life. After conciliar debate over Pelagianism and semi-Pelagianism, Christians such as Caesarius of Arles (470–543) and Gregory the Great (540–604) articulated semi-Augustinian ideas, in which God was thought to start the process of salvation and people accept or reject it. This conciliation avoided the absolute or meticulous predestination characteristic of Augustine. Semi-Augustinian ideas influenced Christianity throughout the Medieval and Renaissance periods, including both Catholic and Orthodox churches.

God restricts divine control over people in order to permit genuine freedom. In particular, God permits freedom to accept or reject the gracious offer of salvation. The self-limitation of divine power over people does not contradict the sovereignty of God because no real limitation on God's power occurs. God wants free responses on the part of people, rather than responses that they could not resist if they wanted to do so. This does not make the world chaotic; God is still in control. God's self-limitation does not include God's knowledge of the future. God foreknows the decisions people make and adjusts accordingly in order to achieve all the goals and promises God gives humanity.

Aquinas reaffirmed semi-Augustinian views of predestination and human freedom, solidifying its ideas for the Catholic Church. Aquinas emphasized the importance of human freedom for understanding the Bible's many injunctions to people for their salvation as well as for living Christlike lives. Although Aquinas lived during the Renaissance, he clearly thought that Scripture emphasized divine grace and people's responsibility for faithfully, hopefully, and lovingly obeying God and God's will, as revealed in Scripture. Aquinas rejected Pelagian and semi-Pelagian ideas, but he considered it biblically and theologically essential to affirm God's expectation for responsible human cooperation with God's grace.

Arminianism

During the Protestant Reformation, Luther vigorously debated the topics of predestination and human freedom with such scholars as Erasmus. Luther, Calvin, and the other reformers rejected Catholicism as being Pelagian or, at best, semi-Pelagian. To Luther and Calvin, the Catholic Church distorted biblical teaching by allowing for any exercise of human freedom that is not determined by God, at least, for their salvation. In wanting to avoid any possibility of works-righteousness, they considered Augustinianism more biblical and true to the spirit of Protestant principles of salvation by "grace alone" and "faith alone."

Christians do not believe they can work for or earn salvation

However, Protestants increasingly thought that Luther and Calvin had gone too far in their rejection of Catholic beliefs. In rejecting one extreme, the reformers had gone to another, focusing responsibility solely upon God for salvation. Some Christians in the Reformed tradition reacted and wanted to return to a less restricted view, considered more true to the balance in Scripture. For example, Arminius thought he was being true to Calvin as well as the Bible by advocating a semi-Augustinian view, which in time came to be known as Arminianism. In the Netherlands, the followers of Arminius wrote a Remonstrance (or response) to the prevailing Calvinist views of predestination and human freedom. A council was called in Dort, located in the Netherlands, known as the Synod of Dort (1618). The Remonstrants expected that they would be recognized as equals, and the synod would be an opportunity to discuss disputed questions. Instead, the synod summoned the Remonstrants to appear before it as defendants, and in due time their doctrines were condemned.

20.4 Calvinism and Arminianism

Although debates about predestination and human freedom have occurred among Christians for centuries, the main differences are often summarized by the distinctions between Calvinism and Arminianism. This particularly applies to Protestant debates, but it also summarizes some of the main differences between the broader historic positions of Augustinianism and semi-Augustinianism, since few describe themselves as Pelagian or semi-Pelagian. Some Christians may be caricatured as being Pelagian, but in reality they usually are not.

20.4.1 Synod of Dort

The following table summarizes the Canons of Synod of Dort.[3] The descriptions for Calvinism represent longstanding demarcations of reformed theology. Often they are referred to as the "five points of Calvinism" that deal with the themes of predestination and human freedom. The first letters of the descriptions spell the acronym "TULIP," also used to summarize Calvinist views. In order to contrast Arminianism with Calvinism, the table provides contrasting descriptions that are added in order to clarify differences with Arminianism.

THE FIVE POINTS

Calvinism (Augustinianism)	Arminianism (Semi-Augustinianism)
Total depravity: Humans begin life with all aspects of their nature corrupted by the effects of sin.	**Universality of sin:** Fallen humanity sins and cannot do good or achieve saving faith without the regenerating power of God.
Unconditional election: God's choice of certain persons to salvation is not dependent upon any foreseen virtue or faith on their part.	**Conditional election:** Election and reprobation are founded on foreseen faith or unbelief (that is, based on foreknowledge).
Limited atonement: Jesus' atoning death was only for the elect.	**Unlimited atonement:** Jesus' death is for all, but only believers enjoy his forgiveness.
Irresistible grace: Those whom God has chosen for eternal life will come to faith and thus to salvation.	**Resistible grace:** Grace represents the beginning, continuation, and end of all good, but grace is not irresistible.
Perseverance of the saints: Those who are genuine believers will endure in the faith to the end. (Cf. the idea of "eternal security"; ch. 22)	**Assurance of salvation:** Grace can preserve the faithful through every temptation so that they may be assured of their salvation, but Scripture does not clearly say people may not fall from grace and be lost.

20.4.2 Comparison

Calvinism places priority on the sovereignty of God. From its perspective, God's preeminence is most important in understanding predestination and human freedom. People, due to sin, are utterly dependent upon God, and God chooses to save some. Jesus dies on behalf of the elect, but not for all. People cannot resist God's decrees. Yet, those who are elect may be assured that God will save them, regardless of the perfect or imperfect ways they live their lives. A common misconception of Calvinism is the idea of "once saved, always saved, no matter what." Calvinists instead affirm the doctrine of *perseverence,* by which God's elect will—by grace—persevere in their faith until the end. Salvation is entirely up to the goodness and graciousness of God. Calvinists find great comfort in their belief that they do not need to do anything to merit salvation. Those who believe may be eternally assured that their faith is from God, since it is God who elects those who will believe and be saved.

A Calvinist contemplating God's predestination and an Arminian contemplating human freedom

Arminianism affirms the sovereignty of God but does not consider it inconsistent with God permitting people freedom to choose or reject God's gracious offer of salvation. All people are sinful and incapable of saving themselves, but the doctrine of total depravity may be misleading in regard to the nature and extent of sin. God elects people to be saved based on foreknowledge of who will accept divine redemption. From this perspective, Jesus indeed died for all and not just the elect. Of course, people may reject God, but that is their choice rather than God's choice. Because of Arminianism's emphasis upon human freedom, it is possible that someone may be saved and later reject it. However, Christians cannot lose their salvation accidentally, like someone might lose a wallet or purse. Someone would have to reject God intentionally and habitually before God would permit people to reject their salvation.

Arminian ideas were condemned in the Netherlands, but they spread throughout Europe. Their influence spread, for example, to Anglicanism and Methodism in Great Britain. Wesley, for example, named a journal *The Arminian* in order to distinguish Methodist beliefs about predestination and human freedom from Lutheran and Calvinist beliefs. In some ways, the appeal of Arminianism represented a moderate view within Protestant theology, which reappropriated historic Christian beliefs. Moreover, it seemed as difficult to affirm Augustinianism in practice as in

A slight difference among friends?

theory. Although people may claim to be Augustinian in theory, they often live their lives as if their choices make a difference in this life and the life to come. When you consider how widespread Arminian beliefs are among Protestants, along with similar beliefs held by Catholic, Orthodox, and Anglican churches, it becomes clear that semi-Augustinian beliefs are the most prevalent among Christians today as well as throughout church history.

20.5 Open Theism

A recent variation of semi-Augustinianism, described as open theism, or open theology, affirms that God self-limits divine power over people in order to permit them a measure of genuine freedom in accepting or rejecting God's gracious offer of salvation. Like semi-Augustinianism, God's sovereignty is not thought to be limited because God chooses to permit people some responsibility for their salvation. Some open theists believe that God self-limits not only power, but also foreknowledge. Others believe that the future is unknowable and thus does not represent a genuine limitation of God's sovereignty. If the future is set in God's mind, open theists contend, people do not genuinely have freedom to decide, and our interactions with God are disingenuous and cannot really affect God or our relationship with God. Prayer, for example, does not make sense if God already knows what we will decide. Of course, prayer from an Augustinian perspective makes even less sense to an open theist, since all has been decreed by God before the world was created. Thus, open theists say scriptural teachings about prayer and other human interaction with God, as well as their understanding of predestination and human freedom, makes more sense if we think of God as well as people as being open to the future.

What did God know, and when did God know it?

In response, Augustinians would contend that open theism further trivializes God's sovereignty. It empowers people but diminishes God. Despite numerous biblical passages to the contrary, not only does God not have control over the world, God does not even know the future. God's plans for the future are general and not specific; likewise, prophecies in Scripture were not specifically foreknown. Similarly, semi-Augustinians would say that open theists go too far in trying to preserve the personal interaction of people in relationship with God, such as in prayer. From a semi-Augustinian perspective, it is not necessary to see a causal connection between foreknowledge and foreordination. Although mystery remains, one does not need to deny God's foreknowledge in order to affirm the genuineness of human freedom.

In considering the claims of open theism, it is important to distinguish it from process theology. Process theology reflects the philosophy of Alfred North Whitehead (1861–1947), who interpreted the world and our lives as part of an ongoing process. Historically, people—Christian and non-Christian—have thought of things in terms of being. Instead, process theologians think of things in terms of process, including that which is spiritual as well as physical. Even Scripture exhibits change and process in all it discusses. From this perspective, God too is thought to be finite and in the process of change as much as people are. Open theism, on the other hand, does not consider God to be finite. God is the same God of the Bible and ancient church creeds—the almighty God, maker of heaven and earth. The prospect of God self-limiting divine power and foreknowledge does not negate the orthodox view of Christianity that open theists affirm.

20.6 Conclusion

Throughout church history, Christians have affirmed their belief in the sovereignty of God and God's gracious provisions for people's lives and for their eternal lives. Christians have also affirmed their belief in human freedom. They have differed in their views of the degree to which people have freedom, but they have affirmed it as crucial to salvation. Salvation is both a gift and a task; it involves divine initiation and human response, which people exhibit in accordance with God's will. The relationship between God's role and the role of people is, of course, ultimately a mystery, which people may not fully understand in this life. Nevertheless, in the context of this mystery, Christians affirm the sovereignty of God and God's grace, and they act responsibly, trusting in God to accomplish salvation despite their lack of understanding.

> **SERENITY PRAYER**
>
> O God, give us serenity to accept what cannot be changed, courage to change what should be changed, and wisdom to distinguish the one from the other.
>
> REINHOLD NIEBUHR (C. 1934)

Views of grace, predestination, and human freedom have significance for more than salvation. They relate to every thought, word, and action people have. They also relate to every circumstance and experience people have. The discussion of grace, predestination, and human freedom, theologically speaking, usually focuses on their redemption. However, it relates to the whole of life: the degree to which God controls it, and the degree to which people control it. This too is a mystery. Yet, Christians must decide what they think about the relationship between God's role and their role. Although they may not want to make such a decision, they do so through their

> **God gives us grace;** it is a gift. God predestines grace and events that happen.
>
> Yet, God permits people freedom of choice for day-to-day life as well as salvation.

day-to-day thoughts, words, and actions, even if they are not consciously aware of it. The more self-conscious Christians are of God's presence and involvement in their lives, the more appropriately they will view the grace of God. The more self-conscious Christians are of their responsibilities as those who are saved, who have become the children of God, the more appropriately they will view their God-given roles. The overall effect will be greater maturity as well as success in living out all God intends them to be. They will also become more aware of all the benefits God graciously desires to bestow upon them.

20.7 Questions for Further Reflection

1. What do you believe is the relationship between God's role in salvation and the role of people?

2. What do you believe about God's role and people's role in the day-to-day aspects of life? of being a Christian? Is it always the same, or might it be different from person to person, from time to time?

3. Which historic view appeals to you most: Pelagianism? Semi-Pelagianism? Augustinianism? Semi-Augustinianism? Open theism? Why?

4. Can you understand views different from your own? Can you appreciate why they believe as they do? What difference does each view make in life? for salvation?

5. Does your theory match your practice? In other words, do you act the way you say you believe? If you act differently than you believe, are you willing to modify your beliefs? your theory?

20.8 Notes

1. For other scriptural examples, see 2 Chr 20:6; Isa 14:26–27; 43:12–13; John 6:37; Acts 7:51; and Rom 9:1–12:16.

2. For other scriptural examples, see Ezek 33:11; Mark 1:15; Luke 7:28–30; Acts 7:51; Eph 1:4; 1 Tim 2:3–4; and 1 Pet 1:1–2.

3. For definitions, see Millard J. Erickson, *Concise Dictionary of Christian Theology* (Grand Rapids: Baker, 1986).

CHAPTER TWENTY-ONE

For God so loved the world that he gave his only Son,
so that everyone who believes in him may not perish
but may have eternal life. Indeed, God did not send the
Son into the world to condemn the world, but in order
that the world might be saved through him.

(John 3:16–17)

WHAT IS SALVATION?

21.1 Introduction

The Gospel of John tells of a man named Nicodemus, who came to see Jesus by night. Scripture describes Nicodemus as a leader of the Jews, perhaps a member of the Sanhedrin, which was the highest leadership in Jerusalem and presided over by the high priest. John does not state why Nicodemus came during the night, but interpreters have speculated. Was he afraid to be seen with Jesus? After all, it was dangerous for anyone to be affiliated with Jesus, regardless of one's status. Being a leader of the Jews would make his audience with Jesus especially risky. Was Nicodemus there at night because he had a busy administrative or personal schedule? Or, was it merely a spur of the moment decision on his part? We may never know the reason, and does it really matter? What mattered most is that Nicodemus came to Jesus at all. Certainly Jesus welcomed him, though he challenged Nicodemus as well. In the context of their discussion, some of the most memorable words of Jesus were spoken. They are as meaningful to us today as they were for Nicodemus.

Nicodemus began his encounter with Jesus by complementing the godliness of Jesus' teachings. Jesus responded with words that were both perplexing and challenging. He said, "Very truly, I tell you, no one can see the kingdom of God without being born from above" (John 3:3). These words are more famously known through the King James Version of the Bible, published in 1611. It says, "Verily, verily, I say unto thee, Except a man be *born again,* he cannot see the kingdom of God" (John 3:3, KJV). In addition to translations that say people must be "born again," other variations of the text say that people must be "born anew." Regardless of the precise wording or translation, Nicodemus was taken aback by Jesus' words. He did not understand what it meant to be born again.

In response, Jesus chided Nicodemus somewhat and, in a roundabout way, other religious leaders who seemed too intellectually dense or spiritually stiff-necked to comprehend, much less accept, his words. Jesus continued:

> Very truly, I tell you, no one can enter the kingdom of God without being born of water and Spirit. What is born of the flesh is flesh, and what is born of the Spirit is spirit. Do not be astonished that I said to you, "You must be born from above." The wind blows where it chooses, and you hear the sound of it, but you do not know where it comes from or where it goes. So it is with everyone who is born of the Spirit. (John 3:5–8, NRSV)

Apparently, Jesus says that salvation comes through both the water of baptism, and through the Spirit. He describes spiritual matters, which Nicodemus has difficulty understanding. Yet, Nicodemus was impacted by Jesus' words, despite the fact that no details are given about the end of his conversation with Jesus that night. Later, when Jesus was being discussed, it was Nicodemus who bravely argued on Jesus' behalf, despite the groundswell among the leaders of the Jews to crucify Jesus (John 7:50–51).

What does it mean to be "born again"?

Near the end of the story of the encounter between Jesus and Nicodemus, John writes the following words, "For God so loved the world that he gave his only Son, so that everyone who believes in him may not perish but may have eternal life" (John 3:16). This verse embodies the gospel—the "good news"—of Jesus' life and ministry. They are the words of salvation, of eternal life. To be sure, there is a great deal more to salvation than being "born again," but it is a great place to start a discussion of the fullness of God's redemption for humanity.

21.2 The Order of Salvation

In Scripture, those who were converted by the good news of Christianity were predominantly adults, as is evidenced by Nicodemus. During the time of the apostolic church—the church recorded in the Bible—most conversions to Christianity seem to be instantaneous rather than gradual. We need to be careful, however, about making first-century experiences of salvation normative for all time. In fact, even as we study the Bible there appear a variety of conversion experiences. Rather than provide a set *ordo salutis,* or "order of salvation," Scripture describes a variety of experiences, uniquely reflecting the gracious work of God for salvation in the lives of individuals as well as groups of individuals. The variety does not seem to exhaust the possible ways people become Christians. On the contrary, it suggests that God works in many wondrous ways in the lives of people, dealing with their salvation in ways specific to them. Certainly it is God's will that all be saved, regardless of particularities in the way it occurs (1 Tim 2:4).

21.2.1 Biblical Background

Is there an "order of salvation"?

Perhaps the first reference to evangelism, after the death, resurrection, and ascension of Jesus, provides one of the best summaries of how people convert to Christianity. On the day of Pentecost, Peter spoke on behalf of the disciples and preached about Jesus to the masses, empowered by the person and presence of the Holy Spirit. In response, the people "were cut to the heart" and asked, "Brothers, what should we do?" (Acts 2:37). Peter said:

> Repent, and be baptized every one of you in the name of Jesus Christ so that your sins may be forgiven; and you will receive the gift of the Holy Spirit. (Acts 2:38)

Note the order Peter describes: Repent, be baptized, and receive the gift of the Holy Spirit. This message is extraordinary for several reasons. First, it reminds us of the importance of repentance and of baptism for the forgiveness of sins. These actions are essential for a holistic biblical understanding of salvation. Second, it talks about salvation as the gift of the Holy Spirit. Here the gift of the Holy Spirit follows baptism, but elsewhere in Acts it occurs in different ways, serving as a caution to us against ordering salvation too rigidly (see Acts 8:16; 10:44; 18:26; 19:5–6). Third, Peter's order of salvation does not specifically mention faith, which elsewhere figures prominently in biblical descriptions of it. Although faith is certainly implied, its absence serves as a caution against describing God's way of salvation too narrowly or dogmatically.

21.2.2 Instantaneous Conversions

In Scripture, most Christians seem to have had instantaneous conversions, such as the three thousand people who converted and were baptized on the day of Pentecost (Acts 2:41). Paul, too, had a dramatic conversion with his vision of Jesus on the Damascus road, which resulted in temporary blindness until Ananias laid hands on Paul and baptized him (Acts 9:1–19). The conversions of most Christians, however, are not documented in the Bible. In fact, there is scriptural evidence that people converted in a variety of ways, sometimes reporting

---

Becoming a Christian is both easy and hard. One the one hand, salvation is God's free gift of eternal life. On the other hand, God wants us to make a total commitment. Salvation is both a gift and a task. It is a relationship with God which, once received, requires continual nurture.

immediate baptism and sometimes not, and sometimes reporting immediate speaking in tongues and sometimes not.

Evangelism!

Throughout church history, evangelism has constituted an important expression of Christian obedience to God and love for others. Indeed, it constitutes a powerful expression of Christian spirituality, albeit not the only one. Without evangelism, Christianity could have never spread the good news of Jesus. The church could never have grown, as God intends it to do. In Christians' zeal to evangelize, however, they have not always done so with sufficient self-awareness of their motives and methods. In addition, they have not always done so with sufficient awareness of how their cultural, political, and sometimes militaristic backgrounds have distorted the gospel message. Colonialism, for example, sent mixed messages to those being evangelized. It was not always clear whether the message of Jesus was being proclaimed, or an entire socio-economic and political worldview that incorporated elements not present in Jesus' teachings. Thus, Christians need to avoid cultural triumphalism or any other evangelistic approach that coerces rather than persuades people of the good news of salvation.

21.2.3 Gradual Conversions

Christians do not agree as to when the disciples were converted to Christianity. Was it when they first decided to follow Jesus as disciples (Matt 4:18–22; Mark 2:13–14)? Was it when they did evangelism, healed the sick, and cast out demons (Luke 10:1–20)? Was it when Peter first declared Jesus to be "the Messiah, the Son of the living God" (Matt 16:16; Mark 8:29)? Was it when Jesus "breathed on them [the disciples] and said to them, 'Receive the Holy Spirit'" (John 20:22)? Was it when Jesus' disciples and other followers experienced Pentecost: "All of them were filled with the Holy Spirit and began to speak in other languages, as the Spirit gave them ability" (Acts 2:4)? If the disciples did not convert to Christianity until well into Jesus' ministry, it would seem that they did not have dramatic conversion experiences. On the contrary, their relationship with Jesus would have grown slowly until they finally recognized him as the Christ—the Messiah. Whenever the disciples converted, Christians agree that they did become true converts, true believers, though their experiences do not provide a prototype or order of salvation, which all subsequent converts must follow.

Is conversion more like a leap or a stroll?

In the decades and centuries after the apostolic period of the church, practices, rites, and rituals became associated with Christianity. Many related to the conversion of new Christians as well as the baptism and nurture of the children of adult Christians into the church, into Christian faith and practice. The practices, rites, and rituals of the church served to nurture young children into Christianity as well as to facilitate the conversion of adults. Scripture, along with the traditions of the church, served to bring a growing number of people to salvation.

Gradual conversions are just as valid as instantaneous conversions, and vice versa. At times, Christians have been tempted to elevate the importance of one type of conversion over another, or to disavow certain types altogether. However, the validity of people's salvation should not have to do with how immediately or protractedly it occurs.

21.3 Church Developments

Until midway through the second millennium, Christians did not focus upon a so-called order of salvation (*ordo salutis*). There was general agreement about how salvation occurred. Of course, there were differences of opinion, even after the schism between the Catholic and Orthodox churches. However, their view of salvation remained largely the same. It was not until after the Protestant Reformation that significant differences arose among Christians with regard to the order of salvation. In fact, some of the more pronounced differences occurred among the Protestants. I will summarize some of the key issues questioned.

21.3.1 Catholicism and Orthodox Churches

After Constantine became ruler of the Roman Empire in the fourth century, Christianity no longer consisted of a persecuted minority. It became respectable, and within decades, Christianity became the official religion of the empire. This relatively quick transition has been praised as well as condemned by Christians and non-Christians alike. Mass conversions occurred to Christianity, not always through a genuine embrace of Jesus as Savior and Lord. Instead, they involved cultural conversions that had more to do with self-advancement or self-preservation than with Christian beliefs, values, and practices. Still, it finally became possible for Christians to reflect upon their centuries of existence and development, which included the development of the church as well as an official canon of Scripture. Over subsequent centuries, Christians developed their doctrines about salvation and just about every other topic imaginable.

Both the Catholic and Orthodox churches have a sacramental view of salvation. That is, they believe that God ordained the church as a means by which God's grace is given to people both for salvation and for growth as Christians. Salvation requires faith, but God also requires the church to serve as the channel through which grace was given, primarily through the seven sacraments of the church. Although there are differences between Catholic and Orthodox Christian views of the sacraments, they are sufficiently the same so that in our present discussion we may focus on the former.

The Catholic Church affirms seven sacraments, thought to be established by Jesus himself as specific means by which God mediates divine grace to people.

Most of the sacraments pertain to people's salvation and for their growth in grace. They include baptism, confirmation, Holy Eucharist (communion), penance (reconciliation), and anointing of the sick. Catholics also believe in the sacraments of holy marriage and holy orders, by which God sanctifies those who marry and those called into full-time ordained ministry. The sacraments themselves guarantee grace not otherwise available to believers, and belief is expected for worthily partaking of the sacraments. Thus, when people are baptized, including infants, they receive saving grace. When people complete confirmation, they receive added grace of the Holy Spirit in their lives. When people partake of Holy Eucharist, they partake of the blood and body of Jesus more realistically than most could imagine, which gives grace to comfort, encourage, and strengthen believers. When people participate in penance (or reconciliation), they confess their sins, intend to amend their lives, make appropriate penance for their sins, and receive grace that empowers them to live in accordance with their

God's representatives for conversion

new resolve. When people receive the anointing of the sick, they receive special healing grace for that which curses them spiritually as well as physically. More will be said about the sacraments in a later chapter.

If people want to become Christians, then they need to seek out those in the Catholic Church who can prepare them for baptism. Their desire to become a Christian does not come from their own initiative but by the prevenient grace of God. Prevenient grace is divinely enabling grace to believe. The pursuit of salvation usually involves communication with a priest, but not necessarily. Most people who join the church do so by being born into it. That is, they are baptized as infants, confirmed, and then take their first communion, having affirmed the Christian faith into which they had been baptized. From the Catholic perspective, most conversions to Christianity occur through a gradual process of nurture and discipleship, either as an infant or as an adult. Yet, it is through the church that God intends for people to be saved and embrace the church. As the Catholic Catechism says, quoting Cyprian of Carthage (d. 258): "No one can have God as Father who does not have the church as mother."[1]

21.3.2 Protestant Views

The Protestant reformers disagreed with the Catholic Church. From their perspective, Catholicism had distorted key biblical principles that distinguished Protestantism. They included "grace alone," "faith alone," and "Scripture alone." Of course, grace alone signified that only God provided salvation, and no one needed the church as a mediator. Faith alone signified that faith formed the most important qualifier of true Christianity, emphasizing people's personal trust in God. Even the principle of Scripture alone signified that the

Bible constituted God's most reliable witness to matters of Christian beliefs, values, and practices—not the Catholic Church or other church traditions. The sacraments (or ordinances) were valued, albeit only two of them—baptism and communion. However, the sacraments did not guarantee divine grace. Instead, faith was the requirement for worthily participating in and benefiting from baptism and communion.[2]

Because of the tendency toward individualism among Protestants, there soon arose a variety of Christian traditions. They varied in many ways, including their views of salvation. As time past, an increasing number of Protestants felt a need to distinguish between the various traditions, and orders of salvation were devised in order to distinguish one from another. Even within particular traditions, there occurred differences of opinion. However, distinctions arose that differentiated one Protestant tradition from another. Below is a chart that identifies some of the differences. Keep in mind that the orders are descriptive more than normative, and there undoubtedly exist differences of opinion with regard to precise orders of salvation. Thus, I used several sources for creating the chart, reflective of various individual theological traditions.[3] Be that as it may, it serves only as a starting point for introducing different Protestant views of the order of salvation.

PROTESTANT ORDERS OF SALVATION

Lutheranism	Calvinism	Arminianism	Wesleyanism
	Election		
	Predestination		
	Union with Christ		
	Effectual calling		
Calling	Effectual calling	Calling	Calling
Illumination			
Conversion*		Faith	Conversion*
		Repentance	
Regeneration	Regeneration	Regeneration	Regeneration
	Faith		
	Repentance		
Justification	Justification	Justification	Justification
		Perseverance	Assurance
Sanctification	Sanctification		Repentance after justification and gradual sanctification
Union with Christ			Entire sanctification
Glorification	Glorification	Glorification	Glorification

* Conversion = faith + repentance.

Comparison

In some respects, each order of salvation takes people to the same goal: glorification (or eternal life) with God in heaven. It is the same place, by the way, to which Catholicism and Orthodox churches take people: glorification. How then are they different? Many of the differences will be discussed throughout the remainder of the chapter. One of the biggest differences has to do with their respective views of predestination and human freedom. Calvinism, for example, places great emphasis upon divine predestination, reflecting Augustinian roots. Election appears at the very beginning of the order of salvation. Lutheranism also emphasizes divine predestination, but it does not appear as clearly in the order of salvation. Arminianism and Wesleyanism reflect semi-Augustinian views of predestination and human freedom, placing emphasis on the responsibility of people to accept or reject God's gracious offer of salvation.

The remainder of the chapter includes a discussion of the various aspects of salvation mentioned above. I will discuss Catholic and Orthodox church views of the various aspects of salvation, along with representative Protestant views. Salvation, it seems, does not involve a single moment or component of redemption. Instead, salvation is a single complex event, involving several dynamics of God's grace in people's lives. Although we may identify salvation with such things as conversion, faith, regeneration, or justification, the whole of salvation involves more. As such, salvation has a relational as well as juridical dimension. That is, it has to do with more than guilt and forgiveness of sin. It has to do with estrangement from God and, in turn, people's reconciliation with God. The dynamic between the material and relational aspects of salvation appear over and over again in understanding salvation, holistically conceived. However, for the sake of this study, I will discuss salvation by looking at its constituent parts.

21.4 Grace, Calling, and Illumination

We discussed grace in the last chapter. It signifies God's unmerited favor and empowerment for salvation as well as for living a Christian life. From an Augustinian view of predestination and human freedom, God's grace governs those who are saved. Calvin, for example, would say that the call of God for salvation is irresistible. Calling represents God's summons to salvation. From Calvin's perspective, God's calling is an effectual calling, that is, it is irresistible. It is based upon God's predestination, which God decreed long before now. Based upon people's divine election, Calvin thought that they obtain union with God, which secures the righteousness of God by virtue of the atonement provided by Jesus. It is salvation completed entirely by God for the elect, since people are dead in sin and utterly incapable of contributing to their own salvation.

From a semi-Augustinian view, God provides prevenient grace to people, enabling them to respond to God's grace and calling to salvation. They may then decide to respond to God, cooperating with divine grace for salvation. Prevenient grace was affirmed by Catholics. It was also affirmed by Protestants like Wesley, who talked about "free grace" rather than "free will," since he never wanted people to think that they somehow earned or deserved the calling and salvation offered by God. Nevertheless, God wants people genuinely to believe in God and to genuinely love God and others.

Luther talked about the illumination he thought people gained after having responded to the calling of God. Illumination involves the presence and work of the Holy Spirit to clarify truths about God and salvation, especially truths found in the Bible. Luther had high regard for the way God wants people to respond intellectually as well as willfully to the calling of God. Christianity did not call for a blind leap of faith. On the contrary, God wants Christians to be well informed and mature in their understanding of spiritual truths.

21.5 Conversion

Do you hear God calling?

Conversion is a turning to God and a turning away from sin. Those who become Christians are called converts, that is, those who are saved (1 Tim 3:6). Conversion involves both faith and repentance. However, conversion-language is not used by all Christians in talking about salvation. Instead, the language of faith and repentance may be used, though the meaning remains much the same. Conversion is thought to bring about a new life and relationship with God, which God enables. To some Christians, conversion is synonymous with salvation. In fact, Christians use many terms for identifying salvation. It may be identified as faith, repentance, regeneration, or justification. All of these terms have, from time to time, been used to describe salvation. The diversity of terms emphasizes the importance of salvation as well as differences in how Christians think salvation occurs, when it occurs, and to whom it occurs.

Which comes first: faith or repentance? Some Christians consider the order important, since placing repentance first, as an act of obedience, makes it appear as if people initiate conversion rather than God. Of course, putting faith first runs the same risk, though Christians do not generally think so. Overall, most consider faith first as a theological topic, though chronologically they occur simultaneously. The two are thought to be inextricably bound up with one another. Saving faith includes repentance, and saving repentance includes faith. Regardless, Christians generally consider both faith and repentance essential to conversion to Christianity. Thus, when Christians preach evangelistically, they usually preach both faith and repentance. To preach repentance without faith is legalism, and to preach faith without repentance is what Dietrich Bonhoeffer (1906–1945) described as "cheap grace."[4] True conversion includes both faith and repentance.

A famous example of conversion is found in Augustine's *Confessions,* one of the most influential books in the history of Christianity as well as Western culture. In it, Augustine tells of his conversion. The book starts out with the famous

Augustine before conversion?

assertion, "The heart is restless until it finds its rest in Thee," or using a more contemporary translation, "Our hearts find no peace until they rest in you."[5] These words, along with innumerable other accounts in church history, have served to convict as well as inspire conversions to Christianity.

We earlier discussed whether conversions (or salvation) occur instantaneously or gradually. We observed that both types of conversions occur in church history, reflecting different theological views of Scripture and the Christian life. However, during the nineteenth century, William James (1842–1910) made religion a study of the behavioral sciences. In The Varieties of Religious Experience, James talks about conversion and related it to two types of people he observed.[6] First, there is the "religion of healthy-mindedness." Such people are generally well balanced individuals who are cheerful and optimistic. Second, there is the religion of the "sick soul." Such people are characterized as having a "divided self" and are pessimistic and anxious. Because of their respective psychological makeups, people with a sick soul must be "twice-born" in order to reunify or renew the divided self as well as be converted to Christianity. Hence a more dramatic or instantaneous experience of conversion may occur. On the other hand, a healthy-minded person may only need to be "once-born"

James' sick-souled Christian?

gradually into the ways of Christianity. James did not speak pejoratively of people with a sick soul, since there were many factors involved with what constituted a sick soul—personal, social, economic, political, and so on. People possessed a myriad of religious emotions and possible interpretations of them. Still, James thought that the majority of people were sick souls who benefited from a "twice-born" conversion to both religious and personal happiness. He thought that personality distinctions may help to explain, in part, why some people experience instantaneous rather than gradual conversion, or perhaps why they feel the need to do so. Although there are many dimensions to religious phenomena, supernatural as well as natural, James thought that behavioral scientific studies of religion, and of Christianity in particular, benefited both our religious and personal understanding.

21.6 Faith

Faith signifies belief in and commitment to someone or something. From a Christian perspective, faith has to do with people's relationship with God.

One of the best known scriptural references to faith is found in Heb 11:1: "Now faith is the assurance of things hoped for, the conviction of things not seen." This verse emphasizes the spiritual reality thought to underlie people of Christian faith. In Scripture, people are encouraged to have faith (2 Chr 20:20; John 6:28–29; Eph 6:16). Most importantly, conversion to Christianity occurs by faith, often referred to in the Bible as justification by faith (Hab 2:4; Rom 5:1; Gal 3:6). By faith—by belief—people receive eternal life (John 3:15, 16; 5:24; 11:25; 12:46; 20:31; Rom 10:9).

Scripture warns that people's faith will be tested (e.g., Matt 9:28; Mark 7:27; Heb 11:8, 17, 36; Jas 1:3; 1 Pet 1:7). In response to such testing, "great faith" is praised (Matt 8:2, 10; 9:18, 28; 14:36; 15:28; Mark 5:28). People are blessed according to their faith (Matt 8:13; 9:29–30; 17:20; Mark 9:23). By contrast, "little faith" or "weak faith" is chastised (Matt 6:30; 8:26; 14:31; 16:8).

Christians are known as "believers," reflecting their faith in God and God's interactions with them. In the Christian life, faith is considered crucial in prayer to God (Jas 1:5–6). The Bible—God's revelation—offers aids to faith (Exod 4:5; Isa 41:20; 43:10; John 1:7; 11:15; 13:19; 14:29; 17:21; 19:35; 20:31). It also offers promises to those who exercise faith (Matt 21:22; John 1:12; 14:12; Heb 4:3; Jas 2:5; 1 Pet 2:6; 1 John 5:14).

> **OBEDIENCE AND FAITH**
>
> But when once Christ had called him, Peter had no alternative; he must leave the ship and come to Him. In the end, the first step of obedience proves to be an act of faith in the word of Christ. But we should completely misunderstand the nature of grace if we were to suppose that there was no need to take the first step, because faith was already there. Against that, we must boldly assert that the step of obedience must be taken before faith can be possible. Unless he obeys, a man cannot believe.
>
> DIETRICH BONHOEFFER, THE COST OF DISCIPLESHIP (1937)

21.6.1 Nature of Faith

In a sense, everyone lives by faith since not all aspects of life have been explained, much less proven. People may not use the language of faith, however, since it sounds too religious. Instead, they live by various assumptions, presuppositions, or axioms of some mathematical or scientific nature. The result is much the same: Not all aspects of their lives can be fully proven rationally or empirically. Certainly, varying degrees of rational and empirical evidence can be amassed for whatever practical, moral, or scientific needs people have. However, they are not certain or finally proven; they do not have complete truth. Thus, they live by faith, whether they like it or not, which is what Christians have said for centuries.

Christians should never have to feel apologetic because they live "by faith, not by sight" (2 Cor 5:7). Christians have generally thought that their faith is reasonable, but faith is not—by definition—certain. Otherwise, it would not be faith; it would be certainty, or rationalism, or empiricism, but it would not be faith. Faith always contains an element of doubt. Although Christians are

Does a mirror reflect all there is to know about ourselves?

exhorted not to doubt God, there will always be an element of uncertainty—by definition—alongside faith. Of course, Christians do not think that they will always live by faith. When they come face to face with God, all will be made known to them. As Paul says, "For now we see in a mirror, dimly, but then we will see face to face. Now I know only in part; then I will know fully, even as I have been fully known" (1 Cor 13:12).

21.6.2 Saving Faith

Throughout church history, Christians have made numerous distinctions with regard to faith. It may refer to historical faith, temporary faith, miraculous faith, saving faith, legal faith, or evangelical faith. Faith may also be paired with other theological virtues, such as "faith informed by love," which emphasizes faith that is animated and instructed by love. However, saving faith is a key Christian belief, especially for the context of our discussion on becoming a Christian. It refers to the true faith of a Christian. Often, saving faith is analyzed in terms of three components: knowledge, assent, and trust.

First, faith includes knowledge about God, Jesus, and the gospel message found in Scripture. Faith is not irrational. There may be non-rational components to it, since saving faith includes volition as well as intellect. However, faith includes content that is historical and subject to verification.

Second, faith includes assent to that knowledge about God, Jesus, and the gospel, even though people may not choose to appropriate that knowledge for their salvation. There is a choice, and it is not merely an intellectual choice. Demons are said to know about and believe in God, and they shudder as a result of it (Jas 2:19). However, they do not choose to accept or appropriate that knowledge for themselves.

Salvation means reconciliation with God

Third, faith includes trust or entrusting the whole of one's life to God, Jesus, and the gospel. Although salvation is a gift from God, it is expected that people choose to accept salvation. Faith is more than intellectual, and it is more than volitional. It also includes the establishment or reestablishment of a relationship with God, which was previously severed. This is why salvation is referred to as reconciliation as well as salvation; people are restored to a right relationship with God as well as right legal or moral status.

21.6.3 Faith Development

We have already discussed how God commends people of great faith and chastises those of little or weak faith. However, Christians have not always thought of faith in terms of growing or increasing it. After all, are not Christians saved by faith, and cannot faith the size of a mere mustard seed move mountains (Matt 17:20)? Sometimes faith is thought of in either/or categories: either people have faith, or they do not have it. Christians talk about growing spiritually or in Christlikeness, but they do not always talk about this in terms of faith development. Yet in Scripture God seems concerned that Christians grow in faith.

Faith development has become a topic of increasing concern among Christians, and a variety of views have arisen with regard to analyzing people's faith. For example, James Fowler uses behavioral scientific studies in order to understand better the faith and faith development people experience. He describes six stages of faith, which reflect patterned operations of knowing and valuing that underlie our consciousness.[7] In other words, it is possible to observe patterns people exhibit in how they live out and express their faith. Such patterns can be analyzed and, to a certain extent, promoted. Such studies may aid Christians in their theological as well as spiritual self-understanding and growth. The topic of faith development is related to how one goes about being a Christian and, more specifically, to Christian spirituality. Both of these topics will be discussed further in the following chapters.

Repentance means to change one's direction . . .

21.7 Repentance

Repentance involves godly sorrow for sin, confession of it, and the resolve to return from sin. The Greek word for repentance (*metanoia*) literally means a turning of one's mind and direction. It is a turn away from sin and toward God. The call to repentance occurs throughout Scripture. It is required of all who turn to God (Ezek 18:31; Hos 14:2; Matt 3:2; Acts 3:19; 8:22). Those who repent receive answers to prayer (2 Chr 7:14), pardon for sin (Isa 55:7), eternal life (Ezek 18:21), comfort (Matt 5:4), the gift of the Holy Spirit (Acts 2:38), and more.

Repentance involves more than confession. Confession alone does not result in a change of heart. True believers must do more than confess sin; they must also want to be reconciled with God. In addition, penitents must resolve to live no longer in service of sin, self, or some other authority. Instead, they must resolve to live in accordance with God's will for their lives. Faith in God for salvation without repentance cheapens the grace of God and the Christian life to which believers are called. This is the "narrow way" of salvation Jesus describes (Matt 7:14), yet Jesus claims it is the most fulfilling (John 10:10).

21.7.1 Different Views of Repentance

Catholics emphasize repentance through the sacrament of penance, also known as the rite of reconciliation. Penance is a virtue as well as a sacrament, and Christians are called to establish a lifelong pattern of confession, confessing one's sins, and amending one's life. Confession is "good for the soul," so to speak, and penance is a matter of justice. Christians are called to make right, inasmuch as it is possible, their transgressions. Sometimes this occurs only between a believer and God, and sometimes it involves making right past injustices. Zacchaeus is a classic example of someone who followed Jesus and then committed himself to compensating financially everyone he had cheated or neglected in his life (Luke 9:1–10). Zacchaeus not only repented, he gave money (with reparations) to those he unjustly treated as a dishonest tax collector.

There are personal benefits to confession and penance

Protestants also emphasize repentance; however, they have not emphasized it uniformly. In some traditions, confession occurs communally more than individually. Worship services include the communal reading of a confession, and then the minister declares the people's forgiveness, based upon the free grace of God for salvation. Other traditions place more emphasis upon individual confession. In revivalism, emphasis is often placed upon individuals repenting of their sin, perhaps confessing while kneeling at an altar after an "altar call." An altar call may include a call to conversion; it may also include a call to repentance after conversion. The latter is significant for Christians in obeying God and in becoming more like Christ.

Regardless of the particular church tradition, all Christians have emphasized the need to avoid "cheap grace." Yes, salvation is a gift, which God provided freely through Jesus and through the continuing work of the Holy Spirit. However, Christians should not view their salvation with a sense of entitlement. Salvation came with a cost, and Christians need to view their discipleship in relationship to God with gratitude, praise, and also a sense of responsibility for how God wants them to live their lives as Christians.

Although Christians, individually and communally, confess their sins, Christian churches, parachurch groups, and other groups of Christians sometimes confess their corporate sins. For example, groups of Christians have been convicted of injustices perpetrated against others due to institutional decisions that were later thought to be unjust or disrespectful to others. Corporately stated confessions have sometimes been made for past decisions, for example, church-wide support of slavery before the Civil War, ongoing racial discrimination, or the unjust treatment of women.

21.7.2 Repentance and Forgiveness

If Christians have been forgiven by God for their sins, they should be willing to forgive others. God calls Christians to forgive others just as God graciously forgave them. Forgiveness has to do with excusing or pardoning someone for a sin or offense. From a Christian perspective, God both pardoned and excused people, due to Jesus' atonement on their behalf. Moreover, God compassionately provided for people's forgiveness and reconciliation with God before people had the chance to repent. So Paul said, "Bear with one another and, if anyone has a complaint against another, forgive each other; just as the Lord has forgiven you, so you also must forgive" (Col 3:13). Forgiving others is so important that Jesus said we were to forgive people "seventy-seven times" for the same transgression, emphasizing the bountiful grace we need to extend to others (Matt 18:22). If someone asks for forgiveness, Christians are to forgive them, no matter how hard it may feel to do so.

Just as people cannot merit their forgiveness by God, Christians should forgive others even if those they forgive have not repented. This seems even more difficult to do, yet the Bible admonishes believers to do so for their spiritual well-being as well as for the sake of becoming reconciled with those who have offended. From God's perspective, forgiveness has more to do with the forgiver than the one forgiven.

21.8 Regeneration

All Christians talk about the regeneration or "new birth" of Christians. It has to do with the rebirth of the mind and will of those who, by faith and repentance, have received the gift of salvation through Jesus (Titus 3:5). From the outset of salvation, the Holy Spirit works to transform believers. They are "born anew" (John 3:3, RSV); they are a "new creation" (2 Cor 5:17). Regeneration involves rebirth and renewal. In a sense, converts to Christianity have new eyes with which to see and new ears with which to hear. Salvation has occurred. The fullness of that salvation, however, has not yet occurred. The good work God begins at conversion continues through the presence and work of the Holy Spirit.

Regeneration conveys an element of mystery about salvation. It conveys the idea that something transcendent has occurred, which cannot be accounted for in human terms. It further conveys the idea that believers have already been transformed in ways that are spiritually real, yet physically may be unobservable. That does not make the transformation less real. Such a transformation may be felt, and maybe not. The reality of it occurs because of God. Thus, only God can make the reality aware to us.

To what degree are Christians made new?

In Catholicism, regeneration is thought to occur at the time of baptism. The sacraments, known as the "mysteries" in the ancient church, are God's chosen means for graciously working in and through the lives of believers for their salvation. In baptism, the regenerating grace of God is thought to cleanse believers from original sin and secure their eternal life (1 Cor 6:9–11; Rom 8:15–17; Gal 5:21–25). Without question, it is a mystery why God should choose such means for regenerating people. Yet just as Christians receive salvation as a gift, they receive it through God's chosen means of baptism. This understanding is sometimes referred to as *baptismal regeneration,* since it views the sacrament of baptism as the means by which saving grace is given to Christians. Some Protestants, as well as Catholics, affirm baptismal regeneration.

Protestants historically place greater emphasis upon the doctrine of justification, which we will study next. Yet, justification is generally thought to occur, theologically speaking, subsequent to regeneration. (For example, see the comparison of Protestant orders of salvation at the beginning of the chapter. Regeneration always appears before justification.) Regeneration and justification may occur simultaneously, from a chronological perspective, but primacy is placed upon the regenerating work of God rather than the imputed work of God. Regeneration emphasizes the divine therapeutic work of God in the lives of Christians—a regeneration that begins at conversion and continues throughout their lives.

21.9 Justification

Justification refers to the way in which a believer has been restored by God to a state of righteousness. Although the New Testament focuses on justification by faith, the Old Testament also affirms it. Of Abraham, it is said, "He believed the Lord; and [the Lord] reckoned it to him as righteousness" (Gen 15:6; cf. Hab 2:4). Throughout the New Testament, Scripture talks about justification by faith. Paul especially emphasizes this way of discussing salvation. He says, "Therefore, since we are justified by faith, we have peace with God through our Lord Jesus Christ" (Rom 5:1), and "Therefore the law was our disciplinarian until Christ came, so that we might be justified by faith" (Gal 3:24; cf. 1 Cor 6:11; Phil 3:9; Heb 10:38; 11:4).

According to legal analogies for salvation found in the Bible, Jesus is a legal substitute for Christians—for those who believe. Jesus' righteousness is imputed to them. God now views them "as if" they are righteous, and they are in a position of right standing before God. The righteousness with which God views people is not due to their own merits. On the contrary, salvation comes entirely by the work of God as a gift through Jesus (Eph 2:8–9). Luther called it "alien righteousness," since God imputed Jesus' righteousness on behalf of Christians; they are "both saved and sinner." From a legal position, Christians stand innocent before the judgment seat of God.

Protestant reformers emphasized justification as a primary way for referring to people's salvation. Luther and other reformers stressed the principle of justification by grace through faith alone. The legal terminology of justification appealed to the reformers, since they thought that people were so helpless with regard to salvation. Because of sin and its depravity, people could do nothing for their salvation. All they could do was gratefully receive the gift of salvation, which only God provides.

Catholics also emphasize justification, affirming that faith demarks the beginning of people's salvation in response to God's gracious offer of it. However, they have a more involved understanding of faith and how Christians are justified by it. Christians are saved by grace through faith, but the grace by which they are saved is mediated through the church, primarily through faithful participation in the sacraments. The sacraments, like salvation itself, are gifts from God. People cannot earn or merit salvation through good works. Nevertheless, God wants believers to act responsibly in obedience to all of God's means of grace and commands for the Christian life. Faith may form the basis of justification (Rom 1:16–17), but it includes good works as well (Jas 2:14–17, 24–26). In the Catholic view, the Bible nowhere explicitly says that Christians are justified by faith alone; in fact, it says just the opposite. The book of James, which Luther initially wanted to take out of the canon of Scripture, says, "You see that a person is justified by works and not by faith alone" (Jas 2:24). Although Catholics affirm that Christians are saved by grace through faith, they emphasize that the scriptural understanding of faith represents a more complex and dynamic reality than Protestants present in their view of justification by faith alone.

God views believers "as if" they are righteous

21.10 Conclusion

Salvation is the gift of eternal life, graciously offered to people. Of course, the value of salvation involves more than the afterlife. It has value for life here and now, and Christians have much from which to benefit. Still, their blessed hope is for life eternal with God in heaven.

People experience salvation in a variety of ways. Some emphasize the instantaneous nature of conversion, while others emphasize its gradual occurrence. Some emphasize various means of grace by which God offers people salvation, while others emphasize that it comes by faith alone. Despite differences of opinion, all agree that salvation occurs only by the love and work of God on our behalf. No one earns or merits their salvation. The fact that God initiates, enables, and completes salvation separates Christianity from other religions of the world that emphasize the necessity of what people do for their enlightenment or self-actualization. True, God expects people to respond in faith, which is their task in salvation. However, salvation ultimately represents a gift of God, secured by Jesus, and affected in the lives of people through the Holy Spirit.

After conversion, salvation is not complete. On the contrary, conversion is the beginning of blessings and challenges for the Christian life. The blessings far outweigh the challenges, yet the challenges contribute to the richness of new life in Jesus. Through the presence and power of the Holy Spirit, amazing things lay in store for Christians. In the next chapter, we will begin to explore the variety of ways that God wants to work in and through the lives of believers.

21.11 Questions for Further Reflection

1. How does one become a Christian? What steps should people take in converting to Christianity?

2. Does conversion occur instantaneously or gradually, or both? Why do you think the way you do?

3. How do you interpret the various orders of salvation? What are the benefits of outlining an order of salvation, and what are its liabilities?

4. What is the nature of faith? saving faith? How crucial is faith to salvation? What is its relationship to the sacraments? repentance?

5. Why is repentance important to salvation? Why may it not be enough to be saved by faith alone?

6. What is the significance of regeneration and justification? What is the relationship between the two?

21.12 Notes

1. Cyprian of Carthage, *De Unitate Ecclesiae*, 6: Patrologiae Latina 4, 519, quoted by U. S. Catholic Church, *The Catechism of the Catholic Church* (2d ed.; New York: Doubleday, 2005), no. 181.

2. See chapter 26 for a more detailed discussion of the sacraments.

3. Sources: Walter A. Elwell, ed., *Evangelical Dictionary of Theology* (Grand Rapids: Baker, 1984); Millard J. Erickson, *Concise Dictionary of Christian Theology* (Grand Rapids: Baker, 1986); Harald Lindström, *Wesley and Sanctification: A Study in the Doctrine of Salvation* (Stockholm: Nya Bokförlags Aktiebolaget, 1946; repr., Wilmore, Ky.: Francis Asbury Press, 1946); and Robert C. Walton, *Chronological and Background Charts of Church History* (Grand Rapids: Zondervan, 1986).

4. Dietrich Bonhoeffer, *The Cost of Discipleship* (trans. R. H. Fuller and Irmgard Booth; 1st Touchstone ed.; New York: Simon & Schuster, 1995), 43–56.

5. Augustine, *The Confessions of Saint Augustine* (trans. Edward B. Pusey; New York: Collier Books for Macmillan, 1961), 11; Augustine, *Confessions* (trans. R. S. Pine-Coffin; Penguin Classics; New York: Penguin, 1961), 21.

6. William James, *The Varieties of Religious Experience: A Study in Human Nature, Being the Gifford Lectures on Natural Religion Delivered at Edinburgh in 1901–1902* (New York: Mentor Book from New American Library, 1958), 76–139.

7. Fowler, *Faithful Change,* 56; cf. James W. Fowler, *Stages of Faith: The Psychology of Human Development and the Quest for Meaning* (New York: Harper & Row, 1981).

CHAPTER TWENTY-TWO

I appeal to you therefore, brothers and sisters, by the mercies of God, to present your bodies as a living sacrifice, holy and acceptable to God, which is your spiritual worship. Do not be conformed to this world, but be transformed by the renewing of your minds, so that you may discern what is the will of God—what is good and acceptable and perfect. (Romans 12:1–2)

LIVING AS A CHRISTIAN

22.1 Introduction

One day Jesus saw the crowds following him. He walked up the side of a mountain and sat down. After his disciples came to him, Jesus began to speak. These teachings have become known as the Sermon on the Mount, and they are some of the most famous words of Jesus. He shared the Beatitudes, proclaiming blessings for those who live according to his rules (Matt 5:3–12). Jesus spoke about the witness of the disciples, and the relationship of his message to Jewish law. He taught about practical piety and about how people ought to pray.

Jesus discouraged public prayers that were ostentatious and wordy. Instead, Jesus encouraged people to pray to God in private. God is personally present with us always and knows all that we need before we pray. With this encouragement to pray, Jesus then taught what has become known as the Lord's Prayer:

> Our Father in heaven, hallowed be your name.
> Your kingdom come.
> Your will be done, on earth as it is in heaven.
> Give us this day our daily bread.
> And forgive us our debts, as we also have forgiven our debtors.
> And do not bring us to the time of trial, but rescue us from the evil one.
> For the kingdom and the power and the glory are yours forever. Amen. (Matt 6:9–13)[1]

After the opening invocation, the prayer includes three petitions for honoring God and three petitions for personal needs. The prayer has become a standard prayer for

The Lord's Prayer

Christians, repeated in personal and public prayer in church. It also serves as a paradigm after which Christians model their prayer.

In the Sermon on the Mount, Jesus continues to exhort people not to worry—not to be of "little faith" (Matt 6:30). He gives many practical examples about how people are to be faithful in following him. In this context, Jesus also proclaims the "Golden Rule," the command to love one's neighbor as oneself. He says, "In everything do to others as you would have them do to you; for this is the law and the prophets" (Matt 7:12; cf. Luke 6:31).

In the midst of his discourse, Jesus makes a startling statement: "Be perfect, therefore, as your heavenly Father is perfect" (Matt 5:48). What did he mean by this? To many of us, the statement seems ludicrous. How can anyone be perfect like God the Father? What of sin? What of the limitations and ignorance of finite human life? Some Christians think Jesus' words mean that we are to be loving toward all, as he commands us (Matt 7:12; cf. Col 3:14; 1 John 4:19). Yet, are we actually supposed to love others perfectly? Other Christians think it means that perfection should be our goal. The Apostle Paul, for example, talks about the Christian life as a race—a race he has begun, and in which he strains, but one he has not yet completed (Phil 3:13). Still, would the performer of miracles, healings, and exorcisms expect anything less than perfection? Is there some sense in which Jesus' words make sense, given the fact that other teachings of the Sermon on the Mount are taken as achievable guidelines for Christian life? Regardless of the interpretation of Jesus' words, the statement challenges readers to take stock of their lives and think carefully about the life to which Jesus calls those who follow him.

Is living the Christian life like a race?

22.2 The Order of Salvation

Being a Christian is not a static state of existence. It is not as if people have received tickets for heaven and no longer need to care about their relationship with God, themselves, and others. On the contrary, the Christian life is dynamic and growing, not static and status quo. In a sense, it is status quo in that Christians have been saved; their salvation is assured. However, God is not content to leave them at that because salvation involves a relationship as well as a right standing before God. Indeed, God has great plans in store for all who become Christians (John 10:10).

In the last chapter, I talked about various orders of salvation. They indicate that salvation does not end with conversion. Salvation encompasses a single, complex event that includes a lifetime relationship with God as well as eternal life with God. A view of salvation associated only with conversion, regeneration, or justification is a truncated view. Salvation also includes various dimen-

> **Salvation may begin** with conversion and baptism, but salvation is a process as well as an event.
>
> Throughout Christians' lives, God's Holy Spirit works to make the fullness of love, holiness, and power evident.

sions of relationship with God after one accepts God's gracious gift of eternal life. Salvation includes this and more!

In the previous chapter we discussed the order of salvation as it is variously understood by Christians. We can now continue to analyze it in terms of various constituent parts. Of particular import are Christian understandings of assurance, union with Christ, sanctification, and glorification. All of these dimensions are as vital to the overall doctrine of salvation as are the dimensions having to do with becoming a Christian.

22.3 Assurance

Christians have the privilege of experiencing assurance of their salvation; however, they do not always experience it or understand that experience the same way. Assurance is generally thought of as the divinely given confidence that believers are saved, that they have become the children of God. Scripture describes Christians as having received "adoption" as God's children, becoming fellow-heirs with Jesus (John 1:12; Rom 8:16–17; 2 Cor 6:18; Gal 4:4–7). How are Christians to understand and experience this assurance?

Some Christians never seem to doubt their salvation. Others, however, struggle with doubt about their relationship with God. Over the centuries, Christians have responded to these doubts in a number of ways. Those ways include reflection over issues of divine predestination and human freedom, inward evidence and outward evidence, permanence of salvation, and so on.

22.3.1 Sources of Assurance

Although God is thought to be the only reliable source of assurance for salvation, Christians have not always felt an immediate sense of the presence of God, confirming their salvation. To be sure, the witness of the Holy Spirit is the most direct assurance of salvation. In becoming Christians, they did not receive a "spirit of slavery" to fall back into sin and despair; instead they received a "spirit of adoption" (Rom 8:15). Paul states that it is the "Spirit bearing witness with our spirit that we are children of God" (Rom 8:16; cf. 1 John 5:6). It is the privilege of Christians that they

God does not intend Christians to live lives of fear

feel or sense their salvation, though the feeling or sensation is not required for salvation. Christians are saved by grace through faith, regardless of one's feeling or sensing of God's presence. Yet, the Bible suggests that it is the privilege of Christians that the Holy Spirit, in God's own way and time, confirms their salvation through an inward, spiritual witness.

Because experience is easily misunderstood, there are other ways Christians may experience assurance of salvation. Catholic and Orthodox churches believe that the sacraments serve as means of grace for their assurance of salvation as well as for salvation itself. As Christians partake of the sacraments of baptism, confirmation, Eucharist, penance, and anointing of the sick, they may know that they receive God's grace in an ongoing fashion, which serves to confirm as well as empower their Christian lives. Regardless of the degree of fidelity or intimacy an individual feels in relationship with God, they have the comfort and encouragement the sacraments afford as God's ordained means of grace.

Protestants do not place the same emphasis upon the sacraments as means of grace, so they have emphasized other assurances of salvation. The most important has to do with the actual teachings of Scripture about salvation. Biblical teachings still reflect the witness of the Spirit, since the Holy Spirit is thought to have inspired Scripture. Thus, when the Bible says that those who have believed are saved, a person may claim that promise, if they have faith in God—even faith the size of a "mustard seed"—for their eternal life. Numerous Scripture passages affirm salvation by faith, so Christians need not live lives of fear and uncertainty, but of assurance (see Rom 10:13; Eph 3:8–9; 1 John 1:9; 5:12–13). The feeling or sense of assurance may occur or it may not; it may grow or it may not. Regardless, assurance of salvation involves claiming the *promises* of Scripture rather than any actual *experience* of such assurance.

Although Christians emphasize salvation as a gift, they also emphasize salvation as a task. Christians are to believe, but they are also to be obedient. Catholic and Orthodox churches focus on obedience in observing the sacraments, and Protestants focus on obedience in obeying Scripture. Neither thinks that such obedience merits their salvation, but they consider obedience and faith inextricably connected. It is a mystery how faith and works are related. Over and over in the Bible and in church history, Christians have warned against works-righteousness, that is, salvation by works. Nevertheless, faith as a gift without faith, or in other words faith as a task, is unknown in Scripture and church history.

Thus, there is an expectation that people who convert to Christianity will manifest different thoughts, words, and actions than they did prior to conversion. They will manifest a lifelong practice of repentance and belief; they will be baptized; they will call upon God; and they will obey God in everything. As such, the witness of various "fruit of the Holy Spirit" (Gal 5:22–23) and the development of Christian virtues reflects a certain witness of our own spirit (and actions). They help to "make your salvation sure," so to speak. This does not mean, however, that Christians become absolutely perfect or sinless in this life. On the contrary, there are thought to be degrees of maturity, which I discuss in the next chapter.

In this life, Christians need to use caution in assessing the degree of change or maturity they can exhibit. While Christians are expected to live more Christlike lives, the degree to which they achieve such a life depends on numerous factors. Conversion alone may not overcome, at least not immediately, the influences of a person's personal and family background, church experience (or lack thereof), social, cultural, economic, and other factors that affect people. Still, Christians have always affirmed the benefits of salvation here and now as well as for eternal life.

Christians exhibit "fruits of the Spirit"

22.3.2 Permanence of Salvation

Scripture promises that nothing can separate us from the love of God in Jesus: "neither death, nor life, nor angels, nor rulers, nor things present, nor things to come, nor powers, nor height, nor depth, nor anything else in all creation" (Rom 8:38–39). No person or force can take away God's salvation (John 10:28). God's will and power keep Christians safe, giving them assurance with regard to the continuation of their salvation. Yet, questions still arise about whether it is possible or even probable that someone might reject their salvation. Christians, after all, sometimes become involved in highly questionable activities, personally and corporately within churches. Although claiming to be Christians, are they rejecting their salvation? God may be able to preserve Christians' salvation, but would God coerce people into remaining Christian if they no longer wanted to be in relationship with God?

Historically, the Catholic and Orthodox churches have considered Christians' salvation conditional upon their continued faithfulness to God and the church. Since God dispenses grace by means of the church and sacraments it distributes to Christians, they need to be responsible in maintaining their fidelity to God. Of course, Christians can never lose their salvation by accident. No one can lose their salvation like they might unintentionally lose their keys or jacket. Christians may become Christians of "little faith" or disobedient in obeying the teachings of the Bible and the church. Such Christians may be considered least in the kingdom of God, but they will not lose their salvation (Matt 5:19–20). God's grace is sufficient to enable, continue, and culminate people's faith; however, Scripture does not guarantee that individuals cannot reject their salvation. Those who intentionally and habitually reject God, after conversion, are thought to go over permanently to

People cannot lose their salvation accidentally, like they may lose a set of keys

pagan unbelief (Heb 6:1–8). Such people are called apostate, being guilty of apostasy—the complete rejection of God and of the church in which they were baptized.

Protestants differ with regard to the permanence of salvation. Luther thought that God cultivated maturity in the lives of believers, which aided in preserving their salvation. However, people could reject their salvation. Similar to Catholic and Orthodox church beliefs, salvation represented a relationship with God, which God would not foist upon those unwilling to accept Jesus as their Savior and Lord. Too much scriptural evidence indicated the possibility of someone rejecting salvation (e.g., Matt 13:20–21; John 15:6; 1 Tim 1:19–20; 2 Tim 2:12; Heb 6:4–6; 2 Pet 2:1, 20–21). After Luther, other Christians such as Arminius and Wesley, who emphasized human freedom more than Luther, affirmed the possibility of rejecting salvation and encouraged Christians to remain faithful. However, they never thought that a Christian need fear apostasy or any unintentional loss of salvation. Although Christians may experience spiritual ups and downs, God's grace is sufficient in the face of trials and temptations for them to remain faithful (1 Cor 10:11–13).

In contrast, Calvin placed more emphasis on the sovereignty of God and the surety of God's election. If people are among the elect, it is impossible for them to lose their election to eternal life. Calvin also thought that too much scriptural evidence indicated the impossibility of someone rejecting salvation (for example, John 6:37, 39; 10:28–29; Rom 8:30, 38–39; Phil 1:6). Thus, if people believed in Jesus for their salvation, they were elect. They may live obedient lives in making their election sure; however, they should be assured that God's gracious election is dependable. Calvin's belief in the perseverance of the saints, however, should not be confused with the popular notion of "eternal security," which reflects the cliché "once saved always saved." Although Calvin believed in the irresistibility of God's election, he acknowledged that people could be mistaken about their faith. Indeed, if people appear to become apostate, such evidence suggests that people wrongly claimed saving faith. They did not lose their salvation; they were never saved in the first place.

22.4 Union with Christ

The language of "union with Christ" appears several ways in church history. In Catholic and Orthodox churches, it generally refers to the mystical union or communion Christians may experience with God. Union with Christ, or mystical union, refers to the highest stage of spirituality Christians achieve toward perfection after first going through various purgative and illuminative stages of spirituality.

In Protestant traditions, union with Christ may also refer to a stage in the order of salvation. In the various orders of salvation, union with Christ ap-

Christians experience communion as much as union with God

pears, but in different places. For Luther, union with Christ occurs after justification, and in some respects is synonymous with sanctification. It emphasizes again the mystery of God's grace in relationship to believers and their salvation. Union with Christ initially occurs between God and people in regeneration, when God regenerates true believers in becoming reconciled with them. The initial union inaugurates the imputation of Jesus' righteousness on the behalf of Christians. Yet, that union continues and provides ongoing grace by God in working in and through believers for their sanctification.

Calvin placed more emphasis on the sovereignty of God in electing irresistibly those predestined for eternal life. He locates union with Christ after the election and predestination of people. It functions to secure the imputation of Christ's righteousness for believers and for their adoption as children of God. All this reflects Calvin's belief that people are so sinful—so totally depraved—that everything regenerative in the lives of believers comes from God alone. After union with Christ, the elect are then effectually called, regenerated, and justified.

22.5 Sanctification

Sanctification is the divine act of making believers holy, that is, bringing regenerate people's spiritual and moral condition into conformity with the legal status established at justification. At the time of justification, believers are made holy, through what some have called *positional holiness.* Christians are holy because of Jesus' righteousness imputed to them (1 Cor 1:30; Heb 13:12). In addition to justification, Christians also experience regeneration, which begins the process of sanctification. Progressive holiness occurs during the Christian life. Throughout both Old and New Testaments, believers have been called to holiness—to conforming to god-likeness, epitomized in the person of Jesus. In the Old Testament, God is recorded as saying, "You shall be holy to me; for I the Lord am holy, and I have separated you from the other peoples to be mine" (Lev 20:26; cf. Exod 19:22; Num 11:18; Josh 3:5; 1 Sam 16:5; 2 Chr 29:5). In the New Testament, the theme of holiness continues. Paul says, "Since we have these promises, beloved, let us cleanse ourselves from every defilement of body and of spirit, making holiness perfect in the fear of God" (2 Cor 7:1). The author of Hebrews says:

> Therefore let us go on toward perfection, leaving behind the basic teaching about Christ, and not laying again the foundation: repentance from dead works and faith toward God, instruction about baptisms, laying on of hands, resurrection of the dead, and eternal judgment (Heb 6:1–2).

Jesus exhorts believers to go on for perfection, and depicted the sanctification and holiness of believers in terms of love (Matt 5:48). The greatest commandment involves love for God and for others:

> One of the scribes came near and heard them disputing with one another, and seeing that he answered them well, he asked him, "Which commandment is the first of all?" Jesus answered, "The first is, 'Hear, O Israel: the Lord

our God, the Lord is one; you shall love the Lord your God with all your heart, and with all your soul, and with all your mind, and with all your strength.' The second is this, 'You shall love your neighbor as yourself.' There is no other commandment greater than these." (Mark 12:28–31)

Does God expect Christians to score a "perfect 10"?

How does sanctification occur? Like salvation as a whole, it involves both a gift and task. On the one hand, only God graciously enables spiritual and moral growth in believers. God sanctifies believers by truth, especially truth as found in the words of Jesus and of the Bible (John 17:17; Rom 15:16). On the other hand, sanctification is a task to which God calls believers. In their sanctification, believers are to be obedient in their faithfulness to God (2 Tim 2:21; 1 Pet 1:2). Although there are different views of sanctification, all believe that God ultimately produces spiritual and moral increase in Christians. They merely believe in different degrees of responsible participation God expects in the process of sanctification.

Given the nature of sanctification as both gift and task, along with other distinctions, there arose various understandings of sanctification in church history. Some views reflect optimism in God's grace to perfect believers, while other views reflect pessimism with regard to the effects of sin and finite human nature in increasing godliness in their lives. Despite these differences, some similarities occur:[2]

- All agree that the Bible teaches sanctification that is past, present, and future.

- All agree that the process of sanctification requires believers to strive to express God's love in their experience.

- All agree that the Bible promises success in this process of struggling against sin, through the power of the Holy Spirit.

Noting these areas of agreement, we will now look at some of the differences between Christian views of sanctification. These differences are important; they impact the expectations Christians have with regard to the degree to which God calls them to be holy. In churches, most of the ministry that goes on has to do with the sanctification and nurture of believers more than the conversion and justification of non-believers. Even in the most evangelistic churches, the majority of time is spent on ministering to the members of the church more than to non-members. To be sure, most churches exhort their adherents to minister to others, through evangelism, compassion ministries, and so on. However, their view of sanctification powerfully influences the way churches envision their lives and activities as Christians.

22.5.1 Catholic and Orthodox Views

Catholic and Orthodox churches think that God wants to *impart* as well as *impute* righteousness, holiness, and perfection in the lives of believers. God graciously provides a variety of ways by which they may grow spiritually and morally. Of course, it is only God who enables such growth to occur, yet God also gives believers the task of obediently following biblical and church teachings that aid in their growth. One of the ways believers grow is through participation in the various spiritual disciplines described in Scripture. They include disciplines in spiritual engagement as well as spiritual abstinence, which will be described more fully in the chapter on Christian spirituality. Another way believers grow is through participation in the sacraments of the church. Faithful observance of the sacraments provides grace to bless, keep, and nurture Christians into greater conformity with Jesus. Catholics and Orthodox Christians, of course, recognize the negative effects of sin and finitude in the lives of believers in their pursuit of holiness. Yet, they have more confidence in the power of God to nurture believers significantly, though not perfectly, to become more Christlike.

In the Catholic Church, believers thought to experience exceptional degrees of holiness and virtuosity are called saints. Such people are thought to live such virtuous, self-sacrificial lives that they are venerated by the church and serve as role models for others. Believers thought to have especially heightened spirituality experience a *beatific vision* of God. The beatific vision represents the most intimate sense of union or communion with the presence and glory of God, short of Christians' glorification with God in heaven.

In Orthodox churches, believers are called to deification (Greek, *theōsis,* "being made God"). In the early church, deification referred to conversion because believers were thought to participate and become like God. It never meant that believers were to become gods. More and more, deification referred to the actual growth in spirituality and morality believers may experience by the grace of God through their faithful participation in the spiritual disciplines and sacraments.

What does it mean to be deified?

22.5.2 Protestant Views

Protestants also emphasize the spiritual disciplines as ways that God sanctifies believers. Exceptional examples of Christians may not be distinguished as saints, but they are referred to as heroes and heroines of spirituality and morality, serving as role models for others. Protestants are hopeful for how God wants to work in and through the lives of believers for their sanctification as well as justification.

For the Protestant Reformers, however, too much emphasis had been placed on an optimistic view of human nature and sin. Moreover, too much importance had been placed on the role of the sacraments—as understood by Catholicism—in perfecting believers in this life. Instead, the reformers believed that the Scriptures revealed people to be exceedingly sinful, incapable of contributing to their justification or sanctification. In such a spiritual and moral predicament, people were utterly dependent on God for every aspect of their Christian life and conversion.

Lutheranism

Luther strongly emphasizes the dependency of people upon the sovereignty of God. Because of the atonement of Jesus, believers receive his alien righteousness as their own righteousness, thus being justifed before God and experiencing union with Christ. Luther referred to Christians as *both righteous and a sinner* (Latin, *simul iustus et peccator*). That is, God imputes righteousness to believers, but they are still sinners. Despite their salvation, believers continue to sin in thought, word, and deed because of the deep-seated effects of sin upon their lives (Rom 3:23; 7:14–25; 1 Tim 1:15).

Despite their ongoing sinfulness, believers may desire and do good works in this life, demonstrating praise and thanks to God for the unmerited gift of eternal life. Such works reflect God's *overflowing love* in the life of believers, due to fullness of the presence and work of God. Such works did not constitute any merit for their conversion or Christian life. In fact, Luther was concerned about the temptation of works-righteousness so much that he discouraged talk of sanctification, lest believers be tempted into thinking that their efforts in pious obedience and good works somehow justify their salvation or exhibit spiritual superiority. Believers' union with Christ assures their justification as well as their sanctification, and they are not to strive for anything beyond accepting the fact that all of life, including eternal life, is a gift. God wants believers to receive the many blessings God desires for them and to live in peace, knowing that their lives are utterly dependent upon God.

Luther's followers largely embraced his emphases on relying solely upon God for both their justification and sanctification. Because people lost their freedom of choice due to sin, there was as little need for the imitation of Jesus as for personal merit for justification. Like Luther, Lutherans still preach and teach biblical laws, but such laws are thought to serve two uses. The *first use* of the law is pedagogical or evangelistic; the law demonstrates the sinfulness of people and their utter need for

Both righteous and sinner?

God's grace. The *second use* of the law is the political or civil use; the law provides guidance on how to govern people in an orderly fashion. Some Lutherans emphasized the experiential dimensions of salvation and came to be known as

Pietists. Although Pietists found great spirituality in the life and teachings of Luther, most Lutherans emphasized his teachings on justification by faith alone and the utter dependence of people upon God's grace.

Calvinism and the Reformed Movement

Calvin also emphasizes the utter dependence of people upon God's grace. In fact, Calvin emphasizes the irresistibility of God's grace and predestination more than Luther. However, Calvin thinks that God wants believers to do more than get used to the fact that all of life, including eternal life, is a gift. God wants believers to give praise and thanks to God, and they may do this through faithful obedience to the laws of the Bible. Unlike Luther, Calvin thinks that there is a *third use* of the law—the didactic or moral use of the law. Scripture provides a norm for conduct, which Christians should obey (Luke 9:23; Phil 3:12; 1 John 1:8–9). They should obey not for the sake of meriting salvation or some other approval from God. Instead, they should be obedient out of praise and thanks to God. If growth in spirituality and morality occurs, they should gratefully acknowledge God rather than themselves for it. Since God providentially orders life, both the good and the bad, Christians are to live obediently and not presumptuously with regard to anything they might achieve of eternal significance.

Like Luther, Calvin thinks that believers are both righteous and sinful, and in this life there will be ongoing struggle with sin, exemplified by Paul's discussion in Rom 7:7–25. Ongoing struggle with sin is the normative Christian life, though God comforts and aids believers in their struggles. However, believers are saved by grace through faith; they should show their praise and thanks to God by obedient living, allowing God to give the increase.

The Reformed movement of Protestantism includes more than Calvin and his followers, but it largely draws from the theology and ethos of Calvin. It appears, for example, in the Presbyterian movement in Scotland and the Puritan movement in England (and later in the American colonies). Such movements emphasize the study of Scripture, the importance of preaching, God's providential ordering of life, and of course, Christian obedience.

Pietism, Quakerism, Wesleyanism, and the Holiness Movement

During the seventeenth and eighteenth centuries, a variety of movements developed in Western Protestantism that placed emphasis upon the experiential encounter believers have with God as well as the imputed relationship they have through the atonement of Jesus. Pietism arose among Lutheran churches in continental Europe, with an understanding of Christianity that emphasizes personal religious experience of salvation and a believer's ongoing relationship with God. Lutherans such as Philipp Jakob Spener promoted Pietism, though his emphasis was largely resisted by Lutheranism. As a result, Pietism was sometimes used as a derogatory term for those who overemphasized personal religious experience and the leading of the Holy Spirit and who underemphasized reason and the intellectual dimensions of Christianity. Nevertheless, Pietism had a far-reaching impact upon Christendom, even if it did not have a long-term effect upon most Lutherans.

The Society of Friends arose in seventeenth-century England through the leadership of Christians such as George Fox. Fox thought that God's "inner light" occurred in all Christians, which confirmed God's presence as well as directed their actions and lives (John 1:9; 8:12; 2 Cor 4:6). Although Fox was thoroughly aware of Scripture, he believed that the presence of God through the Holy Spirit continued to work in and through the lives of Christians—work that sanctified as well as justified believers. In fact, Fox was optimistic with regard to the degree of perfection God worked in believers' lives. Such divine work could be attended by shaking or quaking, thus inspiring the "Quakers" as a nickname for the Society of Friends. Although this term was once used as a derogatory name, the Society of Friends continues to be known by it.

The Pietist impulse continued in England, especially through Wesley and the Methodist movement (yet another derisive term initially given to his followers). Wesley emphasizes that the regeneration that occurs at the time of conversion is to continue throughout believers' lives. Likewise, the repentance that leads to conversion is to continue throughout their lives for their sanctification. Although God could grant a believer's entire sanctification at the time of conversion, most often it occurs subsequent to conversion. If at the time of conversion Jesus became a believer's Savior, then subsequent to conversion it is God's will that Jesus also becomes the Lord of his or her life. Wesley refers to this time of total consecration as entire sanctification, or Christian perfection (1 Thess 5:23–24; cf. Matt 5:48). The consecration by believers is met by the grace of God as a kind of "second blessing." Although people balked at the terminology, Wesley thought he was being faithful both to the teachings and spirit of the Bible, exhorting holiness (2 Cor 7:1; Gal 5:24). Jesus, after all, commanded Christians to love God with their whole heart, soul, mind, and strength, and they were to love their neighbors as themselves. Certainly Wesley thinks that the God of creation, redemption, and miracles could also work in and through the life of believers for their entire sanctification. Wesley does not think that believers would become perfectly sinless in this life. Entire sanctification has more to do with the perfecting of believers' intentions than of their actual performance. However, Wesley is optimistic with regard to the degree of holiness God imparts, working with believers whom God expects to cooperate with divine grace.

Are you a "quaker"?

Over time, numerous church and parachurch groups were influenced by Pietism and Methodism; these became known as the Holiness Movement. Its influence spanned denominations, as it was promoted through revivalism and camp meetings. The promoters of holiness have different names, but their emphases tend to be the same. They include Charles Finney (1792–1875) and Phoebe Palmer (1807–1874). Emphasis is placed upon a personal, experienced relationship with God. Emphasis is also placed on the dynamic, interactive relationship people have with God both in prayer and for living the Christian life. Although it is God who gives the spiritual and moral increase, believers pursue holiness in cooperation with God's grace.

Pentecostalism and the Charismatic Movement

At the turn of the twentieth century, Pentecostalism arose with an emphasis upon Holy Spirit baptism, subsequent to conversion, which empowers believers with the gifts of the Holy Spirit. It was thought that speaking in tongues provided physical evidence of Holy Spirit baptism. Coming out of the Holiness Movement, early Pentecostals used "second blessing" language to describe their experience of tongues and empowerment. Sometimes speaking in tongues was considered a third work of the Holy Spirit, but most considered it parallel with entire sanctification. The net result was that Pentecostals considered Holy Spirit baptism an important part of the sanctifying work of God in the lives of believers.

The Charismatic Movement largely affirmed the emphases of Pentecostalism; however, it had greater influence over existing churches, including Catholic as well as Protestant churches. Early Pentecostals had little influence over existing churches, often being asked to leave. The Charismatic Movement, along with Pentecostal churches, however, has had a growing influence on Christianity as a whole. Due in large part to its influence, a growing appreciation for the person and work of the Holy Spirit in the lives of believers has impacted Christians around the world, emphasizing the sanctifying and justifying grace of God.

> **HOLINESS AND FAITH**
>
> Is God unreasonable in his requirements? Hath he given the command "Be ye holy," and not given the ability, with the command, for the performance of it? . . . Faith is taking God at His word relying unwaveringly upon his truth. The nature of the truth believed, whether joyous or otherwise, will necessarily produce corresponding feeling.
>
> PHOEBE PALMER,
> THE WAY OF HOLINESS

22.6 Glorification

Despite different understandings of the order of salvation, all Christian views point toward glorification. Glorification has a twofold meaning. First, glorification has to do with glorifying God's greatness and goodness (Ps 22:23; Rev 19:5; 22:3). All that we have is dependent upon God, and all that we will receive is dependent upon God. What a celebration of praise and worship it will be to be with God in heaven and to honor God forever!

Second, glorification has to do with how believers will share in God's glory. Since believers are children of God, they are co-heirs with Jesus, and they will share in his glory (Rom 8:17; Col 3:4). In this life, believers must suffer for a while; Scripture alerts them about the suffering they will

Celebrate God!

undoubtedly experience, just as Jesus did. Yet, Paul encourages believers, "I consider that the sufferings of this present time are not worth comparing with the glory about to be revealed to us" (Rom 8:18). If believers suffer the faith, hope, and love God requires for salvation, then glory beyond imagination awaits them in heaven (2 Tim 2:10; 1 Pet 5:1). Indeed, they will reign with Jesus in eternal triumph (Rev 22:5; cf. Dan 7:18, 27).

22.7 Conclusion

Truly salvation provides believers far more than they could have ever imagined. Because of the love of God, manifested through the atonement of Jesus and accomplished through the Holy Spirit, believers experience abundant life here and now and eternal life hereafter.

In this chapter, we studied salvation beyond conversion, beyond faith, and beyond repentance. We studied it in the context of what happens after conversion, and how salvation continues to be important for living the Christian life. Life for believers does not end after conversion; it begins a lifetime of blessings as well as challenges. Being a Christian includes both the assurance of salvation and actual union with Christ. It also involves adventures in divine grace, in which God works to bring believers into greater conformity with Jesus. As such, they may love God more effectively and their neighbors as themselves. To be sure, Christians have various views with regard to the nature and extent to which God sanctifies their lives. However, it is God's will that believers live obedient, abundant lives which are as satisfying to them as they are pleasing to God. Finally, it is also God's will that believers share in glory with God throughout eternity.

22.8 Questions for Further Reflection

1. Does being a Christian represent a finished work of God in the lives of believers? In what sense is it dynamic, challenging, growing?

2. What may Christians expect with regard to feeling a sense of assurance of salvation? Is their salvation dependent on their feeling of assurance?

3. Does God want Christians to grow spiritually and morally? To what degree does God enable that growth, and to what degree does God want believers to act freely and responsibly?

4. Which views of sanctification have the greatest appeal? Why? How may the different expectations affect believers in their sanctification? How may they affect the ministry of a church?

22.9 Notes

1. The last line was added, in some form, by ancient authorities; see Michael D. Coogan, ed., *The New Oxford Annotated Bible* (New Revised Standard Version; 3d ed.; New York: Oxford University Press, 2001), Matt 6:13, n.

2. The following areas of similarity are found in Melvin E. Dieter, et al., eds., introduction to *Five Views on Sanctification* (Grand Rapids: Zondervan, 1987), 7.

CHAPTER TWENTY-THREE

For I am the Lord your God; sanctify your-selves therefore, and be holy, for I am holy. (Leviticus 11:44)

May my meditation be pleasing to him, for I rejoice in the Lord. (Psalm 104:34)

O taste and see that the Lord is good; happy are those who take refuge in him. (Psalm 34:8)

Religion that is pure and undefiled before God, the Father, is this: to care for orphans and widows in their distress, and to keep one-self unstained by the world. (James 1:27)

CHRISTIAN SPIRITUALITY

23.1 Introduction

Spirituality is a term often used to describe the Christian life. It is a general term, and one that is used by religions and movements other than Christianity. Thus, when talking about Christian spirituality, it is important to label it as such. (Given the Christian context of this book, in this chapter spirituality and Christian spirituality will be used interchangeably.) Focusing on spirituality will help us to discuss the breadth and vitality of Christian life, often overlooked in the study of theology. Indeed, the study of Christian spirituality has much to do with the quality of relationship believers have with God, and it is the vitality of that relationship that theology tries to articulate.

From a Christian perspective, what does it mean to be spiritual? This is a difficult question to answer because Christians have answered it in different ways. The verses quoted above give testimony to the varieties of Christian spirituality. Nevertheless, if one were to try to summarize the essence of Christian spirituality, perhaps it could be summarized in one word: love. This word is not simply a cliché or reductionistic portrayal of Christianity. While reference to love seems simplistic, its substance is not simplistic in the Bible. For example, Jesus' reference to the greatest commandment has to do with love for God with all one's heart, soul, mind, and strength, and love for one's neighbor as oneself. Moreover, multiple examples of love and compassion

WORKS OF LOVE

To the Christian, love is the works of love. To say that love is a feeling or anything of the kind is really an un-Christian conception of love. That is the aesthetic definition and therefore fits the erotic and everything of that nature. But to the Christian, love is the works of love. Christ's love was not an inner feeling, a full heart and what-not: it was the work of love which was his life.

SOREN KIERKEGAARD, JOURNALS (1833–1855)

appear throughout Scripture. Yet, perhaps the best known reference to love is found in 1 Cor 13, sometimes known as the "Love Chapter." Here is a portion of it:

> If I speak in the tongues of mortals and of angels, but do not have love, I am a noisy gong or a clanging cymbal. And if I have prophetic powers, and understand all mysteries and all knowledge, and if I have all faith, so as to remove mountains, but do not have love, I am nothing. If I give away all my possessions, and if I hand over my body so that I may boast, but do not have love, I gain nothing.

L–O–V–E

> Love is patient; love is kind; love is not envious or boastful or arrogant or rude. It does not insist on its own way; it is not irritable or resentful; it does not rejoice in wrongdoing, but rejoices in the truth. It bears all things, believes all things, hopes all things, endures all things.

> Love never ends. . . . And now faith, hope, and love abide, these three; and the greatest of these is love. (1 Cor 13:1–8, 13)

This passage provides a starting point, rather than an ending point, in a discussion of love. From a Christian perspective, "We love because he first loved us" (1 John 4:19). Love, then, is a key expression of who God is and how God relates to people. It is also a key expression of how people are to relate with God, themselves, and others. In trying to understand love in its various and best expressions, we begin to understand some of the dynamics of Christian spirituality. However you choose to understand and nurture Christian spirituality, it will somehow include love, both divine and human.

23.2 What Is Christian Spirituality?

Christian spirituality refers to the quality of people's relationship with God, especially as revealed through Jesus, enabled by the Holy Spirit. In Scripture, people's spiritual relationship with God is depicted in a number of ways. It involves knowing God (Jer 9:24; John 17:3), being still (Ps 46:10), becoming holy (Lev 11:45; 2 Cor 7:1), having the mind of Christ (Rom 8:6; Phil 2:5), and conforming one's will and life to Christ (1 Cor 12:3; John 13:34–35). Other descriptions, of course, could be given from the Bible. This is because spirituality is considered so holistic and all-embracing. There is no clear distinction between spiritual and physical, since they are inextricably bound up with one another. For example, Scripture describes spirituality as taking shape through various rites and rituals, and a disciplined life of prayer and action. Although spirituality is a lived experience in relationship with God, it does not occur apart from specific theological beliefs as well as actions for which God holds people accountable.

Emphasis upon God as Spirit and upon people as spiritual occurs throughout Scripture. Over and over again, God is described as Spirit (John 4:24; Acts 17:24; 2 Cor 3:17), and people are described as spirit as well as soul, body, and other descriptions (Job 32:8; Prov 20:27; 1 Cor 2:11; Jas 2:26). So people are to be concerned about spiritual life, spiritual discernment, spiritual restoration, spiritual power, spiritual growth, and so on. Although humans are physical beings, the Bible continually talks about the spiritual dimensions and responsibilities people have.

How is the spirit like the wind?

Ironically, spirituality's contemporary popularity is relatively new. Despite millennia-old emphases on spiritual matters in Christianity and other religions, no book written in English even included the word *spirituality* in the title until the twentieth century.[1] Previously spirituality had been talked about in other terms: holiness, godliness, piety, perfection, mysticism, devotion, higher life, and so on. Regardless of the particular term used, spirituality has always been important in Scripture and to Christians, and it continues to be important today.

> **Spirituality represents intimacy** with God, based upon Jesus Christ's salvation, and the ongoing presence of the Holy Spirit.
>
> Believers experience intimacy in different ways: actively and passively, ecstatically and silently—for everyone, a perfect fit!

23.3 Spiritual Formation and Direction

Spiritual formation reflects the longtime concern among Christians to grow or develop spiritually. In the last chapter, we talked about sanctification and God's desire that believers grow in grace. Their expectations with regard to the degree they expect to grow influences how they go about pursuing spirituality, union with Jesus, holiness, godliness, or however one describes it, by various means or disciplines. Over time, Christians have appealed to more than the Bible for spiritual formation. Powerful role models and spiritual writings appeared in church history, which continue to influence believers today. Likewise, an increasing amount of literature from the behavioral sciences has been used to understand the nature and development of faith, morality, and other dimensions related to Christian spirituality. Familiarity with culture—past and present—has also aided in spiritual formation. Christians draw from a variety of resources in order to grow spiritually in relationship with God, themselves, and others.

Sometimes *spiritual directors* aid believers in spiritual formation. Throughout church history, some Christian traditions have affirmed and utilized individuals who have specifically served to help others develop a more conscious and deep relationship with God. Usually spiritual direction occurs one-on-one, but it can occur in a variety of ways. Sometimes Christians lead others in small accountability groups, which aid spiritual formation. Sometimes these groups occur in churches, and sometimes they occur outside churches. Sometimes they are led by clergy, and sometimes they are led by laity. They exist, in large part, for the purpose of spiritual formation—for aiding the quality of people's relationship with God. Such formation occurs in churches as well, for spiritual formation and the expression of an ever-maturing spirituality is a key goal of the church. It produces individual as well as social benefits, according to the gracious will of God, since love for God is expected to manifest itself in love for others.

How do we grow spiritually?

23.4 Spiritual Disciplines

The spiritual disciplines are the ways Christians discipline their lives for the sake of growing spiritually. Scripture mentions a number of them, most notably prayer. Of course, believers do not cause their own spiritual growth. Likewise, they certainly earn no merit for salvation by participating in the spiritual disciplines. Nevertheless, they are God-given ways that people may demonstrate their praise and thanks to God as well as cooperate with God to the degree to which they believe God permits believers to enter into the process of spiritual formation.

The spiritual disciplines are a set of religious practices that reflect devotion to God. Dallas Willard (1935–) provides a helpful way to categorize the various spiritual disciplines:[2]

DISCIPLINES OF THE SPIRIT

Disciplines of Abstinence	Disciplines of Engagement
Solitude	Study
Silence	Worship
Fasting	Celebration
Frugality	Service
Chastity	Prayer
Secrecy (Confidentiality	Fellowship
Sacrifice	Confession
	Submission

Each of these disciplines provides amazing opportunities for believers to situate themselves in ways to cooperate with divine grace in their lives. The so-called disciplines of abstinence and engagement help Christians to grow in love and intimacy with God. They also help Christians grow in love, intimacy, and ministry toward others.

Those interested in growing spiritually should incorporate the spiritual disciplines in their lives. There is no magic formula that guarantees success. Moreover, some disciplines may prove more effective than others in aiding spiritual formation. Altogether they provide individuals with a breadth and depth of opportunity for experiencing the fullness of God's blessings for their lives.

23.5 Christian Virtues

Virtue is a disposition, habit, or quality that inclines one to do what is right, good, or holy. From a Christian perspective, virtue—from the Greek term meaning "excellence" or "strength"—represents how believers are supposed to be, think, speak, and act. Depending on one's translation of the Bible, however, the word *virtue* may not appear. Instead, it may be described as an "excellence" (Phil 4:8) or "goodness" (2 Pet 1:5). Peter says:

> His divine power has given us everything needed for life and godliness, through the knowledge of him who called us by his own glory and goodness [virtue]. . . . For this very reason, you must make every effort to support your faith with goodness [virtue], and goodness with knowledge, and knowledge with self-control, and self-control with endurance, and endurance with godliness, and godliness with mutual affection, and mutual affection with love. For if these things are yours and are increasing among you, they keep you from being ineffective and unfruitful in the knowledge of our Lord Jesus Christ (2 Pet 1:3, 5–8).

The word *virtue* articulates the most common way Christians throughout church history have described the expected character and life of a Christian. Next we will focus on the development of virtue.

Catholics categorize virtues in two ways. The *theological virtues* are those directly infused by God, for which believers are also responsible. They include faith, hope, and love, and they pertain primarily to the development of believers' knowledge of and relationship with God. In addition, *cardinal virtues* are those for which people are primarily responsible, humanly speaking, given the fact they were created in God's image. They include prudence, justice, temperance, and fortitude, and they pertain to the development of believers' knowledge of and relationship with others. The cardinal virtues reflect Aristotelian philosophy and Greco-Roman culture. It is thought that, despite sin, even non-Christians retain sufficient reason to understand and act morally, even if such understanding and action does not merit salvation.

CHRISTIAN VIRTUES	
Theological Virtues	**Cardinal Virtues**
Faith	Prudence (Wisdom)
Hope	Justice
Love (Charity)	Temperance (Self-control)
	Fortitude (Courage)

As Christians develop all these virtues, they grow more intimately in relationship with God, themselves, and others. The virtues are ways in which to grow spiritually and to express spirituality in thoughts, words, and deeds. Thus, virtues may be seen to represent the highest expression of Christian spirituality, when they have developed to their fullest.

Protestants at the time of the Reformation de-emphasized the virtues, thinking they looked too much like works-righteousness. Although all virtues were thought by Catholics to be enabled—directly or indirectly—by God's grace, Protestants wanted to avoid even the appearance of meriting salvation. Sometimes Protestants have spoken in terms of values rather than virtues. After the Reformation, however, Protestants increasingly appreciated the concept of the virtues, referring to them more in terms of piety and holiness than of virtuosity.

23.6 Varieties of Christian Spirituality

Because of the variety of ways Christians understand and promote spirituality, I will summarize the most prominent expressions of it. This is not to say that there are not more expressions of Christian spirituality that can be found. Indeed, variations have been distinguished by gender, race, and cultural differences, not to mention theological and church variations. Nevertheless, the following expressions provide a broad understanding of how Christians understand and act in ways most meaningful to them in their relationship with God, themselves, and others.

In some ways, the various expressions of Christian spirituality reflect the spiritual disciplines. Over the centuries, some spiritual disciplines have been emphasized more than others. The particular spiritual disciplines emphasized and then shaped particular church traditions. They also shaped the virtues and values emphasized for Christian life.

Although the following summarizations are helpful, there is no such thing as a pure type of Christian spirituality. Instead, individual believers and churches tend to reflect more than one expression. They might reflect one approach more than another, but to a certain extent they might resonate with all of the varieties of Christian spirituality.

23.6.1 Sacramental Spirituality

Christians regularly participated in sacramental observances from the start of Christianity. Those who converted were baptized, and meetings of believers included the ritualistic practice of eating bread and wine, consecrated as Jesus' body and blood (Acts 2:43; 20:7; 1 Cor 10:16; 11:23). In the fellowship of regularly meeting together, Christians in the first-century church made these ritualistic practices, along with others, key components of their understanding and expression of Christian spirituality.

Some Christians claim to experience the greatest sense of intimacy and empowerment by God when participating in the sacraments. This includes Protestants as well as Catholic and Orthodox Christians, though the latter are most often identified with sacramental spirituality. From a Catholic and Orthodox church perspective, God provided the sacraments as a means by which grace, along with other blessings, is given to those who partake. In fact, the sacrament of the Eucharist provides an especially intimate encounter with God. After the elements of bread and wine are consecrated through prayer, they are transformed into the essence of Jesus' body and blood. Participation in Eucharist, then, involves genu-

How might the Eucharist— Communion—help us focus on God?

ine communion—if not union—with God. It is difficult to find much greater intimacy with God than in appropriate participation in the Eucharist.

In addition to intimacy, the sacraments also provide grace to believers. They provide grace for salvation and confirmation of salvation. They also provide grace for growing spiritually and morally through the sacraments of penance and anointing of the sick. Such empowerment is thought to be promised by God for all who faithfully partake of the sacraments. They aid every dimension of life individually and socially, inside and outside the church.

Liturgy

Liturgy refers to any service by people, offered to God in worship. The Greek term translated "liturgy" literally means the "work of the people." In church, liturgies include rites, rituals, or other traditions used in worship services. Different liturgies occur at appropriate times during the liturgical year, that is, different religious observances throughout the church year. Such observances may include Advent and Christmas, and continue through Epiphany, Lent, Holy Week, Easter, and Whitsuntide (Pentecost). The remainder of the church year is described as Kingdomtide (Christ the King), or Ordinary Time. Not every church or denomination celebrates all the special religious days of the year, but some are usually observed, especially

How does liturgy make Scripture more accessible?

Christmas and Easter. Each worship service has specific rites, rituals, and traditions, some more than others. Most often, they include a wealth of scriptural quotes and allusions, centering liturgy on God and God's self-revelation.

Prayer books used in liturgical worship services make extensive use of Scripture. Specific theological and ministerial concerns also influence the types of liturgies, readings, and services used. In preaching, lectionaries are sometimes used for focusing sermons on the whole of the Bible so that no part of it is ever neglected. A lectionary is a compilation of biblical passages for reading throughout the year, which may be used for worship services and personally. For worship services, the lectionary follows a three-year cycle and contains passages from the whole of Scripture. That way passages from throughout the Old Testament, New Testament epistles, and New Testament gospels are preached from on a regular basis. Prayer books may be used for private as well as public devotion. They may also serve as guides for prayer.

Sacramentalism and Protestantism

Some Protestant churches, though not all, resist sacramentalism and liturgy. They may associate it with works-righteousness or religious formality that takes away from their conception of God and salvation, which is more individualistically and personally conceived. Be that as it may, all Christians and churches function with some understanding and practice of the sacraments as well as liturgy. They may not call it liturgy, yet all Christians develop traditions for how they run worship services, music, singing, and other church celebrations that honor God in ways they feel best contribute to their and others' spirituality.

Increasingly, Christians—Catholic, Orthodox, and Protestant—focus upon worship, celebration, and fellowship as central to the life and ministry of the church. After Vatican II (1962–1965), Catholics placed renewed emphasis upon making church worship more meaningful, presenting services in the vernacular and ameliorating them in ways culturally relevant to church members. That included cultural relevance for church members around the world. Protestants continue to reform their worship services in ways that meet the contemporary needs of people. Some find it a happy challenge to modify constantly church services in order to promote Christian celebration and worship.

23.6.2 Contemplative Spirituality

Contemplation is prayerful reflection upon God, which involves the mind as well as will. Meditation is often contrasted with contemplation, since meditation involves more focused reflection upon Scripture or other Christian teachings. However, contemplation emphasizes a deeper, intuitive connection with God that transcends human capability.

Contemplative spirituality assumes all spiritual disciplines for its achievement. The disciplines of abstinence are especially helpful for believers to focus on God by means of solitude, silence, fasting, frugality, chastity, confidentiality, and sacrifice. In fact, the spiritual disciplines are identified so much with contemplative spirituality that they are considered synonymous expressions of spirituality. Protestants who incorporate the spiritual disciplines into their understanding and expression of Christianity refer to themselves more and more as advocates of contemplative spirituality.

Development of Contemplative Spirituality

Some of the earliest Christians advocated contemplative spirituality. For example, the earliest Christians emphasized prayer, fasting, and almsgiving as expressions of spirituality. Due to persecution, some were martyred, which is the ultimate self-sacrifice for the sake of God. Later, Christians became monks as an act of self-sacrifice, which included chastity and monasticism. Within this context, mystical and monastic spirituality arose with the help of such Christians as Origen and Dionysius the Areopagite (ca. 500). The latter emphasized three stages of mystical spirituality: 1) purification (purgative way); 2) meditation (illuminative way); and 3) union with God (unitive way). The final stage corresponds to the grace-aided encounter or communion with God, representing the highest experience of God achievable in this life.

Catholicism provided the greatest leadership in developing contemplative spirituality. Religious orders were officially established in order to provide contexts specifically designed for promoting spirituality and ministry to others. For example, Bernard of Clairvaux (ca. 1090–1153) developed guidelines for monastic spirituality, known as the "Rules of Benedict." Later, Teresa of Avila (1515–1582) and John of the Cross (1542–1591) renewed emphasis upon mystical spirituality. The latter spoke of the "dark night of the soul" that can accompany the spiritual journey of believers. Although contemplative spirituality developed in monastic contexts, it continues to have widespread influence on Christian spirituality.

Christian contemplation has parallels, of course, with other religions and religious movements in the world that employ contemplative and related mystical practices. Christians sometimes employ spiritual disciplines parallel to other religions as well as behavioral scientific studies of spirituality in order to better understand and advance Christian practices. This is because the spiritual disciplines used by Christians ostensibly share characteristics with other religions and religious practices. Prayer, worship, and service to others in expression of one's beliefs are not exclusively Christian. Christians may even benefit from the insights of other religions. Parallels between Christian and non-Christian spiritual practices, however, do not negate the particular nature and significance of Christian prayer, worship, and service. Christians practice the spiritual disciplines with a significant difference. Contemplative spirituality is not merely one form of spirituality thought to be equal with all others. Christians believe that God alone sanctifies as well as enables Christian spirituality.

What is meant by the "dark night of the soul"?

Can icons—or any kind
of artwork—help you
focus on God?

Icon Spirituality

Orthodox churches emphasized contemplative spirituality along with Catholicism. One of the distinctive contributions they made to it was their emphasis upon icons. Icons are images or pictures used to represent Jesus or other saints of the church for the sake of veneration and of helping believers focus on God and the eternal mysteries of the gospel. Usually icons appear painted on flat pieces of wood or another two-dimensional surface, sometimes decorating a church. Icons are intentionally *representations* rather than *realistic* portraits, since Orthodox Christians want to avoid preoccupation with the painting rather than spirituality. They also want to avoid any hint of idolatry. John of Damascus (ca. 674–749) was an advocate of icons for the sake of properly venerating Jesus and the gospel he presented. Iconographic spirituality aided believers in pursuit of deification—of how believers could be lifted into the mystery of communion with God.

Orthodox church architecture, rich in religious symbolism, is thought to contribute to the worship experience of believers. Screens called iconostases, on which icons are placed—wood carvings, ornate crosses, and other Christian artwork—help congregants focus on the worship of God. Chanting and the use of incense are also thought to be aids to Christian spirituality.

Other Christians may not use icons, but they are aware of the ways beauty in paintings, sculpture, architecture, music, and singing can aid them in focusing contemplatively upon God. Catholicism is famous for its artwork, including individual pieces of religious art as well as the artistic construction of churches and cathedrals. All are dedicated to God and are useful in aiding believers in spiritual formation. Protestants have excelled in musical contributions to worship and celebration both in churches and in private spirituality. Certainly art and music, which are a part of the physical world in which we live, may serve spiritual ends for the glory of God as well as for spiritual formation.

Marian Spirituality

In early church history, Marian spirituality arose as believers sought to emulate Mary, the mother of Jesus, as a role model of the Christian life. Believers also considered Mary to be alive and present with Jesus. She was a part of the "communion of saints"—all faithful Christians who died and immediately received the glory of eternal life in heaven. Both Catholic and Orthodox churches venerate Mary as being preeminent among the saints. It is believed that the saints intercede on behalf of those still on earth. Believers ask the saints for prayers of intercession to God for their various needs. This does not mean that Christians pray to Mary and the saints; they only pray to God. However, just as people may ask family members or friends to pray for them, Catholic and Orthodox Christians ask Mary and the saints to pray for them.

In venerating Mary, emphasis is placed upon the portrayal of her faithful, outstanding discipleship as described in the Bible. Women especially identify with Mary as a role model for their lives and for their spiritual formation. However, the preeminence of Mary as a role model is not limited to women, nor is it limited to the early church. Catholic and Orthodox Christians today continue to venerate Mary, ask for her intercession, and follow liturgical practices that involve praying the Rosary. Praying the Rosary is a practice of spiritual devotion that uses a chain of beads for counting prayers and reciting the "Hail Mary," which summarizes the words of annunciation addressed to Mary by the angel and by Elizabeth (Luke 1:28–42).

Why is Mary appealing as a spiritual role model?

23.6.3 Evangelical Spirituality

Evangelism has long been an important expression of the Christian life, and it serves as a way for Christians to be close to God as well as serve others through evangelism. Although evangelism is only one expression of spirituality, some consider it the highest expression. The Great Commission (Matt 28:19–20) serves as the essence of the gospel, spreading the good news of Jesus to all nations. In first-century Christianity, much evangelism was needed since people were only beginning to learn about the life, death, and resurrection of Jesus, and the implication for their salvation and lifestyles.

Throughout church history, Christians have continued to evangelize to varying degrees, depending upon their particular circumstances. After Christianity was accepted in the Roman Empire, renewed emphasis was placed upon evangelism. Mendicant friars, such as the Dominicans and Franciscans, preached salvation, especially to the poor of the Middle Ages. Catholics were the first to send missionaries to the New World within a few decades after Columbus discovered it. Other periods of evangelism include post-Reformation Protestantism, Counter-Reformation Catholicism, revivalistic outbreaks of the seventeenth and eighteenth centuries, including Pietism in continental Europe, Methodism in Great Britain, and the Great Awakening in the American colonies.

Evangelism and Proselytism

Some of this evangelism could be viewed as proselytism, since believers from one Christian tradition were being persuaded to another one. The same could be said of first-century Christians, when Jews were persuaded to convert, and of Roman Christians, when mythology and pagan cults became politically incorrect. Today as well as in the past, Christians need to be careful about when and how they go about the task of evangelism. It should not be undertaken coercively, threatening and demeaning other religious traditions. Nor should evangelism and missions be undertaken in ways that confuse the gospel with the cultural worldview of those spreading the gospel. Too often Christians have mixed persecution, colonialism, and other forms of triumphalism into their ministries. Be that as it may, numerous Christians still consider evangelism the height of spirituality.

Evangelism grew through the nineteenth-century revivals throughout the colonial world, and in the twentieth century with improved means for communicating the gospel through radio, television, and the Internet. New languages were learned throughout the world in order to present the Bible to every nation in their own languages and dialects. Despite the various ways it is accomplished, the "making of disciples" is considered the highest manifestation of Christian faith, hope, and love in relationship to God as well as to others.

Evangelism and Evangelicalism

Since the time of the Reformation, a growing number of Christians refer to themselves as "evangelical" or "evangelical Christians." Although the name is new, evangelicalism traces its origin back to the "good news" (Greek, euangelion) of Jesus. Luther emphasized salvation by grace through faith, which individuals could appropriate without the intermediation of the church. Further emphasizing faith as trust, Luther promoted an evangelistic emphasis previously unfamiliar to people. Calvin and other Reformers followed Luther's lead in spreading the Protestant understanding of the good news of the gospel throughout Europe.

Go, and make disciples!

Over the centuries, a strand of Protestantism has traced its theological and spiritual ancestry back to Luther. Self-proclaimed evangelical Christians claim the many revivalistic traditions of Europe and the rest of the world, including Pietism, Methodism, Holiness Movement, and Pentecostalism. Although the latter movements have their own unique characteristics, they share a family resemblance, reflective of their respective concerns for evangelism. In the twentieth century, evangelical identity reemerged in a variety of manifestations in churches, parachurch groups, ecumenical bodies, and academic institutions. Despite numerous attempts to identify evangelicalism precisely, the identifying feature remains focused upon evangelism as the highest spiritual calling of Christians and churches.

23.6.4 Studious Spirituality

Those who sense God most intimately through the exercise of studying things related to God, especially Scripture, and applying their studies to the needs of humanity through teaching what they have learned exercise studious spirituality. In the Bible, wisdom and knowledge are promoted in both the Old and New Testaments. The entire book of Proverbs, for example, presents a highly practical book of wisdom, which teaches knowledge, discernment, and ethical responsibility (Prov 1:1–7). In the New Testament, the believers in

Berea were thought to be of more noble character because "they welcomed the message [of Paul] very eagerly and examined the scriptures every day to see whether these things were so" (Acts 17:11). Even Jesus emphasized how believers were to love God "with all your mind," which was an addition not found in the *Shema*—the Old Testament passage to which Jesus alluded (Deut 6:4–5). A studious spirituality was considered important to the first-century church, appealing to those who sought to understand, teach, and preach the good news of Jesus.

In the early church, the patristic writers became well-known for their apologetics, which was their way of honoring God as well as the burgeoning Christian movement. Church fathers such as Irenaeus, Clement of Alexandria (ca. 150–215), and Tertullian defended the *rule of faith*—their emergent understanding of orthodox Christianity, based upon the Scriptures as they knew them, along with baptismal formulas, catechisms, and other liturgical writings. Their intellectual contributions were highly valued for defending Christianity against its critics. The early apologists also helped to instruct new believers as well as provide growing breadth in their understanding and communication of Christianity.

Catholic Scholasticism

During the Middle Ages, scholasticism arose, which is a highly rational and logical approach to the study, formulation, and teaching of Christianity. Catholic scholasticism had its roots in an academic renaissance of interest in classical and Christian antiquity. The scholastic study of God and the Bible was a profound expression of studious spirituality.

Study as worship?

Anselm is one of the earliest examples. However, the *Summa Theologica,* written by Aquinas, marks a high point in Roman Catholic scholasticism. Aquinas systematically organizes Christian beliefs, values, and practices by means of Greek thought, especially the writings of Aristotle, while maintaining the superiority of theology. He thinks that a harmony exists between faith and reason, which allows Christians to engage multiple disciplines of study. Aquinas thinks that reason significantly aided Christians in understanding, communicating, and applying biblical truths.

The liability of scholasticism is that it tempts Christians into becoming rationalistic and dogmatic in their religious beliefs, values, and practices. Relying too much upon logic, deduction, system, and syllogistic argumentation robs from the personal, experiential dimensions of Christianity. Protestants think that scholasticism puts too much emphasis upon what people know and do, rather than upon God. However, Catholicism has endeavored to avoid the liabilities of scholasticism, while retaining the insights of Aquinas and other scholars for articulating church beliefs, values, and practices.

Protestant Scholasticism

Protestants and Catholics have a history of scholasticism. After the Reformation, Protestants sometimes became involved with maintaining the theology of their founders rather than pursuing their notion of "always reforming." As a result, there arose Lutheran scholasticism, Calvinist scholasticism, and so on. Nevertheless, Protestantism benefited from the studious passion of its scholastics, emphasizing the importance of scriptural study as well as of teaching it in churches and institutions of higher education. Over the centuries, certain Protestant traditions such as Presbyterianism excelled in studious spirituality, promoting many types of scholarship that influenced the church at large.

Studious spirituality is sometimes promoted more in communal than individual terms. Spirituality is not thought of so much in terms of personal piety, except to the extent that individuals recognize that God alone vouchsafes their positional holiness. Thus, the expression of spirituality occurs more in the context of church, worship, and preaching that focuses believers upon the idea that everyone is part of God's wonderful plans and providence. It is in the context of the church that people best understand their gift of salvation and appropriate responses of giving praise and thanks to God.

To be sure, Protestant scholasticism has its liabilities, which from time to time were met by Pietistic and Holiness reactions. Dogmatic formulations, apologetic zeal, and preeminence placed upon rational formulations of Christianity arose throughout its existence. In the twentieth century, for example, fundamentalist Christianity arose in reaction to the growing modernist movement, characterized by Liberal Protestant and secular principles of biblical interpretation. Fundamentalist Christianity reacted by opposing and sometimes withdrawing from debates, choosing to affirm dogmatically an inerrant Scripture that spoke as authoritatively about science and history as about theology. Spirituality is expressed through the deductive study of the Bible and exegetical preaching. Fidelity to perceived "fundamentals" of Christian belief constitutes the greatest example of spirituality.

23.6.5 Holiness Spirituality

We have already studied the numerous biblical references to how Christians should be holy. In both Old and New Testaments, examples abound as to how Christians are to live Christlike lives. They are not to be conformed to this world; they are to be transformed (Rom 12:2). Such transformation involves total consecration to God and to God's sanctifying grace.

Church history is filled with examples of those who promoted holy living. In the early church, Christians pursued holiness in various ways, both individually and communally. They sought to imitate Jesus, live lives of obedience and virtue, and perhaps become a part of monastic life in order to facilitate growth in God's grace.

Catholic and Orthodox Churches

Catholics have long emphasized holiness a number of ways, through the promotion of the theological and cardinal virtues as well as through participation in the sacraments. Various historic developments in Catholicism aided in the pursuit of holiness. During the Middle Ages, mendicant friars (Franciscans and Dominicans) were itinerant preachers who promoted apostolic lifestyles, pastoral leadership, and education, especially among the poor. Lay spirituality increased through reverence for the saints, pilgrimages, and an increasing amount of Christian literature, such as Dante's *Divine Comedy*. An emphasis on *modern devotion,* which was applicable to laity as well as clergy, stressed the spiritual disciplines. In particular, Thomas à Kempis (1380–1471) promoted greater lay involvement in spirituality by emphasizing the spiritual disciplines in imitating Jesus. His book *The Imitation of Christ* became an all-time bestseller.

Orthodox churches emphasized deification as an expression of holiness. All Christians—not just the clergy— are capable of becoming more Christlike by participating in the mystery of Jesus' divinity. Through ongoing repentance and communion with God, believers are optimistic about the power of God to transform them. Origen, Athanasius, and Cyril of Alexandria (ca. 378–ca. 412) emphasized how prayer, liturgical worship, hymnody, and icons aid people in becoming holy. Their influence has had an impact on the Orthodox churches as well as those in the West.

What does it mean to "imitate Christ"?

Protestantism

After the Reformation, Protestantism morphed into scholasticism, prompting several revitalization movements such as Pietism, Quakerism, Methodism, the Great Awakenings, and the Holiness Movement. Pietism influenced Methodism, which in turn influenced the Holiness Movement. Wesley was the key transitional figure as the founder of Methodism. He emphasizes that God not only called people to become holy, God provides sufficient grace to sanctify them entirely (1 Thess 5:23–24). Although Wesley does not advocate sinless perfection, he thinks that God has the power to impart righteousness to people as well as impute it. Conceiving of entire sanctification (also known as Christian perfection) in terms of love, Wesley thinks it possible for believers to love God with their whole heart, soul, mind, and strength, and their neighbors as themselves, just as Jesus had commanded.

Following Wesley, a growing number of Christians sought to live a *higher life*. The Holiness Movement encompasses a broad number of individuals and churches who believe that God wants Jesus to become more than our Savior. God also wants Jesus to become the Lord of our lives. Although he may become Lord of one's life at the time of conversion, most Christians experience the need for total consecration of their lives to God after a period of spiritual growth and ongoing repentance. At the point of total consecration, God then provides extra grace for the sake of purifying believers' intentions truly love God and others—a second blessing. Sometimes members of the Holiness Movement

Have you ever contributed to Christian charities at Christmastime?

became perfectionist and legalistic in trying to attain lofty expectations of holiness, which distracted from the true goal of loving God and others. However, true holiness is more of a means to love than an end in itself.

23.6.6 Activist Spirituality

Christianity has long had a tradition of actively demonstrating love toward others, especially the poor—those challenged economically, politically, socially, and/or physically. Jesus made service to the poor a core part of his ministry. At the beginning of his ministry, he did not talk about only preaching the "good news" of the gospel. Instead, he defined his early ministry by quoting from Isaiah about how he was to "bring good news to the poor . . . proclaim release to the captives and recovery of sight to the blind, to let the oppressed go free" (Luke 4:18). Jesus seemed to have a preference for ministering to the poor. This did not mean he neglected others; however, the poor had a special place in his heart and ministry.

This care for the poor is prominent throughout church history among Catholics, Orthodox churches, and Protestants. Although it may not always seem the case today, Christians have continuously provided compassion ministries to those who suffer pain or grief. They were often the first to care for the sick, feed the hungry, clothe the impoverished, and provide shelter for the homeless.

Protesting as a spiritual act?

Have they always provided these services? No. However, if one can get past obvious examples of insensitivity and harm Christians committed, one can recognize the remarkable amount of care and service given by them, individually and collectively. Many hospitals, orphanages, academic institutions, and other philanthropic institutions were created by churches long before any government or secular charities offered help.

Social Gospel

The social gospel ministers to others by doing more than offering care for the poor. It also seeks to change societal, governmental, and economic structures that perpetuate unjust and oppressive practices. This movement arose, especially among Protestants, during the nineteenth century. Walter Rauschenbusch (1861–1918) advocated social activism along with Christian discipleship. In his care for people, he thinks that Christians need to care for their spiritual lives as well as their physical lives, just as Jesus modeled in his life and ministry. Rauschenbusch is especially concerned for people in a progressively industrialized world, where the plight of urban workers is especially acute. He stresses justice and hopes for a progressively Christianized world, which influences both the spiritual and physical well-being of people.

The concern to change social, political, and economic policies as well as provide compassionate ministries for those in need was anticipated by various expressions of Christian activism. The fight for the abolition of slavery began in Great Britain, during the eighteenth century, and continued in the United States during the nineteenth century. Abolition in the United States was aided through the efforts of churches such as the Society of Friends and activist Christians such as Lyman Beecher (1775–1863), Charles Finney, and Harriet Beecher Stowe (1811–1896), the author of *Uncle Tom's Cabin.* Lyman Beecher also advocated the prohibition of alcohol along with Frances Willard (1839–1898) and Billy Sunday (1862–1935). Emma Willard (Frances' cousin; 1787–1870), Susan B. Anthony (1820–1906), and the Grimke family were early advocates of women's rights. In all these examples, Christian spirituality was not thought to be something private. Instead, true spirituality involved inward and outward care for the soul—one's own soul as well as others. Moreover, it includes care that does more than minister to the effects of sin. It also needs to include care for changing the structures of society, government, and business that subject people to unjust living conditions.

Liberation Theologies

During the twentieth century, a growing number of Christians became concerned about injustice, oppression, and violence in the world. Such things are considered contrary to the will of God and the teachings of the Bible. In response to people's overwhelming social, political, and economic needs, an increasing number of Christians became political activists as an expression of their Christian spirituality and morality. Some resorted to resistance in order to achieve their goals, though usually passive resistance was used. Martin Luther King Jr., for example, was a pastor who led the Civil Rights Movement in opposition to racial discrimination and other injustices perpetrated against minority ethnic groups. James Cone later articulated "black theology," which advocated in stronger terms the need for liberating people from ongoing racial discrimination, typified by ongoing marginalization and oppression of the black minority. People's spiritual nurture could not proceed without concern for their physical well-being.

Martin Luther King Jr. advocated civil rights as a spiritual act

Around the world, growing Christian concern arose for the desperate plight of the poorest people, which was thought to be so great that major social, political, and economic upheaval might be needed.

Catholic priests such as Gustavo Gutiérrez advocated "Latin American liberation theology," which argued that people may be in as great a need of physical liberation from the bondage of social, political, and economic oppression as of spiritual liberation from the bondage of sin, ignorance, and misery. Marxist philosophy was sometimes used in critiquing governments in power, which represented the worst of social, political, and economic oppression. Revolution may be necessary. For the most part, Latin American liberation theologians expressed their concern that spirituality not be seen only in spiritual terms but in holistic terms that provided liberation for all dimensions of human life—liberation thought to be modeled in Jesus' own counter-cultural life and ministry.

Spiritually speaking, why are issues of equality important?

Another area in need of liberation was that of gender discrimination. The women's rights movement was rekindled by Christians as well as others. Theologians such as Rosemary Radford Ruether argued that Scripture advocated equality for women. Although the Bible was historically interpreted in patriarchal ways, it was actually progressive in terms of how it presented women, providing principles of equality which should affirm and promote women's rights and leadership at all levels inside the church as well as society as a whole. Even if men and women choose to express their freedom in different ways, Christians should be concerned about issues of gender equality in promoting healthy spirituality and morality.

23.6.7 Pentecostal Spirituality

At Pentecost, it is reported that all the followers of Jesus "were filled with the Holy Spirit and began to speak in other languages, as the Spirit gave them ability" (Acts 2:4). They were emboldened to preach, which resulted in thousands of conversions. Throughout the book of Acts as well as in the writings of Paul, the gifts of the Holy Spirit appear over and over, suggesting special empowerment for life and ministry. Various "signs and wonders" attended their lives and ministries (Acts 5:12; 2 Cor 12:12; Heb 2:4; cf. Mark 16:17–18). All these manifestations demonstrated a power and diversity of gifts used by the early Christians. They were considered a reflection of their spiritual relationship with God, with dramatic implications for how they lived and ministered to others.

Throughout church history, Christians have been reported to manifest various signs, wonders, and gifts of empowerment. There is no lack of testimony to miracles, healings, visions, and exorcisms. At times, so-called enthusiasts were met with suspicion, fear, and persecution. At other times, they were met with wonder, joy, and honor, sometimes venerated as saints. For the most part,

Christians were suspicious of those claiming signs, wonders, and gifts of empowerment.

Pentecostalism

At the turn of the twentieth century, Pentecostalism considered itself a renewal of first-century spirituality, reflecting the dynamic work of the Holy Spirit in gifting believers with power to love God and others. Using second blessing language from the Holiness Movement, Pentecostalism talked about the need for believers—subsequent to conversion—to experience Holy Spirit baptism. It was thought that speaking in tongues provided the physical evidence of Holy Spirit baptism. This was the blessing promised by John the Baptist as accompanying the ministry of Jesus (Mark 1:8). Pentecost represented the fulfillment of Joel 2:28–32 with regard to this baptism, and it occurred subsequent to conversion (Acts 2:16–21). Making oneself available to Holy Spirit baptism produced a more intimate spiritual relationship with God as well as divine gifts, which empowered believers beyond their natural abilities to achieve miraculous signs and wonders.

Pentecostals profoundly influenced Christianity throughout the world. Its message spread quickly and appealed powerfully to those appreciative of a stirring sense of the presence and power of God. Churches initially resisted Pentecostal enthusiasm. Thus, Pentecostal churches arose aplenty, advocating the spiritual empowerment available through the gifts of the Holy Spirit. Such gifts include prophecy, healing, working miracles, tongues, interpretation of tongues, wisdom, knowledge, faith, and discernment (1 Cor 12:4–11). Despite institutional resistance to Pentecostalism, its emphasis upon the gifts of the Holy Spirit had widespread influence upon Christians' understanding of their spiritual relationship to God and how God may give them supernatural gifts for demonstrating their love and service to others. It also influenced worship styles in churches, encouraging greater freedom of personal expression in services, types of music played and choruses sung, and manifestation of the gifts of the Holy Spirit.

How free should worship be?

Charismatic Movement

By the mid-twentieth century, emphasis on all the gifts of the Holy Spirit influenced existing churches and denominations without resulting in exclusion or schism. The renewal in such churches of an emphasis on all the gifts as essential to Christian life and ministry is commonly referred to as the Charismatic Movement. Such renewal affected worldwide Catholicism and Protestantism, manifested through the outbreak of speaking in tongues as well as other signs and wonders. Knowledge of one's gift or gifts of the Holy Spirit provides a profound bridge for relating spiritually with God as well as fulfilling one's gifting in relationship to others.

Although speaking in tongues is most often identified with Pentecostalism and the Charismatic Movement, it is not always a required expression of spirituality. It is a blessing to speak in tongues, but Holy Spirit baptism may be manifested in other ways. Sometimes Pentecostals and Charismatics have viewed speaking in tongues as the highest manifestation of spirituality; however, it is not essential to one's spirituality. In some respects, the gifts of the Holy Spirit have more to do with ministry than spirituality. Yet, they powerfully influence their possessor as well as minister to others.

23.6.8 Other Spiritualities

Other spiritualities could be added to the ones already mentioned. Scripture, as well as church history, contains variations of the types of spirituality already mentioned. For example, some emphasize ecumenism as the way to grow spiritually in relationship with God and with others, promoting greater unity and cooperation among Christians. Others emphasize filial spirituality, recognizing that in certain seasons of people's lives, the greatest expression of spirituality may become manifest by caring for one's spouse, children, parents, and other members of an extended family. After all, one does not need to live in a monastery or be a full-time member of the clergy to be spiritual.

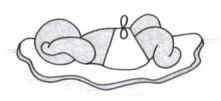

How may changing a diaper be a spiritual experience?

In none of these instances should one form of spirituality be used as an excuse for not participating in one or more other types of spirituality. They are not mutually exclusive. On the contrary, they complement one another in seeking to become more intimate with God and in expressing love for God and others. Although Christians may find themselves in churches that emphasize one or more types of spirituality, they should never consider themselves limited from experimenting with other approaches. It may be that God wants people to find ever new ways of experiencing spirituality, which may prove beneficial in the overarching goal of love toward oneself as well as toward God and others.

23.7 Conclusion

God wants people to believe and to relate with God in ways that foster an ever-growing and fulfilling sense of intimacy. Spiritual formation has been a priority throughout church history, though Christians have understood it and promoted it in different ways. Christians should turn to those beliefs, values, and practices that prove most fruitful in enjoying all the love, joy, peace, patience, kindness, generosity, faithfulness, gentleness, and self-control that God intends for them to experience.

Likewise, Christians should demonstrate their love toward God and others through spiritual disciplines, religious observances, and other gifts of the

Holy Spirit. Christian spirituality is not a passive experience; it includes activities that benefit others as well as individual Christians. For the most part, Christians view spirituality as that which sends them out into the world in order to become more effective, and genuinely Christlike, representatives of God and of the gospel in its holistic concern for people.

23.8 Questions for Further Reflection

1. How do you understand the nature of Christian spirituality?

2. Which spiritual disciplines appeal to you the most? Which have been the most important for your own spiritual development? What are spiritual disciplines you need to incorporate more into your life?

3. What is the relationship between the theological and cardinal virtues, and why are they important to the Christian life?

4. With which view of Christian spirituality do you resonate the most? Why?

5. What can you learn from other views of Christian spirituality? How can you incorporate their views in enriching your own spirituality?

23.9 Notes

1. According to Walter Principe, "The first English title I have been able to find using the term is the translation in 1922 of the first volume of Pierre Pourrat's work [ca. 1922]; in English it bore the title *Christian Spirituality.*" See his "Toward Defining Spirituality," in *Exploring Christian Spirituality: An Ecumenical Reader* (ed. Kenneth J. Collins; Grand Rapids: Baker, 2000), 47.

2. Dallas Willard, *The Spirit of the Disciplines* (San Francisco: HarperSanFrancisco, 1988), 158.

THE CHURCH

God put this power to work in Christ when he raised him from the dead and seated him at his right hand in the heavenly places, far above all rule and authority and power and dominion, and above every name that is named, not only in this age but also in the age to come. And he has put all things under his feet and has made him the head over all things for the church, which is his body, the fullness of him who fills all in all.
(Ephesians 1:20–23)

THE CHURCH

24.1 Introduction

Although we do not know much about Jesus as a young man, the Gospel of Luke shares a provocative story about Jesus at the age of twelve (Luke 2:41–52). Every year Jesus' family traveled to Jerusalem in order to attend the festival of the Passover—the Jewish commemoration of the sparing of the first-born children of the Israelites and their liberation from Egyptian bondage. After Passover, Jesus' parents—Joseph and Mary—left for home with a group of travelers, apparently without knowing whether the young Jesus was with them. When Joseph and Mary realized that Jesus was missing, they returned to Jerusalem. Joseph and Mary found Jesus in the temple—the primary place of Jewish worship—sitting among the teachers, listening to them, and asking them questions. Apparently, all who heard Jesus were amazed at his understanding and answers. His parents, however, were not impressed!

When Joseph and Mary asked Jesus why he had worried them by not following the travelers home, Jesus responded with bewilderment. He said, "Why were you searching for me? Did you not know that I must be in my Father's house?" (Luke 2:49). For Jesus there seemed no place more important to be than in God's house, focusing on the things of God.

Later in life, the temple continued to spark Jesus' passion. In fact, Jesus used a whip and overturned tables in the temple in order to drive out the entrepreneurs that inhibited it from being a "house of prayer" (Matt 21:12–17; John 2:13–22).

Church as "God's house"

Jesus' love for the church appears in the book of Hebrews, where people are encouraged to meet together for the sake of worship, public confession, and provoking each other to love and good deeds (Heb 10:19–25). This regular habit of gathering together helps people in their relationship with God as well as their relationship with themselves and others. Failing to do so jeopardizes their opportunity to experience the abundant life Jesus promised; it also jeopardizes their eternal prospects.

24.2 What Is the Church?

What is the church? Is it the white, steeple-topped building sitting on a prominent corner in town? No, though some people may identify the church with such a building. Most people would say that the church, rightly understood, is the community of people who gather in that building—or anywhere, for that matter. The church is a living and active fellowship of believers, especially those who believe Jesus to be their Savior and Lord. Because the church consists of people rather than a building or organization, the church may meet anywhere and at any time. It may meet in a park or in a storefront; it may meet in suburban America or a faraway jungle. Certainly the church worldwide possesses a variety of sizes, shapes, organizational structures, music, liturgy, rituals, and ministries. With so much diversity, one might wonder what unifies them. What resemblance do churches have with one another?

The Bible describes the church in a variety of ways. In some instances, the church is a local body of believers; in other instances, the church is the universal body of believers. In some instances, the church is a holy institution; in other instances, the church is like a flock of sheep. Perhaps the most significant descriptions of the church in Scripture appear in the rich symbols used to depict the church. For example, the Bible portrays the church in the following ways:

IMAGES OF THE CHURCH

Biblical Symbol	Scripture References
Body of Christ	1 Cor 12:27; Rom 12:5; Eph 1:22–23; 4:12; Col 1:18
Bride of Christ	Rev 21:9; cf. 2 Cor 11:2
Chosen race	1 Pet 2:9
Fellowship in the Spirit	Eph 4:3; Acts 4:32
Holy temple	2 Cor 6:16; Eph 2:21
Household of God	Heb 3:6; Eph 2:19
Flock of God	1 Pet 5:2; Luke 12:32
People of God	1 Pet 2:9, 10
Royal priesthood	1 Pet 2:9
Spiritual house	1 Pet 2:5

The metaphor of the body of Christ is a common one used in the New Testament. In the metaphor, the church is more of an *organism* than an *organization*. It functions as a living, dynamic body of individuals who together are more than the sum of individual believers. Jesus Christ is the head—the source or leader of the body. Yet, he loved the church and sacrificed himself for it (Eph 5:25). Similarly, the church consists of many parts, which serve different functions while also serving one another (1 Cor 12:12–26). Each part should understand and respect other parts, since all work to promote God's kingdom.

References to the church variously refer to it in relationship to God the Father, God the Son, and God the Holy Spirit. All three persons of the Trinity relate to the church, and so we must consider all of them when reflecting upon how God works in the life of the church—past, present, and future. For example, Christians need to be aware of more than the person and work of Jesus in the founding of the church—as crucial as he is for understanding the church. Christians also need to be aware of the person and work of the Holy Spirit, since the Holy Spirit is the primary person of the Godhead with whom people relate today.

Although there exists a rich diversity within Christian churches, one can discern a kind of family resemblance between them. People have long noticed these resemblances and tried to distill the commonality between churches. As early as the time of the ancient church, Christians tried to describe what made a church a church. Many descriptions arose, but how could one fully define the true church?

> **Everyone knows** that the church is not a building; it consists of people who, in God, truly believe.
>
> The church represents the place that God wants believers to flourish, to grow, and to minister to others—a place to give as well as to receive.

24.3 The Marks of the Church

Early terms used by the church to define it may be found in the Nicene Creed. The Nicene Creed used the following terms to describe the church: one, holy, catholic, and apostolic. These descriptions are the marks of the church—those features that constitute the true church of Jesus.

24.3.1 One

The emphasis on the church being *one* signifies that ultimately there exists only one church because there is only one head and Lord—Jesus (Eph 1:22; 4:15; Col 1:18; 2:19). Jesus instituted the church in the New Testament (Matt 16:18; Eph 2:20; 1 Thess 1:1; 1 Tim 3:15), so only those who truly follow him constitute the church. Although there arose various church traditions and denominations, there really exists only one church of Jesus.

As the church grew during the first century, it was inevitable that a variety of churches and church traditions arose. During the time of the apostles, the apostles held consensual authority over the new and growing number of local churches. After the apostles, problems increased in trying to maintain a sense of unity because of the geographical distance between churches, the difficulties of communication, and the increasing linguistic and cultural differences between churches. In time Christians recognized diversity in church beliefs and traditions, but all agreed that, ultimately speaking, there existed only one true church.

It is a task of the church that it should seek out ways in which to act as one unified body of believers (e.g., 1 Cor 1:10; Eph 4:3; Phil 1:27). Today the church worldwide seems anything but united. Yet, Christians throughout church history have sought unity in many ways. The pursuit of unity continues today, often under the name of ecumenism—a topic discussed later in this chapter.

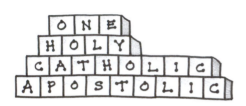

Building blocks of the church: one, holy, catholic, apostolic

24.3.2 Holy

The church is *holy*—set apart for God—because God made it holy through the saving work of Jesus (1 Cor 14:33; 1 Pet 2:4, 9; Rev 11:2). No one considers the church holy because of its preponderance of good works. It is holy because God, who is holy, makes the church holy (1 Cor 1:30; Heb 7:26). Good works do not make the church holy any more than good works make a person holy. Both suffer from the same limitations. God imputes righteousness to the church in that same way that God imputes righteousness to individuals.

The church also has the charge to become holy (Luke 21:19; Jas 1:4; Heb 12:1). Although believers receive the gift of salvation—of God's imputed righteousness—they are not exempt from the obligation of following Jesus, of living like him. Christians corporately as well as individually should endeavor to live Christlike lives.

The church is not the same as the kingdom of God, though the church plays a key role in the emerging reign of God. At times, people have confused the church and the kingdom of God, thinking the church to be a poor reflection of God's reign. The church—like individual believers—is in a process of growth, maturity, and accomplishment. Yet, the church and individual believers experience a genuine foretaste of the presence and power of God in the world.

24.3.3 Catholic

The term *catholic* reflects the universal nature of the church. That is, the church is not restricted in any way due to race, gender, language, culture, or nationality. According to Jesus, "this good news of the kingdom will be proclaimed throughout the world, as a testimony to all nations" (Matt 24:14). Jesus' Great Commission to the disciples clearly included going and making disciples of "all nations" (Matt 28:19). Although Jesus ministered primarily to his native Jewish people, his words and actions applied to anyone who would listen. His example established a trajectory of inclusiveness that inspired and confounded early Christians.

Inclusiveness did not come naturally to the early church. One of the main controversies early Christians experienced pertained to whether the Gentiles— all non-Jews—received the same salvation and blessings as the original Jewish Christians. Paul championed salvation among the Gentiles, without the trappings of Jewish religious tradition. Eventually the council at Jerusalem, led by the Apostle Peter, welcomed Gentile Christians and thus opened the door for a universal conception of Christendom (Acts 10:1–48).

Sometimes people confuse the word "catholic" with the Catholic Church. Historically, the Catholic Church has considered itself the universal church. But the creedal use of the term did not have a particular church institution in mind when the church was described as catholic. All churches consider themselves catholic to the extent that they include everyone in their fellowship.

24.3.4 Apostolic

The *apostolic* nature of the church pertains to the fact that Christians believe the church reflects the earliest teachings of the apostles. Jesus appointed the apostles to preach the gospel and establish the church, empowered by the Holy Spirit (John 16:13; 20:21; Acts 1:8). To the apostolate, Jesus—the chief apostle—gave authority to engage in mission throughout the world (Matt 28:18; Heb 3:1). The called community of the church has a key role to play in the emerging reign of God (Matt 13; 2 Tim 1:1–14; Heb 12:22–28).

Although no one can duplicate the conditions of the first-century church, Christians throughout history tried to replicate the beliefs and practices of the early apostles with their own expression of the church. This replication requires flexibility and creativity, since the church continually needs to reapply itself in order to be relevant to the world around it. Nevertheless, the church tries to maintain a sense of continuity with the first-century church.

Christians challenged the concept of apostolicity during the Middle Ages, when the church experienced its first major schism. The Western church—centered in Rome—believed that its apostolicity extended back to Peter. In addition to its fidelity to apostolic teachings, the church believed that there had been an unbroken line of apostolic leaders who received ecclesiastical authority through the laying on of hands by one bishop

What does it mean to follow the apostles?

of Rome to another. However, in the Eastern churches—centered in Constantinople—Christians believed that the heritage of apostolic authority lay in the

Eastern connection of Orthodox churches. In debate over whether the bishop of Rome had the right to clarify or, perhaps, modify the ancient Nicene Creed, the Western and Eastern churches separated, resulting in the separation of the Roman Catholic and Orthodox churches.

24.4 The Reformation Church

Churches in the Protestant Reformation shifted religious authority away from the church to Scripture. In doing so, they jeopardized the longstanding marks of the church. No longer did the breakaway churches appear to be one or apostolic. Many churches arose, and none of them could claim an unbroken succession of bishops laying hands upon priests, since they separated from the Roman Catholic Church. Protestant churches still affirmed the marks of the church in the Nicene Creed, but they understood them differently—more symbolically. For example, they believed in one universal church, but that did not preclude a variety of local manifestations of it. Likewise, they believed themselves to be apostolic because they reflected the beliefs and practices of the apostles. In fact, Protestant churches considered themselves more apostolic, that is, more faithful to first-century Christianity than the Roman Catholic Church.

Preaching represents the heart of Protestant worship

In order to emphasize their fidelity to biblical or apostolic Christianity, Protestants described other crucial marks of the church. In addition to being one, holy, catholic, and apostolic, the true church also preached the gospel, duly administered the sacraments, and—in some instances—administered church discipline.

24.4.1 Preaching

Protestants separated from the Catholic Church in order to *preach* the gospel—the good news of salvation by grace through faith. They believed that the good news of Scripture needed to be preached in order for a church to be true to its calling. Protestants thought that Catholics had ignored or distorted the pure teachings of the Bible, especially with regard to the nature of salvation and the Christian life. They wanted to restore what they considered a more accurate view of Scripture—the word of God.

Protestants emphasized the importance of preaching in the vernacular, that is, in the language common people used. In the Catholic Church, priests performed parts of the service in Latin, which the laity did not understand. Protestants placed emphasis upon individuals being able to comprehend and decide for themselves with regard to the words of the Bible. Thus preaching of the word of God in a language people understood became the main component of Protestant church services. For this reason, the pulpits from which ministers preach were often moved to the center of churches.

24.4.2 Sacraments

Protestants believed that Catholics inadequately upheld the belief in salvation by grace through faith. This inadequacy appeared prominently in their views of the *sacraments*. From a Catholic perspective, God saves people by grace, but grace is administered to people by means of the sacraments. For salvation, God bestows grace by means of the sacraments of baptism, confirmation, Eucharist, and reconciliation. However, the Protestants emphasized salvation by grace through faith alone. They wanted nothing added to the grace and faith that led to salvation. So, they advocated what they considered the proper celebration of the sacraments, namely, that sacraments served as signs and seals of grace.

Protestants generally agreed that Jesus specifically commanded Christians to practice two rituals or sacraments: baptism and the Eucharist (Lord's Supper). However, they disagreed with regard to how those sacraments should be understood and celebrated. We will investigate different views of the sacraments in a later chapter.

> **CHURCH OF GOD**
>
> Wherever we find the Word of God surely preached and heard, and the sacraments administered according to the institution of Christ, there, it is not to be doubted, is a church of God.
>
> JOHN CALVIN, INSTITUTES OF THE CHRISTIAN RELIGION (16TH CENTURY)

24.4.3 Church Discipline

Some Protestants thought that *church discipline*, rightly understood, should represent one of the distinctive characteristics of a church. This emphasis rose, in part, because Protestants thought they had been wrongly accused of ecclesiastical wrongdoing by the Catholic Church. Their separation from Catholicism marked them as divisive and assertive—both unchristian characteristics. Yet, Protestants believed they responded more purely to the truths of the Bible. Catholics, rather than Protestants, were at fault for unjustly interpreting Scripture and for persecuting Protestants for so doing.

Calvin strongly emphasized the need for meting out discipline in the church. Although God saves people by grace through faith, their salvation does not warrant irresponsible or indulgent lifestyles. The church has the responsibility of monitoring spiritual brothers and sisters for their own sake. Scripture demands church discipline, and Calvin believed that love for one another required just and nurturing discipline of the church body.

Church Discipline and Accountability

The church needs to regulate the conduct of its clergy and laity, based upon its particular view of God, Scripture, and ministry. Too often, people confuse discipline with legalism and sometimes punishment. Yet, discipline is thought to be a constructive part of the accountability the body of Christ—the church—provides all believers. Accountability should occur to promote healthy, holy Christianity. Obviously, abuses can and have occurred in church history. However, that does not distract from the blessings God intends for Christians who demonstrate their love through every means of discipleship.

Christians give thanks that God has forgiven their sins and that they are not judged based upon individual merit. In turn, God asks Christians to forgive others. However, the Bible does not naïvely talk about forgiveness without the need for justice and for correcting wrongs that have been committed. Scripture has much to say about how to go about holding others accountable, especially among members of the church. Of course, a great many sins are listed in Scripture, and Christians are to avoid them as well as prevent them from occurring among members of the church. The Bible mandates holding others accountable, both individually and collectively.

Holding one another accountable

Accountability Guidelines

Although Scripture does not provide extensive guidelines on accountability, it gives helpful principles that Christians may constructively apply today. Principles of church discipline include the need to begin dealing with sin or other problems on a private basis before making issues public (Matt 18:15; Luke 17:3). It also includes provision for gradually drawing in two or three others for the sake of reproof (Deut 19:15; Matt 18:16). If accountability cannot be maintained on a private basis, more public means may be required. Public reproof and other means may be employed, though great caution must be employed throughout (Matt 18:17; 1 Tim 5:20; cf. 1 Cor 5:5; Rom 16:17–19). Keep in mind that church discipline has to do with restoration rather than punishment. Church discipline has the goal of restoration of those who, for one reason or another, transgressed the standards of Scripture or other standards of church and society.

Throughout church history, accountability has been considered important on a variety of levels. First, Christians are accountable to God. The first commandment of the Ten Commandments reminds us, "you shall have no other gods before me" (Exod 20:3). Christians, therefore, need to be responsible in their relationship with God. Second, Christians are accountable to themselves. Christians have not always appreciated or promoted the need for self-accountability, yet they cannot "love their neighbors as themselves" if they first do not love themselves (Lev 19:18; Matt 19:19). Although some Christians consider love for themselves to be sinful, most Christians think that holy and healthy love for others requires the same kind of love for oneself. Third, Christians are accountable to the church—to other believers—and for giving care for other believers. The accountability, of course, needs to be mutual. Just as Christians are to hold their fellow Christians accountable, there needs to be willingness for reciprocated accountability. Finally, Christians are accountable to others—their neighbors. They need to be willing to love and be loved, serve and be served, correct and be corrected. It includes accountability to neighbors both individually and collectively. It is not enough to love and relate to neighbors one-by-one; there needs to be social accountability as well. This includes care for the poor as well as the powerful, for strangers and aliens as well as those next door.

24.5 Types of Churches

Some typologies have been devised in order to analyze, in broad strokes, different types of churches. One typology distinguishes between three historic expressions of the church: body of Christ (Latin, *corpus Christi*), assembly of the elect (Latin, *coetus electorum*), and communion of saints (Latin, *communio sanctorum*). First, the church as the body of Christ focuses on the communal and sacramental dimensions of Christianity, unified

Church discipline is corrective rather than punitive

by the apostolic teachings of Scripture. Liturgical worship plays a key role in this type of church, and it is reflective of Catholic, Orthodox, and Anglican churches. Second, the church as the assembly of the elect focuses on evangelism and discipleship, emphasizing religion of the heart. These churches emphasize the revivalistic and pietistic dimensions of Christianity. Third, the church as the communion of saints focuses on the relevant ministries, services, and social action performed on behalf of others. Activism plays a key role in this type of church, and it is reflective of denominations that emphasize holistic concerns for ministry, for example, as found in the social gospel.

Max Weber (1864–1920) and Ernst Troeltsch (1865–1923) were Germans who studied Christianity historically and sociologically as well as theologically. They draw a contrast between two kinds of church organizations, devising a church-sect typology. A "church" signifies an ideal type that is universal, inclusive, and relatively conservative in terms of preserving historic religion. A "sect" signifies an offshoot that has more particularized concerns, tends to be exclusive, and liberally changes past values and practices. According to Weber, a distinguishing factor between a church and a sect is the mode of membership. The member of a church-type church usually joins by "birth," whereas the member of a sect-type church usually joins by "decision." Troeltsch thinks that the church-type church best helps to preserve historic Christianity; however, the sect-type church helps to bring about valuable vitality and adaptability necessary for the progress of Christianity.

American theologian H. Richard Niebuhr (1894–1962) uses the work of Weber and Troeltsch in talking about the socio-cultural roots of denominationalism—organizations of churches with their own doctrinal and governmental identities. Niebuhr uses the church-sect typology as a continuum with which to analyze the proliferation of denominations, especially Protestant denominations. Niebuhr focuses on the socio-cultural rather than theological reasons for the emergence of denominations. Although theological reasons are usually given for church schism, the socio-cultural reasons—not always admitted or even recognized—are just as important, if not more important, for analyzing the origin and makeup of denominations.

Newer typologies have been developed that help sort out the variety of churches and denominations in the world. Avery Dulles, for example, provides contemporary models of churches: church as (1) institution, (2) mystical communion, (3) sacrament, (4) herald, and (5) servant. He evaluates the strengths and weaknesses of each model in order to develop a better understanding of the nature and ministry of churches. Such attempts contribute to the health and effectiveness of churches as well as to their self-understanding.

Why so many denominations?

24.6 Differences among Churches

It does not take long for a person to realize that there are an awful lot of different Christians and churches in the world. How do we compare and contrast them? Should there ever be disagreement among Christians? Scripture talks about the unity and need for cooperation among Christians, but how can this account for the obvious number and variety of churches in the world? Such questions would take a long time to answer, if done in a way that considers all aspects of Christian and church life.

To begin with, it is naïve to think that there do not occur differences, disagreements, debates, and separations among Christians in the Bible. Sometimes disagreements and confrontations occurred in the New Testament, and often they were resolved. For example, Paul and Barnabas disagreed with individuals from Jerusalem that required Gentile converts to follow the Jewish custom of circumcision. In Acts 15, the heads of the Jerusalem church, under the leadership of James, considered what conditions might apply to the admission of Gentile believers to the church (Acts 15:19–21). In Acts 11, Gentiles had already been recognized as true believers, but that did not prevent debate and conciliation over growing differences of opinion with regard to church values and practices.

A noteworthy example of unresolved difference occurs in the missionary partnership between the apostles Paul and Barnabas. Together, they had served as missionaries throughout the Mediterranean (Acts 13–14). However, Paul and Barnabas disagreed over the inclusion of a young missionary named John, called Mark (Acts 15:36–41). Apparently, Mark had deserted them earlier, and Paul was unwilling to again include the novice in missionary activities (Acts 13:13). The "disagreement became so sharp that they parted company"

(Acts 15:39). Thereafter, the two partners went on separate missionary journeys: Barnabas with Mark, and Paul with Silas.

Differences among Christians occur for a variety of reasons. When they occur due to selfishness, power struggles, or other sinful motivations, then of course such differences are contrary to God's will for Christians and churches. However, other factors influence the formation and development of churches. Calvin, for example, talked about the doctrinal necessity for schism from the Catholic Church, during the Reformation. From his perspective, fidelity to Jesus and the gospel message of Scripture supersedes the authority of any church. Other factors that influence the formation and development of churches include location, language, church-state relations, and other cultural differences. Such differences can preclude churches as well as individual Christians from easily acting in ways that bring about unity and cooperation. Issues of church unity and cooperation will now be discussed in relationship to ecumenism.

24.7 Ecumenism

Ecumenism refers to unity and cooperation among Christians. Jesus prayed that his followers might be unified (John 17:23). The New Testament points out that there is "one body and one Spirit . . . one Lord, one faith, one baptism" (Eph 4:4–5; cf. 2:11–22). Yet, since the schism between the Catholic and Orthodox churches and, certainly, since the Protestant Reformation, the worldwide Christian church has looked anything but unified. The proliferation of Protestant denominations over the past two centuries, for example, leaves us with thousands of different registered churches. So how does ecumenism operate within Christianity?

During the past century, Christians became increasingly concerned about the fragmented nature of the church. Some slowly began to explore ways in which to unify Christian ministries. Willem Adolph Visser't Hooft (1900–1985), a Dutch member of the clergy and a leader in ecumenism, provides a helpful summary of ways in which churches seek to unify. He distinguishes between three types of ecumenism: church-type, doctrinal, and Pietist.[1] *Church-type ecumenism* seeks the actual merger of different churches or denominations into a single institution. Some churches merged during the twentieth century, though the process of unifying has proved more difficult than dividing.

Can the church be "put back together again"?

Doctrinal ecumenism searches for agreement in the area of Christian belief. Perhaps there exist some doctrinal affirmations to which everyone can agree. Throughout church history, numerous creeds, confessions, and covenants arose, expressing significant agreement among Christians, churches, and parachurch organizations. However, such local declarations have failed to capture widespread agreement, much less universal agreement. Even the earliest ecumenical creeds come under attack for being provincial and a distortion of biblical teachings, assuming biblical teachings can escape provincialism. Although there will always be a need to state and restate doctrinal beliefs, such attempts have often resulted in extensive debate over biblical and interpretive minutia, discouraging more than encouraging the ecumenical spirit. In addition, some warn against overemphasizing doctrinal beliefs for the sake of the practice of Christianity, including its lived experience and various religious practices.

Pietist ecumenism emphasizes cooperation for the sake of strengthening church ministry and other Christian activities. Although churches may not be able to agree upon everything, they can cooperate in various ministries that churches and parachurch groups undertake. For example, the World Council of Churches and the National Council of Churches oversee a variety of ministries, which include emphasis upon meeting the physical, social, and other tangible needs of people. Through cooperation, a greater number of people benefit from their ministries. In a similar way, the World Evangelical Fellowship and the National Association of Evangelicals oversee a variety of ministries that include emphasis upon the evangelistic and spiritual needs of people. Through cooperation, a greater number of people benefit from their ministries. Such examples of cooperation constitute very practical ways in which Christians work together ecumenically for the sake of God's kingdom.

Ecumenism seeks cooperation and unity

24.8 Church Governance

Church governance has to do with the particular system of governance used in a particular church or denomination, locally, regionally, and around the world. Scripture talks about various decisions regarding governance in the first-century church. However, there is no overarching type described in the Bible.

Historically, there have been three general types of church government: episcopacy, congregationalism, and presbyterianism. Each view, of course, claims biblical precedent. More than Scripture, however, influenced the development of the different types. The time and location of the founding of a church or denomination, obviously, set boundaries on what could or could not be done in terms of governance. Language differences, church-state relations (or the lack thereof), and other cultural factors impacted church governance just as they influenced other aspects of churches.

Episcopacy refers to a centralized form of church government which has a hierarchical structure that extends beyond local churches. Often bishops oversee regional churches and have authority over theological issues as well as local governance, appointing pastors and other leaders in churches. In Scripture, Paul and Barnabas appointed leaders in local churches (Acts 14:21–23), and elsewhere Paul appointed leaders to churches over which he had oversight (2 Tim 1:6; Titus 1:5). Episcopal governance can become quite large. For example, in the Catholic Church there are priests, bishops, archbishops, cardinals, and even a pope who serves at the pinnacle of ecclesiastical authority.

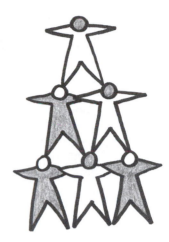

Congregationalism affirms the importance and autonomy of local congregations. Individual congregations are entirely independent, and they are responsible for their own theological identity, governance, and selection of pastors. In Scripture, deacons are chosen by the congregation (Acts 6:3, 5). Elsewhere, local congregations are responsible for church discipline (2 Cor 2:6–7), appointment of special envoys (2 Cor 8:19), and upholding apostolic doctrine (Jude 3). Although congregational governance seems quite ancient, it did not function

Who's in charge?

widely until after the Protestant Reformation. Historically, Baptist churches have been one of the most prominent examples of congregationalism.

Presbyterianism is differentiated by a graded system of governance that includes representative ecclesiastical bodies (for example, presbyteries, conferences, or districts). In Scripture, local congregations are thought to be autonomous but still accountable to apostles and church leaders outside their region. For example, church leaders (elders) in Jerusalem were thought to have authority over the church in Antioch (Acts 15:1–29) as well as special responsibilities elsewhere (Acts 20:17, 28; Jas 5:14). In presbyterian governance, pastors may be chosen by a local church, but the appointment has to be approved by a presbytery. Presbyterian churches represent an obvious example of this graded system of governance that tries to integrate the benefits of episcopacy and congregationalism.

24.9 The Church and the World

One of the ongoing dilemmas the church faces has to do with how Christians should relate with the world around them. How should the church influence the world? In what ways should the church minister to the world? Conversely, how should the church allow the world to influence it? In what ways should the two relate? These questions are more difficult to answer than one might expect. In Jesus' prayer for his followers, he said, "They do not belong to the world, just as I do not belong to the world" (John 17:16). Jesus went on to say, "As you have sent me into the world, so I

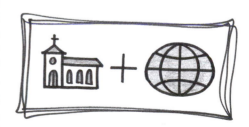

What is the relationship between the church and the world?

have sent them into the world" (John 17:18). The tension between "being in the world" and "not of the world" continues to perplex Christians.

H. Richard Niebuhr also categorized the various ways in which Christians understand the relationship between Christ and culture, or between the church and the world.[2] The first way has to do with "Christ against culture": Christians think of themselves in opposition to culture and the world around them. A common way of opposing the world involves withdrawing from it. Examples include monasteries and Amish communities that withdraw from culture in order to keep themselves pure from the world's temptations.

The second way has to do with the "Christ of culture": Christians think that they must accommodate their beliefs, values, and practices to the contemporary questions and concerns of the world. If this requires substantial changes in their beliefs and practices, such changes are warranted. Christians must be willing to reinvent their religion in order to stay relevant with the best of social, cultural, and scientific developments. Church history is filled with examples of religious groups that gave up historic Christian beliefs for the sake of contemporary concerns, which may or may not have longstanding relevance. Niebuhr gives the example of liberal Protestantism, which reinterpreted Christianity more in terms of modern psychology than biblical teaching.

What does it mean to be "in the world" but not be "of the world"?

The third way H. Richard Niebuhr contends that Christians understand the relationship between Christ and culture has to do with "Christ above culture": Christians think that a synthesis may occur between the best of religion and culture. Christians can learn from and integrate the best the world has to offer, and the world can learn from and integrate the best Christianity has to offer. Niebuhr pointed to Aquinas' use of Aristotelian philosophy as a helpful way in which to conceptualize Christian beliefs and practices. Regardless of whether one agrees with Aquinas' synthesis of the two, many Christians eagerly integrate their beliefs, values, and practices with cultural developments in music, media, computers, business management, demographics, and so on. They see a harmonious blending of the church and the world in these areas of ministry.

The fourth way, in H. Richard Niebuhr's estimation, that Christians understand the relationship between Christ and culture has to do with "Christ and culture in paradox": Christians think that there exists an irresolvable tension between the church and the world. Although Christians must live in the world, they can never become reconciled or compatible with the world. They will always be in opposition to one another. However, Christians should not withdraw from the world because Christ commanded them to live in the world and minister to it. They must be involved if for no other reason than to prevent the wicked and destructive forces in the world from getting out of control. Luther, for example, argued that Christians must act in socially responsible ways for the sake of self-preservation rather than renewal. Ultimately, only God can transform the world. Although some might consider this a pessimistic view of the church's role in the world today, adherents claim that they have a realistic assessment of the world's plight. Until Jesus returns, Christians must patiently live within the inevitable tensions of a sin-filled world in conflict with the church.

The fifth way, according to H. Richard Niebuhr, that Christians understand the relationship between Christ and culture has to do with "Christ the transformer of culture": Just as Christians minister to redeem people spiritually, they also minister to redeem people's social, economic, and political well-being. Christ came to minister to the poor, those who were impoverished in so many ways. So Christians should minister to the holistic needs of people. They should be optimistic with regard to the full extent God wants to minister in the world. *Social gospel* advocates argue that Christians can do much for the physical as well as spiritual well-being of people. In fact, how can one effectively demonstrate Christlike love to people without demonstrating a holistic concern for each and every aspect of their lives?

24.10 Conclusion

Periodically Christian churches come under attack for some mistake or imperfection. No doubt churches around the world exhibit numerous flaws. Yet, the church constitutes the most noticeable, visible witness to Christian beliefs, values, and practices. Although the church may not be perfect, it effectively witnesses to Jesus throughout the world because it is believed that God chose the church—true believers—to fulfill that witness. Christians believe that God ultimately makes the church successful in the world. The church is God's living witness, which is sufficient for the preservation and growth of God's kingdom.

How important is the church? Historically, Christians have said that the church and supporting the church are vitally important. It is as important to individual church attendees as it is to everyone else in the world. Nowhere else provides a better place for an individual to meet and learn about God and to grow spiritually. Likewise, nowhere else provides a better place for believers to demonstrate their love by ministering to the many needs of people in the world.

24.11 Questions for Further Reflection

1. What would an ideal church look like? Do you know of any ideal churches?

2. What kind of church do you attend? Why do you attend? What would make the church better? What could you do to make it better?

3. What are the benefits of regular church attendance? How often do you attend church? What would encourage people to attend more often?

4. What model of the church appeals to you the most? Why?

5. What do you think about the different types of church government?

6. How important is ecumenism? What are the best ways to act ecumenically?

7. What do you think should be the relationship between the church and the world? Is it one of synthesis, paradox, or transformation?

24.12 Notes

1. Willem Adolph Visser't Hooft, quoted by Colin W. Williams, *John Wesley's Theology Today* (New York: Abingdon, 1960), 10.

2. H. Richard Niebuhr, *Christ and Culture* (New York: Harper & Row, 1951).

CHAPTER TWENTY-FIVE

But you are a chosen race, a royal priesthood, a holy nation, God's own people, in order that you may proclaim the mighty acts of him who called you out of darkness into his marvelous light. (1 Peter 2:9)

MINISTRY

25.1 Introduction

When Jesus began his public ministry, he read the following Scripture before his hometown synagogue:

> The Spirit of the Lord is upon me, because he has anointed me to bring good news to the poor. He has sent me to proclaim release to the captives and recovery of sight to the blind, to the let the oppressed go free, to proclaim the year of the Lord's favor. (Luke 4:18–19, citing Isa 61:1–2; 58:6)

In many respects, this passage defined Jesus' ministry. He ministered by bringing good news to the poor, releasing people from captivity, healing those physically challenged, and freeing people who were oppressed in one way or another. Notice that, although the passage begins and ends with proclamation, most of the passage deals with ministering to the day-to-day problems people experience. If you look at Jesus' public ministry, you cannot miss the fact that he spent significant time ministering to more than the spiritual well-being of people. Jesus significantly ministered to the physical, social, economic, and even political well-being of people. The church sometimes overlooks his holistic approach to ministry.

Many Christians have looked to the so-called Great Commission in order to define Jesus' ministry. Before his ascension, Jesus told his followers:

> Go therefore and make disciples of all nations, baptizing them in the name of the Father and of the Son and of the Holy Spirit, and teaching them to obey everything that I have commanded you. And remember, I am with you always, to the end of the age. (Matt 28:19–20)

These words clearly embody Jesus' final exhortation to his followers: Go and make disciples! However, the last words of a person do not necessarily define his or her ministry. Defining words usually come more toward the beginning than the end of a ministry. The final exhortation of Jesus includes evangelism because you cannot make disciples without evangelization, but he places more emphasis upon discipleship, baptizing, teaching, and obedience, representing more of a concern for nurturing than converting people.

Jesus' quotation of Isaiah reminds us that his ministry was multifaceted and balanced in terms of meeting all the needs of people. Throughout church history, Christians have tried to achieve the same kind of balance in ministering to others. Let us look at the various ways Christians have understood and undertaken ministry.

25.2 What Is Ministry?

Ministry refers to the tangible ways in which Christians express their love and service to others by helping their spiritual, mental, emotional, and physical needs. Some consider ministry a formal calling or vocation, but most Christians consider themselves responsible for some involvement in ministering to others.

In the Old Testament, early examples of ministry occurred in the priestly service of the Levites, who had responsibilities for interceding on behalf of people and for representing them before God. In so doing, they oversaw a variety of religious rites for the purpose of intercession and atonement for the sins of people, for example, by offering sacrifices of animals, crops, or other precious objects to God. Priests served as intermediaries between God and people.

God's intermediaries

In the New Testament, Jesus served as the premier example of ministry, reflecting his priestly functions as the Christ. Other ministers in Scripture included the disciples and other followers, whom Jesus sent out to serve the needs of others (Luke 10:1–20; John 20:21). However, even while Jesus was alive, people ministered who were not immediate members of Jesus' entourage. Jesus did not prevent them from ministering, and, in fact, encouraged them to do so (Luke 9:50). When Jesus was no longer present, the disciples and other followers slowly developed their various ministries and churches. As Gentiles joined the church, increasing questions and debates arose with regard to religious beliefs and practices. Most of the debates were resolved. For example, at the council of Jerusalem, the church explicitly welcomed Gentile Christians to their fellowship. As the church grew and spread out into other cultural and national settings, there arose a variety of religious leaders, titles, and functions, which the Bible does not clearly differentiate. Thus, as we will see, various understandings of ministry—ordained and lay—arose throughout church history.

Many of the ministries in Scripture are understood in light of the gifts of the Holy Spirit. Christians in the Bible seemed to think that spiritual gifts represented divinely given empowerments to minister. Of course, there may not be discreet gifts per se—only different ways in which believers ministered. Nevertheless, most Christians have recognized special grace or charisms from God to minister to others.

Although there exists a variety of gifts, Scripture discusses them in the context of being part of one body—the body of Christ. Different parts of the body perform different ministries, but all ministries serve the whole of the body as well as people outside the fellowship of the body. Christians are to understand, appreciate, and value the roles everyone plays and not consider themselves more important or privileged than those with other gifts, talents, and ministries (1 Cor 12).

Scripture mentions different types of ministry, but no consensus arose in church history with regard to how ministry or ministries should be accomplished. People ministered according to giftings and perceived needs rather than specific vocations. Women as well as men served and ministered according to their giftings, though certain limitations were in effect (e.g., Acts 21:9; Rom 16:1–7, 12, 15; 1 Cor 11:5; Gal 3:28). Eventually more formal understandings of ministry arose during the development of the ancient church. We will investigate some of those developments, noting that Scripture does not provide a precise organizational chart for ministry.

25.3 Developments in Ministry

Ancient Christian churches developed in a variety of places, with a variety of languages and cultures, throughout the first century. No wonder such an array of church traditions appeared! We cannot easily summarize the changes in the church and church ministry. We will summarize some of the more important ones, which influenced later church developments.

Most churches had a priest or pastor to lead the church. Although the regular attendees at the church supported its ministries, generally the church gave authority to an individual leader to guide the church. In the New Testament the most basic name given to such leaders was *elder* (or presbyter). Among other responsibilities, elders had governmental oversight over churches.

As churches and church connections grew, various levels of church leaders emerged to assist the elders. Church life became too complex for individual leaders alone. For example, *deacons* (servants, ministers) performed various services, liturgical duties, and social welfare, especially in caring for the poor. These services reflected the ones first performed by deacons in Acts 6:1–6. Over the centuries, deacons and deaconesses have performed many essential ministries in churches, although with varying degrees of authority.

What does it mean to minister?

Bishops (or overseers) also assisted elders, and sometimes the title is used synonymously with elder in Scripture (e.g., Phil 1:1). However, the bishop soon gained the meaning of chief overseer or pastor of a specific geographical area (2 Tim 1:6; Titus 1:5). Similar to the way Paul traveled and administrated church authority over a large area of the ancient Mediterranean world, bishops slowly grew in authority and pastoral oversight over different parts of the ancient church. Some bishops received special honor, such as the bishop of Rome, who eventually received the title of pope.

Ministers were called to a high standard of leadership, regardless of how ministry was conceived. Scripture offers a variety of characteristics expected of those who lead others in the church. For example:

- Hospitable (1 Tim 3:2; Titus 1:8)
- Able to teach (1 Tim 3:2; 5:17; Titus 1:9)
- Not violent, but gentle (1 Tim 3:3; Titus 1:7)
- Not a lover of money (1 Tim 3:3)
- Not quarrelsome (1 Tim 3:3)
- Not a recent convert (1 Tim 3:6)
- Self-controlled (1 Tim 3:2; Titus 1:8)
- Having a good reputation with outsiders (1 Tim 3:7)
- Not overbearing (Titus 1:7)
- Not quick-tempered (Titus 1:7)
- Loving what is good (Titus 1:8)
- Upright and holy (Titus 1:8)
- Disciplined (Titus 1:8)
- Above reproach (blameless) (1 Tim 3:2, 9; Titus 1:6)
- Having one wife [or spouse] (1 Tim 3:2, 12; Titus 1:6)
- Temperate (1 Tim 3:2, 8; Titus 1:7)
- Respectable (1 Tim 3:2, 8)
- Not given to drunkenness (1 Tim 3:3, 8; Titus 1:7)
- Able to manage his [or her] family well (1 Tim 3:4, 12; Titus 1:6)
- Having obedient children (1 Tim 3:4–5, 12; Titus 1:6)
- Not a pursuer of dishonest gain (1 Tim 3:8; Titus 1:7)
- Holding firmly to the deep truths (1 Tim 3:9; Titus 1:9)

This is not an exhaustive list. However, it communicates the importance placed upon the character of ministers and their actions as leaders in churches. The calling to ministry is sacred, and ministers need to be mindful of their responsibilities.

25.3.1 Catholic and Orthodox Churches

The office of *pope* developed gradually as the bishopric of Rome extended its prestige and influence. During the Middle Ages, Pope Gregory VII (1073–1085) proposed the supremacy of papal authority over political as well as ecclesiastical authorities. This proposal came in the wake of the schism between the Eastern and Western churches in 1053, which resulted in the Catholic and Orthodox churches. The Orthodox churches were a consortium of churches, often identified by national or regional identities, for example, Greece, Cyprus, and later Russia. They united, more or less, under the Patriarch in Constantinople, who represented the first among equal patriarchal leaders in the various Orthodox churches.

Priest, minister, pastor

In contrast, the pope exercised supreme jurisdiction over the Catholic Church, which was thought to represent the one true church. The pope may act alone or in conjunction with Catholic councils in defining the beliefs, values, and practices of the universal church. In 1870, Vatican Council I promulgated the doctrine of infallibility, which forms the pinnacle of papal authority. This doctrine asserts that the pope, in proper relationship to Catholic councils, receives divine assistance that results in church pronouncements with regard to matters of church doctrine that do not err. In actuality, such pronouncements have seldom occurred, but they reveal the supremacy of papal authority.

25.3.2 Protestant Churches

The Protestant Reformers believed that the popes had abused their leadership of the church. They usurped the authority of Scripture alone to determine matters of church beliefs, values, and practices. In matters of ministry, Luther uplifted the priesthood of all believers, arguing that people do not need ordained priests for their salvation, nor do they need priests in order for the church to minister. Instead, all Christians must utilize their gifts for the sake of ministering to the needs of others. There existed a greater emphasis upon everyone participating equally, albeit differently, for the sake of God's kingdom.

Whereas Catholics considered vocation to be a specific calling to become a priest, monk, or nun, Protestants considered vocation to include any kind of work—secular or religious. Everyone's work should be considered equally important and valuable to the church—the body of Jesus, which serves many different functions. One might just as well be called to the vocation of a doctor, carpenter, homemaker, or garbage collector as to that of a minister. Certain individual believers might sense a call to full-time ministry, which Luther referred to as the office of ministry. Those involved with the office of ministry function as leaders in churches, overseeing the varieties of church ministries and services. Full-time ministers or pastors should not be considered qualitatively different or better just because they serve in ministry leadership. Appropriate respect should be given to those who lead churches, but all attendees should consider themselves essential participants in the various ministries and services of churches.

25.4 Types of Ministry

Many types of ministry occur within churches and out in the world around them. Certainly all seek to minister on behalf of the kingdom of God, acknowledging a common theme in the preaching and teaching of Jesus (e.g., Matt 6:33; Mark 1:15; Luke 6:20; etc.). The kingdom of God generally refers to the sovereign rule of God in the world. Sometimes Jesus spoke as if the kingdom had already arrived (e.g., Luke 10:9; 17:21). Other times Jesus spoke as if the kingdom would not fully arrive until a future time (e.g., Luke 13:29; 22:18). This tension has led Christians to variously interpret the kingdom of God: some see it only as past or present, and some see it only as future. However, the truth of the matter probably reflects the tension more than one might want to admit. We live in a time of tension—tension involving immediate and future, physical and spiritual realities. The kingdom of God has already occurred in real and powerful ways, especially in the spiritual aspects of our lives. However, the fullness of that kingdom has not yet occurred. It is one of the blessed hopes of Christians that God will someday put everything right in every aspect of our lives and of the world in which we live.

Although Christians do not generally identify the church with the kingdom of God, the two are seen as complementary concepts. To minister on behalf of the church is to minister on behalf of the kingdom of God, though ministry on behalf of the kingdom of God extends far beyond church ministries. Since the kingdom of God is all encompassing, it is no wonder that the ministry of churches throughout the centuries have occurred in a variety of ways. We cannot reduce the ministry of the church to any one word or phrase, unless we talk about the need to love—to love one's neighbor as oneself, the so-called Golden Rule (see Matt 7:12; Luke 6:31). But this love is often interpreted and applied in a variety of ways. Still, we may summarize some of the significant ways in which churches—corporately and individually, officially as churches and unofficially as parachurch groups—have ministered and continue to minister

> **God does not minister** only through pastors and priests. God ministers through everyone who turns to God for salvation.
>
> They minister through their words and actions, spoken and done outside as well as inside the church, because ministry includes everyone.

today. The ministries mirror the various ways Christians envision and live out Christian spirituality.

25.4.1 Evangelical Ministry

Proclamation of the good news of Jesus and of salvation constitutes one of the earliest and lasting ministries of the church. The church could not grow without believers sharing their faith with others and converting them to Christianity. The Great Commission represents one of the oft-cited calls to evangelism, though it calls people to more than conversion. The apostolic and missions work of the early Christians, like that of the Apostle Paul, reflect dramatic growth in conversions during the first century of the church.

Proclamation of the good news, evangelism, missions, church planting, and so on have been part of church ministry throughout the centuries. From time to time, dramatic periods of evangelism and missions occurred. For example, during the seventeenth and eighteenth centuries large evangelistic movements began in continental Europe (Pietism), Great Britain (Methodism), and North America (Great Awakening). Such evangelism continued throughout the nineteenth (Revivalism) and twentieth centuries (Evangelicalism).

You must be born again!

Another example can be found in the Christian emphasis upon missions. Catholicism has a rich history of missions work, establishing local and foreign missions that excelled in service to others as well as in proclaiming the good news. Today Catholicism represents by far the largest Christian church. Protestants too have a rich history of mission work, starting in earnest in the eighteenth and nineteenth centuries. Today many Protestant churches and parachurch groups have thriving missions programs throughout the world.

25.4.2 Sacramental Ministry

As the early church matured, Christians placed an increased amount of emphasis upon the sacraments—the rites or rituals of the church, thought to be instituted by God for the purpose of bestowing grace upon believers. Although we will talk more about the sacraments in the next chapter, they have always played an important role in the ministry of the church, despite the variety of views Christians have about the sacraments. If God intended that certain rites or rituals—such as baptism, Eucharist, and so on—be performed on a regular basis by Christians, an important part of ministry is to perform them in a timely and appropriate manner. Since God bestows grace—unmerited favor and power, freely given—upon believers through the sacraments, Christians must take great care in properly administering them.

Churches that emphasize the centrality of the sacraments for the purpose of ministry are often called sacramental because of how they see God's gracious activity in the lives of people occurring through the sacraments. Catholic and

"Do this in remembrance of me"

Orthodox churches are strongly committed to sacramental ministries, as are many of the Protestant churches with beliefs, values, and practices that reflect those of the earliest Reformers. Sacramental churches tend to value the longstanding traditions of the church, utilizing creeds, confessions, and liturgies that reflect the wisdom of the past. Great value is found in those traditions, sometimes referred to as sacramentals, for their value in obtaining spiritual blessings. For example, the Catholic Church considers the following to be significant sacramentals for public as well as private worship: holy water, sign of the cross, and the Rosary.

25.4.3 Contemplative Ministry

Contemplative ministries refer to those approaches to ministry that emphasize the various spiritual disciplines with the intent of attaining a heightening union or communion with God. Although contemplation represents only one of the spiritual disciplines, it symbolizes the various means of grace available to people who desire greater spiritual intimacy with God. Such intimacy, in turn, helps believers direct their thoughts, words, and actions in ways that allow God to work in and through their lives. For example, we have already looked at Dallas Willard's distinction between disciplines of abstinence and disciplines of engagement (see discussion in ch. 23). Disciplines of abstinence include solitude, silence, fasting, frugality, chastity, secrecy (confidentiality), and sacrifice. Disciplines of engagement include study (especially Scripture), worship, celebration, service, prayer, fellowship, confession, and submission.

Notice that the spiritual disciplines do not necessarily result in the life of an ascetic, though the monastic lifestyles of Christians throughout the centuries provide classic examples of a contemplative approach to ministry. Spiritual disciplines can be undertaken to engage actively in Bible study, prayer, worship, and celebration. Of course, these disciplines of engagement are aided by the disciplines of abstinence. A contemplative Christian life is not a passive life; on the contrary, it actively disciplines through abstinence as well as engagement.

Meditating on God

The tendency of monastics to withdraw from society left them with the reputation of being so heavenly minded that they were of no earthly good. However, many monastics were actively involved in study, worship, service, and prayer, and their accomplishments benefited society as well as the church. Even today, there remains a large number of contemplative Christian ministries, though they tend to occur within the life and ministries of existing churches. The emphasis upon the spiritual disciplines sometimes occurs through spiritual directors, who individually disciple others. This one-on-one approach then influences how individual Christians go on to minister more broadly to others.

25.4.4 Teaching Ministry

The teaching ministry of the church encompasses many emphases upon studying Scripture, scholarly reflection upon Christian beliefs and practices, and teaching them in practical ways for the needs of people. No one church tradition embodies this type of ministry, yet numerous Christians throughout church history served to minister to others through their various studies. Catholic and Protestant traditions of scholasticism provide probably the best as well as the worst examples of a teaching ministry. Scholasticism first arose during the Middle Ages, representing a method and system of thought that embraced all the intellectual disciplines, including the humanities, arts, and sciences as well as theology. It represented a rationalistic approach to the study of Christian beliefs, values, and practices, using logic, deduction, and systematic formulations of theology. Aquinas' *Summa Theologica* in the thirteenth century is a classic example of scholasticism.

Teaching ministry

Protestantism often emphasized the scholarly and teaching aspects of ministry due to its emphasis upon the Bible and the primacy of scriptural authority. Sermons focused on the Bible, and the pulpit, rather than the Eucharistic table, served as the center point of a church. Like Catholicism, Protestantism had its periods of scholasticism, arising during the century after the Reformation, when adherents were still trying to develop an intellectual understanding of their reforming movement. Over the centuries, Protestants have valued and actively promoted the study of Scripture. They were, in fact, the first to promote the various historical and critical methods of biblical interpretation.

25.4.5 Holiness Ministry

The pursuit of holiness is a longstanding emphasis among Christians. The contemplative tradition of Christianity resembles holiness traditions in its use of the spiritual disciplines. Whereas the contemplative tradition seeks greater intimacy with God, holiness traditions seek godliness and moral purity. Holiness traditions look to the spiritual disciplines as means by which God brings believers into greater conformity with the likeness of Jesus, the model of godly living.

Holy?

Early Christians lived ascetic lifestyles in order to pursue holiness. Monastic communities, for example, seriously undertook spiritual disciplines of abstinence in order to purify their lives. Protestant holiness traditions include Methodists, who were optimistic with regard to the degree to which God's grace might sanctify a person entirely. Wesley, for example, believed in the gracious work of the Holy Spirit, subsequent to conversion, that enabled believers to live Christlike lives. Wesley never thought that people would attain perfection in this life, but he was very optimistic with regard to the power of God to transform believers.

25.4.6 Social Activist Ministry

Since the time of Jesus, Christians have always had a focus upon the social, political, and economic well-being of people. But social action was not a primary focus of ministry in churches. Although the principles of social awareness and activism appear in the Bible, there did not arise a consciousness and subsequent conviction in the church to focus upon the elimination of social problems and injustices. Some orders in the Catholic Church placed strong emphasis upon meeting the physical as well as spiritual needs of people, feeding and clothing the poor, establishing hospitals, and ministering to foreigners, prisoners, and other outcasts in society. Moreover, issues of justice repeatedly arose, and the church dealt with them. But an overarching concern for activism on behalf of social problems and injustice did not arise until the nineteenth century.

American theologian Walter Rauschenbusch was a primary representative of the social gospel movement. The social gospel was concerned with the growing social, political, and economic problems faced primarily by urban workers in an increasingly industrialized society. Christians needed to respond to these problems and injustices by working for their rectification, as well as for the spiritual well-being of people. Having a holistic understanding of human needs, proponents of the social gospel advocated social, political, and economic activism on behalf of Christian ministry.

Helping the poor

During the twentieth century, Roman Catholics around the world became increasingly concerned about the poverty and injustices suffered by people, especially in less economically developed countries. Gustavo Gutiérrez advocates liberation theology, which emphasizes the need to liberate people from that which enslaves them socially, politically, and economically before liberating them from their spiritual enslavement. An illustration used by liberation theologians is the exodus, which symbolizes the need to free Israel from its worldly enslavement before it could be fully liberated through the old and new covenants (Exod 1–15). Today numerous forms of liberation theology have arisen. Black theologians, such as James Cone, emphasize the injustices due to racism, especially against blacks. Issues of racism must become a central concern to Christians in order for them to minister effectively on behalf of Jesus. Likewise, feminist theologians, such as Mary Daly and Rosemary Radford Ruether, emphasize the injustices of sexism, which result in the marginalization and oppression of women. Issues of sexism must become a central concern to Christians in order for them to minister effectively on behalf of Jesus.

> **MINISTRY AS TRANSFORMATION**
>
> The church was not merely a thermometer that recorded the ideas and principles of popular opinion; it was a thermostat that transformed the mores of society.
>
> MARTIN LUTHER KING JR., LETTER FROM BIRMINGHAM JAIL (1963)

25.4.7 Charismatic Ministry

Since the gifts of the Holy Spirit—the charismata—always played a role in the development of the church, it is no surprise that there should have arisen a charismatic ministry that emphasizes use of all the gifts, including speaking in tongues and the interpretation of tongues. However, the church does not always accept this charismatic emphasis. For example, Montanus advocated the outpouring of the Holy Spirit through trances and prophetic utterances about the return of Jesus and the need for an ascetic life. The church condemned Montanus and thereafter seemed wary of advocating similar charismatic phenomena. That wariness continued through the Protestant Reformation, when Calvin argued that the ecstatic charismata of the New Testament ceased at the end of the first century. Consequently, most mystical and ecstatic experiences of Christians were kept on the fringe of mainstream churches.

Although Christians often disregard the gifts of the Holy Spirit, they continue to reappear throughout church history. At the turn of the twentieth century, the Pentecostal (and Charismatic) Movement arose, which was the most significant renewal of charismata. Christians increasingly experienced charismata, believing that speaking in tongues gave discernible evidence of Holy Spirit baptism, a work of God's grace subsequent to conversion that empowered believers for ministry. The Pentecostal movement was not so much a theological movement as a popular groundswell of charismatic phenomena. Numerous Pentecostal churches thrive throughout the world.

Although the emphasis upon spiritual warfare does not appear exclusively among Pentecostal and Charismatic Christians, they often emphasize a cosmic struggle at work in the world. The emphasis upon spiritual warfare goes back, at least, to

Actively worshipping God

scriptural references to the struggle between the "flesh" and the "spirit" (Rom 8:38–39; Gal 5:13–26; Eph 6:10–17). Usually spiritual warfare emphasizes the need for prayer in combating satanic and demonic forces who oppose God and God's angelic emissaries. Great diversity exists among Christians with regard to the degree to which demons and angels influence the affairs of people, though an awareness of spiritual beings has always been a part of Christianity.

25.5 Contemporary Concerns

The various ministries of the church demonstrate an ongoing process of interpreting Scripture in light of the changing needs and concerns of people both inside and outside the church. It is not surprising that the emphases of such ministries change regularly in the endeavor to be relevant and effective in response to ministry opportunities. We will consider two of them: missiology, and women in ministry. Missiology is a growing area of concern because of the globalization of the church—the world seems to become smaller all the time and a number of concerns arise. Another concern has to do with women in ordained ministry, since debate continues with regard to the biblical and practical roles of women in the church.

25.5.1 Missiology

Missiology refers to the study of Christian missions and missionary work done around the world, though it may also include cross-cultural ministry inside one's own country. Christians began missions work immediately after the life, death, and resurrection of Jesus, spreading Christianity throughout the Mediterranean region through the ministry of people like the Apostle Paul. Missions have continued throughout the centuries, with greater and lesser degrees of prominence. Of course, in the contemporary world, missionary work has increased among many Christian churches because of the increased opportunities for travel, communication, and innovative means for spreading the gospel of Jesus. Why, then, should missions be a matter of theological concern today? One concern has to do with the globalization of the church and the growing cultural sensitivity—or insensitivity—of the church toward the world.

Although missions work originating from around the world is growing, much of it still comes from the West. As missionaries went out to foreign countries, they took much of their Western culture along with the gospel. Often their cultural understanding of society, politics, and economics became inseparable from their missions work, and they ran the risk of confusing Western culture with the gospel. This confusion tended to ignore or marginalize the indigenous cultures in which missions work was being done. However, a growing number of people in the West and globally think that this enculturation may oppress or even do violence, directly or indirectly, to existing cultures. In light of postmodern concerns about how religious beliefs function as metanarratives that belittle or deny the worldview of others, some fear that those engaged in missions work, as well as evangelism, unfairly impose their world-view upon others.

In response to these concerns, churches have adjusted their approach to missions. Some have opted out of missions altogether, but most have tried to become more sensitive in how missionaries minister. This includes Catholics, Protestants, conservatives, and liberals alike. The tendency among modern missionaries has been to become more aware of the enculturated gospel they preach and teach, and they try to minister without the overt trappings of Western culture. Some missions placed greater emphasis upon ministering to the needs of the poor and oppressed; others placed greater emphasis upon the interreligious dynamics of representing Jesus among other living faiths; and still others placed greater emphasis upon ecological issues that everyone faces today. Most modern missionaries have tried to become more understanding of the beliefs, values, and practices of other cultures—inside and outside their host countries. In turn, they have tried to present what they consider to be the core of Christianity in ways that are relevant and winning, rather than coercive.

25.5.2 Women in Ministry

Women have always ministered along with men. This occurred in the Bible as well as throughout church history. As ordained ministry developed, however, men were thought to be the only appropriate gender to serve in full-time positions of ministerial leadership. For centuries, the exclusively male ordained ministry in Catholic and Protestant churches largely remained unquestioned. However, in the twentieth century, a growing number of Christians challenged this patriarchal orientation and argued for a more egalitarian utilization of both men and women in ordained ministry. Although some churches have settled this issue for themselves, it continues to be a topic of debate among the greater Christian world. Even if some churches ordain women, a practical problem remains with regard to how accepting local churches are of female clergy leadership. Let us take a look at two representative sides of the debate.

The historic perspective of many Christian churches with regard to women's ordination to full-time ministry in the church is that they should be restricted from positions of leadership over men. This patriarchal view has much to support it in Scripture as well as in church history. For example, the Bible suggests that God created order and structure in the world that extended to the relationship between men and women (Gen 1–2). Moreover, the explicit teachings of Scripture enforce the leadership of men over women (1 Cor 11:4–5, 8; 14:33b–35; 1 Tim 2:11–14). Just as Jesus is the "head" of the church, men should serve as the head over women in the family, church, and society so

Women as ordained ministers?

that God's intentions may remain intact (Eph 1:22–23; cf. 1 Pet 3:1–5). However, men should never abuse their authority over women, just as Jesus never abused his authority. Instead, men should help women to discover their complementary relationship to men so that women might achieve the full potential God intended for them to have in proper submission.

During the twentieth century, Christians increasingly questioned traditional views in light of an increased awareness of scriptural teachings and the increased sense of call among women to ordained ministry. Although growing feminist concerns about women's rights may have served as an impetus, Christian advocates for an egalitarian view of women in ministry argue that the Bible offers ample support for women in the ministry of the early church, as well as support for women in full-time ministry today. Several scriptural arguments can be made in support of the ordination of women, though the following arguments do not necessarily build upon each other. For example, some argue that the Bible offers numerous positive female role models in addition to those of men: Deborah (Judg 4–5), Esther, and Priscilla (Acts 18; Rom 16). Patriarchalism is not consistently present in Scripture, as can be seen, for example, in the writings of Paul (cf. 1 Cor 11:4–5, 16, vis-à-vis, 14:33b–35). Perhaps the subordination of women occurred as a result of the fall rather than as a part of God's creation (Gen 3:16); just as we seek to overcome the other effects of the fall, we should seek to overcome the subordination of women. Another egalitarian approach argues that biblical principles promote equality (Gen 1:27–28; Gal 3:28). Since the Bible promotes a just society, free from any kind of oppression, Christians should promote equality between men and women (1 Pet 2:13–14, 18; 3:1). Although much of the Bible suggests a hierarchical relationship between men and women, the trajectory of Scripture promotes the equal opportunity of men and women to utilize all the gifts and talents bestowed upon them by God.

25.6 Conclusion

Some caricature the study of theology as being detrimental to Christian faith and ministry. No doubt this concern arises out of sincere, albeit misplaced, concern for how one's "head" may interfere with one's "heart," so to speak. Christianity has always recognized that we are to love God with our heads as well as our hearts, souls, and strength. So the best ministry (practice) should be aided by the best theology (theory). It should be no wonder that theology, rightly understood, is very concerned about issues of ministry because it is in ministry that many Christian beliefs are applied. Theory and practice are independent of one another, and theological studies benefit from the lessons of Christian ministry as much as Christian ministry benefits from theology.

Few Christians would consider theological study as an end in itself. Instead, Christians desire their beliefs and values to bear fruit in practice, including the practice of ministry. Christians may have different beliefs about the nature and extent of ministry, but all desire to serve God and others in the world.

25.7 Questions for Further Reflection

1. With what types of ministry are you familiar? In your experience, what types of ministry have been most effective?

2. Who has responsibility for ministry in the church? What should the role of laity be in assisting the ministry of churches?

3. To what degree should ministry be directed toward individuals and individual needs? To what degree should ministry be directed toward society and societal needs?

4. What do you think is the best blend or balance of ministries?

5. In what types of ministries have you been involved? In what types of ministry would you be interested in becoming involved? What are specific things you can do to become more involved in ministry?

6. What do you think about women in full-time, ordained ministry?

CHAPTER TWENTY-SIX

For I received from the Lord what I also handed on to you, that the Lord Jesus on the night when he was betrayed took a loaf of bread, and when he had given thanks, he broke it and said, "This is my body that is for you. Do this in remembrance of me." In the same way he took the cup also, after supper, saying, "This cup is the new covenant in my blood. Do this, as often as you drink it, in remembrance of me." For as often as you eat this bread and drink the cup, you proclaim the Lord's death until he comes.
(1 Corinthians 11:23–26)

THE MEANS OF GRACE

26.1 Introduction

On the night Jesus was betrayed, he had a last supper with his disciples. This meal proved to be a profound event for the disciples as well as for Christians throughout the centuries. It occurred at a time of great stress. Many of Jesus' followers had already left him because he would not provide the miracles, food, or political insurgency they sought. Even the disciples felt unease because Jesus' public teachings had become increasingly critical of the religious as well as political leaders of the country. People were out to get him! Moreover, Jesus himself had become more difficult to understand. With all the success and reputation Jesus had gained, he seemed unimpressed by it. In fact, Jesus seemed more intent upon preparing the disciples for a challenging future, which they did not really want, than preparing them for a developing ministry with him.

At the supper, Jesus said and did many things that transformed their worldview and lives forever. He taught them and prayed for them to be both faithful and at peace in the face of impending tragedy. Jesus especially reminded them about how love was to lie at the center of their lives and actions in relation to others. He washed their feet as a sign of humility and to demonstrate how they should seek to serve rather than be served. Jesus told the disciples that they were to follow his example. He also spoke of how the disciples, in their own ways, would deny him. Finally, Jesus indicated that one of the twelve disciples—Judas—would betray him to the religious and political leaders, who would in turn crucify him.

In the midst of these discourses, Jesus performed something quite remarkable. He took some bread and wine, blessed them, served them to his disciples, and talked about them as his body and blood. Mark records the following:

> While they were eating, he took a loaf of bread, and after blessing it he broke it, gave it to them, and said, "Take; this is my body." Then he took a cup, and after giving thanks he gave it to them, and all of them drank from it. He said to them, "This is my blood of the covenant, which is poured out for many." (Mark 14:22–24)

Matthew and Luke provide similar accounts of Jesus' words and actions (Matt 26:17–29; Luke 22:7–20). What did they mean? How were the disciples to model them? How significant were Jesus' words and actions for the life of the church? for individuals?

Throughout church history, a number of rites and rituals became crucial to the lives of Christians, individually and corporately. The ritual above came to be known as communion or holy communion, the Eucharist, or the Lord's Supper—for reasons that will be described later. Every Christian tradition, regardless of whether they formally follow any rituals, have some understanding and teaching about them. To some they are means of divine grace; to others they are symbolic remembrances of God's divine activities. To all, they are important for understanding the beliefs, values, and practices of Christianity.

The Last Supper

26.2 Channels of Grace

What is grace? We have already discussed the nature of divine grace, when we talked about divine predestination and human freedom. Grace is the unmerited favor with which God deals with people. It is also the outflow of God's goodness and generosity, which may divinely empower people and groups of people.

What are the means of grace? They are the divinely instituted channels or ways by which God conveys blessings and empowerment to people. The means of grace are sometimes divided into two categories: first, the formal, instituted, or specific means of grace; and second, the informal, prudential, or general means of grace. The former are usually referred to as the sacraments or ordinances of the church. They will constitute the extended discussion of this chapter. On the other hand, informal means of grace probably occupy the majority of time and involvement on the parts of individual Christians and the church. All the means of grace are thought to be started, continued, and culminated by the gracious work of God, since only God brings about eternal results. Yet, God describes these means in the Bible for our benefit and use. If we wish to grow spiritually or live more effectively as Christians, God provides these means as ways by which we may situate ourselves to receive grace and achieve our intended goals. God gives the spiritual increase, but—like Paul—we are to plant and water the seeds of grace (1 Cor 3:6). It is a mystery, finally, with regard to the admixture of divine grace and human responsibility. Nevertheless, most Christians recognize certain divinely ordained means of grace, in which all may participate, regardless of the particular ways in which they believe grace works in and through the lives of believers.

The power of prayer

The informal or prudential means of grace include spiritual disciplines. They include disciplines of engagement: study, worship, celebration, service, prayer, fellowship, confession, submission, and accountability. They also include disciplines of abstinence: solitude, silence, fasting, frugality, chastity, confidentiality, and sacrifice. If people wish to grow spiritually in love for God and others, they may pray to God or study Scripture. They may fast, or spend time in solitude and silence, meditating on God or the Bible. It is believed that God works in and through such means to comfort and encourage people as well as to guide and empower them, according to God's will. The result is greater maturity, personally and spiritually, and greater effectiveness in loving God and others.

Wesley talked about both instituted and prudential means of grace. Among the prudential means of grace, he thought that small accountability groups were one of the more profound ways God intends to help individuals mature and to empower them as a group to minister more effectively to the needs of others. Wesley organized small accountability groups into numerous levels of accountability, making it possible for large numbers of church members to find the level of accountability that best suited their spiritual needs. However, he encouraged people ever to go on toward Christian perfection, utilizing the various means of grace along with total consecration to God so that God might meet that consecration with grace to sanctify people entirely. From his perspective, there was no holiness without "social holiness," that is, without the community of the church and small accountability groups to help individuals grow more Christlike. One should not think of spirituality in individualistic terms, but rather as something done within the community of believers.

26.3 The Sacraments (Ordinances)

As I mentioned before, the sacraments are religious rites and rituals that are the formal means of grace. They are thought to be outward signs instituted by God to impart inward or spiritual grace. Augustine described the sacraments as visible signs of divine things. Sacraments are generally performed as liturgical rites, usually performed in churches, along with rituals or ritualistic practices that reinforce the wording of rites formalized by churches.

The sacraments are a mystery; they represent how God works graciously in and through the mundane elements of life.

When believers faithfully participate in the sacraments, they both honor God and make themselves available for a more abundant life.

In ancient Greek churches, the sacraments were called *mysterion,* which means "mystery." This name aptly conveyed the mystery of how God spiritually worked in and through rituals of the church for salvation, Christian nurture, and ministry. God often works spiritual realities through physical realities. Despite the presence of sin, the physical world has always been a part of God's good creation, and God uses the world and historical events that occur for the sake of self-revelation and for ministering spiritually in people's lives. From time to time in church history, Christians have been tempted to devalue the interdependence between spiritual and physical realities, emphasizing spiritual, inward Christianity over physical, outward manifestations of it. Yet, God seems to have no problem relating the two.

As Christianity moved throughout the Roman world, the mystery of the sacraments was translated in Latin into *sacramentum,* which means "set apart as sacred, oath, command." This name conveyed that Christians were to be faithful in performing the liturgical practices of the sacraments described in Scripture. The sacraments became more holy, as well as more expected in the life of the believer. When combined, mystery and command convey a richer meaning of the sacraments than either aspect does alone. Christians would do well to keep both aspects of the sacraments in mind. If too much emphasis is placed on sacraments as mystery, the practice of the sacraments may diminish, making ritualism expendable. However, that would also diminish important tangible, visible ways God works in and through the lives of people. Likewise, if too much emphasis is placed on sacraments as a command or oath, the sacraments might diminish into mere formality, removing the dynamic of God's gracious work.

26.3.1 Catholic Church

Over time, the ancient and medieval churches developed an elaborate understanding of the sacraments, generally known as sacramentalism. Early Christians thought there were possibly an unlimited number of sacraments. However, the number of formally recognized sacraments was eventually limited. They were thought to work *ex opere operato,* which in Latin means "by the work performed." This meant that God ordained the sacraments as the means by which grace was bestowed rather than upon the virtuousness of the person or persons administering the sacraments. Thus, when by faith people received the sacraments, blessed by priests, they received grace from God, which they would not have otherwise received. After all, grace comes from God and not from human performance or merit. It was important that the tangible sign of the sacraments be administered by a priest. Such a priest needed to be duly appointed and trained by the church to administer properly the sacramental elements, liturgical format, and accompanying words and actions. After all was said and done, what a blessing to receive such grace, and people participated in the sacraments as often as they could.

Catholics believe that there are seven sacraments administered by priests in the church. They serve a variety of functions; however, most of the sacraments enable the salvation and discipleship of believers, especially the first five listed below. Altogether, the seven sacraments include the following:

1. Baptism

2. Confirmation

3. Holy Eucharist

4. Penance (reconciliation)

5. Anointing of the sick (and dying)

6. Marriage (matrimony)

7. Holy orders

Baptism is the ritual for initiating Christians into the Catholic Church. Baptism regenerates people, infants as well as adults, from the guilt of original sin by their sharing in Christ's death and resurrection, represented in the baptismal ritual. In fact, deferring infant baptism too long is considered spiritually disastrous. More will be said about baptism later in the chapter.

"Go therefore and make disciples of all nations, baptizing them . . ." (Matt 28:19)

When infants are baptized, it is expected that their believing parents will enroll them in *confirmation* class when they reach the age of reason. The age of reason refers to the time in children's growth when they are considered sufficiently adult to act responsibly and confirm the faith into which they were baptized. It occurs approximately at the time of puberty, when children in biblical times were thought to come of age as adults. The term "confirmation" describes a period of instruction on the catechism, which today consists of a variety of oral and written instructions on salvation, the Catholic Church, and important aspects of being a Christian. It also describes the ritual that commemorates the completion of such training. Adolescents are trained in Scripture, church doctrine, and other relevant topics on Christian living. Confirmation is the sacrament of Christian maturity, and it is conferred upon participants after their successful completion of catechetical training. Trainees are known as catechumens, and they receive the sacrament of confirmation at the end of their training, during their first celebration of the Eucharist. Those who believe in Jesus as adults and want to be baptized go through similar catechetical training, only as adult learners.

Holy Eucharist, a term derived from a Greek term meaning holy "good grace," refers to the sacramental ritual reflective of the last supper Jesus had with his disciples. In Catholicism, it is sometimes known as the Holy Sacrifice of the Mass. Holy Eucharist, or Eucharist, is performed as the climax of public worship, when by faith church attendees participate in the sacrament. Like confirmation, it is expected that duly appointed priests of the Catholic Church properly present the elements of bread and wine in churches. It is "closed communion" because only those who have successfully completed catechetical training may participate in the Eucharist. Like baptism, more will be said about the Eucharist later in the chapter.

The sacrament of *penance* has to do with the pardon of sins after salvation. It is also known as the Order of Penance, or the Rite of Reconciliation. After people become Christians, they may continue to sin. When those sins occur, it is expected that they repent of them, confess them, and perform words or acts of penance for them. The sacrament of penance involves confession to the Catholic Church (usually to a priest), suitable satisfaction through acts of contrition, and the amendment of life through the resolution not to continue in the sin. The sacrament of penance helps Christians maintain healthy spiritual growth, which affirms their obedient response to sin as well as God's merciful forgiveness. After penitents have duly exhibited contrition and confession, and performed acts of penance or satisfaction, priests act on behalf of God in granting absolution for their sins. Interestingly, the sacrament of penance was known as the "second baptism" in the ancient church. It called for a second, inner conversion of believers toward a life more consecrated to God.

What are the benefits of confessing sins?

The sacrament of *anointing of the sick* primarily has to do with the biblical injunction to anoint with oil and pray for those who, for one reason or another, are sick or possibly dying (Jas 5:14–16). It is not just for those who are about to die, though it has spiritual as well as physical benefits for them. It is for anyone to be taken at any time for his or her physical and spiritual well-being. This sacrament is often given in conjunction with penance so that both body and spirit have full opportunity for healing by God's grace.

Marriage is a holy union between a man and a woman, and the sacrament of marriage is considered a divine gift (or charisma) to them (1 Cor 7:7). Although two people decide to marry, it is God who blesses the unity and indissolubility of the marriage. Properly, marriage should be between two baptized people. The primary purpose of marriage is procreation and the proper education of children. However, there are secondary purposes as well, which benefit the physical, emotional, and social needs of a man and a woman. Scripture

"Therefore what God has joined together, let no one separate" (Matt 19:6)

embodies the relationship and love of Jesus for the church as both a symbol and role model for marriage (2 Cor 11:2; Rev 19:7).

The sacrament of *holy orders* is the ordination of clergy in the Catholic Church, which God instituted and advances for the ministry of the church. God empowers those who become priests and enables them to fulfill properly the responsibilities of the office. Generally, holy orders are thought to be given by God in perpetuity. Ordination occurs through the laying on of hands by those who fulfill the apostolic succession of priesthood, extending back to the Apostle Peter. Ordained priests carry on the teachings of the apostles as well as the succession of their leadership in the church. The pope represents the succession of Peter's leadership in Rome. Thus, the pope has far-reaching apostolic authority for the spiritual as well as ecclesiastical direction of the Catholic Church.

26.3.2 Orthodox Churches

Orthodox churches have similar views of the sacraments, observing most Roman Catholic sacraments and orders. Sometimes they use different names for the sacraments. For example, they speak of chrismation instead of confirmation; confession and repentance instead of reconciliation or penance; anointing with oil or holy unction (healing) instead of anointing of the sick and dying; and ordination instead of holy orders. In addition to the seven aforementioned sacraments, Orthodox churches also talk about the following in sacramental terms: fasting, almsgiving, and monasticism. All are thought to be biblical and to have been continuous church practice since the time of the first-century.

The angelic life of a monk

Since the schism of 1053, the Orthodox and the Catholic churches have considered each other dissident churches. They do not formally recognize, among other things, the genuineness of their respective claims to apostolic succession and ecclesiastical authority, particularly that of Catholic papal authority. With regard to the administration of the sacraments, neither Orthodox nor Catholic churches recognize the authority of the other to administrate them properly. In view of that, Orthodox churches developed their own rituals, liturgies, ecclesiastical polity, and spiritual heritage that reflect their distinctive beliefs, values, and practices.

Variations in the observance of sacraments include distinctive rituals, for example, for funerals and monasticism. Orthodox churches will perform a special Rite for the Part-ing of the Soul from the Body at the time of death and, later, in honor of the de-ceased. These rituals serve more to commemorate than to pray for the dead. Orthodox churches also honor those called to a life of monasticism. Monastics include monks and nuns who sequester themselves in monasteries for the sake of prayer and contemplation for the world as well as for themselves. This calling is honored with sacramental rituals that honor their "angelic life" vocations.

26.3.3 Protestant Views

At the time of the Reformation, Protestant reformers such as Luther and Cal-vin thought that the Catholic Church had abused its ecclesiastical authority in a number of ways. One way related to the sacramentalism that had developed. Protestants thought that Catholics placed too much emphasis upon the *form* of the sacraments, suggesting that they believed the church's rituals actually saved people. Protestants thought Catholics placed too much emphasis on what people did for salvation rather than what God did. Protestants wanted to return emphasis to the *content* of the sacraments, which focused on people's salvation by grace through faith. The sacraments were not the means by which people were saved; people were saved by faith, personally entrusting their lives to God's grace for salvation. Therefore, the sacraments needed to be reformed by reinstituting the importance of individual repentance and faith, and relying upon God's direct grace rather than the church as God's way of mediating saving grace.

Protestants also disagreed with Catholics with regard to the number of sacra-ments. Catholics believed in seven sacraments, which they considered rituals es-tablished by the first-century church. While Protestants did not reject the spiritual benefits of rituals and biblical truths they communicated, they thought that Jesus formally instituted only two sacraments: baptism and communion. Sometimes other practices were considered sacramental, for example, penance and foot washing, but only two practices were recognized as sacraments. Thus, they believed that the proper administration of sacraments included a quantita-tive view of the sacraments as well as a qualitative view of them.

Although there was general agreement among Protestants with regard to the number of sacraments, there were disagreements about their proper na-ture and administration. Disagreements arose early in the Reformation, and they became sources of debate as well as identifying points of theological dif-ference. Because the practice of the sacraments is something everyone can see, touch, and taste, sacramental differences sometimes distinguished Christian traditions and subsequent denominational developments. Let us look at some of the primary developments in Protestant views of the sacraments. Afterward, we will look more specifically at the sacraments of baptism and communion.

Sign and Seal: Although Luther rejected Catholic sacramentalism, he still had a respectful view of the sacraments. Emphasizing baptism and commu-nion, Luther advocated a view of the sacraments as both a "sign and seal" of

God's grace in the lives of believers. As a sign, the sacraments symbolized the work of Jesus for our salvation. However, they were more than symbols of a transcendent reality. As a seal, sacraments were identifying marks and proof of God's gracious work in and through the lives of believers. The sacraments themselves did not save people, though God chose to use them as part of our understanding and appropriation of the fullness of salvation. They gave people assurance of divine grace, comfort in times of trouble, and helped to strengthen faith.

Calvin and the Reformed tradition shared similar views with Luther, emphasizing the sacraments as signs and seals of divine grace. Calvin thought that there existed a spiritual presence in the administration of the sacraments, which did not occur at other times. Calvin and Luther reasserted the sense of mystery, present in earlier Christian traditions, of God working divinely through physical, everyday aspects of life. Sometimes Christians in this tradition talk about speaking and living sacramentally. People's physical, everyday words and actions may demonstrate love to others as effectively as more traditional aspects of ministry, such as preaching and evangelism. When Christians understand the sacramental nature of life, they realize that all aspects of their day-to-day lives may reflect and communicate God's teachings and values, serving as a means of grace to others.

What is meant to be a sign and seal?

Symbolic Memorial: Ulrich Zwingli (1484–1531), a Swiss contemporary of Luther, advocated a more thoroughgoing view of the symbolic nature of the sacraments. According to Zwingli, the sacraments served as ways to remember or commemorate the salvation of God through the person and work of Jesus. The sacraments are symbolic memorials rather than special occasions of grace. Grace was always available from God, and Christians did not need to perform any particular rites or rituals to secure more. Instead, Christians participate in the sacraments in order to give praise and thanks to God, and to act in obedience to Jesus' teachings as a role model. The sacraments have a special blessing for those who take part in them, but no greater grace is available than is available any other time. After the Reformation was underway, Zwingli and Luther met in order to resolve some of their theological differences; however, they did not agree with regard to the sacraments.

The Anabaptists, who formed independent churches in continental Europe that promoted Protestant principles, were more rigorously symbolic than Zwingli. They were also more rigorous than Luther in advocating the Protestant principles—grace alone, faith alone, and Scripture alone. Nothing but grace, through faith, saved people, and the sacraments were only efficacious for adults who could adequately exercise responsible faith. Anabaptists advocated the Protestant principle of Scripture alone more exactly than did the founding reformers. Luther thought that the Anabaptists were too extreme in their narrow, individualistic interpretations of Reformation principles. However, their emphasis upon the symbolic nature of the sacraments has had widespread influence upon Protestant views.

Spiritual View: Some Protestants agreed that the sacraments were symbolic rather than mystically capable of securing added grace for believers. For example, Kaspar Schwenkfeld (1490–1561), a German contemporary of Luther, also disagreed with several of Luther's beliefs. With regard to the sacraments, Schwenkfeld not only thought the sacraments were symbolic, he thought that the very practice of the sacraments ran the risk of confusing people into thinking that they, rather than God alone, had something to do with their salvation. Spirituality should be an ongoing part of believers' lives rather than something promoted on special occasions. Thus, Schwenkfeld had a spiritual or spiritualized view of the sacraments. In order for people to avoid the temptation of falling into the mistaken view of salvation by works,

Can you imagine no sacraments?

Schwenkfeld abandoned sacramental rites and rituals. Since people were saved by grace through faith, the addition of rites and rituals did more to confuse and tempt people than aid them in faith.

During the seventeenth century, George Fox and the Society of Friends in Great Britain advocated a similar spiritualized view. Fox thought of all of life as sacramental. The person, presence, and work of God's Holy Spirit permeated all of life. No rite, ritual, or clergy deserved more recognition than the multitude of ways God works in and through people. Grace was always available, especially through the inner light of the Holy Spirit. Fox did not celebrate the sacraments in order to emphasize to individuals as well as the church that God's grace was continuously available to those who looked to God as their Savior and Lord.

26.4 Baptism

Baptism is an act of initiation. Usually Christians use water in the rite of baptism, speaking a Trinitarian formula "in the name of the Father and of the Son and of the Holy Spirit" (Matt 28:19). Jesus was baptized early in his public ministry (Matt 3:13–17; Mark 1:9–11; Luke 3:21–22; cf. John 1:29–34). John the Baptist regularly baptized in his ministry, and it was John who baptized Jesus, though he thought Jesus should baptize him. However, Jesus considered

The Holy Spirit descending like a dove on Jesus

it right for him to be baptized by John as a sign of obedience to God, as well as to be a role model for others. It was during Jesus' baptism that his sonship was pronounced by God the Father. Moreover, at Jesus' baptism the presence of God the Holy Spirit in the life of Jesus was revealed.

Jesus baptized those who repented and believed in him (Luke 18:15–17). He also instructed his disciples to baptize others. The Great Commission, of course, emphasizes Jesus' exhortation to make disciples, baptizing them, and teaching such to obey everything Jesus commanded them (Matt 28:19–20). When the disciples began to evangelize and establish the church, baptism was a prominent part of their ministry (Acts 2:38–39). Paul also made baptism a major focus of his missions work (Rom 6:3–5; Gal 3:27–28; Eph 4:4–6; Titus 3:5).

The Greek word for baptism (*baptizein*) means "to dip in water," "to wash," or "to purify." Many examples of baptism occur in the New Testament; however, the circumstances were diverse. As a result, a variety of Christian views arose concerning proper ways to baptize. Because baptism is such a visual event and because it has such importance in sacramentalism, differing views of it caused extensive debate and varying degrees of divisions among Christians. We will look at some of the issues pertaining to the sacrament of baptism.

26.4.1 Efficacy of Baptism

What does baptism accomplish? Of what is it efficacious, or what does it do? Certainly it serves as initiation into the church—the body of true believers. In the history of the church, it has also been thought to be a part of God's plan of salvation. For example, Catholics believe that baptism cleanses people of original sin, as they understand original sin. It regenerates them as Christians through divine grace, making them children of God and heirs of eternal life. This view is sometimes referred to as *baptismal regeneration* because it is believed that baptism is the means by which God brings about saving grace to people (John 3:5; Titus 3:5). The ritual itself does not save people; only God does so. Yet, God effects that salvation by grace through faith, on the part of the church as well as individuals, using the sacrament of baptism. Thus, Catholics consider it important to baptize infants, especially if there are complications at childbirth. Baptism regenerates infants, ensuring their eternal well-being.

Some Protestants, as well as Catholics, affirm baptismal regeneration. Luther believed in it, despite the fact he championed the Protestant principle of salvation by grace through faith alone. Luther saw no necessary conflict in affirming the importance of grace and faith along with the biblically mandated need to be baptized. To him, grace, faith, and baptism were inextricably bound up with one another. There was no true faith without baptism and vice versa. Other Protestant traditions affirm baptismal regeneration along with Lutheranism. This viewpoint reinforces the need to baptize infants, since God disperses salvific grace by means of baptism. Without question, this represents a mysterious dialectic of divine initiation and human response. Yet Luther and other Protestants considered it essential for God's plan of salvation.

Most Protestants consider baptism to be a sign or symbol of grace and faith rather than the means of them. New believers are to be baptized out of a sense of obedience, following the role model of Jesus and the disciples. After all, the Bible repeatedly wants new believers to be baptized. From a Reformed perspective, there is the expectation that extra grace is available to the believer at the time of baptism, which serves to seal the reality of salvation, but it is not regenerative grace. From a more symbolic perspective, baptism serves as a public testimony, without superadded grace for an individual. In either case, baptism is important for aligning oneself publicly with God as well as a particular church or denomination. It is also important for the spiritual nurture of a new believer, commemorating a decision for God that may provide assurance of salvation and encouragement for living a Christlike life for years to come. However, baptism is more exemplary than a means by which regenerative grace occurs.

26.4.2 Types of Baptism

When and to whom should baptism be given? Generally, there are two main views of when and to whom baptism should be given. They are infant baptism and believer's baptism. The differences have been topics of debate as well as divisiveness during church history.

Infant Baptism

Infant baptism, also known as *paedobaptism* (Greek for "child" + "baptize"), is the baptism of infants. It constitutes a sign of the new covenant of faith, analogous to the old covenant marked by the circumcision of infant boys in the Old Testament. Colossians 2:11–12 draws an explicit comparison between circumcision and baptism. Although there do not appear to be explicit references to infant baptism in the New Testament, some have argued that the Bible speaks only of adult converts because of its focus on the first generation of Christians, and because insufficient time had passed to fully describe second-generation practices. Furthermore, the book of Acts records several examples of the baptism of entire households once the head of a household was converted (Acts 16:5, 14–15, 31–33; 18:8; cf. 1 Cor 1:16). The conversion of Cornelius provides a wonderful example of solidarity on the part of a household, in which everyone converts and is baptized when the head of the household becomes a Christian (Acts 10:23–48). Although it is not explicitly stated that infants were baptized in Cornelius' household, it is significant that the entire household converted to Christianity together. No one was denied baptism in his household or in other households that converted *en masse*.

The blessings of infant baptism

By the beginning of the second century, Christians regularly practiced infant baptism. Rites and rituals were soon developed for the baptism of infants, and the practice continued uninterrupted for more than a millennium. It is especially important for Catholics to baptize infants because of their sacramental belief that an infant is regenerated at the time of baptism. Although Catholics believe that infants must continue to be nurtured and confirmed in their faith, baptism initiates infants into the eternal as well as temporal church of God.

Many Protestants also baptize infants. However, Protestants differ in terms of their expectations with regard to what infant baptism accomplishes. Those who affirm baptismal regeneration like Catholics believe that infants are cleansed from original sin and given eternal life. Although the infants may not have developed conscious faith, the faith of their parents and of the church make the sacrament of baptism effective in the lives of infants. They also expect infants to grow into mature faith through confirmation or other means of Christian discipleship. Some who do not affirm baptismal regeneration may not consider infants regenerate, but they do believe that God graciously endows grace that infants would not otherwise receive. In this way, baptized infants have advantages that other infants do not have in their spiritual growth. Finally, Protestants who have an entirely symbolic view of the sacraments may still baptize infants. Their reasons for baptism are similar to those above, though there is no expectation of superadded grace. Instead, it is an obedient commemoration of what God has already accomplished on our behalf for salvation and the expectation of it for the infant.

Believer's Baptism

Believer's baptism is the conviction that only those who have made credible professions of faith, normally adults and children, but not infants, should receive baptism. This view of baptism, which respects the responsible faith true believers have in response to the gracious gift of salvation offered by God, expects people to have reached an age of reason or accountability before being baptized.

Advocates of believer's baptism contend that in the New Testament the only explicit examples of baptism seem to occur in adult converts. Only among more mature believers do we find credible testimonies to faith in the gospel message of Jesus leading to baptism. Like the thief on the cross, a person is saved by his or her profession of faith (Luke 23:43). Throughout the book of Acts, *converts* are said to have been baptized: including at Pentecost (Acts 2:41), in Samaria (Acts 8:12), the Ethiopian eunuch (Acts 8:38), Paul (Acts 9:18), Lydia (Acts 16:15), the Philippian jailer (Acts 16:33), Corinth (Acts 18:8), and Ephesus (Acts 19:5). Believer's baptism supporters argue that baptismal practice should be based on clear-cut teaching in Scripture rather than on general evidence such as that provided by household baptisms. Finding arguments from silence unconvincing, they place their confidence only in explicit teaching and example of Scripture.

Interestingly, a tradition of *infant dedication* arose among Protestants who support believer's baptism. Infant dedication usually involves special prayers in church by a pastor and others who want to give thanks for their newborns and to dedicate them publicly to God. They also dedicate themselves, individually and collectively as a church, to raising infants in a Christian environment, conducive to the growth of faith in Jesus for their salvation. It is not clear how the tradition of infant dedication arose; however, it functions similarly to the practice of infant baptism in other churches.

Believer's baptism expects a credible profession of faith

26.4.3 Modes of Baptism

How is baptism to be performed? While Christians universally use water in baptism, different traditions use the water in different ways or *modes*. The Greek words for baptism (*baptismos* and *baptisma*) suggest washing or dipping in water; however, the degree to which one is immersed in water is not clear from the terms themselves. Those who advocate believer's baptism usually prefer complete immersion. Those who advocate infant baptism do not require immersion in water as necessary for baptism but may apply water by sprinkling (aspersion) or pouring (affusion) as well as immersion. Baptism involves clear imagery of dying and rising again (Rom 6:3–5; Titus 3:5), but this can be understood in different ways with respect to mode. For many, the mode of applying the water is not as critical to the proper administration of baptism as is the meaning of the rite.

Over the centuries, many modes and rituals have arisen, which become very important to individuals and individual churches. Sometimes the sacramental practices are recognized by other Christians; sometimes they are not. Some churches do not recognize the baptism of others and insist on *rebaptism*, that is, baptizing someone appropriately for the first time. Anabaptists, for example, derive their name from the words to "baptize again." They reject infant baptism and require that believers be rebaptized after credible professions of faith in God for their salvation. Finally, other modes and rituals have arisen with regard to baptism; however, Christians need to be careful about being overly scrupulous about them. They may become embroiled in religious minutiae that hinder more than help Christianity.

26.5 Communion

Communion is the sacrament of eating bread and drinking wine in commemoration of the death and resurrection of Jesus. It follows the pattern of the last supper Jesus had with the disciples before his betrayal and arrest. Communion is the central sacrament of the Christian church because it centers on the gospel message of Jesus. Christians believe that Jesus instituted the sacrament and called for its duplication (Luke 22:19–20). The breaking of bread and drinking of wine in commemoration of Jesus occurred throughout the New Testament.

Communion is known by many names. Each one contributes to the overall meaning and significance of the sacrament to Christians. It is known as *Eucharist* or Holy Eucharist, which means "good grace." The term suggests thanksgiving on behalf of the church for the grace God bestows upon Christians. Communion is also known as the *Lord's Supper,* which emphasizes how Jesus instituted the sacrament and how his teachings and actions at the last supper are crucial to Christians today. Even the name *Communion* or *Holy Communion* emphasizes the communion or fellowship believers have with God during the sacrament. However, communion is not individualistic because there is also a communal dimension of the sacrament in the church, among true believers in Jesus.

In Catholicism, Holy Eucharist occurs at the end of Mass—at the end of worship. Holy Eucharist forms the climax of church services, and worship would not be complete without its celebration. In addition to Holy Eucharist, Catholics refer to it as Holy Communion, Most Blessed Sacrament, Bread of Life, Sacrament of Love, and Sacrament of Unity. Each name signifies an even richer understanding of the sacrament.

Participants in communion first examine themselves

26.5.1 Preparation for Communion

Because of the sacredness of communion, it is important for Christians to partake of the sacrament in a worthy manner. Scripture says,

> Whoever, therefore, eats the bread or drinks the cup of the Lord in an unworthy manner will be answerable for the body and blood of the Lord. Examine yourselves, and only then eat of the bread and drink of the cup. For all who eat and drink without discerning the body, eat and drink judgment against themselves. (1 Cor 11:27–29)

The interpretation of this passage has varied throughout church history. What does an unworthy manner mean? What does judgment mean? It is clear that participation in communion should not be undertaken without seriously considering the repentance, faith, and consecration God expects on the part of those who partake of Jesus' body and blood.

Most Christians consider participation in communion as an opportunity to examine themselves with regard to all aspects of their lives in relationship to God and others. It is a time of prayer and devotion to God. It is also an opportunity for growth in self-awareness, intimacy with God, and to be challenged to live a more Christlike life. Some church leaders have used communion as an opportunity for evangelism. Just as Christians need to use the celebration of the sacrament as an opportunity for improving the quality of their relationship with God, it may also serve as an opportunity to appeal to those who have never converted to Christianity. God would certainly not want someone participating in communion without first accepting the salvation it represents.

26.5.2 Real Presence

How is Jesus present in communion? Hebrews 9:12–14 suggests that the ritual elements of communion are the same as the body and blood of Jesus. In offering the bread and wine to the disciples, Jesus said, "this is my body . . . this is my blood" (Matt 26:26, 28). In interpreting these passages, many in the ancient church took Jesus' words very seriously. They thought that believers somehow ate the body and drank the blood of Jesus. Yet how could this be? Non-Christians were mockingly critical of Christians for being cannibalistic. Thus, articulating their understanding of the sacrament of communion became a high priority. Yet, various viewpoints arose over time. These are summarized below.

Transubstantiation

The Catholic Church developed the doctrine of *transubstantiation,* which maintains that God divinely transforms the bread and wine of Holy Eucharist. This interpretation of Scripture suggests that the elements of bread and wine are changed mysteriously, albeit in a real sense, into the body and blood of Jesus. After a priest of the Catholic Church consecrates the elements in prayer, the essence of the bread and wine transform into the real "substance" or essence of Jesus' body and blood. The appearance of the bread and wine remain the same; such things are secondary "accidents" or "species" of their unseen essence. They may maintain the same size, shape, color, and taste, but they are no longer the same. The elements now serve as a divine means by which God comforts, encourages, and empowers believers as well as commemorate Jesus' life, death, and resurrection. From a human perspective, believers eat and drink what appears to be bread and wine. From God's divine perspective, they eat and drink the body and blood of Jesus. Only the doctrine of transubstantiation interprets adequately, with sufficient literalness, the words of Jesus to eat his body and drink his blood. To believe anything else is to trivialize the words of Jesus instructing his disciples to his disciples and all he commands them to observe regularly in remembrance of him and of the salvation he provided. Holy Eucharist, after all, represents an ongoing celebration of Jesus' salvific work for humanity.

Consubstantiation

Consubstantiation is the view that Jesus is spiritually present in a special way during the sacrament of communion. Jesus is always present, of course, but his presence ensures special grace for believers in their partaking of communion. Consubstantiation preserves the mystery of communion in that it does not explain how the sacrament serves as a means of grace not otherwise available to Christians. Yet, it is thought that Jesus is present in a more intimate way than usual and that special grace is available to comfort, encourage, guide, and empower those who participate in communion.

Luther's view is identified with consubstantiation, though he did not coin the term. He disagreed with the Catholic view of transubstantiation. It seemed too magical to Luther. From his perspective, transubstantiation placed too much emphasis on what people did rather than on what God did. Luther described the real presence of Jesus during the sacrament of communion as spiritual in nature. Yet, he thought that great mystery surrounded communion, and that people received grace in the sacrament that they would not otherwise have. To Luther, grace existed all around the elements of communion—above, below, and beside the bread and wine. Christians, then, should often partake of communion, both because of the memorial it serves as well as the gracious benefits it offers participants.

Memorial Meal

Those who view communion as a *memorial meal* consider it a symbolic commemoration of the death and resurrection of Jesus. Jesus is really and spiritually present during the ordinance.[1] From the perspective of a memorial meal, Jesus is thought to be no more present than at any other time. Christians become more focused upon Jesus and his significance for their lives in partaking of the bread and wine. Those advocating this position hold that certainly there is a special blessing in such a commemoration, and that Christians should often participate in communion. However, believers receive no superadded grace through their participation.

Zwingli promoted the view of communion as a memorial meal. From his perspective, a symbolic view of the sacraments enhanced rather than detracted from their significance. Speculation about what happens during communion detracted from the things clearly known by Christians about God's work in their lives. Certainly God provided for their salvation through Jesus, and God continues to work in and through their lives via the Holy Spirit. God's grace is always available to people. People should celebrate that constancy. Thus, communion reminds us not of special grace available only at certain times but of how grace is available always and everywhere.

The importance of remembering Jesus

26.5.3 Modes of Communion

How is communion performed? That depends on whether a church's view of the sacraments emphasizes the mystery of the sacraments or the commemorative aspect. The former view is sometimes referred to as "high-church," and the latter view is sometimes called "low-church." Such terms, of course, are relative to a particular church, denomination, culture, and so on. However, they are helpful in distinguishing between different types of church practices. Although the characterizations of high church and low church pertain to the whole of a church's worship and celebration practices, they often center on a particular view of communion. So-called *high-church* worship practices include more rites and rituals, liturgy, and formal procedures pertaining to communion. So-called *low-church* worship practices exercise greater simplicity and freedom, characterized by greater degrees of informality with regard to how communion takes place. For example, high-church communion may follow rites and rituals that have existed for centuries, whereas low-church communion may frequently vary with no set wording or liturgy for its observance. High-church worship occurs most frequently within the Catholic, Orthodox, Anglican, and some Lutheran and other mainline Protestant traditions. Low-church worship occurs most frequently within the varieties of Protestant or independent churches and denominations that formed after the Reformation.

How often does or should communion occur? High-church traditions partake of communion regularly. Each worship service serves the sacrament of bread and wine. Catholic Churches, for example, may provide Holy Eucharist on a daily basis, and laity as well as clergy partake of it as often as possible because of the benefits they believe it provides. Low-church traditions have widely varying traditions with regard to administering communion. Some may administer Eucharist once a week, once a month, once a quarter, semi-annually, or only annually. Some may never administer it at a traditional Sunday morning worship service. Instead, they may only administer it at a Sunday evening service or mid-week evening service. On occasions, clergy may administer communion to individuals who are shut-ins or ill, or perhaps for such special occasions as weddings. In each instance, their view of the sacraments powerfully affects the frequency as well as the ways they administer communion.

Closed and Open Communion

Churches and denominations that consider the sacraments to be special means of grace, which God would not otherwise bestow upon Christians, exercise close oversight over the administration of communion. Often it is expected that participants in communion be either baptized or a member of the church from which they receive the elements of bread and wine. This practice is known as *closed communion* because it is not left up to individuals to decide whether they are worthy partakers, and we have already discussed the scriptural warning to those who partake of communion unworthily (1 Cor 11:27–28). Churches may also consider themselves responsible for approving those who are worthy. This is especially true of churches and denominations that consider themselves to partake literally of the body and blood of Jesus. In these instances of high-church worship, only those approved by a church or denomination may receive the elements of bread and wine.

Other churches and denominations, usually from a low-church view, permit individuals greater freedom in deciding when and where they may partake of communion. Since they emphasize a more symbolic understanding of the sacraments in general, they allow more liberty in all aspects of the administration of communion. Generally, the view of *open communion* requires only that individuals discern for themselves whether they are worthy to partake of the bread and wine. Such churches and denominations welcome all, based upon individual affirmations of faith in Jesus for their salvation.

Elements of Communion

How, specifically, is communion to be performed? In what modes or ways is it administered? Bread and wine, of course, have been used throughout church history. However, there are numerous variations on these. For example, different types of bread have been used. Sometimes this includes a loaf of bread from which pieces are pulled either by clergy or by individuals. Other times individual pieces of bread, wafers, or even crackers are used by churches. Sometimes Christians drink from a common cup, from which everyone drinks. Other times individual cups of wine are provided. More noticeable has been the use of grape juice instead of wine—fermented grape juice—to signify the blood of Jesus. Grape juice was first used instead of wine when processing advances made it possible to store grape juice. "New wine" is sometimes referred to in the New Testament along with old wine (e.g., Matt 9:17; Mark 2:22; Luke 5:37–39; Acts 2:13). Consequently, there seemed to be no necessary reason why new wine—grape juice—could not be used along with old or fermented wine for communion. As there occurred a growing awareness of personal and social problems related to alcoholism, churches and denominations sometimes adopted the use of grape juice in lieu of wine. In serving the elements, references were made to partaking of the bread and cup rather than the bread and wine, thus avoiding confusion over using grape juice rather than wine. Nowadays grape juice is commonly used in low-church observances of communion. The "lower" the church tradition, the greater the liberty churches may use in observance of the sacrament. However, Christians of all views have high regard for partaking of communion and do not partake of them frivolously, regardless of their choice of elements.

How do you prefer to take communion?

Usually bread and wine are served consecutively: first, the bread is provided and eaten, and then the wine is provided and drunk. Sometimes the laity only eat the bread, while the clergy consume both bread and wine. In some observances of communion, the bread and wine are partaken simultaneously through intinction, when the bread is dipped into a common cup and then both are consumed. In Orthodox churches, priests may administer sacramental wine from the chalice with a spoon directly to the mouth of recipients. Due to contemporary health concerns, discretion is often used with regard to using a common cup, regardless of the particular mode of participation.

26.6 Conclusion

From the first century until today, Christians believe that God ordained specific means of grace by which they may benefit from the comfort, encouragement, guidance, and empowerment available to them from God. If people want to know God better and grow in grace in relationship to God, they may participate in the various beneficial ways God indicates through Scripture. General or informal means of grace benefit Christians on a daily basis. Sometimes known as spiritual disciplines, they include disciplines of engagement and abstinence. Faithful, hopeful, and loving participation in these spiritual disciplines serve as the means by which God graciously works in and through people's lives.

Specific or formal means of grace, known as the "sacraments" in high-church traditions and "ordinances" in some low-church traditions, serve as special means of grace to Christians. In Catholic and Orthodox churches, there are thought to be at least seven sacraments by which God guarantees special presence and grace to all who worthily participate. The sacraments include baptism, confirmation, Holy Eucharist (communion), penance, anointing of the sick, holy marriage, and holy orders. In most Protestant traditions, only two sacraments are recognized: baptism and communion. In all churches, the sacraments are thought to be special religious observances, ordained by God, for the salvation and nurture of Christians, commemorating how God graciously provides for the holistic needs people have.

26.7 Questions for Further Reflection

1. How does one grow in grace? What would one do if he or she wanted to grow closer to God, or grow spiritually as a Christian?

2. Do you participate in the disciplines of engagement: study, worship, celebration, service, prayer, fellowship, confession, submission, and accountability? Or, do you participate more in the disciplines of abstinence: solitude, silence, fasting, frugality, chastity, confidentiality, and sacrifice? Which are most important to you?

3. Do you participate in the specific means of grace, that is, the formal sacraments (or ordinances) of the church? How many sacraments do you think there are? What should be your attitude when you partake of them? What should you expect from God by participating in the sacraments?

4. Have you been baptized? Why is it important for a believer to be baptized?

5. Do you partake of communion? What attitude should a believer have when partaking of the bread and wine of the sacrament? What are the benefits of partaking of it?

26.8 Notes

1. Some memorialists prefer to refer to communion and baptism as *ordinances* rather than sacraments in order to distinguish their understanding of these practices from the previously mentioned sacramental views.

THE FUTURE

But about that day or hour no one knows, neither the angels in heaven, nor the Son, but only the Father. Beware, keep alert; for you do not know when the time will come. It is like a man going on a journey, when he leaves home and puts his slaves in charge, each with his work, and commands the doorkeeper to be on the watch. Therefore, keep awake—for you do not know when the master of the house will come, in the evening, or at midnight, or at cockcrow, or at dawn, or else he may find you asleep when he comes suddenly. And what I say to you I say to all: Keep awake.
(Mark 13:32–37)

ESCHATOLOGY

27.1 Introduction

One day Jesus and his disciples visited the temple in Jerusalem. For one reason or another, the disciples pointed out the buildings of the temple to Jesus. In response, he totally amazed his disciples by telling them that all the stones would one day be thrown down! It was a familiar belief among people who lived during the first century that the world would come to an end due to some cataclysmic event. Thus, the interest of the disciples was piqued, especially since they hoped that Jesus would physically establish his kingdom on earth!

Later, on the Mount of Olives, which overlooks the temple site, the disciples privately asked Jesus about the end times. They asked, "Tell us, when will this be, and what will be the sign of your coming and of the end of the age?" (Matt 24:3). Jesus responded in several ways. First, he began by warning his disciples. In fact, and as we shall see, Jesus warned them about several things in his eschatological discourse. Second, he alluded to horrific events that would occur—wars, rumors of wars, famines, and earthquakes. However, such events were "but the beginning of the birth pangs" (Matt 24:8).

Perhaps more important than the horrific events Jesus foretold were the warnings. They are as relevant now as they were for the disciples two millennia ago. First, Jesus said, "Beware that no one leads you astray" (Matt 24:4). No doubt he was concerned that the disciples not become preoccupied with fantastic theories about the end times. Throughout history, people have been fascinated with predicting the end of the world. Even today people are as guilty of this diversion as anyone!

Second, Jesus warned about future perils to Christians: hatred, torture, and death because of their Christianity. Due to these perils, he further warned that "many will fall away . . . betray one another and hate one another. . . . the love of many will grow cold. But the one who endures to the end will be saved" (Matt

Is the end near?

24:10, 12–13). Jesus was more concerned about the status of their relationship with God and others than about predicting the end of the world.

Finally, Jesus said, "But about that day and hour no one knows, neither the angels of heaven, nor the Son, but only the Father" (Matt 24:36). Despite the fact that he alludes to many future events—vile as well as victorious—Jesus places more emphasis upon our preparedness now than upon our anticipation for the future. True, Jesus promised that he would physically return to establish his kingdom. However, in the meantime, people should be ready for Jesus' return at any time, since not even he knew the precise time of the end of the world. Jesus said, "Therefore you also must be ready, for the Son of Man is coming at an unexpected hour" (Matt 24:44).

27.2 The Scriptural Setting

Eschatology is the study of "last things" or "the end times" (Greek, *eschata*). In the Old Testament, not much emphasis was placed upon predicting the future. However, there was complete confidence that God was in control of the future as well as the present. To be sure, there are passages that suggest future events—both in terms of the immediate future as well as the end times. The latter half of the book of Daniel, chapters 6–12, for example, has been interpreted by some in reference to the final eschaton (Matt 24:15). For the most part, the Old Testament focuses on God's promises and the hope believers have in the present and future fulfillment of those promises.

In the New Testament, there emerge notable developments in teachings about the end times. Jesus appears as the Messiah, the promised one; he articulates heaven and hell more clearly than is found in the Old Testament; and Jesus' teachings on the kingdom of God (also known as the kingdom of heaven) figure prominently throughout the Gospels. In some ways, Jesus talks about the kingdom as not yet present; in other ways, Jesus talks about the already present kingdom of God. Which is it? The disciples were not entirely sure. They were, however, excited about the imminent possibility of the kingdom's establishment by Jesus.

The appearance of Jesus is the *parousia* (Greek), the "coming" or "advent" of the incarnate God. So when Jesus talks about his return, it is also referred to as his parousia or, in this instance, the *second coming* of Christ. Jesus speaks of his return at the time of his ascension. Likewise, his second coming is referred to, discussed, and anticipated in various places throughout the New Testament (Matt 26:64; Luke 21:27; Acts 1:11; Heb 9:28). Most notably, it appears in the book of Revelation, which is also known as the Apocalypse (Rev 3:11; 16:15; 22:20). In Greek, *apokalypsis* means "disclosure, unveiling, or revelation." In this context, it refers to the revelation of God's sovereign control over the final destiny of humanity and, indeed, all of creation.

Throughout church history, it has been a matter of debate with regard to how apocalyptic literature should be interpreted. To be sure, the book of Revelation contains a great deal of dramatic imagery. It is not a matter of whether imagery and symbolism exist in Revelation; it is a matter of how much is there and how historically literal its writings are. Since every interpreter recognizes symbolism, varying degrees of relish have been exerted in interpreting it. Adding to the complexity of the interpretation process is the realization that, historically speaking, Hebrew writers tended to write with great drama in their apocalyptic writings, whereas Greeks were more literally precise in how they understood apocalyptic literature. These distinctions exacerbated the degree of precision with which people could predict the future.

How are we to understand apocalyptic literature?

Some interpreters of Revelation have provided safeguards, which may be of help in developing eschatology, that is, doctrine about the end times. Shirley Guthrie Jr. (1927–2004) provided four such safeguards. He suggested the following:

- We must not want to know too much.

- Biblical language about the future is primarily symbolic.

- There is no consistent biblical picture of the future, but a development in its thought.

- The best insight we have into what God will do is found in looking at what God has already done.[1]

First, we must not want to know too much. People seem to have an innate desire to know and, perhaps, control the future, especially the end times. But they must not want to know more than God has revealed. Second, biblical language about the future, that is, apocalyptic language, is primarily symbolic. There may be literal and historical references that are made, and they may be predictive of the future. However, even the most literal and historical interpreters of the future recognize numerous symbols and symbolic meanings in the biblical texts. The very nature of predicting the future, especially the distant future, requires symbolism. Of course, the symbolic nature of apocalyptic literature does not mean it is not predictive of the future. Third, there is development in what Scripture says about the end times. Scripture is thought to contain progressive revelation. God reveals more and more to people as they read through the Bible. Finally, the best insight we have into what God will do is found in looking at what God has already done. Although we may not be able

How much can we know about the future?

to predict the future as well as we would like, we have faith and hope in the love, grace, and mercy that God has already revealed.

Certainly it is no easy task to interpret the book of Revelation. Indeed, a variety of theories arose in church history, attempting to explain the book's significance, as well as the significance of other New Testament references to the end times. Often, the degree to which apocalyptic literature is thought to be symbolic, vis-à-vis, literally and historically predictive of the future, distinguishes one view of eschatology from another. In order to simplify the various theories, we will look at three primary views of the millennium.

27.3 Historical Developments

Biblically, the millennium (Latin, "thousand years") refers to a thousand-year reign of Jesus in the book of Revelation, written by the Apostle John. Although the symbolic or literal reference to the millennium in Rev 20 forms just one part of eschatological theories about the end times, its name has come to summarize the various viewpoints. We will discuss the following theories as they formally developed in church history: amillennialism, postmillennialism, and premillennialism.

Development in millennial theories of the end times was a complex process. They did not happen all at once. Biblical and theological emphases interacted with cultural and ideological emphases. Despite the complexity in their development, it is possible to summarize the gist of their respective views of the end times.

27.3.1 Amillennialism

In the ancient church, the Nicene Creed established clear affirmations with regard to the end times. It states the following about Jesus' second coming: "Jesus Christ . . . will come again with glory to judge the living and the dead. His kingdom shall have no end"; and it further states, "We look forward to the resurrection of the dead and the life of the world to come."[2] The ancient church clearly looked forward to the physical return of Jesus, judgment, and the establishment of his kingdom without end. It also looked forward to the resurrection and eternal life beyond the life we now know. Although the ancient creeds do not provide much specificity with regard to the end times, people believed and hoped in the second coming of Jesus to the world and its final consummation.

In this context, Augustine was noteworthy in developing a doctrine of eschatology that gained wide acceptance. Although he did not coin the term, Augustine's eschatology became known as *amillennialism,* which means "no

> **Jesus Christ promised** to return, physically and with the full manifestation of his kingdom.
>
> Till then, he is more concerned about how we live our lives than with our speculating when he will come for the second time.

millennium." That does not mean that he doubted the second coming of Jesus and the final establishment of God's kingdom. On the contrary, like the Nicene Creed, Augustine anticipated the physical return of Jesus. The overwhelming testimony of Scripture pointed to this blessed hope. However, he did not think that a strictly literal or historical interpretation of apocalyptic literature in the Bible represented the appropriate approach to the biblical texts.

In interpreting apocalyptic literature—John's vision in the book of Revelation in particular—Augustine thought a symbolic or allegorical method of interpretation was the most appropriate. Much that was said had the semblance of prediction about the end times, but literal or historical interpretations inadequately communicated the overall sovereignty as well as mystery of the final fulfillment of God's promises throughout Scripture. One could try to decipher Revelation and make detailed predictions about the future; however, Augustine considered that an unreasonable and less faithful rendering of the text. Instead, Augustine thought that Revelation served as a glorious vision of God, filled with images that encouraged Christians with regard to their affirmations about Jesus' second coming and eternal kingdom. His symbolic interpretation of Revelation and, more specifically, the millennial kingdom in Rev 20, did not mitigate Christians' eschatological expectations. Augustine did not think, however, that Christians should become mired down in unproductive speculation in trying to predict the future, especially since Jesus himself claimed that no one knew the day or hour of the end times, including him.

Later in church history, variations on the basic themes of amillennialism arose. Although different names were used, they generally argue that the eschatological references in Scripture were thought to refer to past events or to events that were being fulfilled in the first century, rather than to future events. They include names such as realized eschatology, inaugurated eschatology, and preterist ("past") view of eschatology. Such interpreters looked at the book of Revelation and saw in them matters that occurred and were fulfilled during the first century. Jesus' life and ministry actually initiated the kingdom of God. The destruction of Jerusalem and the persecution of the Christians may have served as events that sparked a need for hope in God's sovereign control of the world. In response to that need, God graciously gave John a series of visions to encourage the first-century church to persevere until the end times. The visions were not intended to predict future events.

A minority of amillennialists hold that all of Scripture is to be demythologized in order to ascertain the existential values embedded within the texts. From this perspective, Christians are not to anticipate the return of Jesus.

Since salvation is primarily for people here and now, they should focus on the present rather than the future. This view tends to deconstruct both the transcendent and eschatological meaning of the Bible.

Throughout church history, amillennialism as it was conceived by Augustine has constituted the majority view among Christians. It has been held by Catholics, Orthodox Christians, and most Protestants after the time of the Reformation. Alternative views of eschatology were developed primarily by Protestants, but amillennial beliefs and values persisted. To this day, amillennialism remains the predominant worldwide view of Christian eschatology, though other views may receive more attention.

Amillennialists are not end times clock-watchers

With regard to the future, amillennialists are hopeful of Jesus' return and the final establishment of his kingdom. Although they do not necessarily expect a literal millennial reign on earth, they do expect the final consummation of creation. In the meantime, the situation of the world may become worse; it may also become better. Since they interpret apocalyptic literature primarily as symbolic or allegorical, they remain neutral with regard to their expectations about world events. Christians should not spend their time speculating. Instead, they should prepare for the end times, faithfully loving God and others without becoming distracted by unhelpful conjecture.

27.3.2 Postmillennialism

Postmillennialism is the view that Jesus will return after (or post) the establishment of his kingdom on earth. There are, of course, different understandings of how Jesus' kingdom will be established. Regardless of these specific differences, postmillennialists emphasize the establishment of the kingdom here and now.

Postmillennialism as a movement arose after the Protestant Reformation. Although there have always been postmillennial tendencies in Christians throughout church history, it was not until after the Reformation that formal eschatological doctrines arose. There is no chief representative of postmillennialism, since it did not initially arise as a specific doctrine. Instead, it arose out of belief and hope in God's powerful, gracious work in all aspects of the world today. If God is a God of miracles, healing, and resurrection, then God can work powerfully in transforming both individuals and society. Thus, a cautious optimism arose with regard to how God might work to establish his kingdom on earth here and now through the obedient efforts of the church in the world. It was not an unrealistic optimism, since sin and its effects—direct and indirect—pervade the world in which we live. However, postmillennialists have reason to expect and work for a better world, based upon the guidance and empowerment of God's Holy Spirit.

Some point to Calvin as an example of postmillennialism, since he wanted to construct a theocratic state in Geneva where the church and civil government functioned cooperatively. The leaders of the church had authority and input for matters of the civil government, and leaders of the civil government had authority and input for matters of the church. Puritan reformers had similar hopes for the Anglican Church in England, just as the early Puritans in the American colonies had theocratic hopes for the new world.

Support for postmillennialism grew at the same time the Enlightenment developed in the Western world. Although the Enlightenment's optimism in humanity and progress made postmillennial ideas attractive, Christians believed they had sound biblical and experiential support for their eschatology. As transformers of culture, postmillennialists thought they could evangelize individuals as well as progressively Christianize the world in which we live.

In interpreting apocalyptic literature, postmillennialists believe that symbolism and allegory best represent Scripture. The book of Revelation, for example, expresses present as well as future hope for establishing the kingdom of God. They expect Jesus to return someday, and, in the meantime, they would faithfully serve to usher in kingdom values and practices in anticipation of that day. Out of obedience to and belief in the sovereignty of God, millennialists think a great deal can be accomplished here and now. The so-called millennium is not to be thought of in terms of a literal thousand-year reign, since it is not known how long people will tarry on earth. However, the second coming of Jesus is expected and anticipated, based upon repeated statements about it throughout the New Testament.

Progress!

Developments in postmillennial expectations continued throughout the nineteenth and twentieth centuries. In the nineteenth century, proponents of liberal protestantism and the social gospel optimistically believed in both the transformation of individuals through salvation and the transformation of society through obedient, Christlike activism. As an expression of spirituality, postmillennialists engaged in compassion ministries, where the symptoms of sin, bondage, ignorance, and misery existed. They also engaged in advocacy ministries, where the causes of such problems were addressed institutionally as well as individually, trying to overturn the poverty, injustices, and persecutions perpetrated upon people. This holistic approach to Christian life and ministry was thought to be at the core of the gospel message of Jesus.

In the twentieth century, various liberation theologies emerged with similar optimism with regard to the degree to which societal problems as well as the problems of sin may be transformed. They are, in a sense, theologies of hope. For example, James Cone advocates racial justice and equality for blacks as well as other ethnic groups; Gustavo Gutiérrez advocates economic justice and equality for the poor of the world; and Rosemary Radford Ruether advocates gender justice and equality. All advocate the need for political as well as spiritual activism in living out the gospel message of love for others. Just as God liberated Israel from physical bondage in Egypt (Exod 1–15), and later liberated people from spiritual bondage through the death and resurrection of Jesus, Christians are to provide the same holistic ministry to the world. They may do so, knowing that God is with them as salt and light in the world, which impacts society as well as individuals.

With regard to the future, postmillennialists are cautiously optimistic. They balk at being accused of unrealistically assessing the many and, apparently, growing problems of the world in which we live. Empirically speaking, it is not always easy to argue that the world is getting better and better. Indeed, one could easily make the counterargument. All the advances in learning, science, and technology only seem to make us better at sinfully hurting one another, individually and socially. Our quantity of knowledge does not necessarily seem to have helped us in terms of improving its quality. Nevertheless, postmillennialists think there are more reasons for hope than despair, given their belief in the presence and ongoing work of God through the Holy Spirit. They are not utopian, but they think we should value all aspects of the world in which we live. Since God initially directed people to have dominion over the world (Gen 1:28), we should seek to do so regardless of circumstances or ideas that might lead one to despair over the world in which we live.

> ### REAL CHRISTIAN LOVE
>
> Real Christian love is founded on commitment to a more just society and action to bring it about.
>
> GUSTAVO GUTIÉRREZ,
> A THEOLOGY OF LIBERATION

27.3.3 Premillennialism

Today one of the most publicized views of eschatology is known as *premillennialism*. Premillennialism is the view that Jesus will return to earth prior to the establishment of his kingdom on earth. Although they differ as to where, when, and how Jesus' second coming will occur, proponents of premillennialism agree that Jesus will return before the establishment of his thousand-year kingdom. They argue that the earliest patristic writers espoused premillennial views, but that these views were largely eclipsed until modern times by the amillennial views of Augustine.

Proponents of premillennialism argue that their views existed among the earliest patristic writers and that their views were eclipsed by the amillennial views of Augustine. From time to time, Christians have speculated about the identity of the antichrist—the demonically motivated individual described in Revelation as the harbinger of the end times. Among Protestants after the Reformation, the antichrist has often been identified with one or more Catholic popes, though others have been counted among possible candidates.

Despite its precursors, premillennialism did not arise as a formal doctrine of eschatology until the nineteenth century. Premillennialists generally take a literalistic approach to biblical interpretation, including apocalyptic literature. Symbolism and allegory invariably occur throughout Scripture, including apocalyptic literature. However, there remains a great deal more that is literally and historically accurate regarding both past events and future events. Thus, apocalyptic literature, especially as found in the book of Revelation, should be studied and used in preparing for the future, if not actually predicting it.

One frequently debated aspect of the premillennial scheme concerns the identity of the antichrist—the demonically motived individual described in Revelation as the harbinger of the end times. Among Protestants since the Reformation, the antichrist has sometimes been identified with one or more of the Catholic popes. In more recent times, a host of other historical figures have been labeled as the antichrist. Most contemporary premillennialists believe this ominous end-times figure has yet to be revealed.

Predictions about the end of the world have existed among Christians throughout church history. Even in the New Testament, people mourned that their anticipation of the imminent second coming of Jesus had not occurred. In response to such laments, the Apostle Peter is recorded as having said the following:

> First of all you must understand this, that in the last days scoffers will come, scoffing and indulging their own lusts and saying, "Where is the promise of his coming?" . . . But do not ignore this one fact, beloved, that with the Lord one day is like a thousand years, and a thousand years are like one day. The Lord is not slow about his promise, as some think of slowness, but is patient with you, not wanting any to perish, but all to come to repentance. (2 Pet 3:3–4, 8–9)

In the ancient church, Christians sometimes predicted the imminent end of the world. As a result, they sometimes threw themselves zealously into evangelism, lived ascetic lives, sold or donated all their possessions in order to wait for the return of Jesus. The belief that Jesus will come again any moment has profound influences upon how people live their lives.

Societal and world affairs could arguably be said to influence the regularity of such doomsday expectations. However, that would trivialize the regularity of hope and anticipation found among Christians, based upon the testimony in Scripture. To be sure, first-century Christians had to be assuaged in their disappointment about the delay of Jesus' second coming. To a certain extent, Christians seem to struggle with ongoing disappointment over God's apparent delay in the final establishment of his kingdom. Nevertheless, the New Testament consistently affirms the coming kingdom of God, though the majority of Scripture advises patience as well as preparedness. Christians are to be cautious in what they prophesy, though there seems to be an inherent human desire to know the future.

Do wars and rumors of war portend the end?

Premillennialists believe that Scripture communicates vital clues to understanding the signs of the times and for recognizing key indicators of Jesus' second coming. In the book of Revelation and in the latter half of Daniel, a discerning interpreter can determine the plans God laid out for ushering in the end times.

Early nineteenth-century Christians called Adventists followed William Miller (1742–1849), who predicted the second coming (advent) of Jesus in approximately 1843. Although Miller repeatedly had to recalculate Jesus' return, the Adventist movement continued with an urgent sense of the imminent establishment of the kingdom of God. Adventists continue to live with a sense of urgency about the second coming of Jesus.

Because the end times are foreshadowed in Scripture with wars, rumors of wars, famines, and earthquakes, premillennialists tend to live with a sense of nervous tension, putting off conventional life activities in expectation of Jesus' second coming. Insults, hardships, persecutions, and calamities that occur are thought to be inevitable rather than challenges to overcome. Accordingly, there is not the same sense of urgency for ministering to this-worldly concerns. Instead, zeal is placed on prophetic study and evangelism rather than on more mundane matters.

Pretribulationism

In the mid-nineteenth century, John Nelson Darby (1800–1881), a founding member of the Plymouth Brethren in England, promoted what came to be known as *dispensational theology*. Dispensationalism, generally speaking, interprets Scripture as containing several dispensations or eras in which God uniquely related to people from one dispensation to the next, from the time of creation to the final judgment. With regard to eschatology, Darby argued that the church currently lives in the final dispensation before the millennium—the thousand-year reign of Jesus on earth. Prior to the millennium, Jesus would secretly rapture Christians from the world, after which there would occur seven years of tribulation. Because the rapture is thought to occur prior to the tribulation, this view of eschatology is known as *pretribulational premillennialism* or, simply, *pretribulationism*.

The rapture, which comes from the Latin word *raptus* ("carried off"), is thought to occur in 1 Thess 4:17, among other places in the New Testament, where those who are alive will be "caught up in the clouds" with Jesus (cf. Matt 24:21–30). In 1 Thess 4:15–17, the Apostle Paul says:

> For this we declare to you by the word of the Lord, that we who are alive, who are left until the coming of the Lord, will by no means precede those who have died. For the Lord himself, with a cry of command, with the archangel's call and with the sound of God's trumpet, will descend from heaven, and the dead in Christ will rise first. Then we who are alive, who are left, will be caught up in the clouds together with them to meet the Lord in the air; and so we will be with the Lord forever.

The rapture is thought to be an unexpected and, relatively speaking, secret event. Of course, there is bound to be amazement and confusion when masses of Christians disappear.

After the rapture, the people remaining on earth will have to deal with the dramatic removal of Christians from the world along with cataclysmic events of earthly tribulation and divine wrath. The idea of such a seven-year period of tribulation derives from Dan 9:20–27, where an "anointed one" (or messiah) arises and then is cut off for a period of time (cf. Dan 7:23–28; 8:14; 12:5–12). Dispensationalists interpret this seven-year period as a time of diverse troubles, after which the world as we know it will come to an end in a multi-national battle called Armageddon, probably near a mountain of Megiddo in Israel (Rev 16:16). Jerusalem and its presumably rebuilt temple will be destroyed (Matt 24:21–30). Then Jesus will visibly return as conquering king, along with Christians, to establish on earth a thousand-year reign of Jesus (Rev 20:1–7). Only after that time will the final judgment and the eternal kingdom of God occur.

Darby zealously promoted dispensationalism in England and the United States. During the twentieth century, *The Scofield Reference Bible*—the first readily accessible study Bible—did much to promote pretribulational, premillennial eschatology. After the reinstitution of Israel as a nation in 1948, speculation was rekindled about the end times. For example, dispensationalist Hal Lindsey (1929–) wrote a very popular book entitled *The Late Great*

Rapture!?

Planet Earth, which promoted a dramatic interpretation of the end times, characteristic of pretribulationism.[3] Thereafter, people made the rapture a focal point of conjecture, resulting in literary, musical, and cinematic media that popularizes this type of eschatology.

Alternative Views of the Tribulation

As premillennial eschatology became more prominent, variations in its basic beliefs emerged. Most notably, adherents questioned the nature and timing of the rapture. What was its nature, and when precisely would it occur? Traditional dispensationalists assert that the rapture will occur prior to the tribulation. It would be forewarned by such portents as the coming of an antichrist and the "mark of the beast," some sort of designation placed upon those who oppose God (Revelation 13:16–18). The most common alternative views of pretribulationism are posttribulationism and midtribulationism.

Posttribulationism arose because it was thought that Scripture does not teach a private rapture prior to the second coming of Jesus. Instead it occurs at the end of the tribulation, when Jesus returns. Hence, this viewpoint is known as posttribulationism. Look, they say, at the same passage

Will the world come to a final cataclysmic end?

in 1 Thess 4:15–17. Posttributionists argue that the meeting of Jesus "in the clouds" was a public event, attended by "a cry of command, with the archangel's call and with the sound of God's trumpet." Jesus' description of his second coming also speaks of a very public event: "For as the lightning comes from the east and flashes as far as the west, so will be the coming of the Son of Man" (Matt 24:27). Although Christians will be spared the "wrath of God," they will experience the seven years of tribulation (Rev 20:11–15). For this reason, they must be more prepared than ever for the coming of the end times, lest they be tested and tempted unnecessarily, due to the incorrect belief that God would exempt them from it.

Midtribulationism makes a distinction between the "tribulation" people would experience due to calamities that result from the presence of sin and evil in the world, and the "wrath of God" by which God will judge and punish unbelievers. Since midtribulationists do not think that God would unjustly punish the faithful, God would spare them from all of it. Drawing upon Dan 9:25–26, it is thought that the tribulation will be divided in half, and Christians will not need to endure divine wrath, destruction, and desolation (cf. Dan 7:25; 8:14; 12:7, 11–12). Instead they will be raptured midway through the tribulation. Consequently, Christians need to be prepared for the signs and calamities of the first half of the tribulation, but they will be spared God's punishments.

Because of the degree of specificity with which premillennialists believe that apocalyptic passages in the Bible can be interpreted, debates over different views of the tribulation deal with minute differences in Scripture passages. Yet, their respective views of the future resemble the larger views of millennialism above. Pretribulationism expects an imminent rapture, while posttribulationism and midtribulationism expect tribulation at the very least, if not divine wrath before the return of Jesus. Consequently, adherents to the former eschatological view take less interest in the preparing for or caring for troubles that arise in life because only God can set these right. Before things become too bad, believers will be raptured. However, advocates of the latter two eschatological views take more interest in preparing for or caring for troubles that arise because they expect that they—as well as others—may have to endure quite a bit before the world comes to an end.

27.4 Conclusion

Contemporary concerns about world eschatology focus on both the biblical evidence—the immediate cause of their beliefs—and the effects of their beliefs. For example, using H. Richard Niebuhr's typology of "Christ and culture" (see discussion in ch. 24), we may ask: is our eschatological theory commensurate with the way we want to practice in culture, society, and the world? Does our view of the end times reinforce or diminish the ways we want to be in the world? The practices of our theories should not be determinative of them. However, it is irresponsible biblically and theologically to ignore the relationship between the two.

There is no consensus in church history with regard to particular views of millennialism. There is consensus, however, with regard to the belief and hope in Jesus' second coming. Overall Christians have been united in their expectation of the coming kingdom of God in fullness and glory. The Apostle Paul says, "For it is written, 'As I live, says the Lord, every knee shall bow to me, and every tongue shall give praise to God'" (Rom 14:11).

27.5 Questions for Further Reflection

1. How should apocalyptic literature in the Bible be interpreted? How literally and historically predictive is it?

2. Do you think that the world will come to an end? How do you think it will happen? How soon? To what extent do you think that Scripture foretells the end of the world?

3. What effect does the impending end of the world have on you now? Should it have an effect? How should you live, knowing that Jesus may come again? How should Christians relate to the world, given their beliefs about the end of the world?

4. How should you view world events? How relevant or irrelevant is apocalyptic literature for making personal, social, and governmental decisions?

5. Should Christians bother with caring for the poor, for injustice, and for peace, or should they see such troubles as inevitable and irredeemable signs of the end times?

27.6 Notes

1. Shirley C. Guthrie Jr., *Christian Doctrine* (Atlanta: John Knox, 1968), 384–88.
2. "Nicene Creed," *Encyclopedia of Christianity*, 300.
3. Hal Lindsey, *Late Great Planet Earth* (Grand Rapids: Zondervan, 1970).

CHAPTER TWENTY-EIGHT

Then I saw a new heaven and a new earth; for the first heaven and the first earth had passed away, and the sea was no more. . . . And I heard a loud voice from the throne saying, "See, the home of God is among mortals. He will dwell with them; they will be his peoples, and God himself will be with them; he will wipe every tear from their eyes. Death will be no more; mourning and crying and pain will be no more, for the first things have passed away."
(Revelation 21:1, 3–4)

HEAVEN AND HELL

28.1 Introduction

When Jesus spent time with the disciples, he spoke with them about many things. He spoke of heaven and earth. He spoke of God's grace and people's responsibility. He spoke of faith and love. During the three or so years Jesus spent with the disciples, he undoubtedly grew fond of them, with their respective strengths, weaknesses, personalities, and quirks. Undoubtedly, the disciples had grown quite fond of Jesus as well. Their relationship included several dimensions: master/servant, teacher/disciple, friend/friend. Certainly intimacy had grown between them to a depth we may not easily comprehend.

Jesus is our friend

On the night Jesus was betrayed and arrested, he spent time with his disciples at a last supper. It was an amazing time of fellowship, teaching, and encouragement, and the events of that night irrevocably changed Jesus' relationship with his disciples and, indeed, all of history. Leonardo da Vinci's painting entitled "The Last Supper" immortalized the occasion. The words that were spoken and the events that occurred that night had long-term effects upon the disciples as well as upon the church.

The book of John records a prolonged farewell discourse and prayer on behalf of the disciples. His words could not help but move the disciples to a myriad of thoughts and feelings, ranging back and forth between jubilation and despair. Jesus' first words begin with reference to both. He said:

Jesus Christ spoke more about life here and now—about how God graciously works to make our lives abundant.

Still, the blessed hope of all believers is eternal life with God in heaven, full of peace, joy, and life resplendent.

> Do not let your hearts be troubled. Believe in God, believe also in me. In my Father's house there are many dwelling places. If it were not so, would I have told you that I go to prepare a place for you? And if I go and prepare a place for you, I will come again and will take you to myself, so that where I am, there you may be also. (John 14:1–3)

Although Jesus spoke much about what it means to be, think, speak, and act as a Christian in the here and now, everything was predicated on the fact that someday all who believe in him will live eternally in heaven. This is certainly the most blessed hope of the gospel message of Jesus. Without diminishing the present significance of his teachings, Jesus spoke of his glorification and of how his disciples would share in it in the future. It is easy for us as humans to doubt that, after life is over, there will be an afterlife. Yet, Jesus makes it crystal clear that heaven is no "pie in the sky bye and bye." It is real, and he is specifically talking with the disciples about heaven in order to bolster them, especially since Jesus knew the trials and temptations they would soon face.

Not only did Jesus assure his disciples of eternal life and heaven, he made it clear that he personally would make it happen. Heaven would not be a mystical, amorphous place that lacked a personal sense of who we are. On the contrary, we would retain our identity—new and improved—and we would continue in a quality relationship with Jesus as well as other believers for eternity!

In this chapter, we will investigate Christian views of death and the afterlife, and of heaven and hell. Although some of the topics discussed may cause discomfort, the overarching focus in Scripture is upon hope, blessing, and eternal life through Jesus Christ.

28.2 The Scriptural Setting

Scripture speaks much of life, death, resurrection, judgment, and eternal life. Almost by definition, religions speak of such issues, that is, essential issues of life and the afterlife. Therefore, this final chapter draws upon passages from all of the Bible.

In the previous chapter, I gave several cautions to readers about how to interpret apocalyptic literature. Although many of the passages mentioned in this chapter are not a part of that biblical genre, they still reflect issues that are of a transcendent or future nature. Thus, many of the cautions remain in effect. We must curb the predictable desire to know about every detail of our lives to come. It is not wrong to ask such questions, of course. However, we should not be

How do we unlock the secret of the end times?

presumptuous about what we can expect to know. God does not reveal everything to us, and Christians believe that there are holy and healthy reasons for this. Like a parent who does not share all information with a child, some things are best left unknown until a later time.

We must remember that a great deal of information about personal eschatology is symbolic in nature. That does not mean that the future is only symbolic or mythical. Scripture says that our future is firmly established, but the particular details of it may remain unclear. Christians believe in heaven and hell, for example, but their symbolism and imagery are more sophisticated than many realize.

Caution needs to be taken in the study of what the Bible has to say about heaven and hell. Not everything is revealed at once. Revelation is given progressively, so that the New Testament may give crucial insights about heaven and hell not found in the Old Testament. It is important, then, to read Scripture in its appropriate context. This involves recognition of the historical, literary, and cultural contexts of Scripture. But clarity about these topics arises when the whole of the Bible is studied.

Heaven and hell are difficult and, at times, emotional topics of study, but people should be encouraged. All that God has done has been for humanity's well-being. As Jeremiah says, "For surely I know the plans I have for you, says the Lord, plans for your welfare and not for harm, to give you a future with hope" (Jer 29:11).

28.3 Humanity's Future

In talking about humanity's future, it is helpful to break the subject down into parts more easily studied and valued. Although the various topics will be studied separately, they cannot be fully understood without reference to the other aspects of our future. Taken alone, some aspects may sound downright depressing. Taken together, they sound downright inspiring.

28.3.1 Death

When it comes to talking about people's future, the one undeniable reality with which everyone must deal is death. Basically speaking, death is the cessation of life in this world as we know it. There are medical definitions of death, of course, which help us come to grips with technical, physiological aspects of the event. However, from a Christian perspective, so much more than physiology is involved in understanding the nature and implications of death.

According to Scripture, death is the result of sin (Gen 2:16–17; 3:19). More specifically, it is part of the curse of God upon humanity for their failure to remain in right relationship with God. The Apostle Paul traces the curse of sin and death to Adam and Eve (Rom 5:12–21). There has never been Christian consensus, however, with regard to the spiritual and physical interconnectedness of death. However, it is thought that death signals more than the cessation of physical life. It also signals the need for concern about our spiritual lives.

Because of its linkage with sin, death is not something to be welcomed in and of itself. On the contrary, people are justified in dreading it and the unknowns of life hereafter. When people die, they suffer from the effects of the curse of sin upon humanity. Christians believe and hope in their eternal lives, but that does not diminish the sense of loss and grief that they naturally experience. Jesus wept, for example, when his friend Lazarus died (John 11:35). Moreover, all the Gospels recount the anguish Jesus experienced in the garden of Gethsemane on the night he was betrayed and arrested. He prayed that God might remove the "cup" of his crucifixion, and that his death might be avoided (Matt 26:39). However, Jesus chose to be obedient to God's will in fulfilling his providence.

The Grim Reaper

From a human perspective, the afterlife is an impenetrable mystery without the revelation of God, especially in Scripture, about God's provision of redemption. However, in God's revelation, we discover that the problems are more complex than we might have imagined. There is something that people must fear more than physical death: spiritual death or second death (Rev 2:11; 20:6, 14; 21:8). It refers to the final or eternal state of someone who dies apart from the salvation offered by God. Jesus said, "Do not fear those who kill the body but cannot kill the soul; rather fear him who can destroy both soul and body in hell" (Matt 10:28). The spiritual dimension of death communicates an eternal as well as a temporal reality, which heightens the concern people should have for the afterlife.

In providing for salvation, Jesus not only lived, he also died a physical death. Through his resurrection, however, the Bible says that divine victory occurred over the sting of death. The Apostle Paul says:

> "Death has been swallowed up in victory." "Where, O death, is your victory? Where, O death, is your sting?" The sting of death is sin, and the power of sin is the law. But thanks be to God, who gives us the victory through our Lord Jesus Christ. (1 Cor 15:54–57)

Death is not the final word for Christians. After Christians are saved, they die to sin (Jas 1:15). Hebrews 2:14–15 says that, through his death and resurrection, Jesus conquered "the one who has the power of death, that is, the devil, and free[d] those who all their lives were held in slavery by the fear of death." Death is not to be made light of; it is still a part of the curse, and it involves uncertainty, pain, and grief. Consequently, the prospect of death—both temporal and eternal—should prompt people to repent of their sins, believe in Jesus for their salvation, and live a life reflective of his teachings.

Rest in Peace

Christians, then, have a healthy degree of respect for death and for its implications for understanding the consequences of sin and its effects. They do not minimize its sense of curse, nor do they glorify it. Nor are they tormented by it. In the end, death serves as a reminder that the visible world is not all there is, and God has amazing plans in the future as well as the present for those who accept Jesus as their Savior and Lord.

28.3.2 Intermediate State

What happens to people after they die? Do they resurrect immediately and meet God, or do they continue in some alternative form of existence until the time of the resurrection? Scripture suggests that people have potential for some kind of consciousness after death; however, it does not clearly and consistently present a view on the subject. Of course, this has not prevented Christians from speculating about a possible intermediate state of existence after people experience temporal death. Perhaps confronted with the grief of death and attending a funeral service, questions arise. Throughout church history such questions have generated several views of what happens to people after they die.

Purgatory

Catholics believe that people are immediately aware of their salvation or damnation after death. Those who are saved receive eternal life in heaven, and those who are not saved do not. However, not all Christians immediately receive the fullness of glory. Not all Christians have lived commendable lives on earth, and God expects them to do penance, if they did not do so in life. They will eventually go to heaven; however, God wants their lives purged from unconfessed sin and related transgressions before receiving the fullness of eternal life in heaven.

Such people go to a place called *purgatory,* where they atone for sins of commission or omission for which they were not accountable on earth. Although purgatory is not explicitly mentioned in the Bible, Catholics point to 2 Macc 12:39–46 as well as passages that talk about ongoing consciousness after death (e.g., Luke 16:19–31) and that suggest that people's works will be tested (1 Cor 3:10–15; cf. Matt 12:36–37; 2 Cor 5:10). The existence of purgatory was affirmed by the Catholic Church and defined at the Council of Trent (1545–1563). Purgatory is not considered a "second chance" for salvation; only Christians go to purgatory. However, God wants those saved by grace to be accountable for the grace they receive, allowing God to purify them before finally appearing before God. Once purified, Christians go to heaven, and, after the final judgment, there will be no further need for purgatory.

For reasons such as these, Catholics venerate those who have died, especially the saints of the church—those thought to go immediately to heaven. In fact, Christians may ask saints who have died to intercede on their behalf. Just as people sometimes ask others to pray for them, Catholics believe that Mary, the mother of Jesus, as well as other Christians already in heaven, aid us as prayerful intercessors with God. So when people talk about "praying" to Mary or a saint, it is for the sake of imitating, venerating, or asking for intercession. This does not mean that Mary and the saints are worshipped. On the contrary, only God is worshipped, and it is only God to whom we pray and from whom we receive divine grace. However, believers may ask Mary and the saints in heaven to intercede on their behalf.

Intercessory Prayer

Just as those in heaven may intercede for people on earth, Catholics believe that intercession may be made on behalf of those in purgatory. It is believed that a spiritual union exists between those in heaven, those in purgatory, and those who are believers on earth. This "communion of saints" enables the ongoing dynamic of prayer and intercession that aids those in purgatory as well as those on earth. So although Christians may die, there continues a lively communion of saints, which gives a foretaste of the fullness of eternal life in heaven.

Soul Sleep

Luther rejected much of Catholicism, and he rejected most of what was believed about the communion of saints. He rejected the veneration of Mary and the saints as people's intercessors before God. Instead, Luther emphasized the direct, immediate access Christians have to God and God's grace. He also rejected belief in purgatory, thinking it corrupted the gospel message of salvation by grace through faith without any admixture of good works or the need to be purged of anything after death. Jesus' atonement for sin was sufficient, and there was no need for purgation in the afterlife.

After death, Luther believed that people experienced soul sleep. This belief reflects several biblical passages where the dead are described as being asleep (Matt 6:9–10; 9:24; John 11:11; 1 Cor 15:6; 1 Thess 4:15). According to Luther, there was no place of purgation, which he associated with anguish due to a works-righteousness view of salvation. Instead, he thought that death was a state of unconscious sleep, even if the physical body deteriorated. In this soul-like sleep, one had no conscious awareness until the final resurrection and judgment.

How is death like sleep?

Luther had also rejected the idea of indulgences, which referred to the remission of temporal punishments of sin for which people were accountable either in this life or in purgatory. During his lifetime, Luther thought that the Catholic Church had abused its ecclesiastical authority by selling indulgences to people, either for themselves or for those who had died. However, Luther considered this belief to be as unjust as it was unbiblical. His belief in soul sleep took the place of purgatory, the communion of saints, and its attendant beliefs about a conscious existence after death.

Disembodied State

Calvin also disagreed with Roman Catholic beliefs about the afterlife. However, he was not convinced that people's souls slept, as Luther believed. Like Roman Catholics, Calvin thought that people continued to be conscious even after death. For example, he looked to passages in Scripture that suggest ongoing awareness, dialogue, and creativity (e.g., Luke 16:19–31). There was also the possibility of hearing and understanding preaching after death (1 Pet 3:19). Thus, Calvin argued that people continue to be aware and responsive, even after their body dies. They continue to live in a kind of disembodied state of existence until the time of their resurrection.

Of course, belief in a disembodied state of existence remains a mystery to us while we are alive. Christians generally avoid speculation about such a state; it conjures images of ghosts and other paranormal phenomena. The Bible discourages involvement with paranormal phenomena, including spiritism, mediums, wizardry, witchcraft, and other occult-like activities (Lev 19:31; 20:6, 27; Isa 8:19–20). Although people may continue to exist in a disembodied state after death, they are no longer in meaningful communication with us.

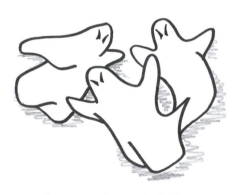

Ghosts are better left alone

No Intermediate State

Another view of the afterlife is that there is no intermediate state. After people die, they immediately cease living in time and space, as we know them, and live in eternity. Their next awareness will be that of God, the resurrection, judgment, and—for believers—eternal life (2 Cor 5:6–9). There is no waiting period or soul sleep.

On the cross, Jesus spoke to the penitent thief beside him. When the thief asked Jesus to remember him when he came into his kingdom, Jesus responded, "Truly I tell you, today you will be with me in Paradise" (Luke 23:43).

Paradise originally referred to the garden of Eden, and, of course, it could be interpreted as being the place where the righteous wait until the resurrection. In Christian writings, paradise is often associated with heaven (2 Cor 12:4; cf. Rev 2:7). Many Christians consider this option the most persuasive, since it avoids speculation that does not necessarily help people in the present. It is better to focus on the clear teachings of Scripture about the present and future than to become preoccupied with speculation.

28.3.3 Resurrection

Resurrection is one of the great affirmations of Christianity. The word resurrection comes from *resurrectio* (Latin, "a rising again from the dead"), and, when used in a Christian context, it refers to how all who have died and who are alive will resurrect before the final judgment. The resurrection has to do with more than rising from the dead. It has to do with a self made anew, which all will receive. The resurrection includes all of a person—physical as well as spiritual. It does not have to do with the concept of the immortality of the soul, which reflects Greek philosophy. The Greeks promoted a spiritualized view of immortality and the afterlife in which only the soul survived physical death. However, Christianity emphasizes that the resurrection includes the body as well as other dimensions of who people are (1 Cor 15). It is a holistic view of how people will live in eternity.

The resurrection refers to what happened to Jesus after his crucifixion and death. He appeared before his disciples as well as others, appearing and disappearing in extraordinary ways (Matt 28:9–10; Luke 24:31, 36–43; John 19:20–29). Obviously, Jesus' body surpassed anything people currently possess. He did not appear as a ghost. Jesus' body was substantial. The disciples could recognize him, and he retained physical remnants of the crucifixion. Jesus talked and ate with them. Yet obviously he was made new. The Apostle Paul describes Jesus as the first among those who resurrect from the dead (1 Cor 15:20). Jesus' resurrection was unlike the rising again of Jairus' daughter and Lazarus, whom Jesus brought back to life, since both the young girl and Lazarus would eventually die again. In a sense, they were resuscitated back to life but not strictly resurrected. Jesus was the "first fruits" of resurrection, which all may receive for eternity (1 Cor 15:23).

Jesus embodies and guarantees resurrection!

Before Jesus, the resurrection was discussed in the Old Testament (Job 19:25–27; Isa 26:19; Dan 12:12). However, resurrection was not something universally accepted by the Israelites. The Sadducees, for example, rejected belief in the resurrection and challenged Jesus about it (Matt 22:23–33). Jesus responded by appealing to the words of God in

Exod 3:6, arguing that the patriarchs were not dead. They were alive, resurrected from the dead (Luke 20:37). Over and over again, Jesus encouraged people by preaching and teaching about the gift of eternal life God offers to people. To be sure, so much of what Jesus said was about the relevance of salvation here and now. In fact, Paul talks about the resurrection life as the life Christians live now in obedience to God (Phil 3:10).

The idea of an afterlife is not unique to Christianity. Almost every religious tradition has some notion of life after death. Of course, the Western religions of Judaism, Christianity, and Islam have similar concepts of a resurrected life after death. On the other hand, Greek philosophies—like some Eastern religions—have both monistic and reincarnational traditions of the afterlife. Monists, for example, Hindus and Buddhists, believe that ultimately there exists only one reality, which is spiritual. The present life, more or less, is illusory. Salvation or, as they would say, enlightenment comes through means by which we can escape the transitory illusions of life as we think we experience it now. Instead we need to become one with the all-pervading, undifferentiated, spiritual oneness of the universe.

Until we experience enlightenment, we are trapped in our present existence, which is characterized by a cycle of birth, death, and rebirth. Known as reincarnation or transmigration, people and other forms of life are reborn, based upon their past lives. The power—sometimes known as karma—produced by the decisions and actions of people's past lives determines the quality of rebirth. Such karma can be thought to have great deterministic influence upon people before they achieve release from the illusions of the world.

Christianity, on the other hand, affirms the eternity of people's physical as well as spiritual existence. It may be an existence that is renewed, but it is a tangible existence nonetheless. Christianity also affirms the eventuality of God's justice and how people are resurrected for judgment (John 5:28–29; Acts 24:15). People who resurrect and are judged will receive reward and punishment that is tangible and not merely ethereal.

In anticipation of judgment, some Christians believe in a first and second resurrection. Premillennialists (see discussion in ch. 27), for example, who take a more literal approach in interpreting apocalyptic literature, understand Rev 20 as exactingly predictive of various resurrections as well as the millennium. Reference to a first resurrection in Rev 20:5 refers to the resurrection only of Christian believers. A second resurrection will occur for unbelievers. Other interpreters, however, understand apocalyptic literature as powerful descriptions of God's sovereign control of life events rather than explicit predictions of the future. In this understanding of Scripture, references to resurrection are indeed literal, but they refer to the general resurrection of all people rather than particular resurrections that ultimately include everyone.

28.3.4 Judgment

From a Christian perspective, judgment is an event of divine justice. It is the occasion of God's ruling upon the innocence and guilt of people and also of nations (Rom 2:1–11; 1 Cor 3:10–15). Their consciences and their actions will be evaluated, and, if necessary, condemned (Rom 2:12–16). In this life, it may seem as if people get away with murder, so to speak. However, Scripture says that God is not mocked; people will reap what they sow (Gal 6:7). Sometimes Jesus is associated with judgment, since he is empathetic as well as just when it comes to ruling on people's eternal state (1 Thess 5:2; Phil 1:10; 2 Pet 2:9). Because of the holiness and justice of God, divine judgment will eventually be meted out to all in order to bring about a fitting and fair sense of closure.

Christians, of course, do not need to fear judgment. Because of the salvation that Jesus wrought on the cross, his righteousness takes the place of our own at the judgment seat of God. God imputes righteousness to people due to Jesus' salvific work on our behalf. As a result, Christians receive fully the gift of salvation at the time of judgment. It will be a time of rejoicing rather than a time of regret, sorrow, and damnation.

Here comes the judge!

Judgment and Accountability

Will there be no sense of accounting for Christians at the judgment seat of God? There has been no consensus throughout church history, but there have been several views put forward. Catholics' belief in purgatory emphasizes that all people—including Christians—must make amends for sins that were unconfessed or for which no penance or amends were made in life. Although people are saved by God's mercy and grace, God's holiness and justice demands accountability, even if it is not eternal. In purgatory Christians will be accountable "for every careless word" they speak (Matt 12:36).

Others believe that, because of Jesus' atonement, God will look upon the sins of believers as if they never existed. Jeremiah 31:34 records God as saying, "for I will forgive their iniquity, and remember their sin no more." Psalm 103:12 says, "as far as the east is from the west, so far he removes our transgressions from us." These verses suggest that the atoning blood of Jesus is sufficient to wipe away all accounting of the sins of Christians. It is as if God has a case of divine forgetfulness, and Christians will receive nothing but the rewards of salvation. In contrast to God's forgetfulness of Christians' sins, what of their good works? Since no one is saved by their good works, it is presumed that they were all done out of praise, thanksgiving, and obedience to God. Like the faithful described in Rev 4:10–11, Christians are imagined as throwing their crowns of achievement before God in heaven.

Still others believe that there may be a divine accounting of our lives, even if our salvation is secure. God will welcome believers by grace, yet God will also review their lives, praising when appropriate and likewise reproving unrighteousness. A review of people's works, so to speak, would not merit their salvation, but it would evaluate their works as fruits of faith. When Scripture speaks of God's forgiveness, the eternal reward of true believers is secure. However, that does not preclude the relevance of those biblical passages which talk about accountability at the time of judgment. Similar to Catholicism, believers may go through a time of disclosure, answerability, and healing. They will not go to purgatory to be purged of sin, but they will go through a therapeutic experience of salvation.

In what sense is salvation therapeutic?

Judgment and Justice

Is the judgment of God's righteousness commensurate with the mercy of God's love? Ultimately, Christians believe that this is a decision only God can make. After all, God's ways are not our ways (Isa 55:8). Yet, verse after verse of Scripture affirms the holiness, righteousness, impartiality, and justice of God (Zeph 3:5; John 5:30; Rom 2:2). Such attributes are not considered incommensurate with God's love, grace, mercy, and forgiveness. God's concern for justice applies to the present life as well as the life to come.

In this life, God permits confusion, injustice, and calamity more than we wish. In the afterlife, however, God demands a final accounting. Certainly people will receive retributive justice, that is, justice that is due their actions. Based upon God's just judgment, God will distribute rewards and punishments impartially. Presumably, if people choose to reject God's gracious offer of salvation, God will not force them beyond their will. Instead, God will permit them to remain forever apart. As we will see, Christians see that separation as hellish and as an eternal place of damnation. For those who accept God's gracious offer of salvation, there will be an eternity of blessing in fellowship with God.

28.4 Hell

After judgment, hell is the place to which God sends people in punishment of their sin and unbelief in God. It is a place that Scripture describes as a place of anguish and separation from God. The descriptions of hell vary, yet they conjure unimaginable damnation for those who, one way or another, reject God. After reading about hell, no one should want to run the risk of an eternity spent there.

One must be careful with how one imagines hell, just as one must be careful with how one imagines heaven—the place of eternal reward, happiness, and fellowship with God. As with other theological descriptions, human language falls short of completely conceptualizing what hell and heaven are like. As we shall see, descriptions of heaven include that of a temple, a city, a kingdom, and the dwelling place of God. As impressive as these descriptions are, most consider the totality of heaven to include more than a temple, a city, and a kingdom, though certainly Christians expect it will be the dwelling place of God. Moreover, such language is symbolic, since it describes a transcendent reality, which has no exact representation in human and earthly forms. Heaven is actually considered much better, more diverse, and more expansive than the words Scripture uses to describe it. Few people balk at the idea that heaven is "bigger and better" than the biblical descriptions of it, yet they may well balk at the idea that language about hell suggests an existence far worse—if not precisely the same—as biblical descriptions of it.

28.4.1 Imagery of Hell

Hell does not immediately appear in the Bible. Certainly everyone dies. However, the nature of the afterlife was not clearly and consistently articulated in Scripture. Instead there occurred a development—a progressive revelation—about the afterlife, especially regarding hell. In the Old Testament, people are not thought to go to heaven and hell per se. Rather, they are thought to go to *Sheol,* which is Hebrew for "death" (Job 30:23; Eccl 8:8), or "the grave" or an unseen state (Job 17:13; Ps 49:15; 141:7; Eccl 9:10; Hos 13:14). Sometimes death is referred to as "the pit" (Job 33:18; Ps 28:1; 30:9; 88:4; 143:7; Isa 14:15; 38:17; Ezek 26:20; 32:18). Overall the nature of death was nondescript; it was not clearly a place of punishment or of reward.

The New Testament presents a clearer, albeit not perfectly clear, description of the afterlife; in particular, descriptions of hell varied. Jesus used the Greek word *Gehenna* to describe the place of eternal damnation, alluding to the Hebrew name for a valley next to the city of Jerusalem, where trash was dumped and kept burning (Matt 5:22, 29–30; 10:28; Mark 9:43, 45, 47; Luke 12:5). The Greek word *Hades* is also used to describe hell; however, it may be used as much to describe the realm or abode of the dead as to describe the place of eternal punishment (Matt 11:23; Luke 16:23). Although development in the concept of hell occurs in the Bible, it is clear that by the time of Jesus the biblical writers believed in the existence of places of eternal reward—heaven—and of eternal punishment—hell.

Here are some of the ways Scripture describes hell. It is a place where people are thrown outside the kingdom of God, where there is darkness, weeping, and gnashing of teeth (Matt 8:11–12; cf. Jude 13). Hell is described as a fiery furnace (Matt 13:49–50), eternal fire (Matt 18:8–9), eternal punishment (Matt 25:46), unquenchable fire (Mark 9:42), and "where their worm never dies, and the fire is never quenched" (Mark 9:48). It is described as a place of torment and agony, separated from the place of divine reward by a great chasm of sorts, so that no one may cross over between the two (Luke 16:22–26). Perhaps the most awful descriptions of hell are those in which God's vengeance will be directed against "those who do not know God and on those who do not obey the gospel of our Lord Jesus. These will suffer the punishment of eternal destruction, separated from the presence of the Lord and from the glory of his might" (2 Thess 1:8–9). The prospect of eternal separation from the presence

Fire and brimstone!

of God may constitute the worst part of hell, despite the vivid imagery of fire and brimstone. The personal dimensions of belief and reward as well as of unbelief and punishment outweigh the physical dimensions of reward and punishment.

Hell is described in the book of Revelation as a bottomless pit (Rev 9:1). It is also described as a lake of fire, where there will be no rest, but torment every "day and night forever and ever" (Rev 20:10; 14:11). Since Revelation states that there will be a new heaven and a new earth in conjunction with John's vision of heaven as the "new Jerusalem," it is not clear what will constitute day and night (Rev 21:1–2). In heaven, it will be God rather than the sun that provides light (Rev 22:5). In sum, the reality of hell and the prospect of eternal punishment is more important than the particular conception we have of it.

Not only people will suffer hell. Revelation states that the devil—Satan—along with demons and other minions of the devil will be damned to hell (Rev 20:10). All who reject God at various times and in various places receive the just punishment of hell. The finality of hell is reflected in descriptions of it as the "second death" (Rev 21:8).

28.4.2 Degrees of Punishment in Hell

Will there be degrees of punishment in hell? Images of different levels of hell come to mind when reflecting upon, for example, such classic descriptions of hell as found in Dante's *Inferno*.[1] The deeper you go into "the pit of hell," due to

The devil made me do it!

the severity of your sins in life, the worse is your punishment! It is not easy to forget such creative literary descriptions, and such descriptions may have more to say about degrees of punishment than does the Bible. It does not seem that Scripture gives a clear response to the question of whether or not there are degrees of punishment in hell. Scripture, as we have seen, gives various descriptions of what hell is like, and thus individuals may experience hell differently than others. Let us look at different Christian points of view with regard to this difficult topic.

Catholics believe that there are levels of hell. Just as distinctions are made between venial and mortal sins, distinctions are made between levels of punishment. Although Catholics believe that people are saved by grace through faith, mediated through the church, they also believe that belief in God and obedience are inextricably bound up with one another. There are numerous verses to support degrees of torment in hell (Matt 11:16–24; 23:14; Luke 12:46–48). Likewise, unbelief is compounded by disobedience, and people's damnation in hell reflects grades of punishment.

Certainly some sins in the Bible are thought to be more severe than others, though all are accountable for sin in their lives, regardless of its severity. Still, Scripture refers to the punishment of some being greater than that of others. The Old Testament residents of Sodom and Gomorrah, for example, are said by Jesus to receive less punishment than those who explicitly reject the gospel message he preached (Matt 10:15; cf. Gen 19). Similarly, Jesus states that the non-Israelite cities of Tyre and Sidon would be judged less severely than Israelite cities, since the former would have been more repentant and faithful, if they had received the same preaching and teaching heard by the latter. The principle seems to be that more is expected, spiritually speaking, from those who have received the most (Luke 12:47–48). Thus, punishment may be greater for some than others. However, it may also be that, while the punishments may differ, the experience of punishment may seem the same, varying to the degree to which people are aware of and understand their punishment.

On the other hand, many Christians do not bother with reflecting upon degrees of torment or, indeed, degrees of heavenly bliss. Although Scripture contains language of eternal differentiation, the overwhelming gospel message is for choosing God and eternal life or rejecting God and experiencing eternal damnation. The gospel proclaimed in Scripture overwhelmingly specifies the principle of salvation by divine initiation. If salvation is by grace through faith and not by merit, there is no need for considering degrees of heavenly bliss or of hellish damnation. Focusing upon the degrees of reward or punishment distracts people from the essence of the gospel, which is graciously given by God.

28.4.3 Justice of Hell

What of the justice of hell? Does it seem fair that God should damn someone for eternity, along with Satan, based upon the decision or decisions made during their finite existence? What of people who never heard of Jesus, or lived before his time? What of those who may have never heard the gospel message presented in a way they could adequately understand and appreciate for its eternal significance? After all, is not God ultimately responsible for people's eternal well-being, since God created everyone and everything with all their potential faults and sins?

Christians talk about hell in terms of justice and how there are just reasons for why God punishes people, even if it means eternal punishment. Since God gave people freedom, they were given choices with regard to whether they would live in accordance or in opposition to their consciences, if not to the explicit gospel message of Jesus. Was God fair? From a human perspective, it is not immediately apparent how decisions made during a limited period of time—given other limitations in length of life and quality of life (for example, mental, emotional, and physical capacities)—could deservedly damn a person for eternity. Appealing to mystery does not really satisfy, even if people are willing to accept that it is not possible to know fully the mind and actions of God.

There must be some analogy with which to understand the justice and fairness of God with regard to eternal damnation.

How long must one suffer?

Scripture speaks of the impartiality and justice of God in many places; God "desires everyone to be saved and to come to the knowledge of the truth" (1 Tim 2:4). Just quoting the Bible, however, may not be of much comfort, at least not emotionally. The suffering in this life, especially of the young, innocent, and weak, can be overwhelming; thus, how much more horrific does eternal damnation seem for such people. Still, most people can understand that justice is a good thing, even if punishments sometimes seem more extensive than the original crime. Furthermore, most people can understand that some people have committed crimes in this world that seem incapable of adequate restitution in this life or in the life to come. Justice in and of itself can always appear severe, yet virtually no one says that justice should not occur. Since justice does not always occur in this life, God guarantees that justice will occur in the afterlife.

Perhaps a problem with our conceptions of hell is that it is always seen in terms of damnation and torment rather than in terms of grace and mercy. C. S. Lewis talks a great deal about hell and heaven in his writings, sometimes thinking "outside the box" with regard to usual Christian views of the subjects.[2] For example, with regard to hell, Lewis suggests that God created hell out of mercy toward those who did not want to spend eternity in the presence of the divine. God created hell as a place to live. If hell seems too hellish, it is because this is what those who live there make it, rather than what God makes it. If there is a lock on the doors to hell, Lewis says, they are locked on the inside rather than the outside. Moreover, he suggests that people in hell—some way or another—will be given as many opportunities for salvation as are needed. Lewis expects that people in hell will always be welcome in heaven; however, he doubts that many will be willing to do what it takes to extricate themselves from hell, regardless of how hellish it may be.

28.4.4 Alternative Views of Hell

While most Christians affirm the reality of hell, despite its dire image, other views of hell exist. Some think of hell as limited in time; it is not a place of eternal punishment but of punishment limited in time and severity to fit individual guilt. This view is known as *conditional immortality* or *annihilationism,* since people are thought to cease to exist after divine justice is fulfilled. This annihilation is sometimes interpreted as the "second death" (Rev 21:8). Hell conceived in terms of limited punishment is thought to be more in line with the justice and mercy of God.

Other views of hell take a more personal approach, emphasizing biblical imagery of separation from God and eternal regret. The personal dimensions of hell are thought to be more important than the physical, dramatic imagery of hell. Others demythologize the imagery altogether and refuse to speculate about the afterlife. The imagery of hell represents a less sophisticated religious worldview, no longer relevant or persuasive to modern people. They deconstruct apocalyptic literature and replace it with an existential sense of urgency for living faithful and obedient lives in the present. Finally, some completely do away with the concept of hell, arguing that only universal salvation corresponds to the justice and mercy of God. Although Scripture talks about judgment and eternal damnation, references to God's love and forgiveness supersede them.

28.5 Heaven

Heaven is the final state or place of those who receive eternal life from God, characterized by reward, happiness, and fellowship with God and others. It is the final dwelling place of the saints—those who truly believe (Rev 21; 22; John 14). Although so much of Christianity has to do with the present importance of salvation, there is always the reality lying behind the present promises of a future, eternal promise of heaven. Our immediate lives are not all that there is; there is an afterlife. Heaven is the abode that God prepares for those who will receive it as a divine gift.

Like our discussion of hell, we must beware of becoming overly preoccupied either with the thought of heaven or descriptions of it. If we become preoccupied with the thought of heaven and of our hope of it, we may forget to live in the present. As the cliché goes, we may become so heavenly minded that we are of no earthly good. The longing for heaven is a desire God inspires within us. However, we are not to become obsessed with it and other spiritual matters without remembering the here-and-now relevance of spirituality. Correspondingly, we should not become narrowly preoccupied with descriptions of heaven. Like the discussion of hell, we need to be cautious about how we understand heavenly imagery.

28.5.1 Imagery of Heaven

The most important part about the imagery of heaven is that it represents the final and full reconciliation between God and those who have turned to God in faith and received the gracious gift of eternal life. Heaven is a place of fellowship, where God consummates the entire good God desires to give people. It constitutes the "kingdom of heaven" (Matt 5:3). More intimately, Christians will experience heaven as their parent's house (John 12:2), where they will receive a "crown of glory" (1 Pet 5:4). Catholics refer to the encounter with God as the "beatific vision," where the fullness of knowledge and love of God permeates our existence.

Perhaps some of the most compelling images of heaven have to do with the elimination of present pain and suffering. In heaven, Scripture says that people will be like angels, who neither marry nor die (Luke 20:35–36). There will be no hunger or thirst, since God will meet their needs (Rev 7:16–17). There will no longer be any tears or crying (Rev 3:17; 21:24). There will no

Heaven: We can only imagine

longer be any pain or sorrow, and the curses upon humanity will be removed (Rev 21:4; 22:3). God will physically live with humanity, providing for all their needs: light, food, drink, and well-being, since heaven will be like a grand banquet (Matt 22:2; Rev 22:5). Certainly the image of heaven is intended to communicate the most wonderful place imaginable to spend eternity.

Keep in mind, however, that there are many popular images of heaven, which are entirely unbiblical. For example, some paintings as well as modern cartoons sometimes envision people sitting on clouds, strumming harps, and—at best—singing songs continuously in praise to God, while pudgy cherub-like angels float around with little fluttering wings. While people will undoubtedly praise God in heaven, this imagery will inspire few people. Most consider it quite unappealing and undesirable. Such images make heaven seem unimaginative, stagnant, and boring. No wonder some people have no desire to experience it!

Images of heaven are of that, ultimately speaking, which transcends human abilities to comprehend fully and appreciate. Scripture certainly gives us clues as to what heaven is like, and those clues are wonderful. However, even biblical imagery cannot inspire the fullness of what God has planned for people in heaven. For example, the Bible describes people in heaven in ways that seem unfamiliar to us. People there are described as wearing white robes, waving palm fronds, and worshipping God in a temple day and night (Rev 7:13–15; 21:1). Scripture also describes heaven as the dwelling place of God (Luke 11:2; Acts 7:49), the kingdom of God (Luke 13:29), and the "new Jerusalem"—an

Probably not what heaven looks like

ethereal city with bejeweled gates (Rev 21:15–21; 22:14). However, if we look at the imagery too closely, we may not be impressed by it. For example, do we really want to wear robes? Will heaven involve nothing more than worshipping God day and night? Do we want to live in a square-shaped city, with each side approximately 1,500 miles in length, with walls seventy-five yards high (Rev 21:15–17)? Although the city will be constructed of gold and jewels, would we not want a little extra space, with some rivers and lakes, grass and trees, and room to roam? Obviously, the descriptions of heaven are intended to inspire us rather than give a precise description. However, like the imagery of hell, we should not become preoccupied with the specificity of the imagery, lest we become distracted by minutiae rather than the transcendent nature of heaven and the wonderfulness God intends for us. Perhaps, the best way to describe the surpassing nature of heaven is found in 1 Cor 2:9: "But, as it is written, 'What no eye has seen, nor ear heard, nor the human heart conceived, what God has prepared for those who love him.'"

28.5.2 Degrees of Reward in Heaven

Are there degrees of recognition and reward in heaven? Some verses say that we are to store up for ourselves "treasures in heaven" (Matt 6:20), as if we could create some kind of spiritual capital. Paul talks about a man—possibly himself—"caught up to the third heaven," suggesting the possibility of levels of heaven (2 Cor 12:2). Certainly the fantastic imagery of Revelation describes varieties of peoples, creatures, places, and experiences in heaven. Finally, does it not seem unfair that some who, in this life, live exceedingly saintly lives would not receive special recognition or reward in the afterlife?

Catholics suggest that there are degrees of reward in heaven, based upon the merit they received on earth in faithful obedience to God. The Bible suggests rewards in heaven in a number of places (Matt 25:14–30; 1 Cor 3:14–15; 15:40–58; cf. Dan 12:2). Some believers are singled out as saints in this life, based upon their virtuousness or upon their suffering, martyrdom, or other self-sacrifice on behalf of God. Those who immediately enter heaven upon death become a part of the communion of saints in heaven who will enjoy fellowship with angels as well as other believers. In heaven, people will continue to pray as intercessors for those on earth and in purgatory. They will also grow in their knowledge and other human potential, and in their enjoyment of fellowship with God—their eternal beatific vision.

Protestants are not as clear in their views of heaven. Because of their historic emphasis upon salvation by grace, without the admixture of merit, there has tended to be a more egalitarian view of heaven. To be sure, Protestants recognize and venerate—in their own ways—saints of the church. However, such veneration has more to do with this life than with the afterlife. If, in fact, Protestants talk about good works on earth, they embody works of obedience and praise to God, rather than merit. Sometimes an allusion is made to the imagery in Rev 4:10, where twenty-four elders throw their crowns before God, giving God all glory. Similarly, Christians in heaven are thought to throw the crowns of their accomplishments in deference to God, no matter how bejeweled their crowns may have become through good works on earth. Despite such imagery, Protestants have tended to emphasize the equality rather than hierarchy of reward in heaven. Since it is God alone who saves people, why detract from the gospel by reintroducing a preoccupation with merit and good works for the sake of what they can get out of these in heaven? Like the parable of the workers in the vineyard, Jesus said that those who worked the least would receive the same wage or recompense as those who worked the most (Matt 20).

Is there growth in heaven? Will heaven be a place of perfect peace and contentment, or will it be a place of new knowledge, insight, and challenge? Catholics, more than Protestants, talk about the dynamic progress that may occur in heaven, since we will be surrounded by God and others with an infinite number of creative and loving possibilities. Who knows the fullness of what God has planned for those in heaven? Because Protestants, relatively speaking, have tended not to engage in conjecture about the afterlife, their conceptions of it may not seem as dynamic or creative as is justified. Surely, if people continue their self-consciousness in the improved environment of heaven, there is reason to suspect that heaven will not be a static place of complacent existence. On the contrary, people will continue to be challenged and enthused in ways that fulfill them as well as please God.

28.5.3 Justice of Heaven

At first, most people would wonder why it is important to talk about the justice of heaven. What is wrong with wanting an eternity of reward, happiness, and fellowship with God? It is much easier to question the justice of hell and the prospect of eternal damnation, regardless of how one conceives it. Yet, how could someone enjoy heaven, knowing that others did not? Moreover, how could God enjoy heaven, knowing that some human beings did not? After all, did not Paul suggest that he would sacrifice himself to damnation if it would result in the salvation of others (Rom 9:13)?

C. S. Lewis again offers insights about the afterlife, which address questions about the justice of heaven as well as hell. With regard to heaven, Lewis understands that some people castigate the pursuit of heaven as being the height of self-interest, self-centeredness, and sin. After all, if one wants to go to heaven in order to benefit from it or to avoid the liabilities of hell, is not selfishness at the heart of salvation rather than faith, hope, and love? Lewis uses an analogy. He asks if a person is selfish to want to breathe, eat, and drink. Of course they are not because the essence of their existence depends on breathing, eating, and drinking. In a sense, people were created by God to breathe, eat, and drink. Likewise, Lewis states that people were made for heaven; people are at their best when they pursue God and heaven. Certainly, there is tremendous grief when not everyone goes to heaven, and great efforts are made to convince others to be saved. However, Lewis reminds us that one of the great aspects of being created in the image of God is freedom. People do not go to either heaven or hell without it reflecting their choice to do so. People in heaven or hell are not there because of divine coercion. Despite misconceptions that sometimes creep into Christian thinking, the afterlife cannot be separated from people's choices any more than it can be separated from God's initiative.

> **PEOPLE'S NATIVE HEAVENLY LAND**
>
> Blessed is the pilgrim, who in every place, and at all times of this his banishment in the body, calling upon the holy name of Jesus, calleth to mind his native heavenly land, where his blessed Master, the King of saints and angels, waiteth to receive him. Blessed is the pilgrim who seeketh not an abiding place unto himself in this world; but longeth to be dissolved, and be with Christ in heaven.
>
> THOMAS À KEMPIS,
> THE IMITATION OF CHRIST
> (15TH CENTURY)

28.5.4 Alternative Views of Heaven

Why would someone imagine heaven to be anything different than the wonderful images provided in the Bible? Like their understanding of Scripture's picture of hell, some Christians think that images of heaven in Scripture provide symbolism that bears no resemblance to an afterlife. What apocalyptic literature says about the future in the Bible has already been realized in past events or understandings, and people should focus upon living Christlike lives now and not focus on the future. Like the Sadducees, they deny the resurrection, yet contend that the importance of following God now is manifestly present in Scripture as well as in the needs of people and of nations today.

Other Christians say that, without sufficient evidence of the future, we should remain silent in our uncertainty about the end times. There may be a heaven, and there may be a hell. Heaven and hell, however, should not be prominent in our thinking and acting. Instead, we should focus upon the present, being more concerned about the present work of God in our lives as well as upon the salvation God achieved through the person and work of Jesus. Christianity should make a difference in the world now, socially as well as individually, and those should be our priorities. Whether Scripture should be demythologized for the sake of existential authenticity or for psychological self-actualization, emphasis should be on the here and now, and not on the hereafter. Perhaps our eternal life may be nothing more than God's memory of us and our faithful obedience to God.

28.6 Conclusion

Although so much of Christianity focuses upon the present-day relevance of Christian beliefs, values, and practices, the prospect of eternal life in heaven remains an essential part of biblical teaching and church history. The blessed hope of Christians is spending an eternity in heaven with God and other believers, both past and present. The curse of death will finally be overcome, and Scripture promises that there will be no more hunger, thirst, pain, sorrow, or tears. Instead there will be a blessed experience of reward, happiness, and growth beyond our wildest imagination.

It is easy to become mesmerized and distracted by speculation about the afterlife with regard to a possible intermediate state, resurrection, judgment, heaven, and hell. Of course, such musings should convict the unbeliever of sin and encourage the believer with divine love and grace. However, they should never distract a person from the importance of salvation here and now, nor from the fact that God's presence and power works toward loving ends in meeting the challenges people face now. God is not the least bit indifferent to our personal and social needs. God fully knows the pain and suffering, the impoverishment and injustice that both Christians and non-Christians experience in life. That is why God sent Jesus to provide salvation, and the Holy Spirit to be forever present and empowering on our behalf, in this life and in the eternal life to come.

28.7 Questions for Further Reflection

1. What thoughts do you have about death? Why do some people find it difficult to talk about it? What questions do you have about death?

2. What happens after death? How much should people speculate about the possibility of an intermediate state? Why do you think the way you do?

3. What is the nature of resurrection? Why is it more important to think in terms of resurrection rather than of immortality?

4. How does the prospect of judgment make you feel? How does Scripture help you develop a constructive view of judgment?

5. How do you respond to the Christian belief in hell? What is your view of it? Does the belief in hell help or hinder people in thinking about God?

6. How do you respond to the Christian belief in heaven? Does the prospect of heaven appeal to you? Can one ever be "too heavenly minded to be of earthly good"?

28.8 Notes

1. Dante Alighieri, *The Divine Comedy [Inferno, Purgatorio, Paradiso]* (ed. David N. Higgins; trans. C. H. Sisson; New York: Oxford University Press, 1998).

2. See C. S. Lewis, *The Problem of Pain* (London: Centenary, 1940); *The Great Divorce: A Dream* (London: Geoffrey Bles, 1945); and *The Last Battle* (Chronicles of Narnia 7; London: Bodley Head, 1956). The view of hell I describe comes primarily from Lewis's book *The Great Divorce,* which is a work of fiction that represents his musings on hell rather than his fixed views.

FROM THEORY TO PRACTICE

When I teach students a new topic, I often begin by first asking them about it. But I do not ask what they believe; instead I ask how they live in relationship to the topic. When I find out how they actually live, then I tell them what they believe. For example, if I teach about Scripture, I do not ask students what they believe about it because they often claim to have lofty views about Scripture. What I want to know is: How often do they read it? Do they ever read the Bible outside of church? How often do they factor it into their day-to-day decisions? Once students answer these questions, I tell them what they truly believe about Scripture.

Very often people experience a disconnect between what they believe and value and what they practice. Another way of saying it is that we have a problem with theory and practice. *Theory* (Greek, *theoria,* "a looking at") pertains to the intellectual way we think about and articulate our most basic beliefs and values. From a Christian perspective, it includes what we think about God in relationship to our lives and to the world in which we live (namely, our theology). *Practice* (Greek, *praxis,* "practice, action") pertains to how we apply those beliefs and values. Some individuals are better theoreticians than practitioners, and other people are better practitioners than theoreticians. It is the presumption of this book that theory and practice are inextricably bound up with one another. Although this book focuses more on the theory—theology—of historic Christianity, there has always been a concern for how it works out in practice.

Theory & Practice

How does theory relate to practice, and vice versa?

> **It is not always easy** to combine theory and practice. Life is confusing as well as difficult, though we try to do our best.
>
> We pray that God will aid us in believing and valuing aright, and in living our lives with love and justice, which is a noble quest.

It is not always easy for us to be consistent in living out what we believe, and there are a number of possible explanations for this. Some people do not have the leisure, discipline, or inclination to reflect upon what they believe and value. From a Christian perspective, there are also the problems of sin, ignorance, bondage—spiritual and physical—and different types of human misery that prevent sufficient reflection upon and practical application of people's beliefs and values.

Even if we are not aware of our most basic beliefs and values, they still profoundly affect us. Whether unconsciously or subconsciously, they powerfully impact what we think, say, and do. Thus, it is important for us to become increasingly aware of what drives us from within. In the words of the Greek philosopher Socrates, "The life which is unexamined is not worth living."[1]

Although in this life people may never attain complete consistency between theory and practice, they can at least build bridges between the two. We should become more aware of our basic beliefs and values in order that we may become more effective practitioners. Likewise, if our practice is better than our theory, we may need to modify our beliefs and values. Sometimes practice needs to inform our theory, and other times theory needs to inform our practice. In fact, it can be argued that the best theories are shaped by the best practices, and vice versa. This involves learning—learning that seeks to integrate rather than separate theory and practice.

Socrates having a bad hair day

In this book I have tried to help you gain a greater awareness of the historic ways in which Christians have believed and valued God and God's relationship to them. Of course, it is not enough just to know about theology—to know about the theory of things. You must decide for yourself about what you believe and value. No one will mature spiritually or personally if they just mirror their parents, friends, church, or culture. Their practice—their lives—will also suffer from a lack of reflection. Thus, I encourage people to examine themselves and to live the kind of life that they want and that God wants. Remember that it is not enough for you to say you believe in God if that belief makes no difference in your values or life.

Fortunately, from a Christian perspective, we are not all alone in the struggle to reconcile theory and practice. God is always present, working graciously in and through the lives of people for their well-being—in this life and for eternity. This book has invited you to explore God and Christian theology anew, and I hope new learning and practice will result from it that is pleasing to God as well as to those who read this book.

Notes

1. Socrates, in Plato, *Apology,* in Classics of Western Philosophy (ed. Steven M. Cahn; 3d ed.; Indianapolis: Hackett, 1990), 54; cf. 41–56.

GLOSSARY

adoptionism   a subordinationist view of Jesus, considering him inferior to God because Jesus was a human adopted by God the Father. *See also* **monarchianism**.

age of accountability (or age of reason)   the time when young people are thought to become responsible for their salvation and moral decisions.

allegorical interpretation   an approach to biblical interpretation that seeks meaning in symbols or allegories rather than literally.

amillennialism   the view that Jesus will come again, but that the Bible does not present the details of the end times, providing more symbolic than literal descriptions of the millennial kingdom of God.

Anabaptist   a sixteenth-century movement of the Protestant Reformation that emphasized rebaptism, a literal reading of Scripture, and the separation of church and state; from Greek *ana* 'again' and *baptizō* 'baptize'.

analogical (language)   language that speaks of God by way of analogies, parallels, or symbols rather than directly. *See also* **apophatic (language)**.

angel   a heavenly or supernatural being who praises and serves God.

Anglican   related to the Church of England, which was founded in the sixteenth century as a "middle way" between Roman Catholicism and continental Protestantism; part of the worldwide Anglican Communion.

anointing of the sick   the sacrament or practice of anointing and praying for the healing of those who are sick or dying.

anthropology, Christian   the study of Christian teaching related to humanity; from Greek *anthrōpos* 'human'. *See also* **humanity**.

apocalyptic   a *genre* or type of biblical literature that deals with the end times, often characterized by dramatic imagery.

apocryphal/deuterocanonical books   certain writings, created during the intertestamental period, that are contained in the Roman Catholic Bible but not in the Hebrew or Protestant Bibles; see complete list in the Appendix.

Apollinarianism   the belief concerning the person of Christ that in the incarnation Jesus received a new soul—the divine Logos or Word—that displaced his human soul.

apologetics   the defense or justification of belief in God and Christianity; from Greek *apologia*.

apophatic (language)   language that refers to God negatively or by way of denial, that is, in terms of how God differs from human beings. *See also* **via negativa;** **analogical (language)**.

Apostles' Creed   an eighth-century creed that was thought to be based upon the most ancient apostolic teaching.

apostolicity   close association with Jesus' apostles and other early leaders of the church; apostolicity, association with the apostles, is considered one of the four marks of the church, though it is understood various ways.

arguments for the existence of God   various arguments (or "proofs") for God's existence that appeal to the existence, order, and purpose found in the universe.

Arianism   theology of Arius, who advocated a subordinationist view of Jesus, considering him inferior rather than equal to God the Father. *See also* **monarchianism**.

Arminianism   theology of James Arminius, who disagreed with Calvinism by emphasizing conditional election, unlimited atonement, and the resistibility of grace.

assurance   divinely given confidence that believers are saved.

atonement   a sacrifice that brings about reconciliation (literally, an "at-one-ment") between God and people; Jesus' death on the cross for others. *See also* **exchange**, **exemplar**, **rector**, and **victor** motifs of atonement.

Augustinianism   the theology of Augustine, who emphasized the sovereignty of God, the utter sinfulness of people, and their unconditional dependence upon God for salvation; Augustine profoundly influenced the early development of theology.

authority, religious   refers to the God-given right and power to command and be obeyed.

baptism   the Christian ritual of washing, purifying, or dipping in water, often considered the sacrament of initiation or incorporation into the church.

baptism, believer's   the limitation of the rite of baptism to people who are thought to have reached an age of accountability and who make a profession of faith.

baptism, Holy Spirit (or baptism by/in/of/with the Holy Spirit)   the special outpouring of the Holy Spirit that occurred at Pentecost; some hold that it continues to occur in believers subsequent to conversion, as evidenced by the gifts of the Spirit.

baptism, infant   the application of the rite of baptism to infants; also known as *paedobaptism;* from Greek *paidos* 'child' and *baptismos* 'baptism'.

Baptist   a member of a church and/or denomination that emphasizes believer's baptism (see baptism, believer's), usually having a congregational form of church government; the Baptist tradition developed from the sixteenth-century Anabaptists and seventeenth-century Puritans and Separatists.

Bible   the sacred book of Christianity; from Greek *biblia* 'book'. *See also* **Scripture**; see complete list of biblical books in the Appendix.

biblical theology   an approach to theology that organizes the theological teachings according to prominent biblical themes. *See also* **historical theology, philosophical theology, practical theology,** and **systematic theology**.

bondage (of the will)   the belief that rather than possessing a free will, people are in bondage to sin, Satan, and/or addictive habits.

born again (or born anew, born from above)   referring to a Christian believed to be spiritually reborn or born from above (John 3:3, 7).

calling   God's summons to salvation or to a particular kind of service such as full-time ministry.

Calvinism   the theology of John Calvin, who emphasized the sovereignty of God, the total depravity of humanity, and the need for unconditional election and irresistible grace for salvation.

canon   the standard by which ancient writings were identified as sacred writings; the accepted body of scriptural writings; from Greek *kanōn* 'rule', 'measuring rod'.

catastrophism   the scientific notion that many of earth's geological features formed as a result of past catastrophic activities such as floods, earthquakes, volcanoes, and meteors.

Catholicism   various Catholic Church traditions, the main representative of which is the Roman Catholic Church. *See also* **Roman Catholicism**.

catholicity, catholic   the universal nature of the church, not restricted with regard to race, gender, language, culture, or nationality; catholicity is regarded as one of the traditional marks of the church.

Charismatic Movement   a Pentecostal renewal movement, influencing a wide variety of churches and denominations in the mid-twentieth century, that emphasized the expression of the whole complement of spiritual gifts, including speaking in tongues. *See also* **spiritual gift**.

charisms   *see* **spiritual gift**.

Christ   the designation of Jesus as the Messiah, the coming deliverer foretold in the Old Testament; Greek *Christos* = Hebrew *mashiah* 'the anointed one'.

christocentric   Christ-centered; in theology, that which focuses on Jesus Christ as the preeminent revelation of God.

Christology   the theological study of the person and work of Jesus Christ.

church   the gathering or community of believers in Jesus Christ; in Scripture the church refers both to local bodies and to the universal church.

church discipline   the church's role of monitoring and regulating the beliefs and practices of its members, both positively through discipleship and negatively through the imposition of various sanctions.

church history   the record of the historic figures and events related to the church, beginning with their biblical roots.

Communion, Holy   the commemoration or sacramental meal based on the last supper Jesus shared with his disciples; also referred to as the Eucharist or the Lord's Supper.

compatibilistic freedom   *see* **freedom, compatibilistic**.

confirmation   the sacrament or celebration of Christian maturity, following a period of instruction or catechism, that normally includes an affirmation of the faith into which one is baptized and participation in Holy Eucharist.

congregationalism   a form of church government in which churches are individually constituted and independently governed.

Congregationalist   a member of a church communion that has a congregational form of church government.

consubstantiation   the belief that Jesus' body and blood are spiritually present in a special way in the bread and wine of communion. *See also* **memorial meal** and **transubstantiation**.

contemplation   prayerful reflection upon God, which involves the mind as well as the will.

contextual   pertaining to theological reflection that occurs within the milieu of a particular culture or historical setting, including the particularities of the people doing the reflection themselves.

conversion   the act of turning to God in faith and turning away from sin in repentance.

cosmological argument an argument for God's existence based upon cosmological (*a posteriori*) grounds, that is, evidence from the empirical world; from Greek *cosmos* 'world'.

cosmology, Christian the Christian study of the world; from Greek *cosmos* 'world'.

creation all that God has brought into being, including all forms of life.

creation *ex nihilo* the belief that God has brought all into being "out of nothing"; Latin *ex nihilo* 'from nothing'.

creationism the view that God created the universe and its life forms; there are various views of creationism.

death, physical the cessation of physical life.

death, spiritual separation from God in this world or eternal separation from God in eternity.

deduction the method of reasoning that derives conclusions from the logical and necessary consequences of premises, for example, by means of syllogisms; reasoning that proves or explains general laws or principles. *See also* **induction**.

deism the belief that God created the world and left it and everyone in it to live according to its natural laws and potentialities.

demon an evil spirit, usually thought to be a fallen angel.

demythologization the task of interpreting the Bible according to the existential relevance of its religious or "mythical" significance rather than historically.

denomination an organization of churches around shared doctrinal and governmental distinctives.

deposit of faith the Catholic notion of the sum of revelation and tradition embodying the earliest statements of Christian beliefs, values, and practices that was passed from the apostles to the succession of bishops and that shaped the later creeds.

devil *See* **Satan**.

dialectical pertaining to the form of reasoning in which conclusions become apparent from the tension between divergent viewpoints; this can occur through dialogue, synthesis, or paradoxically by the grace of God.

dichotomy (view of humanity) the view that human nature consists of only two distinct parts, body and soul. *See also* **trichotomy (view of humanity)**.

discernment, spiritual gift of the supernatural ability to determine the spiritual or divine origin and veracity of prophetic claims.

dispensationalism   the theological position that emphasizes that God works different ways during the multiple periods (dispensations) of biblical history; it is normally characterized by a literal interpretation of Scripture and the expectation of an imminent return of Jesus Christ.

Docetism   the view concerning the person of Christ that Jesus was exclusively divine and merely appeared to be human.

doctrine   Christian beliefs or teachings, communicated objectively through propositional statements. *See also* **dogma**.

dogma   official teachings or doctrines, sanctioned by churches or other Christian organizations.

double predestination   the belief that God determines both those who will be saved and those who will be condemned before they are born. *See also* **predestination**.

dramatic motif of atonement   *See* **victor (or dramatic) motif of atonement**.

Ebionism   the belief concerning the person of Christ that Jesus was not divine in essence but merely a human being on whom the Holy Spirit descended at his baptism.

ecclesiology   the theological study of the church; from Greek *ekklēsia* 'assembly', 'church'.

ecumenism   the desire and promotion of unity and cooperation among Christians.

egalitarianism   the theological belief that men and women share an equal relationship, with neither subordinate to the other.

election   God's decision in choosing people or groups of people for salvation or service on God's behalf.

entire sanctification   the Wesleyan or Pentecostal belief in a second work of grace beyond conversion that leads to moral purification and love for others.

environmentalism, Christian   the conviction that God has given humans "dominion" over God's good creation (Gen 1:28), and that they are consequently responsible to care for and preserve the world.

episcopacy   a centralized, hierarchical form of church government in which bishops oversee the local churches within a given region.

Episcopalian   a member of the Anglican Communion in the United States. *See also* **Anglican**.

eschatology   the study of the future things, events to occur in the end times; from Greek *eschata* 'last things'.

eternity that which is distinguished from time, having no beginning or end; in Christian thought, the realm in which God exists.

Eucharist, Holy *See* **Communion, Holy.**

Eutychianism the belief concerning the person of Christ that the human nature was overshadowed by and absorbed into the divine nature and thus effectively eliminated.

evangelical revivals outbreaks of evangelism and discipleship that occurred in the seventeenth and eighteenth centuries in continental Europe (Pietism), Great Britain (Methodism), and the American colonies (the Great Awakening).

evangelicalism the modern Christian movement that emphasizes proclamation of the "gospel" or "good news"; more broadly, the term is used to include the Protestant Reformers, evangelical revivals, and similar movements that emphasize evangelism.

evangelism the Christian practice of telling the gospel or "good news" in the hope of converting people to trust in Jesus as their Savior and Lord and to repentance of their sins; from Greek *euangelion* 'gospel', 'good news'.

evolution the scientific theory pioneered by Charles Darwin that life on earth evolved or slowly developed from simple to more complex life forms. *See also* **theistic evolution.**

ex nihilo *See* **creation** *ex nihilo.*

exchange (satisfaction) motif of the atonement the belief that Jesus brought about salvation by offering himself in death as a substitute for the person being saved; the unrighteousness of the person is exchanged for the righteousness of Jesus; also known as penal or substitutionary atonement. *See also* **atonement.**

exemplar (moral influence) motif of the atonement the belief that Jesus' death brought about salvation by setting an example of obedience to his heavenly Father. *See also* **atonement.**

existential emphasizing the personal dimensions of life; finding truth through personal subjectivity or participation in "reality" (existence).

experience, inner or religious generally, observation of or participation in events as a basis of knowledge; specifically, the self-disclosure of God within a person's inner spirit or mind as a source of authoritative religious knowledge.

faith belief in and commitment to someone or something, involving knowledge, assent, and trust; one of the three theological virtues of Catholicism.

feminist theology an approach to Christian theology that seeks to counter the injustices of sexism and the oppression of women and to reconstruct Christian thinking on the basis of gender equality.

fideism   the view that religious knowledge is based on a non-rational commitment (or "leap") of faith rather than on the evidence of reason or sense experience. *See also* **volitional justification of belief.**

foreknowledge   God's prescience or foresight concerning future events.

foreordination   the view that God renders events certain before they occur in time.

forgiveness   excusing or pardoning someone for a sin or offense.

foundationalism   confidence in certain fundamentals that are thought to provide rational and empirical foundations for religious knowledge (for example, inerrant Bible). *See also* **modernism (modernity).**

fourfold sense of Scripture   four medieval ways of interpreting Scripture (literal, allegorical, moral, and anagogical).

freedom, compatibilistic   the belief that humans are free to act only in ways that are compatible with God's foreordination or decreeing of what will eventually occur.

freedom, human (free will)   the belief that humans are free, to a significant degree, to make choices that determine their behavior.

fundamentalism   a conservative theological movement of the early twentieth century that rejected the historical criticism of the Bible and insisted on specific doctrines or "fundamentals" of the Christian faith such as the inerrancy of Scripture and the virgin birth of Christ.

general revelation   the revelation or knowledge of God and his will that is available to people at all times and places, especially through God's creation. *See also* **special revelation.**

gifts of the Spirit   *See* **spiritual gift.**

glorification   the final state of a Christian in the order of salvation, sharing in God's glory in heaven.

glossolalia   *See* **tongues, speaking in.**

gospel, Gospel   the "good news" about salvation and reconciliation with God that come through faith in Jesus Christ and repentance from sin; one of four accounts of Jesus' life in the New Testament.

governance   God's maintenance of creation; God's rule through Jesus, to be fully manifested in the end times; oversight of the church through various kinds of church polity.

grace   God's unmerited favor toward the believer and God's empowerment for salvation or for living the Christian life.

Great Awakening the revivalist movement of the eighteenth-century American colonies that emphasized evangelism and the importance of religious affections or experience.

heaven the abode of God and the angels; the final state or place of those who have received eternal life from God.

hell the final state or place to which God sends unrepentant demons and people in punishment of their sins and unbelief in God.

hermeneutical circle the process of interpreting one's own cultural context and religious biases as one interprets the Bible, and vice versa; awareness of the degree to which both the interpreter and the material interpreted influence the interpretive process.

hermeneutics the theological study of the methods of biblical interpretation. *See also* **interpretation of Scripture**.

historical criticism (or historical critical method) the method of biblical interpretation that attempts to identify the historical context of events, people, and culture that lie behind the biblical texts and out of which they emerged.

historical theology an approach to theology that studies its development from biblical times to the present.

Holiness Movement a nineteenth-century American renewal movement that emphasized revivalism and the pursuit of holy living.

holy set apart to be godly, whole, pure, perfect; used of God's sacred character; one of the marks of the true church.

holy orders the Catholic sacrament of the ordination of clergy. *See also* **ordination**.

Holy Spirit the Spirit of God; the third person of the Trinity, being fully divine and fully personal.

hope the expectation of the present and future promises of God; it is one of the three theological virtues of Catholicism.

humanity the highest of God's created beings, made in God's image for relationship with God; due to sin, people are in need of the salvation provided by God.

icon an image or picture representing Jesus or one of the saints used by Orthodox Christians as an aid to worship.

illumination the Holy Spirit's work of clarifying truths about God and salvation.

image of God the presence of the divine likeness in human beings created by God, often understood in terms of humanity's higher capabilities of religious, rational, social, and linguistic interaction; Latin *imago Dei,* "image of God."

immanence   God's presence, nearness, or ubiquity in relation to humans. *See also* **transcendence**.

immortality   the belief that the human soul continues after death, whether unconditionally or in conjunction with the resurrection of the body.

incarnation   embodiment in flesh; specifically, the belief that Jesus, while remaining fully divine, became at the same time fully human.

indefectibility of the church   the Catholic and Orthodox belief that the church will never cease to exist, but will continue to safeguard God's truth in the world.

induction   the method of reasoning that investigates experiential or observable data, and then logically establishes general laws or principles. *See also* **deduction**.

inerrancy   the view that the Bible is unerringly truthful; in its most stringent form, the view that the Bible does not err in any respect, including in its statements about history, geography, and science.

infallibility   the view that Scripture neither misleads nor is misled, especially in fulfilling the purposes for which God intended it to be written.

inner light   the Quaker belief that God's Holy Spirit gives believers personal illumination about God's will for their lives and actions.

inspiration of Scripture   the belief that Scripture is "God-breathed" (2 Tim 3:16) or "inspired" and that God specially communicates to us through the words that have been preserved in the Bible.

intelligent design   the view that the world, especially the biological world, is too complex to be explained without postulating an intelligent designer, and that the evolution of living organisms by random mutations alone is mathematically implausible. *See also* **teleological argument**.

intermediate state   the belief that after death people continue in an intermediate form of existence until the time of the resurrection; alternative explanations of the intermediate state include purgatory, soul sleep, and disembodied consciousness.

interpretation of Scripture   refers to the exegesis or understanding of Scripture. *See also* **hermeneutics**.

irresistible grace   the belief that God's grace in bringing elect people to conversion cannot be thwarted; one of the core beliefs of Calvinism.

justice   the virtue of giving to everyone what is rightly due to them, involving both individual and social fairness; one of the cardinal virtues of Catholicism.

justification   the way in which believers are restored by God to a state of righteousness.

kenosis   Jesus' "emptying" himself of his divine rights and privileges so that he might live genuinely as a human being; Greek *kenōsis* 'emptying'.

law   a body of injunctions prescribed by God to regulate behavior; specifically, the law given to Moses on Mount Sinai.

liberal Protestantism (liberal theology)   the nineteenth-century theological movement that emphasized the primacy of religious experience over divine revelation in reformulating Christian doctrine in contemporary terms.

liberation theology   a twentieth-century theological movement emphasizing the need to confront social, political, and economic injustices and to bring about physical as well as spiritual liberation.

limited atonement   the belief that Jesus' death and resurrection provides atonement only for the elect; one of the core beliefs of Calvinism.

liturgy   the arrangement of rites, rituals, and church traditions used in worship; literally, from Greek *leitourgia* 'work of the people', 'service'.

Lord's Supper   *See* **Communion, Holy.**

Lutheranism   a branch of the Protestant church founded by Martin Luther, the initiator of the Protestant Reformation of the sixteenth century, emphasizing the authority of Scripture alone, and salvation by grace alone, and salvation through faith alone.

magisterium   the teaching authority of church magistrates or leaders, especially of the Roman Catholic pope, cardinals, and bishops.

Mariology   the study of Mary, the mother of Jesus, and her importance for Christian beliefs, values, and practices.

marks of the church   a group of essential characteristics of the true church, defined in the early Christian centuries, that include unity, holiness, catholicity, and apostolicity.

matrimony, holy   marriage; one of the seven sacraments of the Catholic Church.

means of grace   divinely instituted channels or ways by which God conveys blessings and spiritual empowerment to people. *See also* **spiritual disciplines** and **sacrament.**

memorial meal   the Lord's Supper viewed as a symbolic commemoration of the death and resurrection of Jesus. *See also* **consubstantiation** and **transubstantiation.**

Messiah   *See* **Christ.**

metanarrative   in postmodern discussions, a narrative or account of reality illegitimately claiming superior or absolute status. *See also* **narrative, postmodernism (postmodernity).**

Methodism a branch of the Protestant church founded by John Wesley that emphasizes evangelism, social concern, and holy living. *See also* **Wesleyanism**.

methodology, theological the body of methods and procedures by which theology or biblical studies are done, resting on basic assumptions about knowledge, revelation, language, and humanity.

midtribulationism the view that the rapture will occur midway through the tribulation. *See also* **rapture**.

millennialism (various understandings of) the thousand-year reign (millennium) of Christ spoken of in Rev 20.

minister *See* **pastor**.

ministry the service to God rendered by an individual or church, including tangible expressions of love and service to others.

miracle an extraordinary achievement or event that exceeds natural agency.

missiology the study and practice of missions and missionary work around the world.

modalism the belief that God is a single person who appears in various personages (or modes) but never ceases to be one. *See also* **unitarianism**.

modernism (modernity) a worldview that emerged during the Enlightenment in the West that emphasizes individualism, confidence in reason, objective truth, and claims of universal truth based upon past authorities, including the church and Scripture.

Monarchianism the early antitrinitarian belief that God is a single being and a single person, with Jesus understood as either a subordinate, adopted being or a mode of expression of the one divine person. *See also* **Arianism** and **adoptionism**.

Montanism the second-century theology of Montanus, an apocalyptic teacher who emphasized ecstatic utterances, visions, and trances.

moral governance motif of the atonement *See* **rector (moral governance) motif of the atonement**.

moral influence motif of the atonement *See* **exemplar (moral influence) motif of the atonement**.

mortal sin in Catholic theology, a more serious sin that results in spiritual death. *See also* **venial sin**.

mystery in the New Testament, that which is not fully revealed or understood; Greek *mystērion* 'mystery'.

narrative   in postmodern discussions, an account or a story that legitimately communicates reality or truth from a given perspective. *See also* **metanarrative** and **postmodernism (postmodernity)**.

Neo-orthodoxy   the twentieth-century theological position that rejected liberal Protestantism and advocated a dialectical approach to the Bible in which Scripture is thought to reveal not propositional truth so much as it enables us to encounter God in a personal and intimate way. *See* **dialectical**.

Nestorianism   the early belief concerning the person of Christ that there were two separate persons in the incarnate Jesus, the Christ, with Jesus bearing or carrying God within himself rather than becoming or being God.

New Testament   the second and later part of the Christian Bible that deals with Jesus and the founding of the Christian church. *See also* **Old Testament** and the Appendix.

Nicene Creed   the first ecumenical summary of Christian beliefs; what is commonly known as the Nicene Creed, initially drafted at the Council of Nicaea (325), was in fact promulgated by the Council of Constantinople (381); it is also called the Nicene-Constantinopolitan Creed.

old-earth creationism   a harmonization of the biblical account of creation with the scientific account of evolution that views the earth as billions of years old.

Old Testament   the first and earlier part of the Christian Bible that contains the Hebrew Scripture, dealing with the creation of the world and the history of the Jewish people. *See also* **New Testament** and the Appendix.

ontological argument   an argument for God's existence based purely upon the rational (*a priori*) idea of perfection rather than on empirical (*a posteriori*) evidence. *See also* **arguments for the existence of God.**

open theism (or open theology)   the belief that God self-limits foreknowledge as well as foreordination in order to permit human beings to have a measure of genuine freedom in accepting or rejecting God's gracious offer of salvation.

order of salvation (Latin *ordo salutis*)   a temporal order of events purporting to describe the steps or stages by which people are saved, typically involving elements such as regeneration, justification, conversion, sanctification, and glorification.

ordinance   something ordained by God or Jesus; a sacrament. *See also* **sacrament**.

ordination   the corporate recognition of and setting apart of a person for a particular ministry in the church; one of the seven sacraments of Catholicism (Holy Orders).

original sin   the primal sin of Adam which has consequences for the entire human race. *See also* **transmission of original sin**.

Orthodox churches   the churches that originated in the East, which united more or less under the patriarchate of Constantinople, and are today represented by autonomous national churches (e.g., Greek and Russian Orthodox).

orthodoxy   the body of beliefs, values, and practices representative of the historic or widely accepted views of the Christian church, for example, based upon ecumenical councils from Nicaea (325) to Chalcedon (451); also, the theology of Orthodox churches.

paedobaptism   *See* **baptism, infant**.

paradox   an apparent contradiction; a true statement that exhibits a sometimes irresolvable tension between divergent concepts or realities; e.g., the doctrine of the trinity.

Parousia   *See* **second coming of Jesus**.

pastor   a religious leader or overseer of a local church congregation. *See also* **priest**.

patriarchalism   a system of hierarchical relations that gives men authority over women.

Pelagianism   the theology of Pelagius, who denied original sin and held that Adam's sin affects subsequent humanity only as a bad example and that each person is capable of living a life pleasing to God.

penance   the practice of making personal satisfaction for one's sins through acts of humility and contrition; one of the seven Catholic sacraments, also know as reconciliation.

Pentecost   the Jewish feast at which the Holy Spirit was poured out upon all believers, empowering them (Acts 2:1–4).

Pentecostalism   an early twentieth-century movement that emphasized a baptism of the Holy Spirit subsequent to conversion that empowers believers with spiritual gifts, especially speaking in tongues.

perseverance   the belief that God's grace powerfully preserves those elected to salvation, enabling them to persevere in their faith and avoid falling away; one of the core beliefs of Calvinism.

philosophical theology   an approach to theology that interacts with important philosophical themes. *See also* **biblical theology, historical theology, practical theology**, and **systematic theology**.

Pietism   a renewal movement within seventeenth-century German Lutheranism that emphasized the importance of religious experience in salvation and the need to live devout lives.

pneumatology the theological study of the Holy Spirit; from Greek *pneuma* 'spirit'.

polity church government; the body of beliefs and practices related to how the church should be organized and governed.

postmillennialism the belief that Jesus will come again after God's millennial kingdom has been established in the world.

postmodern theology an approach to theology, influenced by postmodernism, that emphasizes practical reflection and rejects models of "Christian" modernity that claim rational universality based on "objective" truth.

postmodernism (postmodernity) a contemporary worldview that debunks traditional accounts (metanarratives) of reality, considers truth to be culturally relative, and emphasizes the need for the comparison of a host of perspectives (or narratives) in a context of humility and tolerance toward others. *See also* **metanarrative** and **narrative**.

posttribulationism the view that the rapture will occur at the end of an endtimes period of tribulation. *See* **rapture** and **tribulation**.

practical theology an approach to theology that organizes topics around the application of Christian beliefs to the church and the world. *See also* **biblical theology, historical theology, philosophical theology**, and **systematic theology**.

praxis the practical and social application of Christian theory or theology.

predestination the belief that God determines those who will be saved before they are born. *See also* **double predestination**.

premillennialism the belief that Jesus will return prior to the establishment of God's millennial kingdom in the world. *See also* **tribulation**.

Presbyterianism a branch of the Protestant church, founded in the sixteenth century, that emphasizes reformed theology and a presbyterian (elder-directed) form of church government. *See also* **reformed theology**.

pretribulationism the view that the rapture will occur prior to an end-times period of tribulation. *See* **rapture** and **tribulation**.

prevenient grace God's initiating grace that precedes people's decision to follow God, enabling them freely to accept or reject God's offer of salvation.

priest in Anglican, Catholic, and Orthodox churches, a religious leader or member of the clergy who presides over a local parish or congregation and administers the church's sacraments.

process theology an approach to theology, influenced by the process philosophy of Alfred North Whitehead, that conceives of everything, including God, in terms of change or "becoming" rather than static "being."

progressive creationism   the view of divine creation which holds that within the course of evolutionary development, God periodically steps in and creates entirely new life forms *de novo* (Latin, "anew").

progressive revelation   the view that God gradually reveals aspects of God's divine nature as well as God's covenant relationships with people, especially in Scripture, with later revelation being built on earlier revelation.

prophecy   words spoken on behalf of God that may include both the forth-telling of God's will and the foretelling of future events.

Protestant   a member of any of several church denominations that affirm the principles of the Reformation. *See* **Protestant Reformation**.

Protestant Reformation   the reform movement in the sixteenth century that separated from the Roman Catholic Church and affirmed the principles of justification by faith alone, the priesthood of all believers, and the primacy of the Bible as the only source of revealed truth.

providence   God's sovereign sustenance, governing, development, and care for all aspects of God's creation and creatures.

purgatory   in Roman Catholic theology, the place where believers go after death to atone for sins for which they were not held accountable in this world.

Quakerism   *See* **Society of Friends**.

rapture   the belief that Christians will be "carried off" (Latin *raptus*) to heaven by God sometime before, during, or after a time of end-times tribulation. *See also* **tribulation**.

reason   the mental capacity, which some consider religiously authoritative, to think logically and critically in the pursuit of truth.

reconciliation, divine   the reuniting of people with God, which God graciously initiates. *See also* **penance**.

rector (moral governance) motif of the atonement   the view that Jesus' death for sin was a statement regarding the seriousness of sin rather than a penal sacrifice, and that God provides salvation by executive clemency rather than by demanding legal satisfaction. *See also* **atonement**.

Reformation   *See* **Protestant Reformation**.

Reformed churches   Protestant churches that adhere to the theology of the Protestant Reformation, and particularly to **Calvinism**.

reformed theology   *See* **Calvinism**.

regeneration   the "new birth" or renewal of the mind and will of those who, by faith and repentance, have received the gift of salvation through Jesus (Titus 3:5).

repentance   a turning away from sin and toward God, involving godly sorrow from sin, confession of it, and resolve to avoid sin.

reprobation   God's decision in choosing people or groups of people for damnation. *See also* **election** and **double predestination**.

resurrection   the bodily raising of people from the dead; specifically, Jesus' rising from the dead.

revelation   the revealing, unveiling, or uncovering of knowledge about God. *See also* **general revelation** and **special revelation**.

revivalism   the evangelistic movement begun in the nineteenth century that used camp meetings or other mass forums to emphasize the need for individuals to make personal decisions to follow Jesus.

Roman Catholicism   the teaching and polity of the Roman Catholic Church, that branch of the church that recognizes the pope as the vicar of Jesus Christ and the successor of Peter. *See also* **Catholicism**.

sacrament   a religious rite ordained by Jesus Christ and believed to be a formal means of receiving God's grace. *See also* **baptism; Communion, Holy;** and **ordinance**.

sacramentalism   the belief that God's grace is bestowed upon people primarily by means of the sacraments, rather than being bestowed directly.

salvation   the redemption of people by God, involving forgiveness of sin and reconciliation to God through the atonement of Jesus and the work of the Holy Spirit.

sanctification   God's work of bringing believers into greater conformity with the likeness of God, progressively enabling and empowering them to act in ways that reflect God's love, holiness, righteousness, and justice.

Satan   the devil; a powerful angelic creature who rebelled against God and continues to lead spiritual opposition to God's purposes in the world; from a Hebrew word meaning "accuser" or "adversary."

satisfaction motif of the atonement   *See* **exchange (satisfaction) motif of the atonement**.

scholasticism   a highly rational and logical approach to the study, formulation, and teaching of Christianity; there have been both Catholic and Protestant manifestations of scholasticism.

Scripture   the sacred writings of Christianity; Latin *scriptura* 'a writing'. *See also* **Bible**.

second coming of Jesus   the Christian teaching regarding the return or final 'coming' (Greek *parousia*) of Jesus in the end times.

Semi-Augustinianism the belief that God graciously initiates, continues, and completes salvation while allowing people the freedom to accept or reject salvation.

Semi-Pelagianism the belief that the grace of God and human freedom work cooperatively in bringing a person to salvation.

sin an offense against God, which may include active rebellion against God and God's laws or unbelief and passive indifference to God; sins may be of an individual, social, and institutional nature.

sinlessness of Jesus the belief that, although tempted, Jesus never sinned.

Social Gospel the late nineteenth-century movement that sought to address the physical, social, political, and economic well-being of people as well as their spiritual well-being.

Society of Friends renewal movement of sixteenth-century England that emphasized the importance of the "inner light" of the Holy Spirit; also known as Quakers due to the quaking or shaking phenomena experienced by adherents.

sola fide the Reformation tenet that people receive salvation by faith alone, apart from good works; Latin for 'by faith alone'. *See also* **Protestant Reformation**.

sola gratia the Reformation tenet that God saves people by grace alone, apart from human efforts; Latin for 'by grace alone'. *See also* **Protestant Reformation**.

sola scriptura the Reformation tenet that the Bible is the sole authority for establishing Christian beliefs, values, and practices; Latin for 'Scripture alone'. *See also* **Protestant Reformation**.

soteriology the theological study of salvation; from Greek *sotēria* 'salvation'.

soul the essential life or self of a person, which has been variously understood by Christians and non-Christians.

soul sleep the belief of Luther and others that following death the soul enters into a state of unconscious sleep, with no awareness until the final resurrection and judgment.

special revelation the revelation or knowledge of God and his will that is uniquely given by God, especially through Scripture. *See also* **general revelation**.

spiritual disciplines a set of exercises developed for the sake of spiritual growth or formation, including such practices as directed prayer, fasting, study, worship, solitude, and contemplation.

spiritual gift a special quality and ability given supernaturally by the Holy Spirit that enable the believer to minister to others and build up the church, including such endowments as prophecy, miracles, speaking in tongues, teaching, evangelism, and serving; sometimes called a *charism*.

spiritual warfare direct, supernatural conflict, whether by angels or humans, with Satan and demons, involving fervent prayer and, on some occasions, exorcism.

spirituality, Christian the quality or intimacy of a person's relationship with God, sometimes described in terms of qualities such as love, holiness, piety, and perfection.

substitutionary atonement *See* **exchange (satisfaction) motif of the atonement**.

systematic theology an approach to theology in which Christian beliefs, values, and practices are arranged in an orderly and comprehensive manner. *See also* **biblical theology, historical theology, philosophical theology,** and **practical theology**.

teleological argument an argument for God's existence based upon the evidence of order and design found in the empirical world. *See also* **intelligent design**.

temptation an enticement to evil or sin; a test of faith and commitment.

theistic evolution the view of divine creation that holds that the evolutionary process is the means by which God's creative purposes are fulfilled. *See also* **evolution**.

theodicy the defense or justification of God's power and goodness in a world in which evil exists.

theology the systematic study of God and God's relationship to the world; Greek *theos*, "God," and *logos*, "word, discourse, study, science." *See also* **biblical theology, historical theology, philosophical theology, practical theology,** and **systematic theology**.

time the linear sequence of events or processes that includes past, present, and future; in Christian theology traditionally thought of as a part of God's creation.

tongues, speaking in the spiritual gift of being able to speak in a language the speaker has never learned (1 Cor 12:10); the modern charismatic phenomenon of ecstatic utterance; also known as *glossolalia;* from Greek *glōssa* 'tongue' and *lalia* 'chatter'. *See also* **Charismatic Movement** and **spiritual gift**.

total depravity the belief that the inherent sinful nature of humans in their fallen condition affects and corrupts every aspect of their personality, including the intellect, the emotions, and the will; one of the core beliefs of **Calvinism**.

tradition   the body of beliefs, values, and practices passed down from one generation to the next; in Catholic theology, the authoritative body of beliefs and practices not contained in Scripture that have been passed down by the church.

transcendence   God's surpassing otherness, exceeding the ability of finite humans to comprehend and articulate. *See also* **immanence**.

transmission of original sin   the belief that original sin and its effects are transferred from one generation to the next, either by virtue of a person's actual solidarity with Adam or because Adam represented the person in the original sin.

transubstantiation   the belief that God miraculously transforms the bread and wine of communion into the essence of the body and blood of Jesus. *See also* **consubstantiation** and **memorial meal**.

tribulation   the end-times period of crisis that some believe will immediately precede the return of Jesus and the final manifestation of God's kingdom; sometimes referred to as the *great tribulation*. *See also* **rapture**.

trichotomy (view of humanity)   the view that human nature consists of three distinct parts: body, soul, and spirit. *See also* **dichotomy**.

Trinity   the belief that God is one in essence, yet exists as three equal yet distinct persons—Father, Son, and Holy Spirit.

unconditional election   the belief that God chooses individuals for eternal salvation not based on any condition of faith or merit foreseen in them; one of the core beliefs of **Calvinism**.

union with Christ   the mystical union or communion believers may experience with God; the connection with God believers experience as a part of their salvation.

unitarianism   the antitrinitarian belief that God is one in essence as well as in personality.

venial sin   in Catholic theology, a less serious sin that weakens the spiritual well-being of a person; contrast **mortal sin**.

via negativa   the "negative way" of speaking about God that emphasizes how God is dissimilar to human beings. *See* **apophatic (language)**.

victor (or dramatic) motif of the atonement   the belief that Jesus' death brought about salvation by means of its dramatic victory over sin, death, and demonic bondage. *See also* **atonement**.

virgin birth   the belief that Jesus was conceived in the womb of Mary by the Holy Spirit rather than by normal sexual union; Mary thus gave birth as a virgin.

virtue   a morally excellent quality or trait; a disposition, habit, or quality that inclines people to do what is right, good, or holy.

virtues, cardinal   in Catholic theology, those virtues for which people are primarily responsible: prudence (wisdom), justice, temperance (self-control), and courage.

virtues, theological   in Catholic theology, those virtues infused by God: faith, hope, and love.

volitional justification of belief   the idea that belief in God is warranted as an act of the will rather than as a matter of reason or experience. *See also* **fideism**.

Wesleyan quadrilateral   in Wesleyan theology, the four sources of religious authority, including the primary source of Scripture and the secondary sources of tradition, reason, and experience.

Wesleyanism   the theological system of John Wesley, the founder of Methodism, who advocated contextualization, human cooperation with divine grace, and holy living. *See also* **Methodism**.

Word of God   God's expression of truth, either in Jesus or in Scripture.

young-earth creationism   a view that the earth was created no more than several thousand years ago, based on a strict biblical chronology and a literal, twenty-four-hour interpretation of the days of Gen 1.

THE BOOKS OF THE BIBLE

Old Testament (Hebrew Bible)

Genesis
Exodus
Leviticus
Numbers
Deuteronomy
Joshua
Judges
Ruth
1 Samuel
2 Samuel
1 Kings
2 Kings
1 Chronicles
2 Chronicles
Ezra
Nehemiah
Esther
Job
Psalms
Proverbs
Ecclesiastes
Song of Solomon
Isaiah
Jeremiah
Lamentations
Ezekiel
Daniel

Hosea
Joel
Amos
Obadiah
Jonah
Micah
Nahum
Habakkuk
Zephaniah
Haggai
Zechariah
Malachi

Apocryphal/Deuterocanonical Books

Tobit
Judith
Additions to Esther
Wisdom of Solomon
Sirach (Ecclesiasticus)
Baruch
Letter of Jeremiah
Prayer of Azariah and the Song of the Three Jews
Susanna
Bel and the Dragon

1 Maccabees
2 Maccabees
1 Esdras
Prayer of Manasseh
3 Maccabees
2 Esdras
4 Maccabees

New Testament

Matthew
Mark
Luke
John
Acts
Romans
1 Corinthians
2 Corinthians
Galatians

Ephesians
Philippians
Colossians
1 Thessalonians
2 Thessalonians
1 Timothy
2 Timothy
Titus
Philemon
Hebrews
James
1 Peter
2 Peter
1 John
2 John
3 John
Jude
Revelation

NAME INDEX

SUBJECT INDEX

SCRIPTURE INDEX